FIRE PUNCH

2

STORY AND ART BY
TATSUKI FUJIMOTO

CHARACTERS

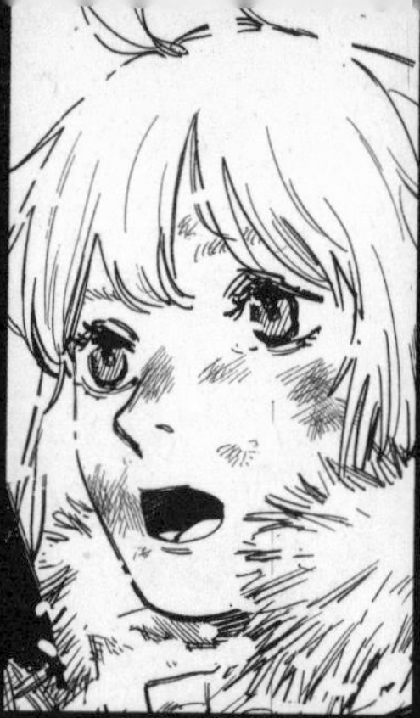

SUN

A Blessed with the power of electricity. Agni saves his life.

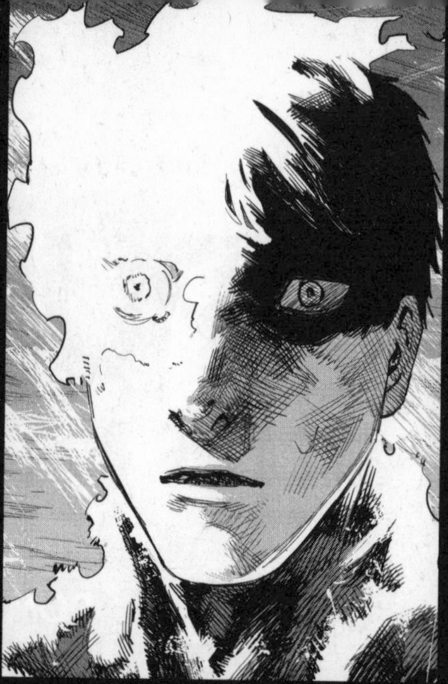

AGNI

A Blessed with the power of regeneration, his little sister is killed by Doma, who engulfs Agni in flames that will never extinguish.

JUDAH

A soldier of Behemdorg who is a Blessed with the power of regeneration.

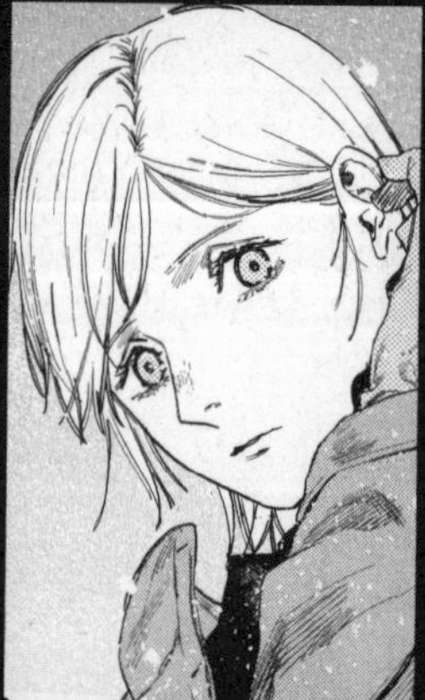

NENETO

A girl taken to Behemdorg with Sun.

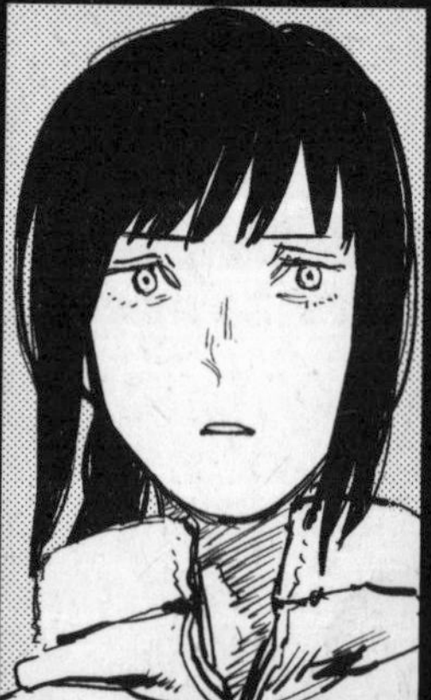

IVAN

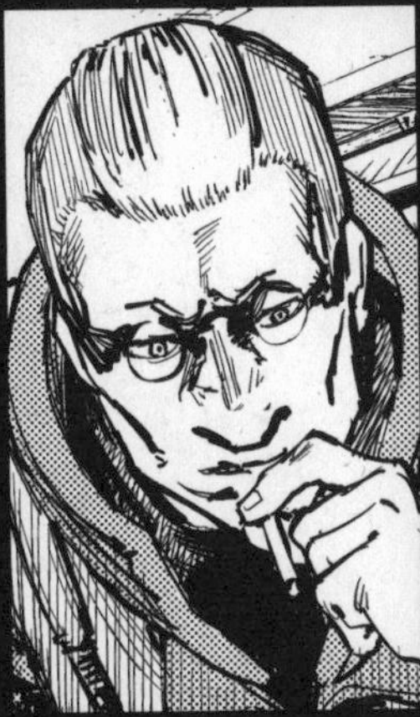

A soldier of Behemdorg, and Jack's little brother.

JACK

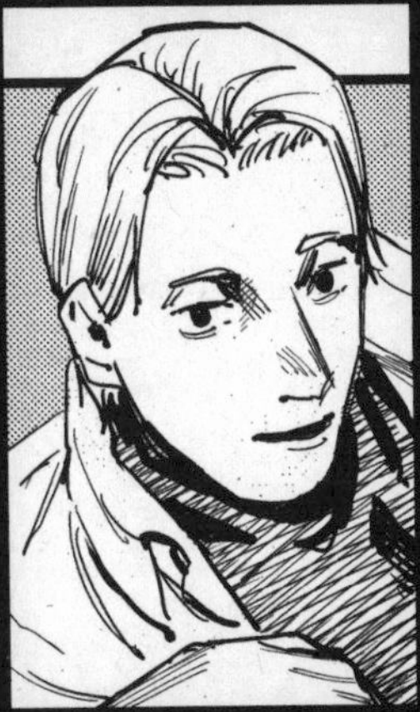

A soldier of Behemdorg who is a Blessed with the power to heal wounds.

TOGATA

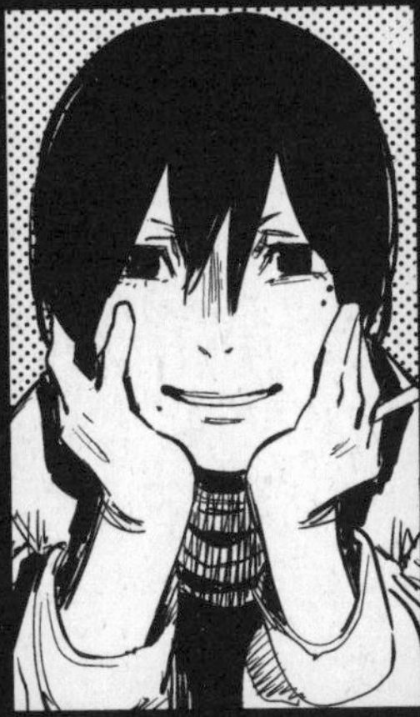

A mysterious girl who is trying to film a movie starring Agni.

DOMA

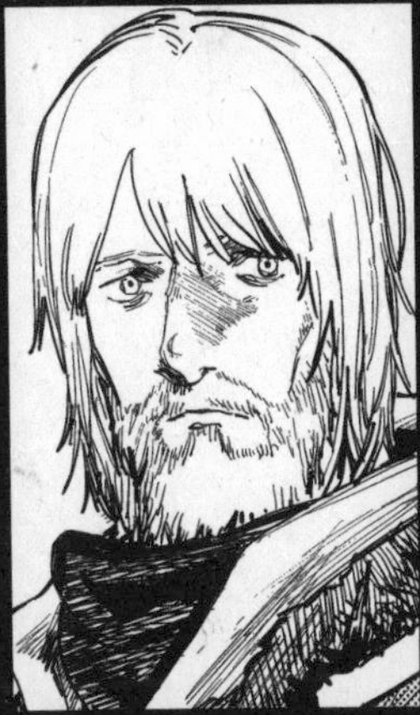

A soldier of Behemdorg who is a Blessed with the power of fire.

STORY

Humans who possess unique powers are called Blessed, and currently their world is encased in snow, starvation and madness thanks to a Blessed called the Ice Witch. Siblings Agni and Luna are two of these Blessed, who have the power of regeneration. With no living relatives, they struggle to survive.

One day they're attacked by Doma, a Blessed soldier of Behemdorg—the kingdom seeking to defeat the Ice Witch—whose flames won't go out until they've completely consumed their fuel. Luna loses her life, but before she does, she tells Agni he must live, giving him the will to carry on. Because Doma's flames are burning him alive, he must continue to regenerate, making his life a living hell.

Eight years pass, and Agni has learned how to control the flames engulfing him. He sets out on a journey seeking revenge against Doma, and now that he's been reunited with his long-desired target, what will be his next move?!

FIRE PUNCH

STORY AND ART BY
TATSUKI FUJIMOTO

CHAPTER 9

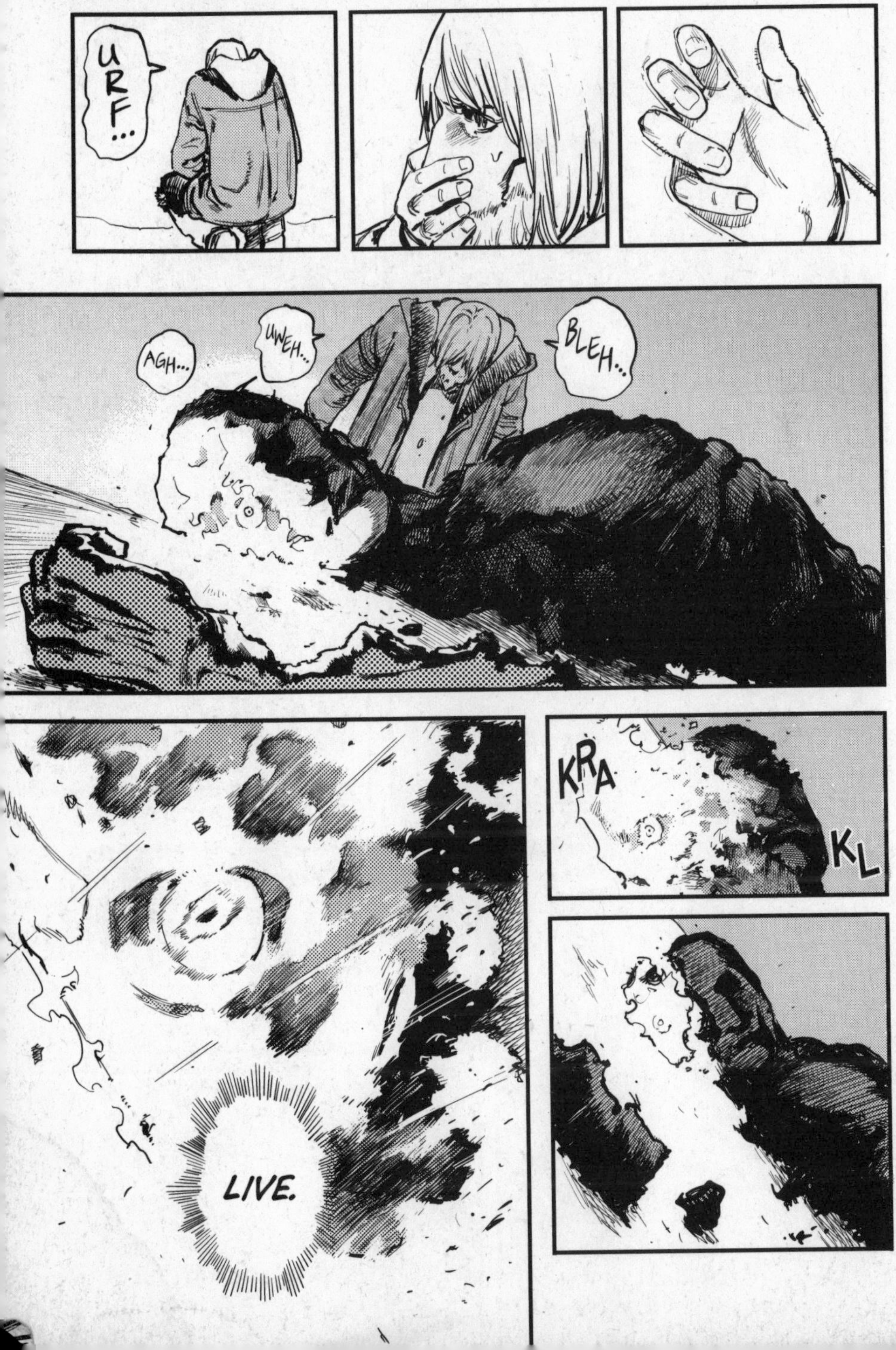
URF...
BLEH...
UWEH...
AGH...
KRA
KL
LIVE.

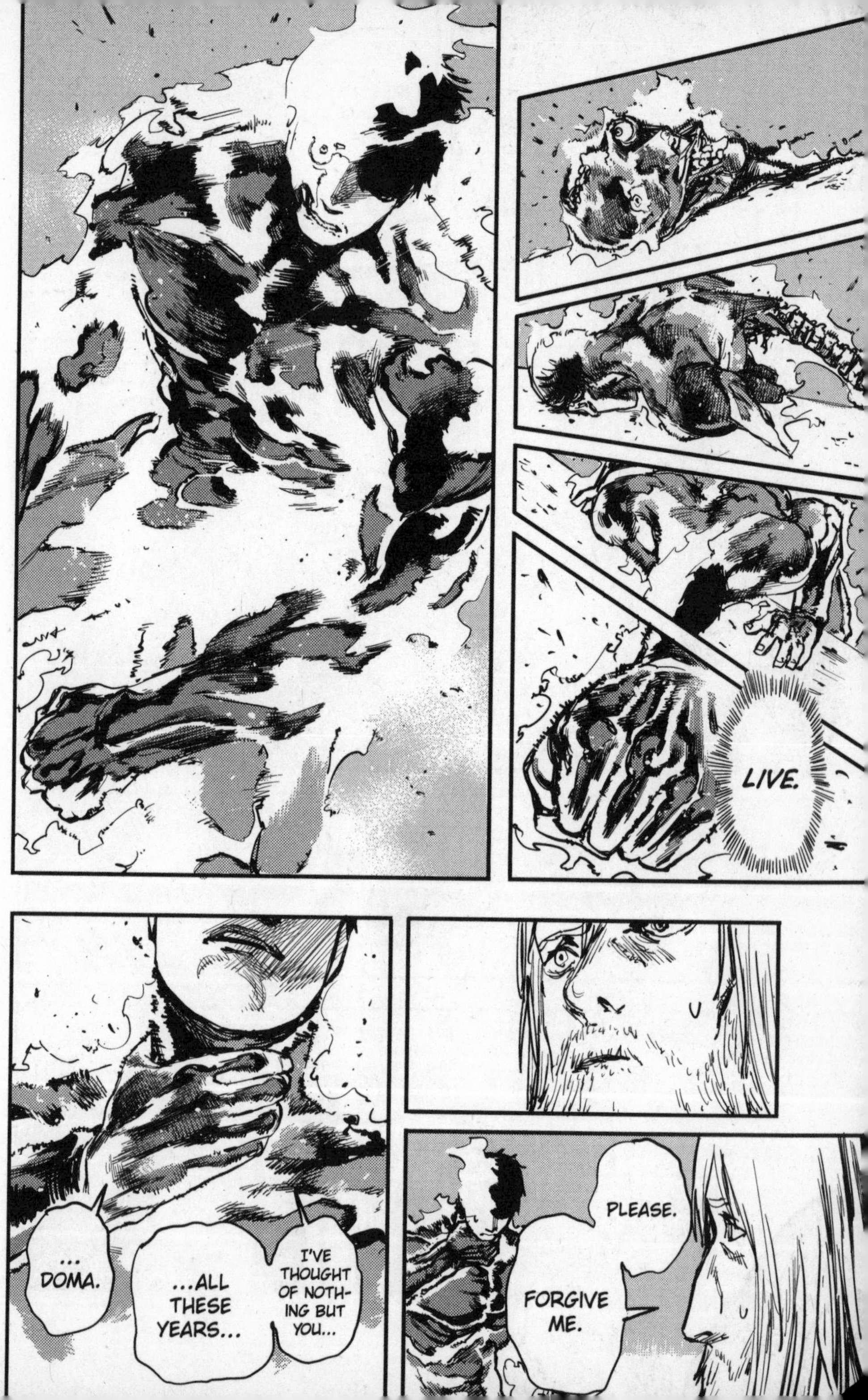
LIVE.
PLEASE.
FORGIVE ME.
I'VE THOUGHT OF NOTH-ING BUT YOU...
...ALL THESE YEARS...
...DOMA.

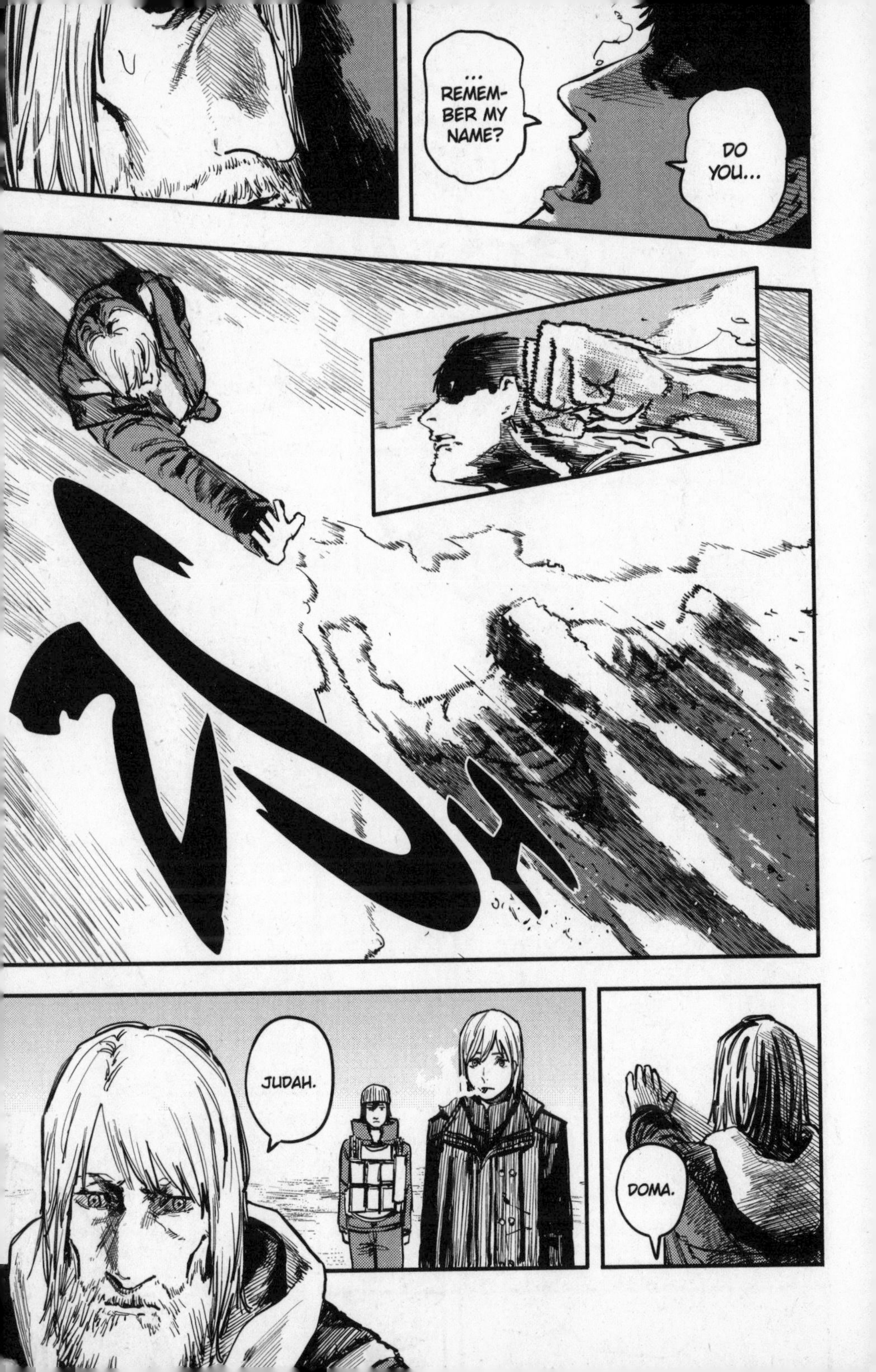
DO YOU...
... REMEMBER MY NAME?
DOMA.
JUDAH.

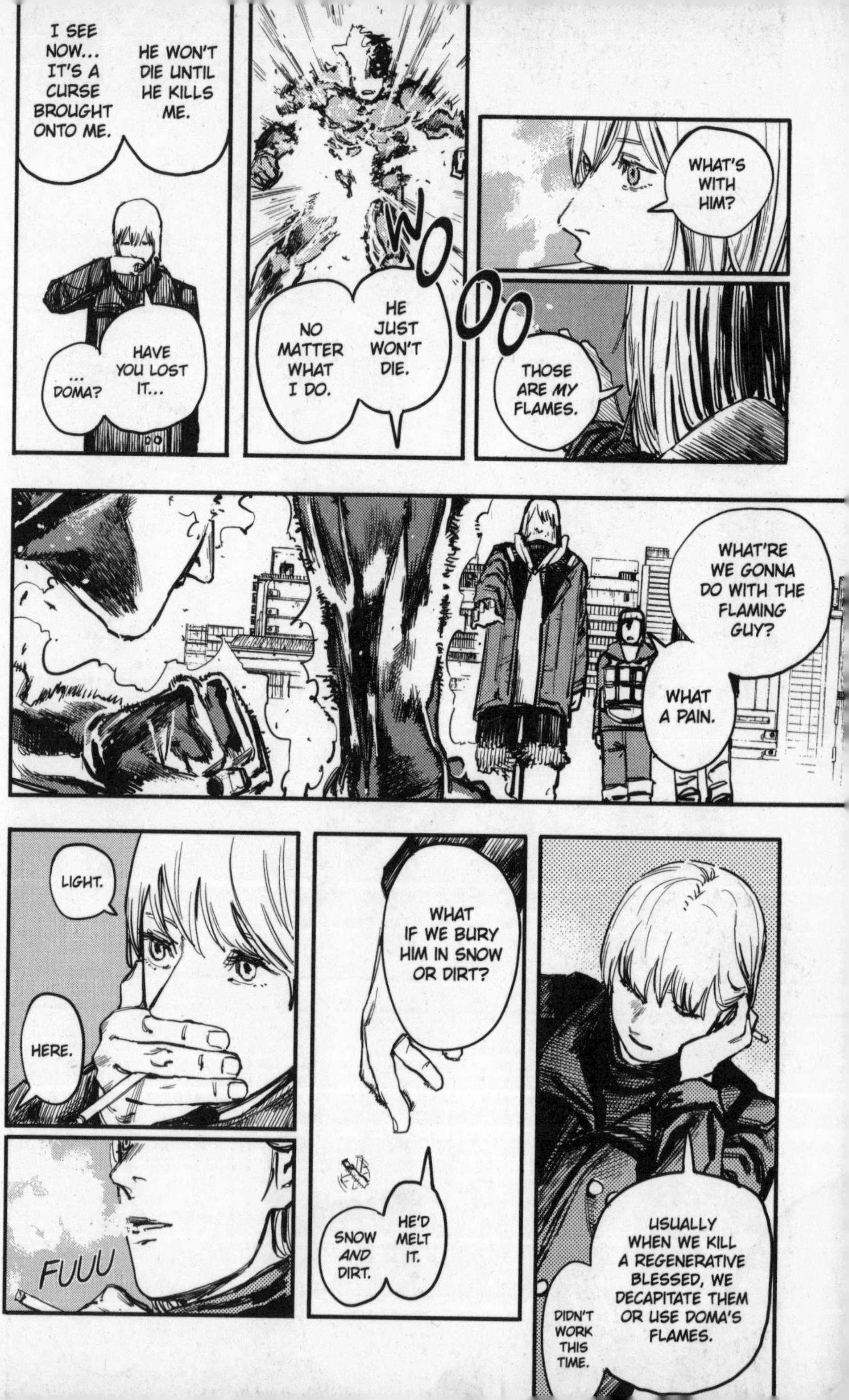
WHAT'S WITH HIM?
THOSE ARE MY FLAMES.
WOOO
HE JUST WON'T DIE.
NO MATTER WHAT I DO.
HE WON'T DIE UNTIL HE KILLS ME.
I SEE NOW... IT'S A CURSE BROUGHT ONTO ME.
HAVE YOU LOST IT...
... DOMA?
WHAT'RE WE GONNA DO WITH THE FLAMING GUY?
WHAT A PAIN.
USUALLY WHEN WE KILL A REGENERATIVE BLESSED, WE DECAPITATE THEM OR USE DOMA'S FLAMES.
DIDN'T WORK THIS TIME.
WHAT IF WE BURY HIM IN SNOW OR DIRT?
HE'D MELT IT.
SNOW AND DIRT.
LIGHT.
HERE.
FUUU

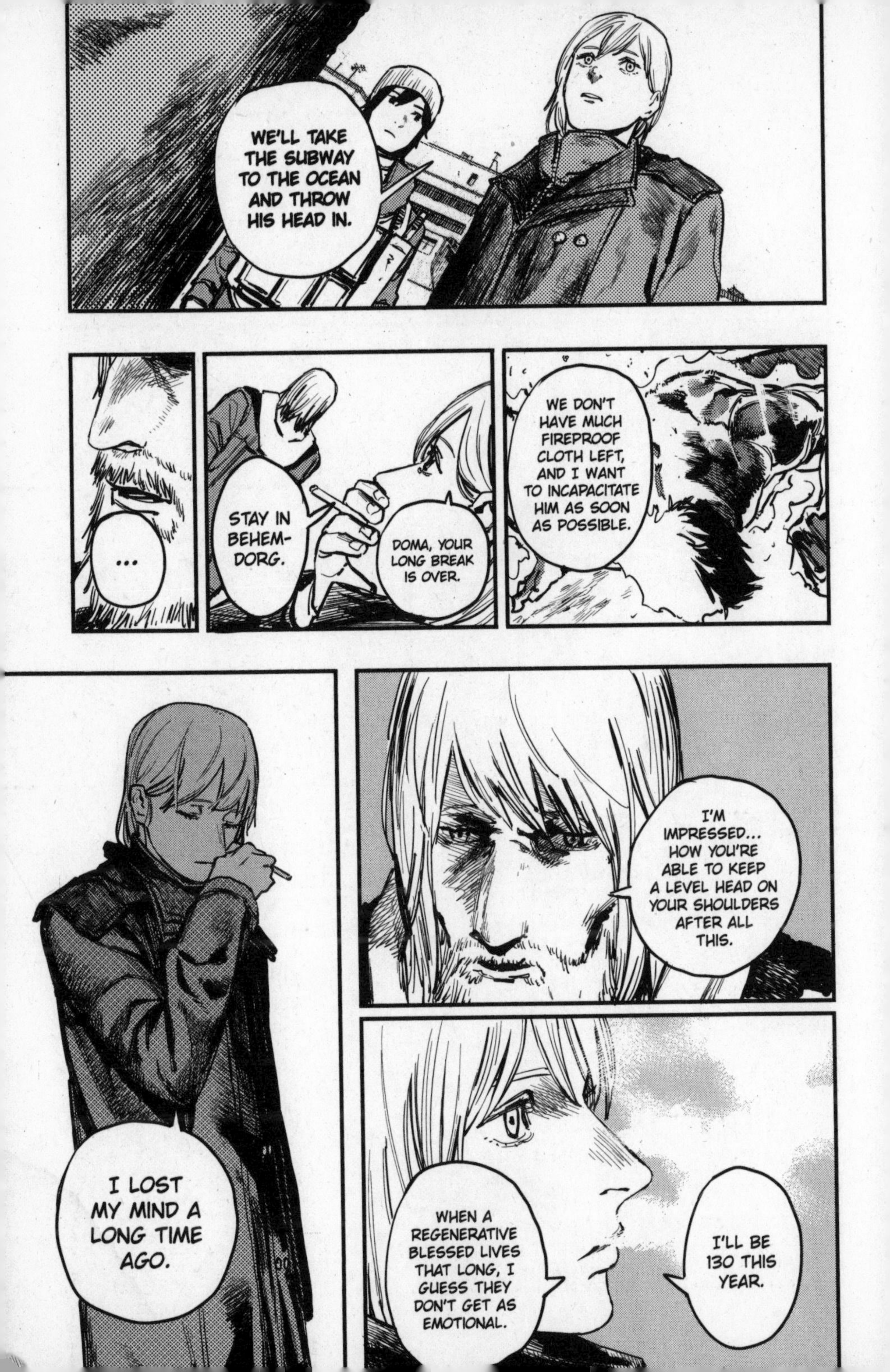
WE'LL TAKE THE SUBWAY TO THE OCEAN AND THROW HIS HEAD IN.
WE DON'T HAVE MUCH FIREPROOF CLOTH LEFT, AND I WANT TO INCAPACITATE HIM AS SOON AS POSSIBLE.
DOMA, YOUR LONG BREAK IS OVER.
STAY IN BEHEM-DORG.
...
I'M IMPRESSED... HOW YOU'RE ABLE TO KEEP A LEVEL HEAD ON YOUR SHOULDERS AFTER ALL THIS.
I'LL BE 130 THIS YEAR.
WHEN A REGENERATIVE BLESSED LIVES THAT LONG, I GUESS THEY DON'T GET AS EMOTIONAL.
I LOST MY MIND A LONG TIME AGO.

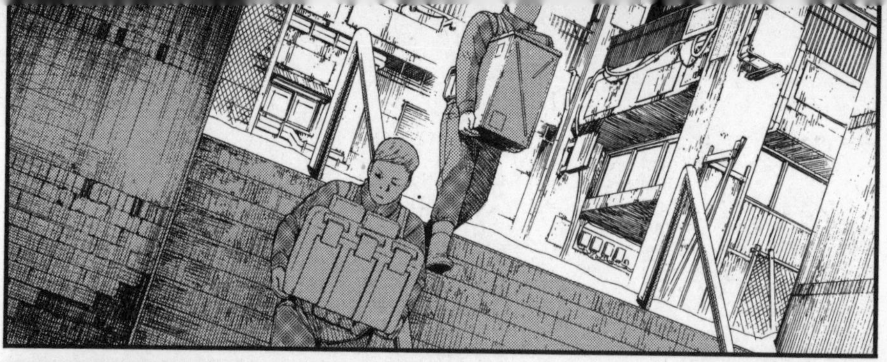
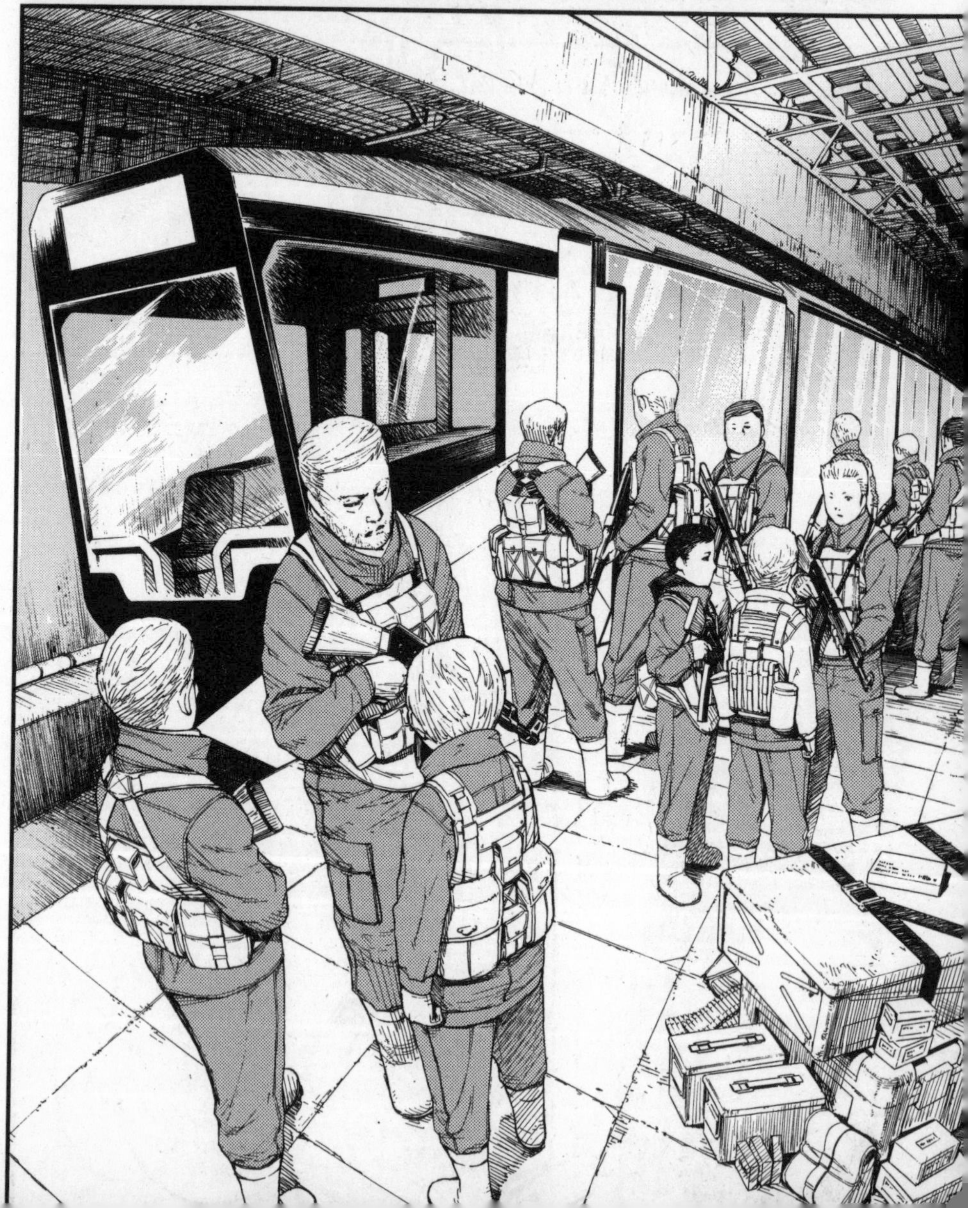

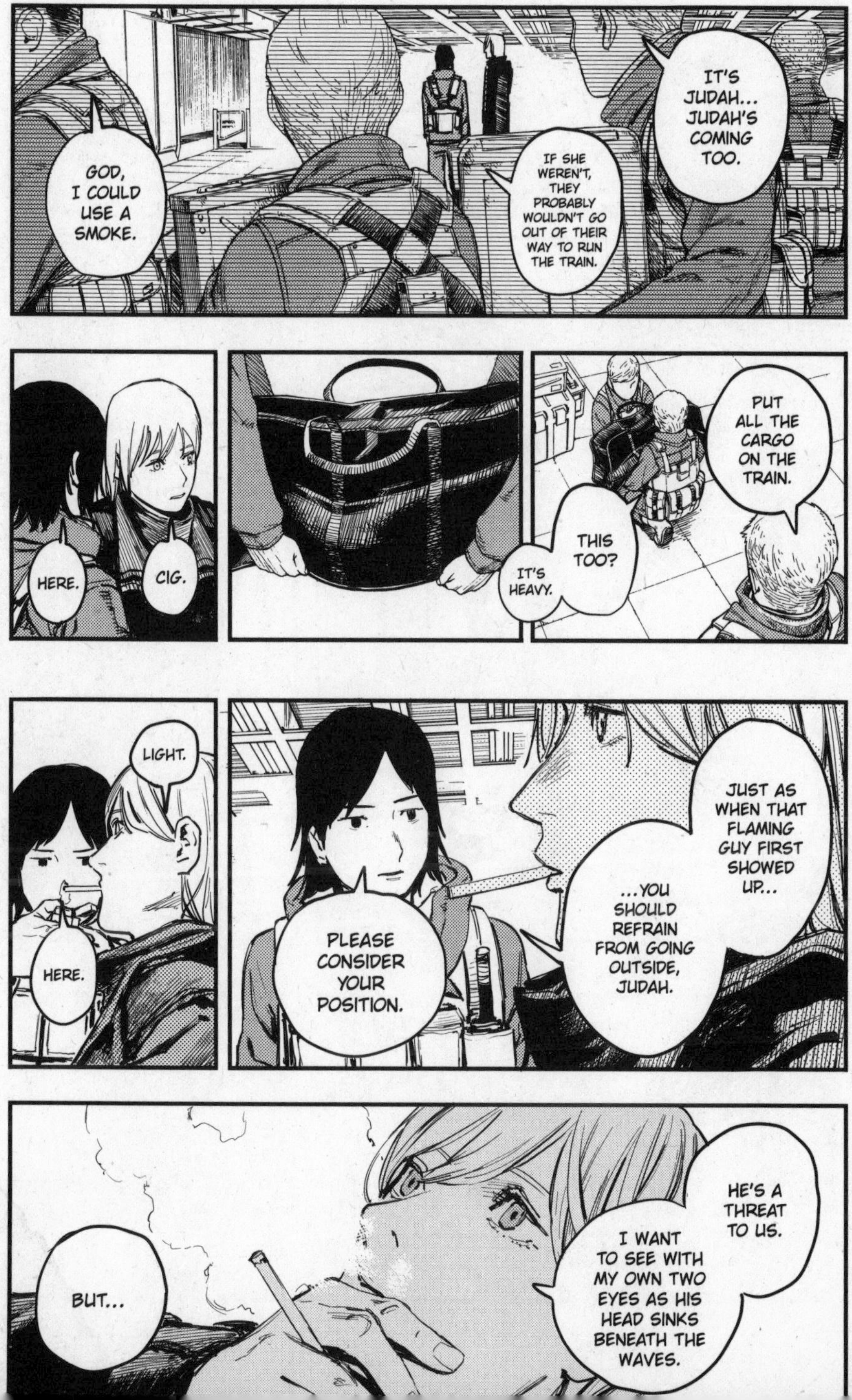
IT'S JUDAH... JUDAH'S COMING TOO.
IF SHE WEREN'T, THEY PROBABLY WOULDN'T GO OUT OF THEIR WAY TO RUN THE TRAIN.
GOD, I COULD USE A SMOKE.
PUT ALL THE CARGO ON THE TRAIN.
THIS TOO?
IT'S HEAVY.
CIG.
HERE.
JUST AS WHEN THAT FLAMING GUY FIRST SHOWED UP...
...YOU SHOULD REFRAIN FROM GOING OUTSIDE, JUDAH.
PLEASE CONSIDER YOUR POSITION.
LIGHT.
HERE.
HE'S A THREAT TO US.
I WANT TO SEE WITH MY OWN TWO EYES AS HIS HEAD SINKS BENEATH THE WAVES.
BUT...

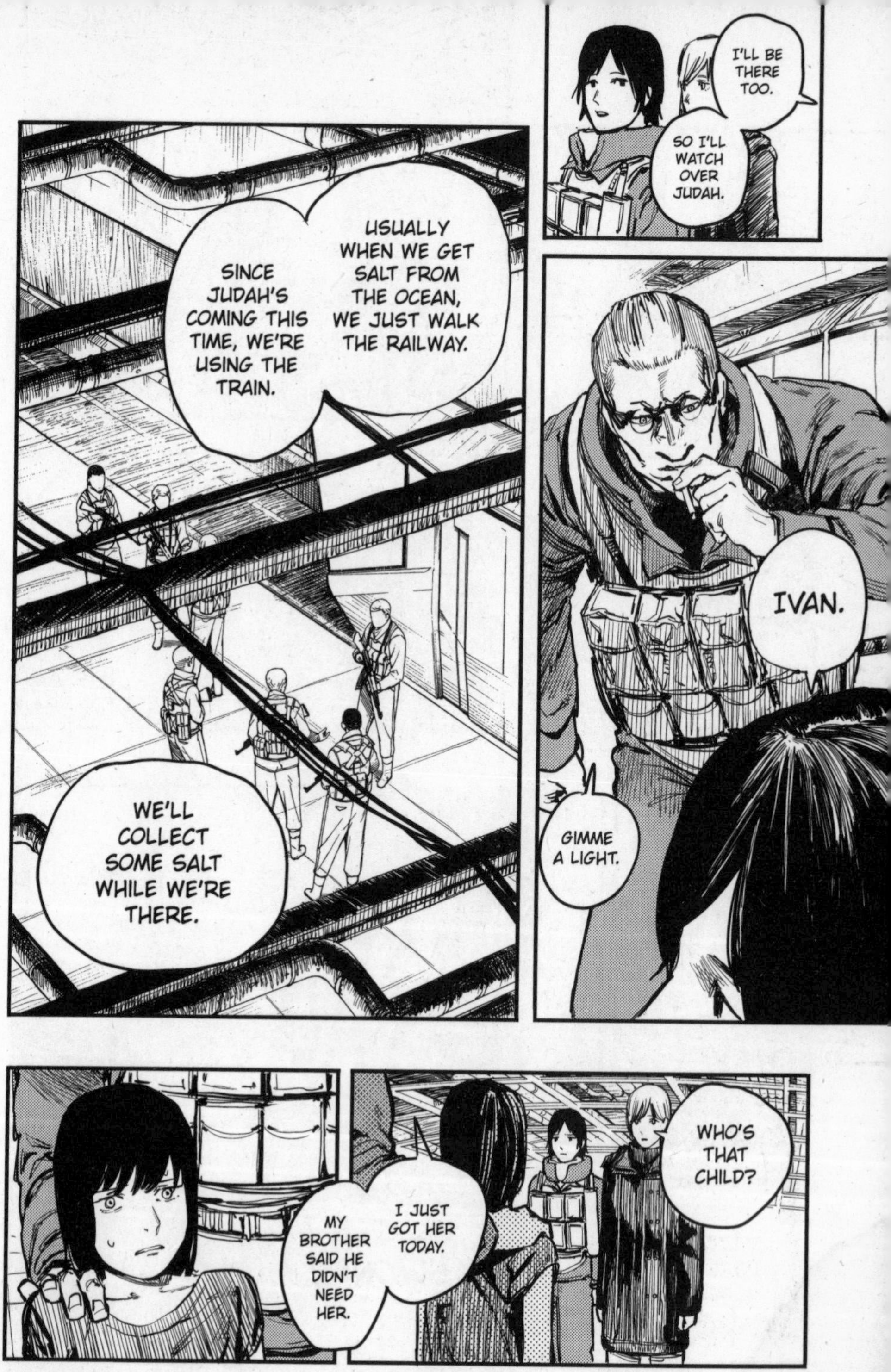
I'LL BE THERE TOO.
SO I'LL WATCH OVER JUDAH.
IVAN.
GIMME A LIGHT.
USUALLY WHEN WE GET SALT FROM THE OCEAN, WE JUST WALK THE RAILWAY.
SINCE JUDAH'S COMING THIS TIME, WE'RE USING THE TRAIN.
WE'LL COLLECT SOME SALT WHILE WE'RE THERE.
WHO'S THAT CHILD?
I JUST GOT HER TODAY.
MY BROTHER SAID HE DIDN'T NEED HER.

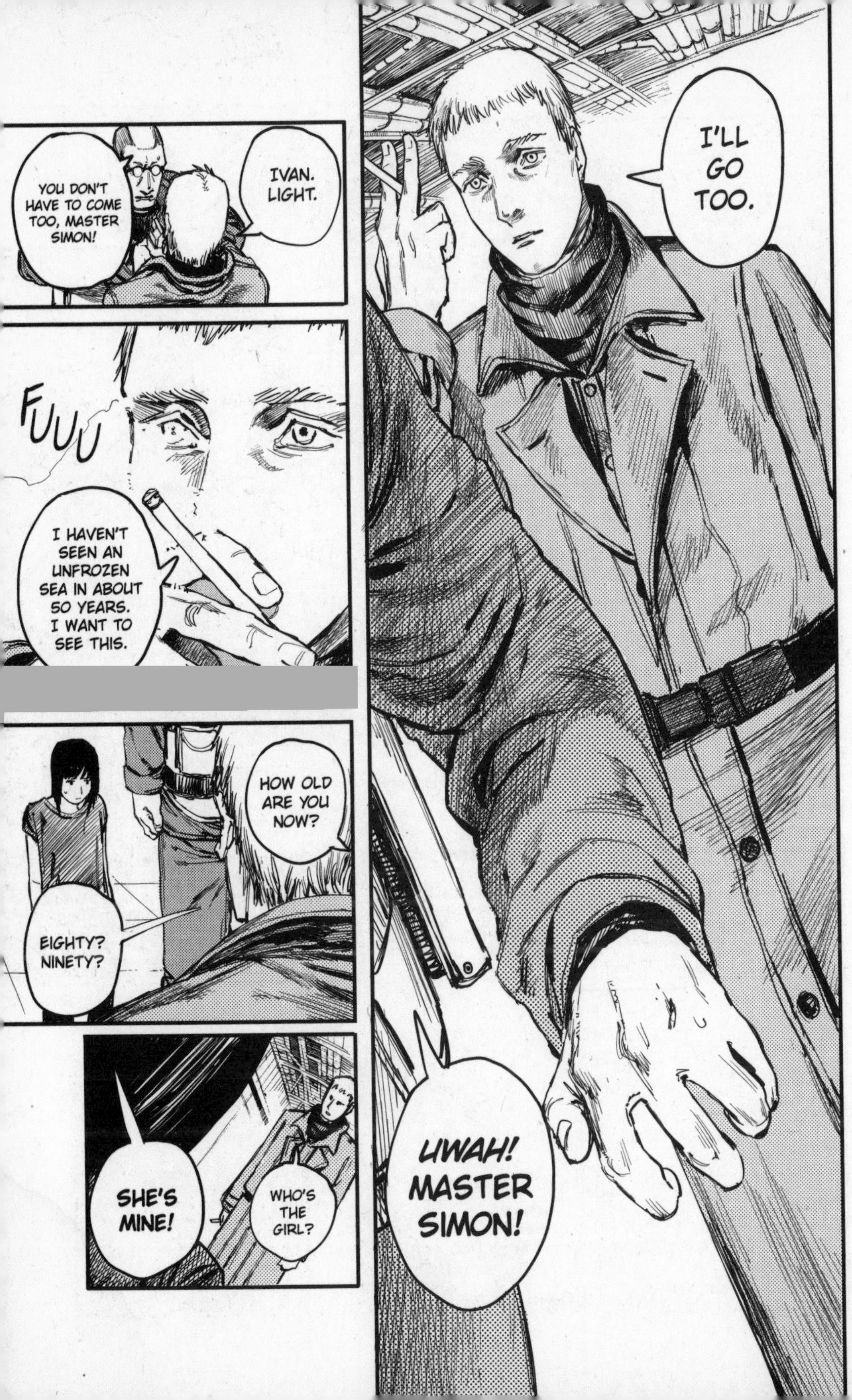
I'LL GO TOO.
UWAH! MASTER SIMON!
IVAN. LIGHT.
YOU DON'T HAVE TO COME TOO, MASTER SIMON!
FUUU
I HAVEN'T SEEN AN UNFROZEN SEA IN ABOUT 50 YEARS. I WANT TO SEE THIS.
HOW OLD ARE YOU NOW?
EIGHTY? NINETY?
WHO'S THE GIRL?
SHE'S MINE!

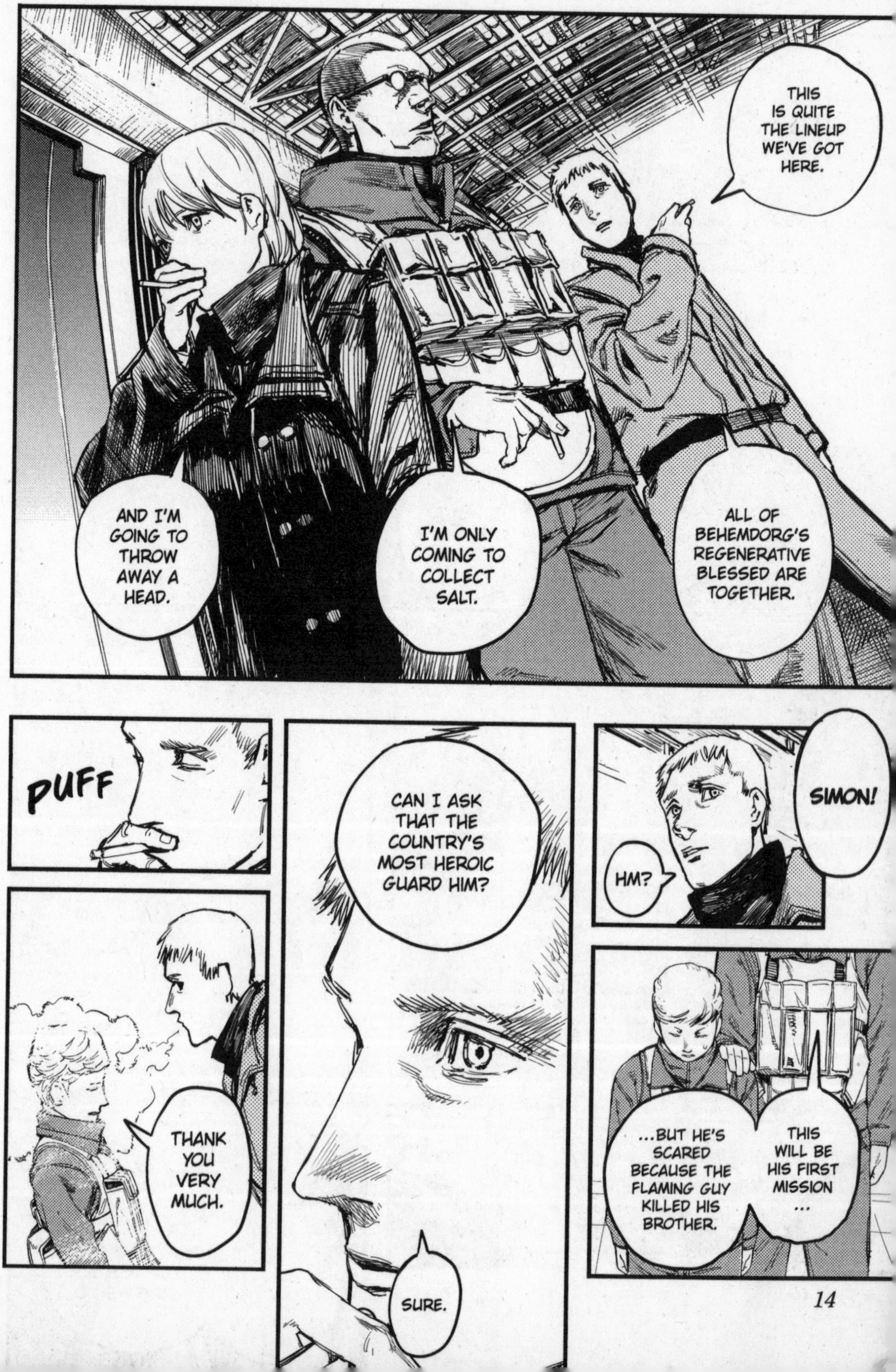
THIS IS QUITE THE LINEUP WE'VE GOT HERE.
ALL OF BEHEMDORG'S REGENERATIVE BLESSED ARE TOGETHER.
I'M ONLY COMING TO COLLECT SALT.
AND I'M GOING TO THROW AWAY A HEAD.
SIMON!
HM?
THIS WILL BE HIS FIRST MISSION ...
...BUT HE'S SCARED BECAUSE THE FLAMING GUY KILLED HIS BROTHER.
CAN I ASK THAT THE COUNTRY'S MOST HEROIC GUARD HIM?
SURE.
PUFF
THANK YOU VERY MUCH.

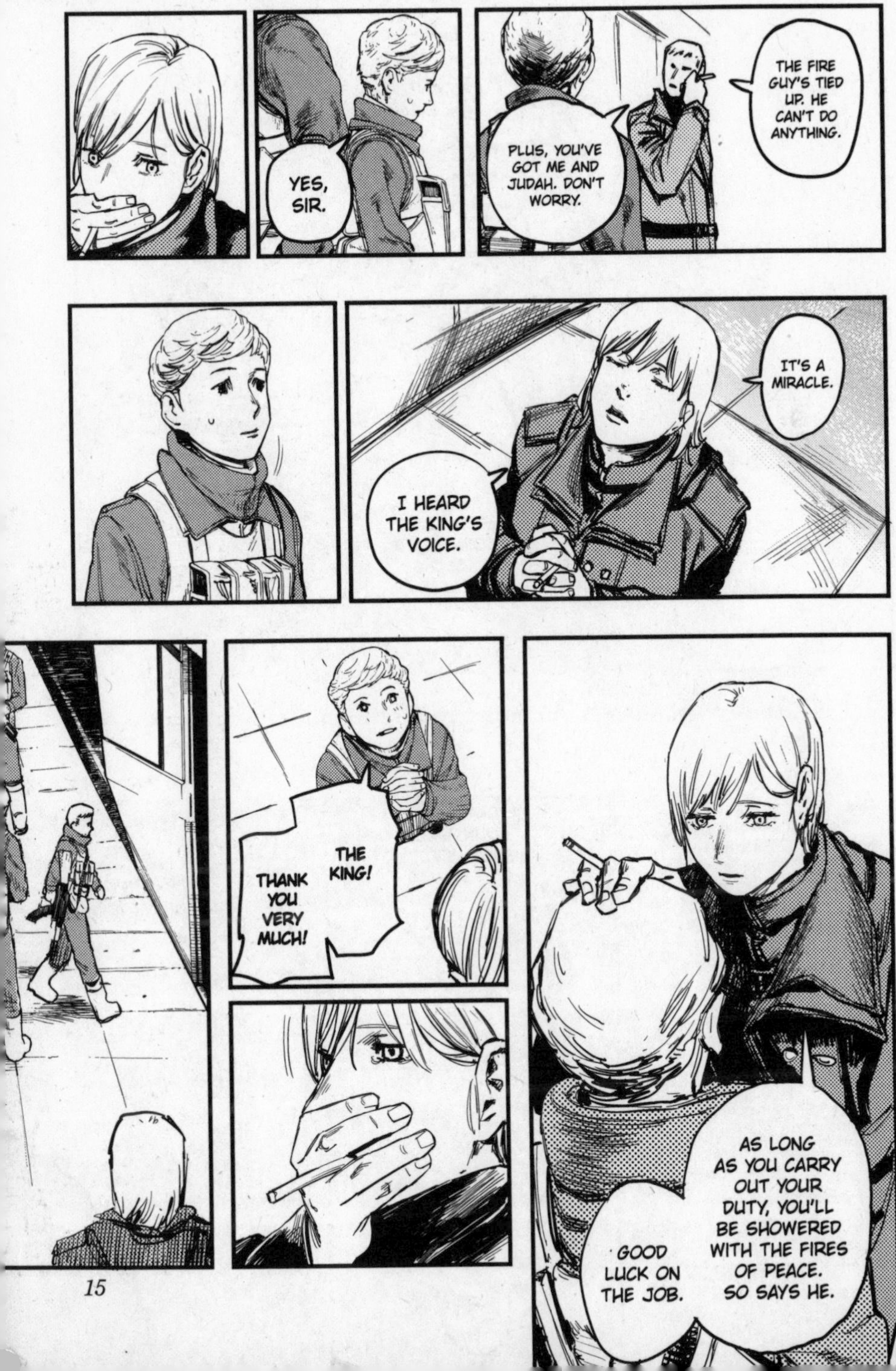
THE FIRE GUY'S TIED UP. HE CAN'T DO ANYTHING.
PLUS, YOU'VE GOT ME AND JUDAH. DON'T WORRY.
YES, SIR.
IT'S A MIRACLE.
I HEARD THE KING'S VOICE.
AS LONG AS YOU CARRY OUT YOUR DUTY, YOU'LL BE SHOWERED WITH THE FIRES OF PEACE. SO SAYS HE.
GOOD LUCK ON THE JOB.
THE KING!
THANK YOU VERY MUCH!

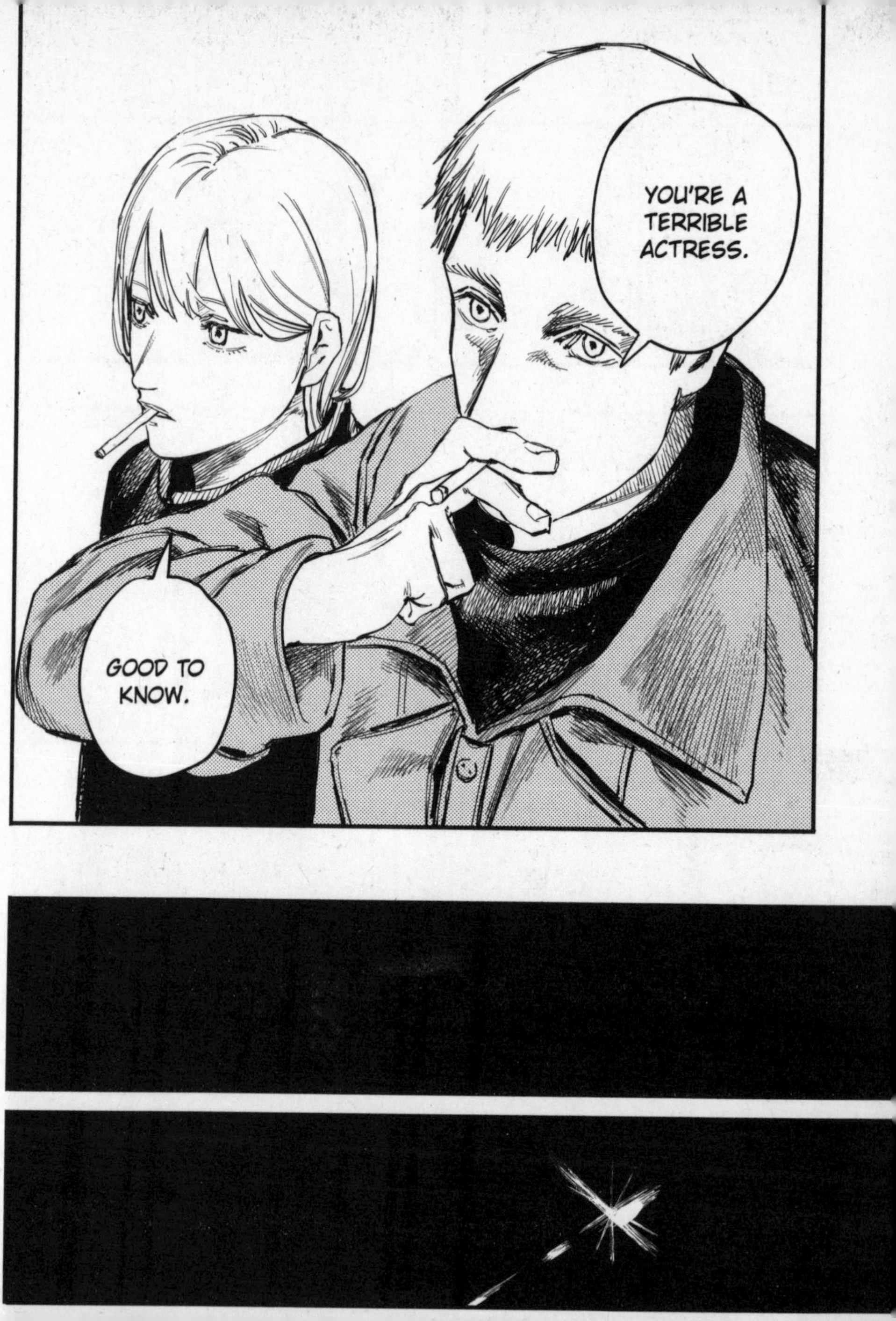
YOU'RE A TERRIBLE ACTRESS.
GOOD TO KNOW.

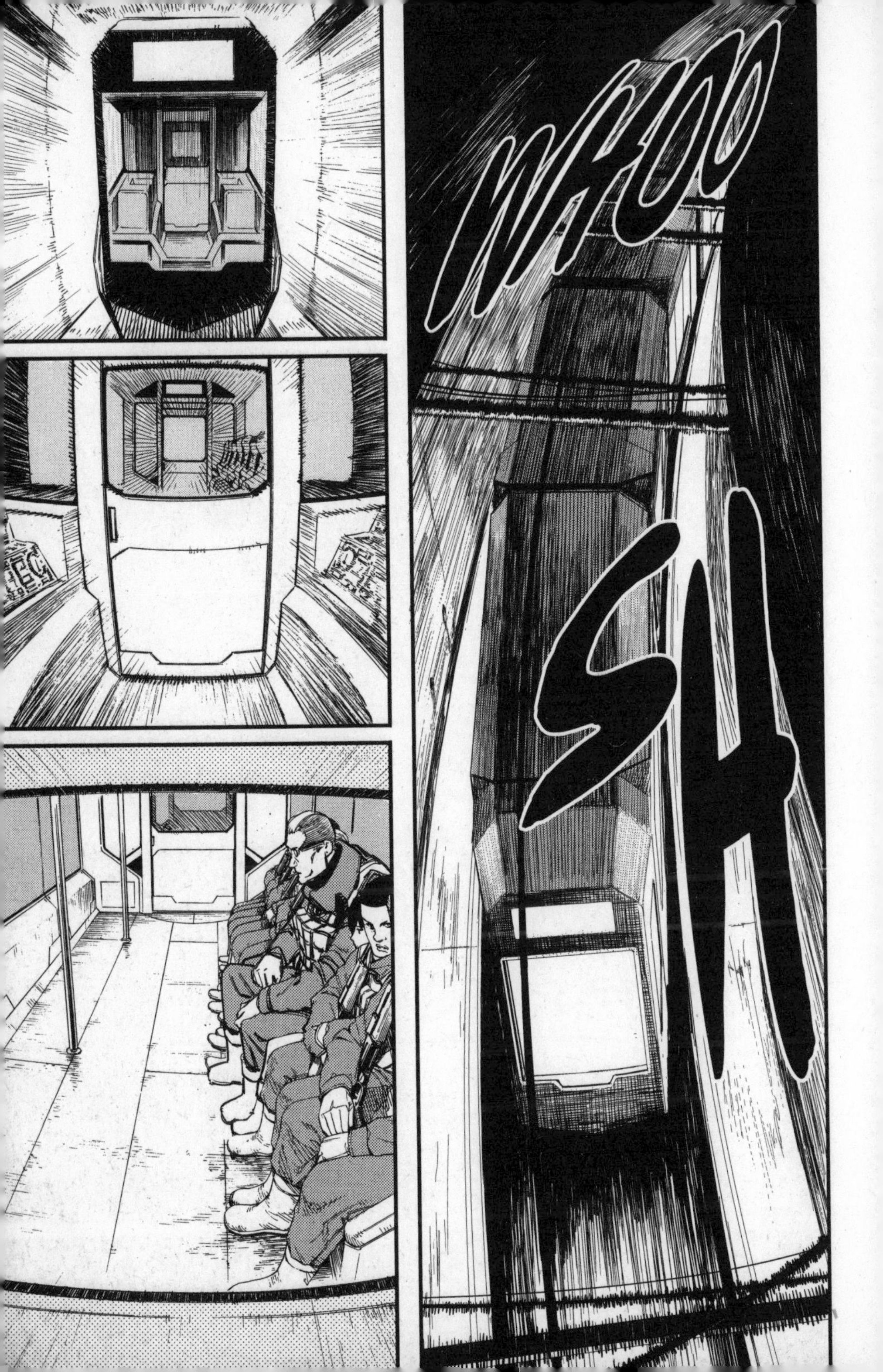
WHOOO
SH

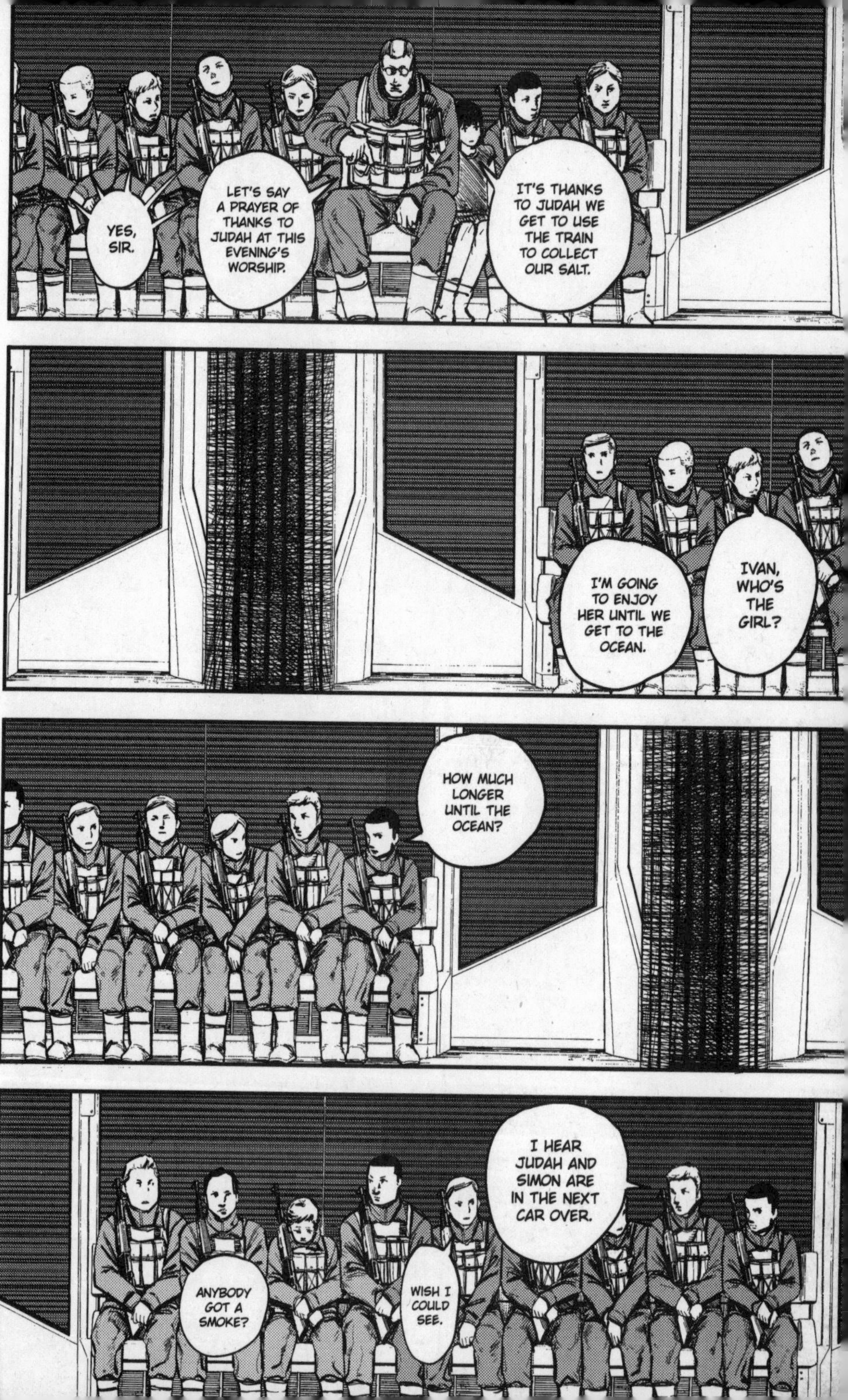
IT'S THANKS TO JUDAH WE GET TO USE THE TRAIN TO COLLECT OUR SALT.
LET'S SAY A PRAYER OF THANKS TO JUDAH AT THIS EVENING'S WORSHIP.
YES, SIR.
IVAN, WHO'S THE GIRL?
I'M GOING TO ENJOY HER UNTIL WE GET TO THE OCEAN.
HOW MUCH LONGER UNTIL THE OCEAN?
I HEAR JUDAH AND SIMON ARE IN THE NEXT CAR OVER.
WISH I COULD SEE.
ANYBODY GOT A SMOKE?

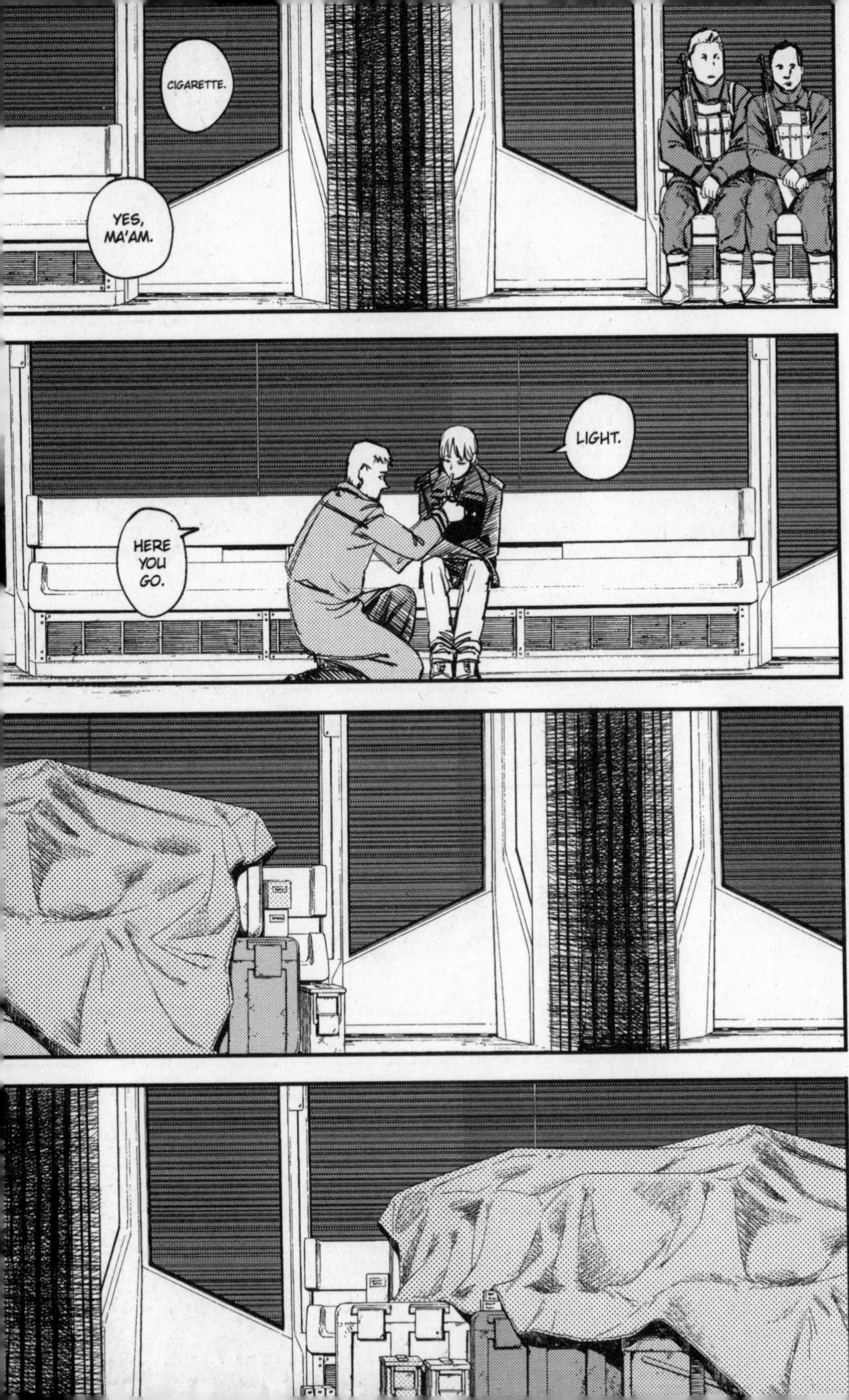
CIGARETTE.
YES, MA'AM.
LIGHT.
HERE YOU GO.

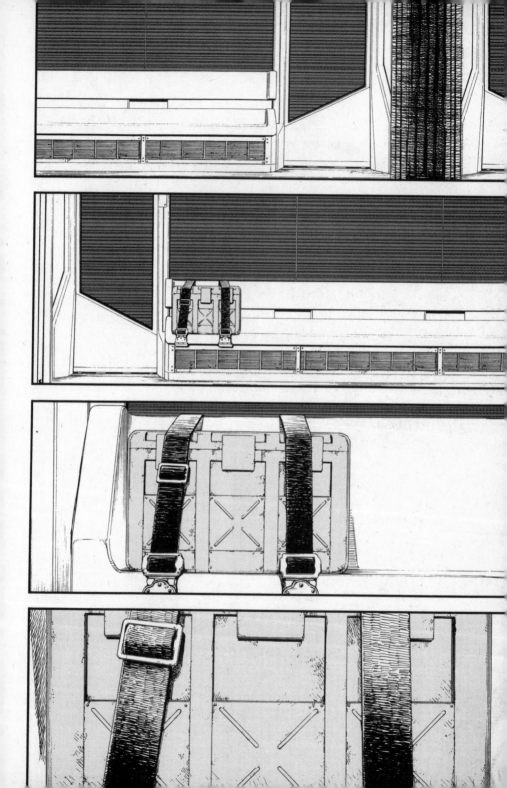

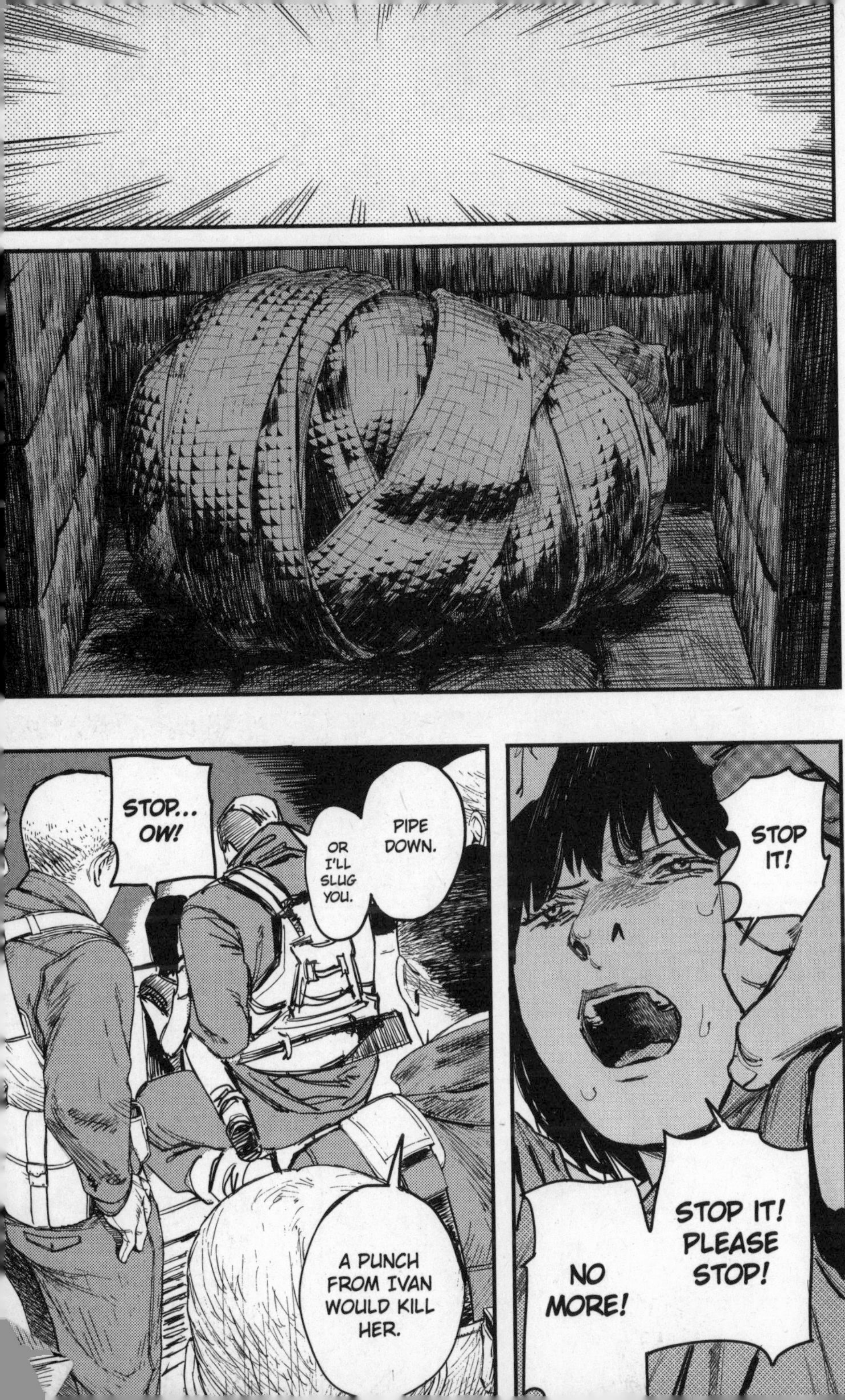
STOP IT!
STOP IT! PLEASE STOP!
NO MORE!
PIPE DOWN.
OR I'LL SLUG YOU.
STOP... OW!
A PUNCH FROM IVAN WOULD KILL HER.

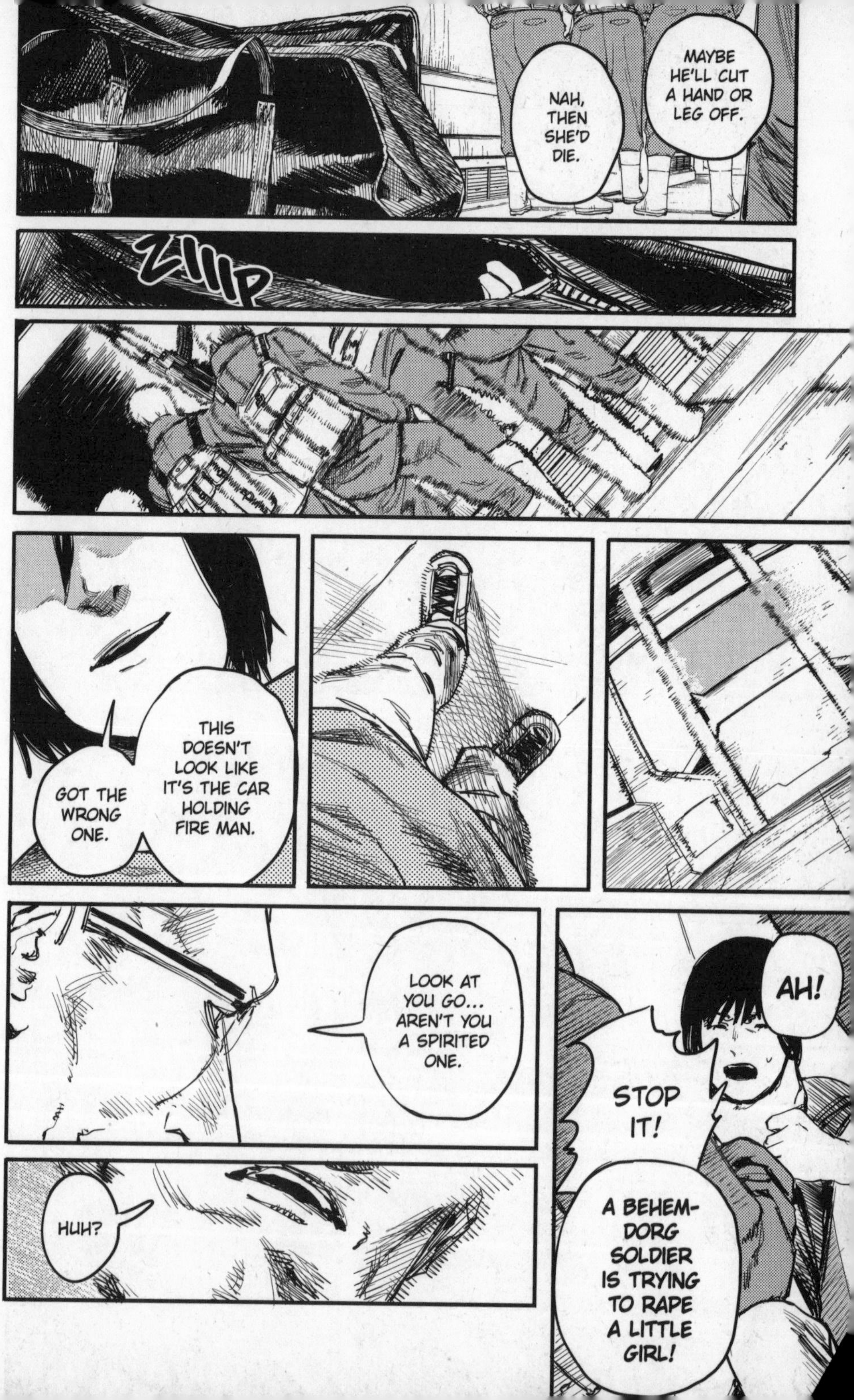
MAYBE HE'LL CUT A HAND OR LEG OFF.
NAH, THEN SHE'D DIE.
ZIIIP
THIS DOESN'T LOOK LIKE IT'S THE CAR HOLDING FIRE MAN.
GOT THE WRONG ONE.
AH!
STOP IT!
A BEHEM-DORG SOLDIER IS TRYING TO RAPE A LITTLE GIRL!
LOOK AT YOU GO... AREN'T YOU A SPIRITED ONE.
HUH?

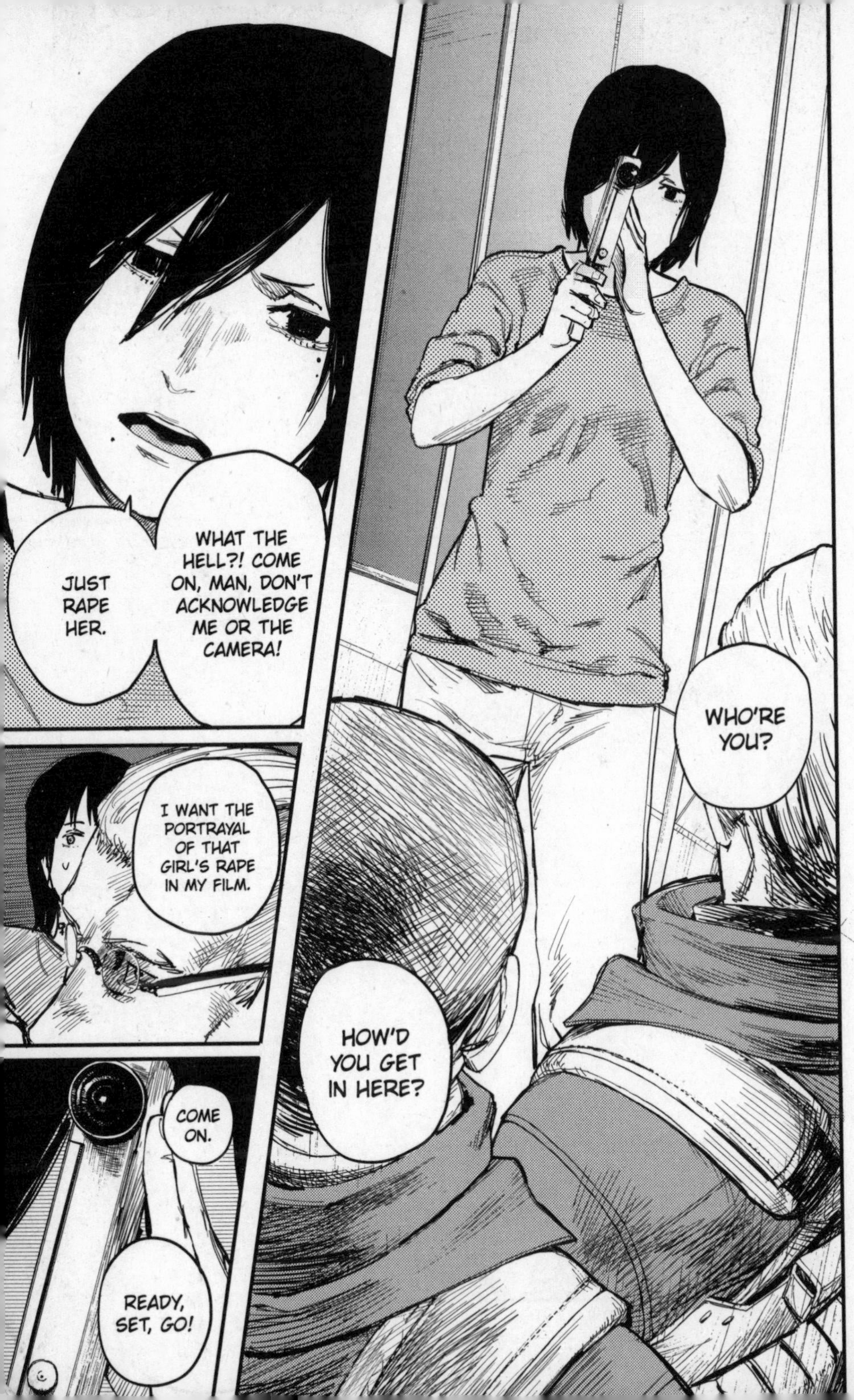
WHO'RE YOU?
HOW'D YOU GET IN HERE?
WHAT THE HELL?! COME ON, MAN, DON'T ACKNOWLEDGE ME OR THE CAMERA!
JUST RAPE HER.
I WANT THE PORTRAYAL OF THAT GIRL'S RAPE IN MY FILM.
COME ON.
READY, SET, GO!

FIRE PUNCH

CHAPTER 10

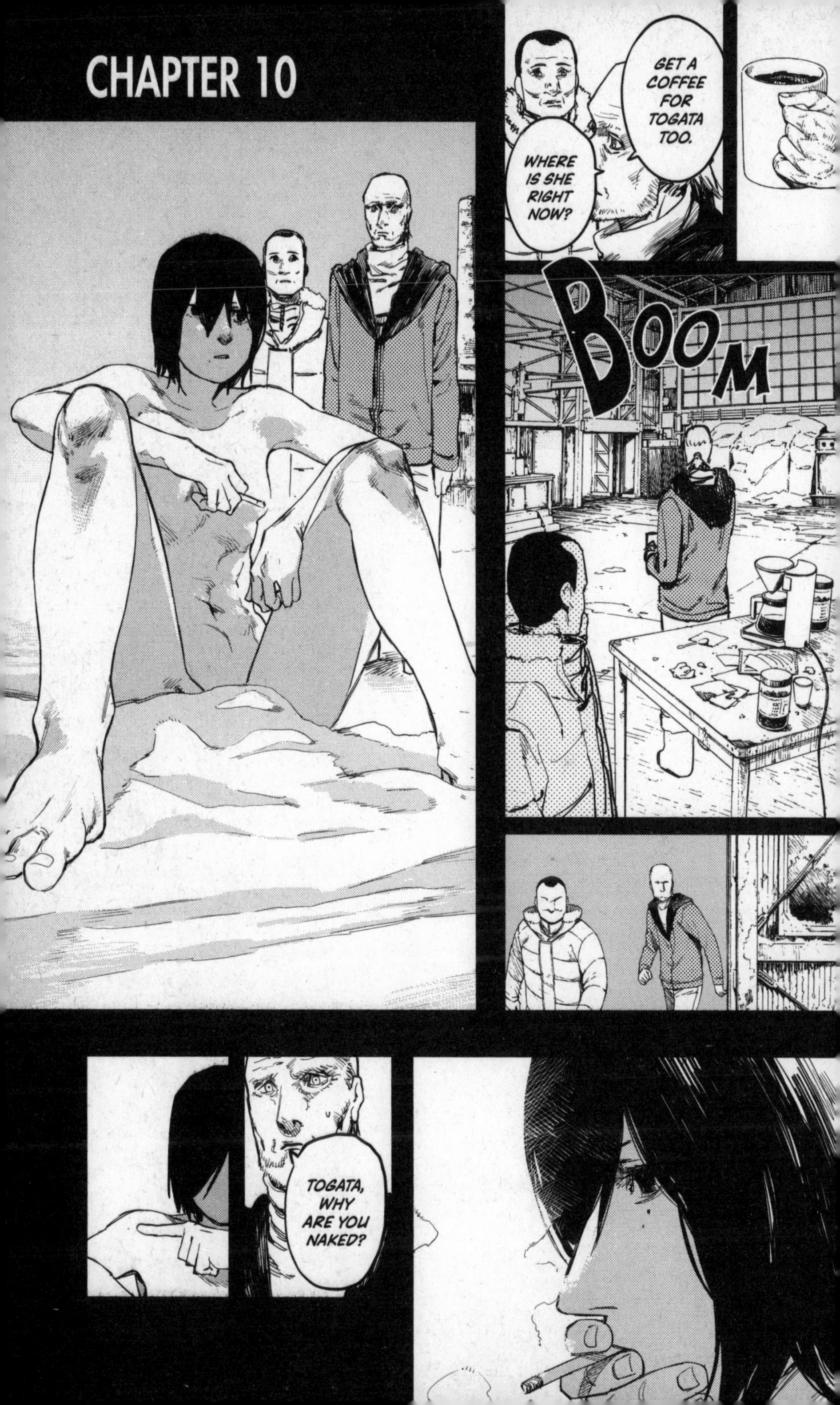
GET A COFFEE FOR TOGATA TOO.
WHERE IS SHE RIGHT NOW?
BOOM
TOGATA, WHY ARE YOU NAKED?

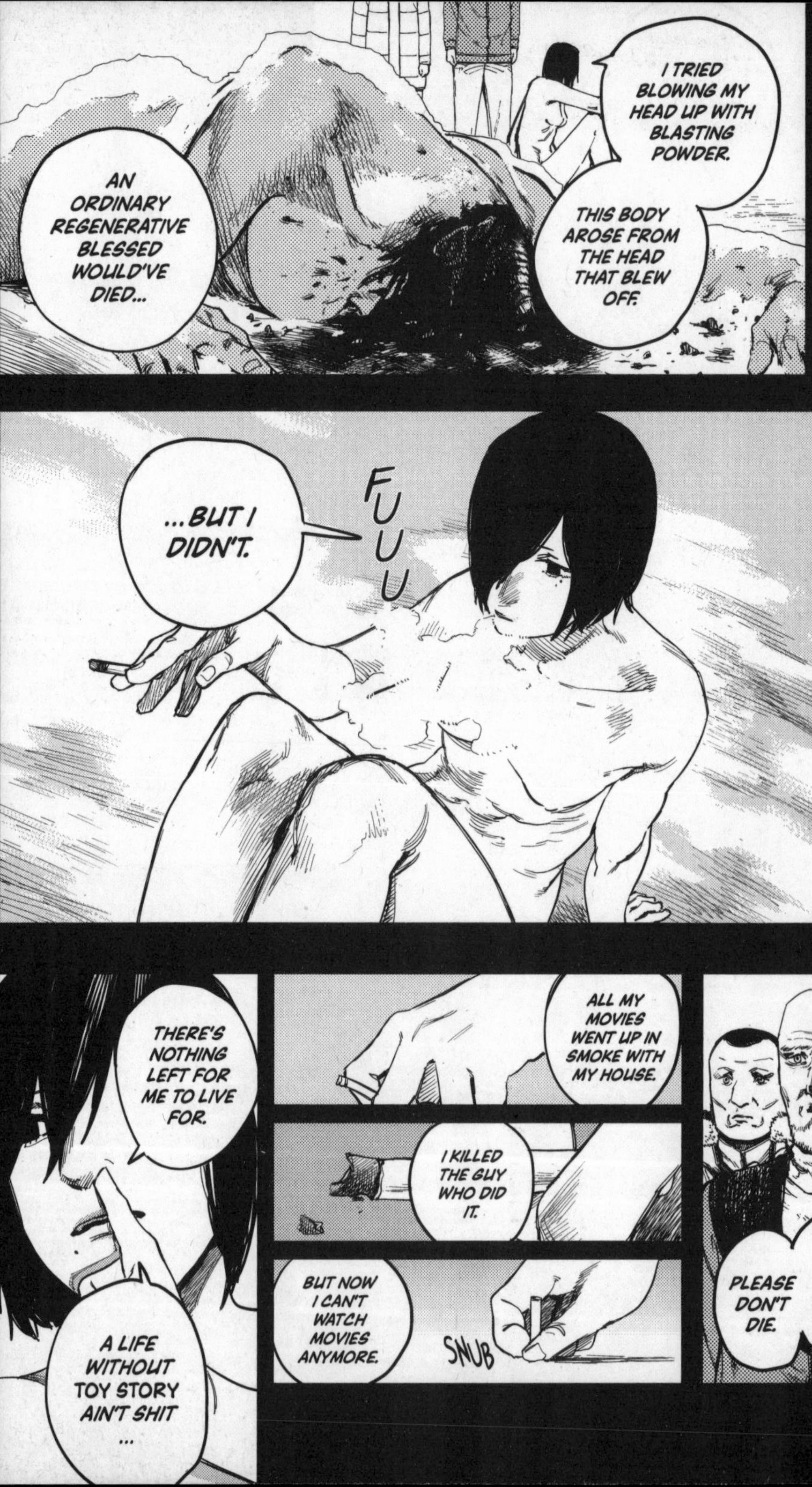
I TRIED BLOWING MY HEAD UP WITH BLASTING POWDER.
THIS BODY AROSE FROM THE HEAD THAT BLEW OFF.
AN ORDINARY REGENERATIVE BLESSED WOULD'VE DIED...
FUUU
...BUT I DIDN'T.
PLEASE ... DON'T DIE.
ALL MY MOVIES WENT UP IN SMOKE WITH MY HOUSE.
I KILLED THE GUY WHO DID IT.
SNUB
BUT NOW I CAN'T WATCH MOVIES ANYMORE.
THERE'S NOTHING LEFT FOR ME TO LIVE FOR.
A LIFE WITHOUT TOY STORY AIN'T SHIT ...

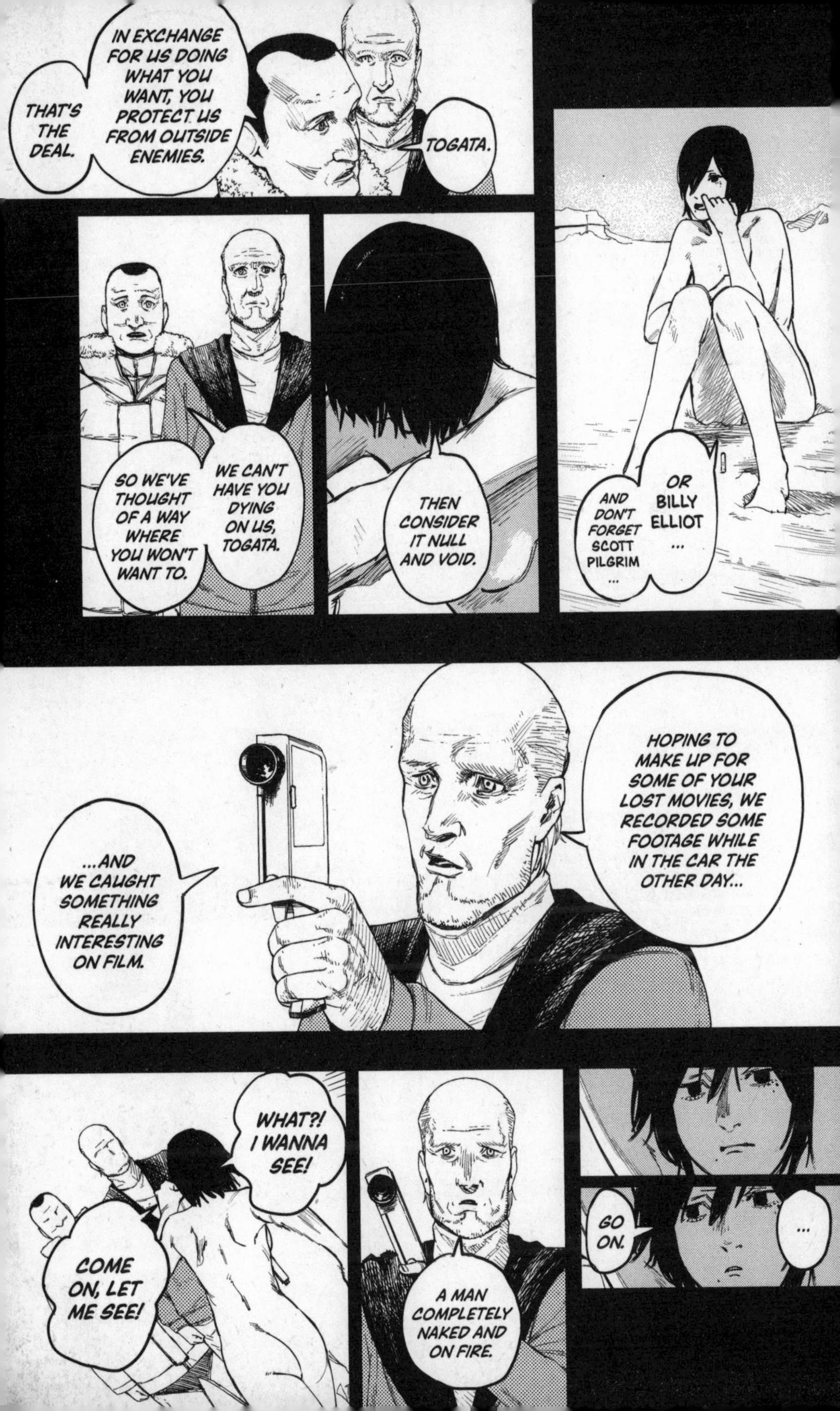
OR BILLY ELLIOT ...
AND DON'T FORGET SCOTT PILGRIM ...
TOGATA.
IN EXCHANGE FOR US DOING WHAT YOU WANT, YOU PROTECT US FROM OUTSIDE ENEMIES.
THAT'S THE DEAL.
THEN CONSIDER IT NULL AND VOID.
WE CAN'T HAVE YOU DYING ON US, TOGATA.
SO WE'VE THOUGHT OF A WAY WHERE YOU WON'T WANT TO.
HOPING TO MAKE UP FOR SOME OF YOUR LOST MOVIES, WE RECORDED SOME FOOTAGE WHILE IN THE CAR THE OTHER DAY...
...AND WE CAUGHT SOMETHING REALLY INTERESTING ON FILM.
...
GO ON.
A MAN COMPLETELY NAKED AND ON FIRE.
WHAT?! I WANNA SEE!
COME ON, LET ME SEE!

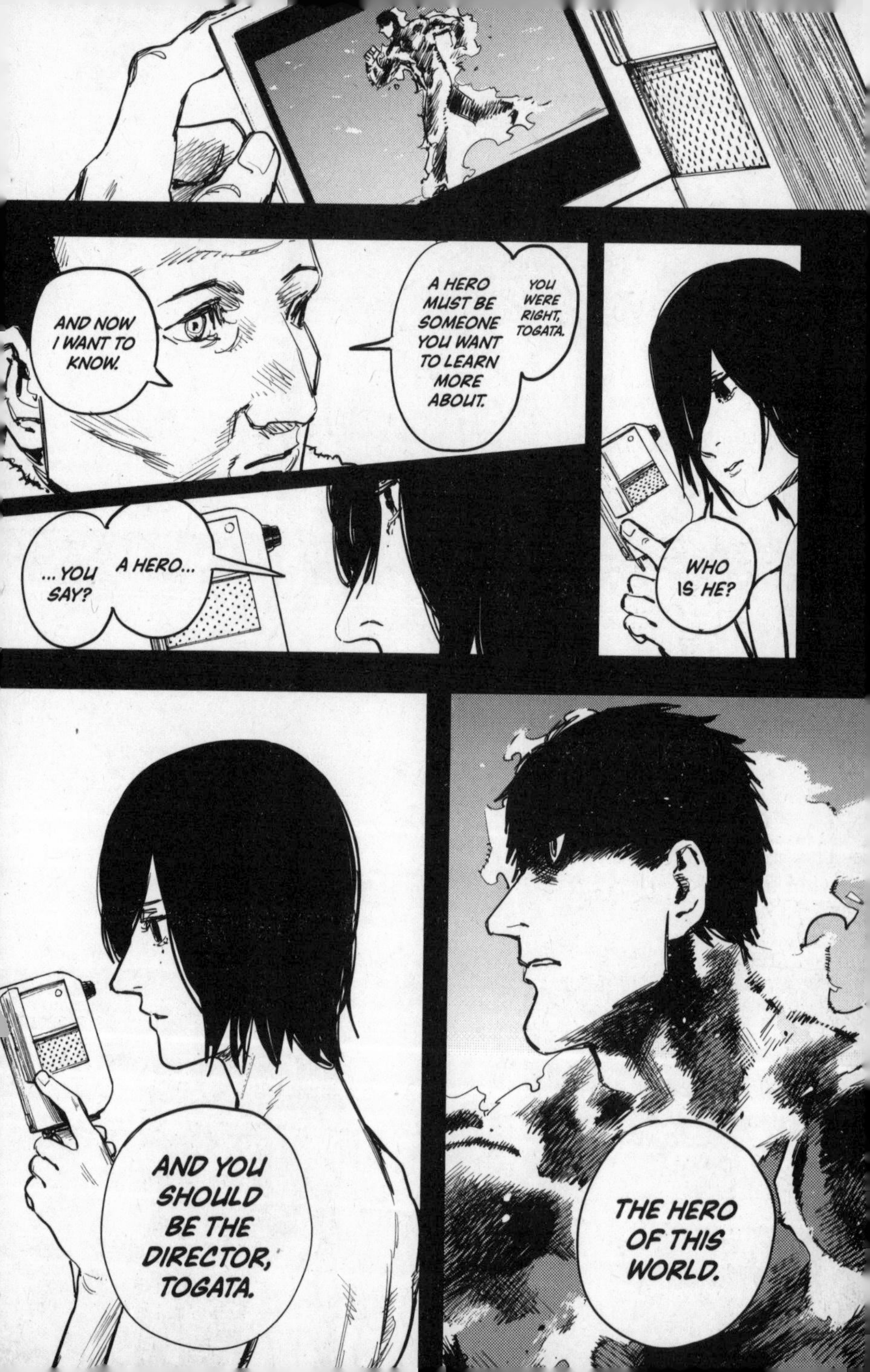
WHO IS HE?
YOU WERE RIGHT, TOGATA.
A HERO MUST BE SOMEONE YOU WANT TO LEARN MORE ABOUT.
AND NOW I WANT TO KNOW.
A HERO...
...YOU SAY?
THE HERO OF THIS WORLD.
AND YOU SHOULD BE THE DIRECTOR, TOGATA.

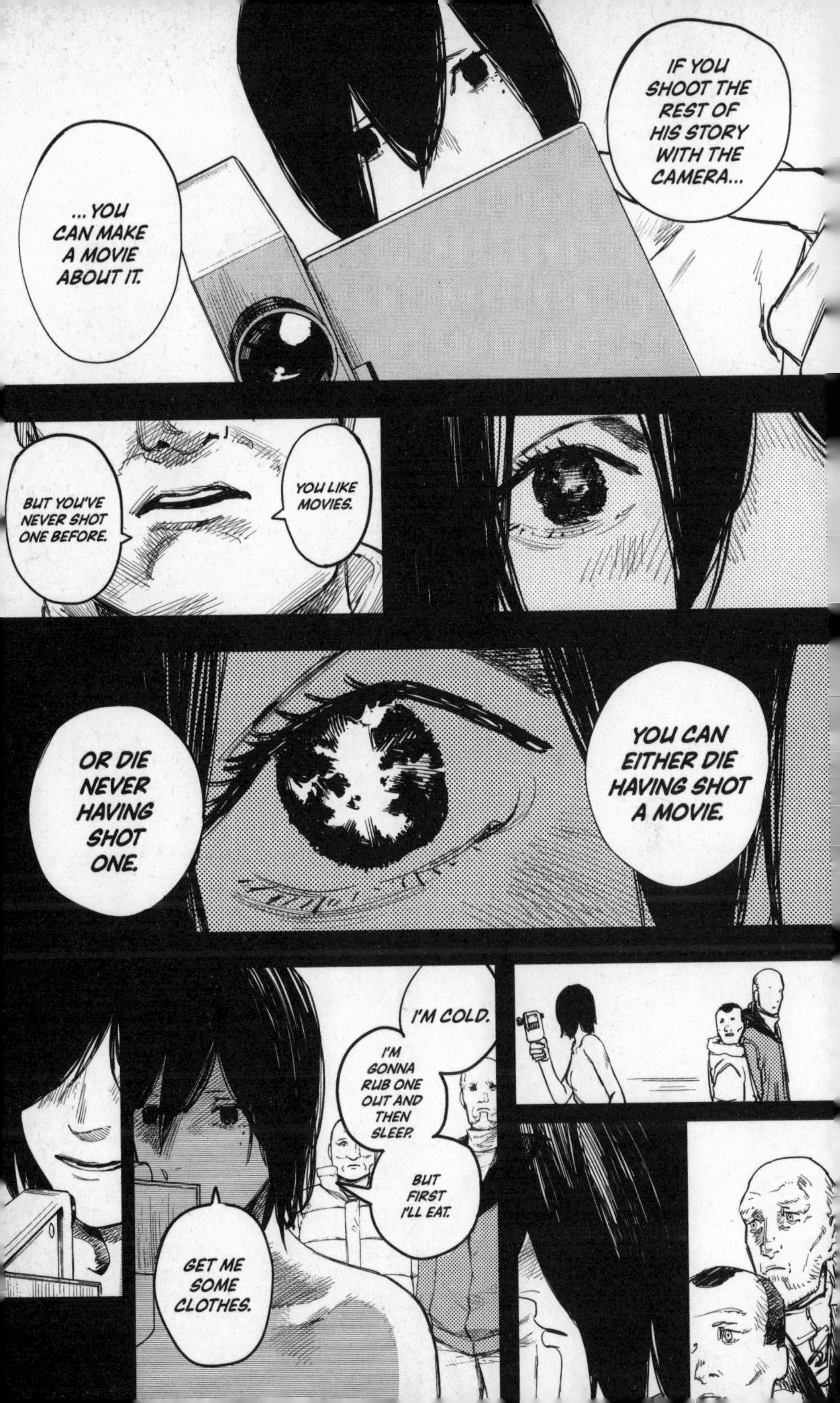
IF YOU SHOOT THE REST OF HIS STORY WITH THE CAMERA...
...YOU CAN MAKE A MOVIE ABOUT IT.
YOU LIKE MOVIES.
BUT YOU'VE NEVER SHOT ONE BEFORE.
YOU CAN EITHER DIE HAVING SHOT A MOVIE.
OR DIE NEVER HAVING SHOT ONE.
I'M COLD.
I'M GONNA RUB ONE OUT AND THEN SLEEP.
BUT FIRST I'LL EAT.
GET ME SOME CLOTHES.

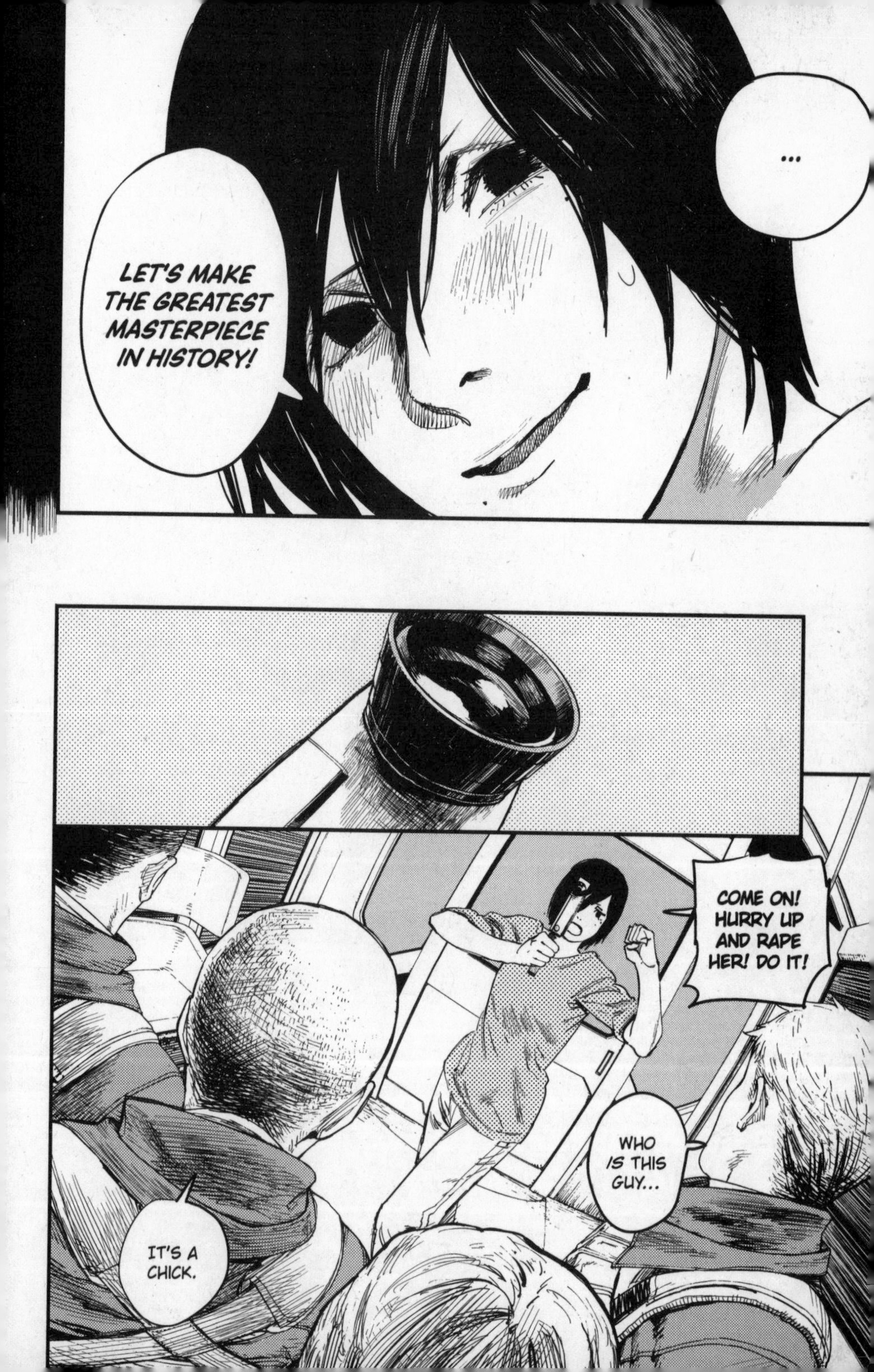
...
LET'S MAKE THE GREATEST MASTERPIECE IN HISTORY!
COME ON! HURRY UP AND RAPE HER! DO IT!
WHO IS THIS GUY...
IT'S A CHICK.

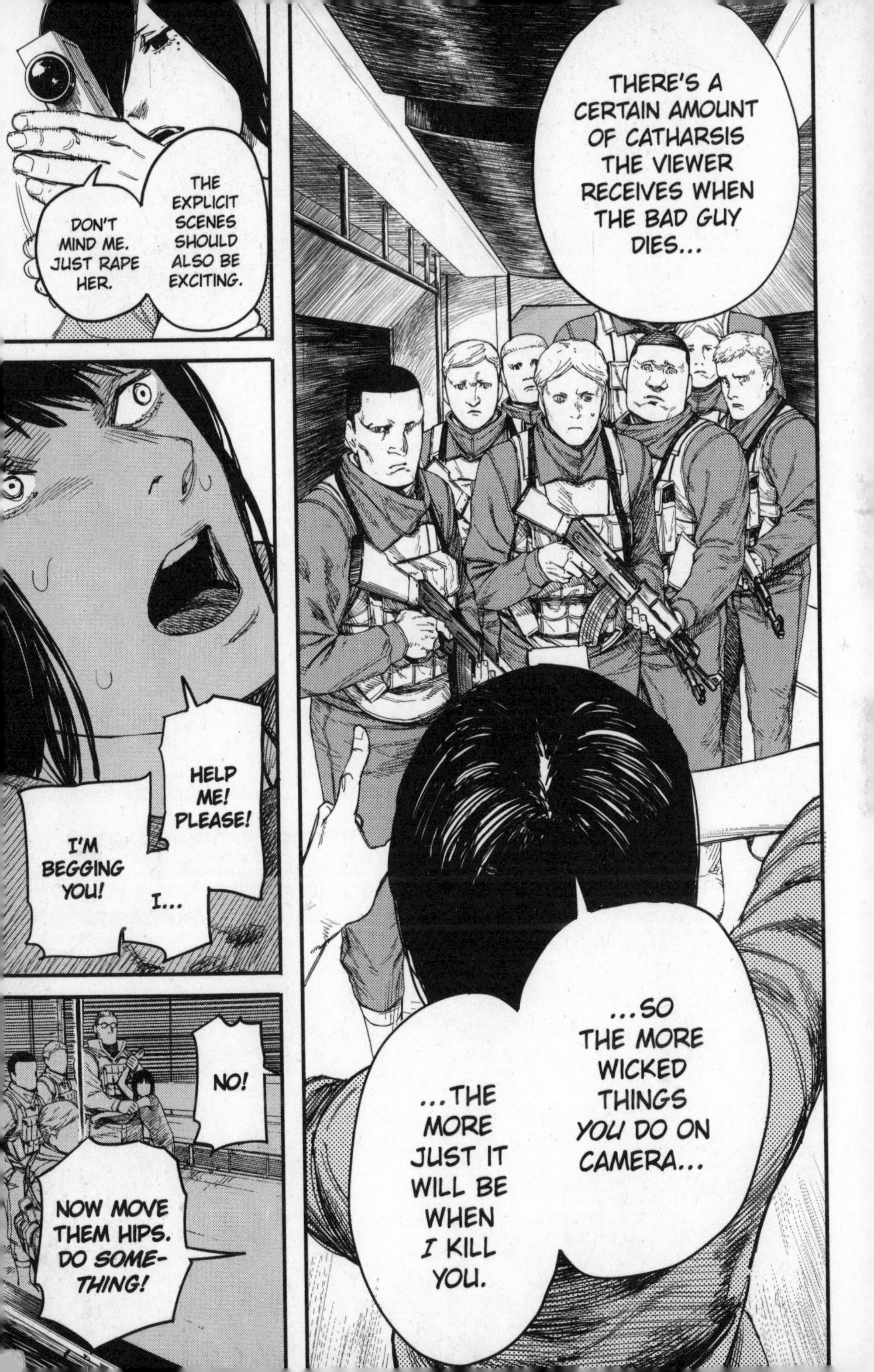
THERE'S A CERTAIN AMOUNT OF CATHARSIS THE VIEWER RECEIVES WHEN THE BAD GUY DIES...
...SO THE MORE WICKED THINGS *YOU* DO ON CAMERA...
...THE MORE JUST IT WILL BE WHEN *I* KILL YOU.
THE EXPLICIT SCENES SHOULD ALSO BE EXCITING.
DON'T MIND ME. JUST RAPE HER.
HELP ME! PLEASE!
I'M BEGGING YOU!
I...
NO!
NOW MOVE THEM HIPS. DO *SOME-THING!*

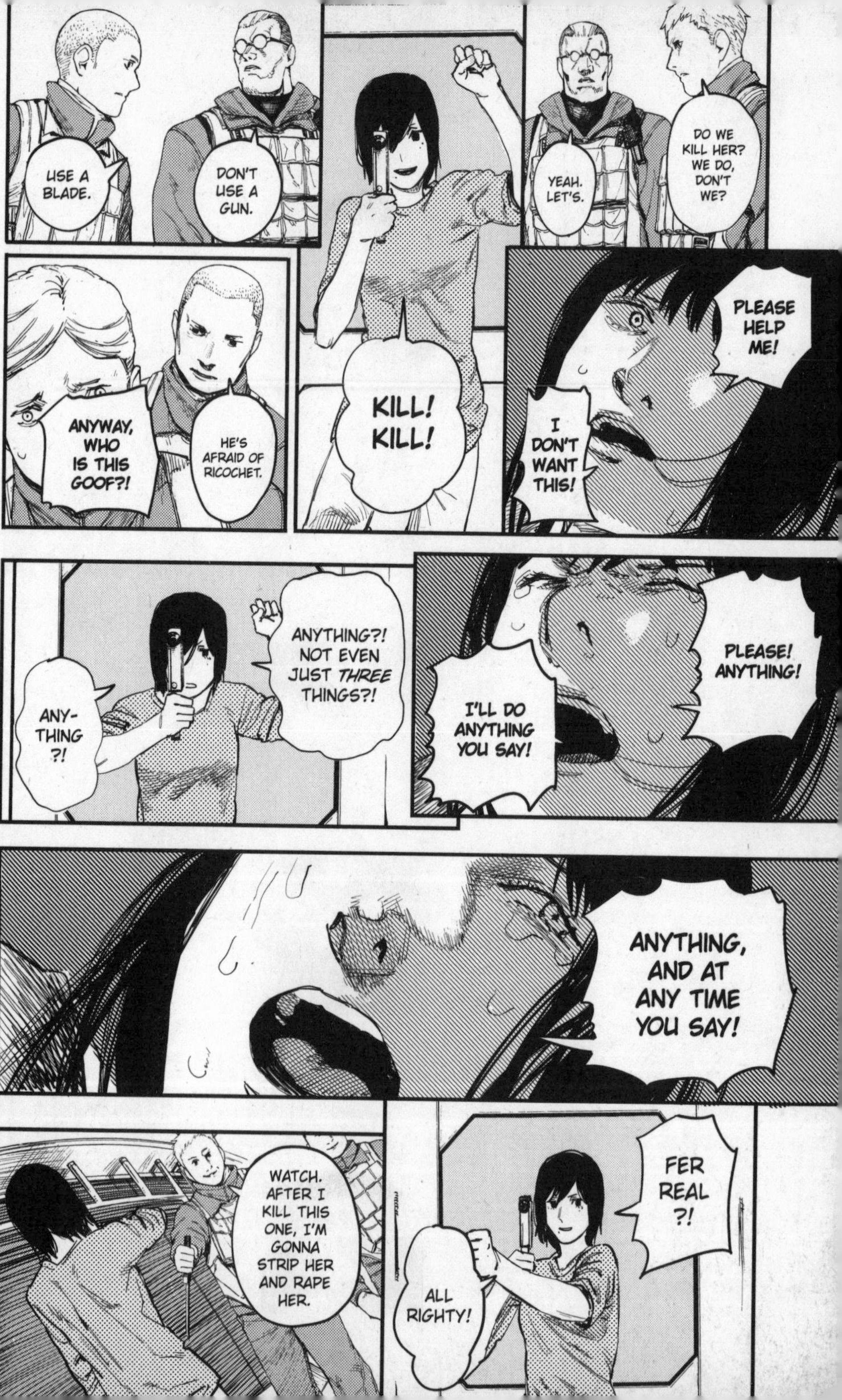
DO WE KILL HER? WE DO, DON'T WE?
YEAH. LET'S.
PLEASE HELP ME!
I DON'T WANT THIS!
KILL! KILL!
DON'T USE A GUN.
USE A BLADE.
HE'S AFRAID OF RICOCHET.
ANYWAY, WHO IS THIS GOOF?!
PLEASE! ANYTHING!
I'LL DO ANYTHING YOU SAY!
ANYTHING?! NOT EVEN JUST *THREE* THINGS?!
ANY-THING?!
ANYTHING, AND AT ANY TIME YOU SAY!
FER REAL?!
ALL RIGHTY!
WATCH. AFTER I KILL THIS ONE, I'M GONNA STRIP HER AND RAPE HER.

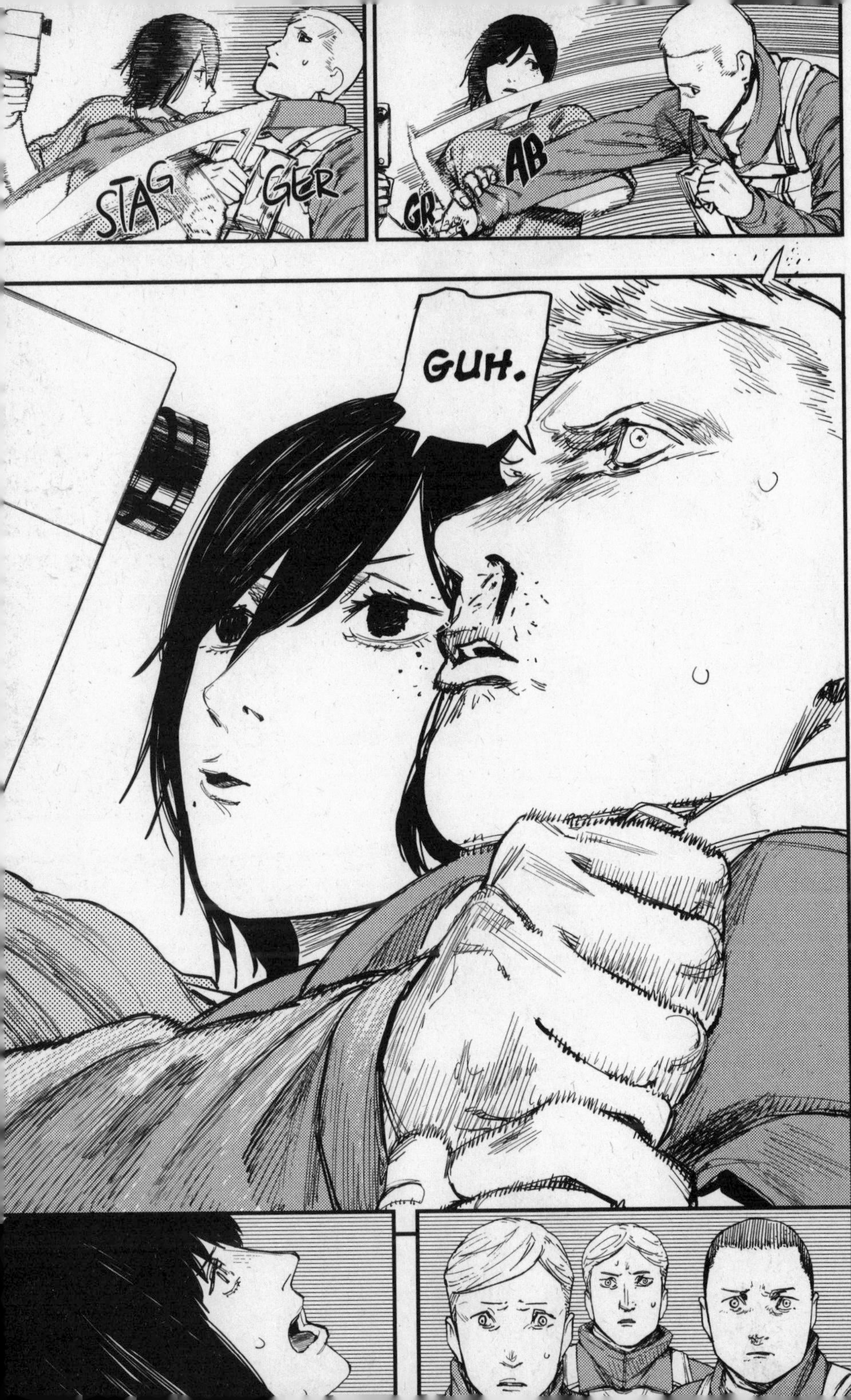
GRAB
STAGGER
GUH.

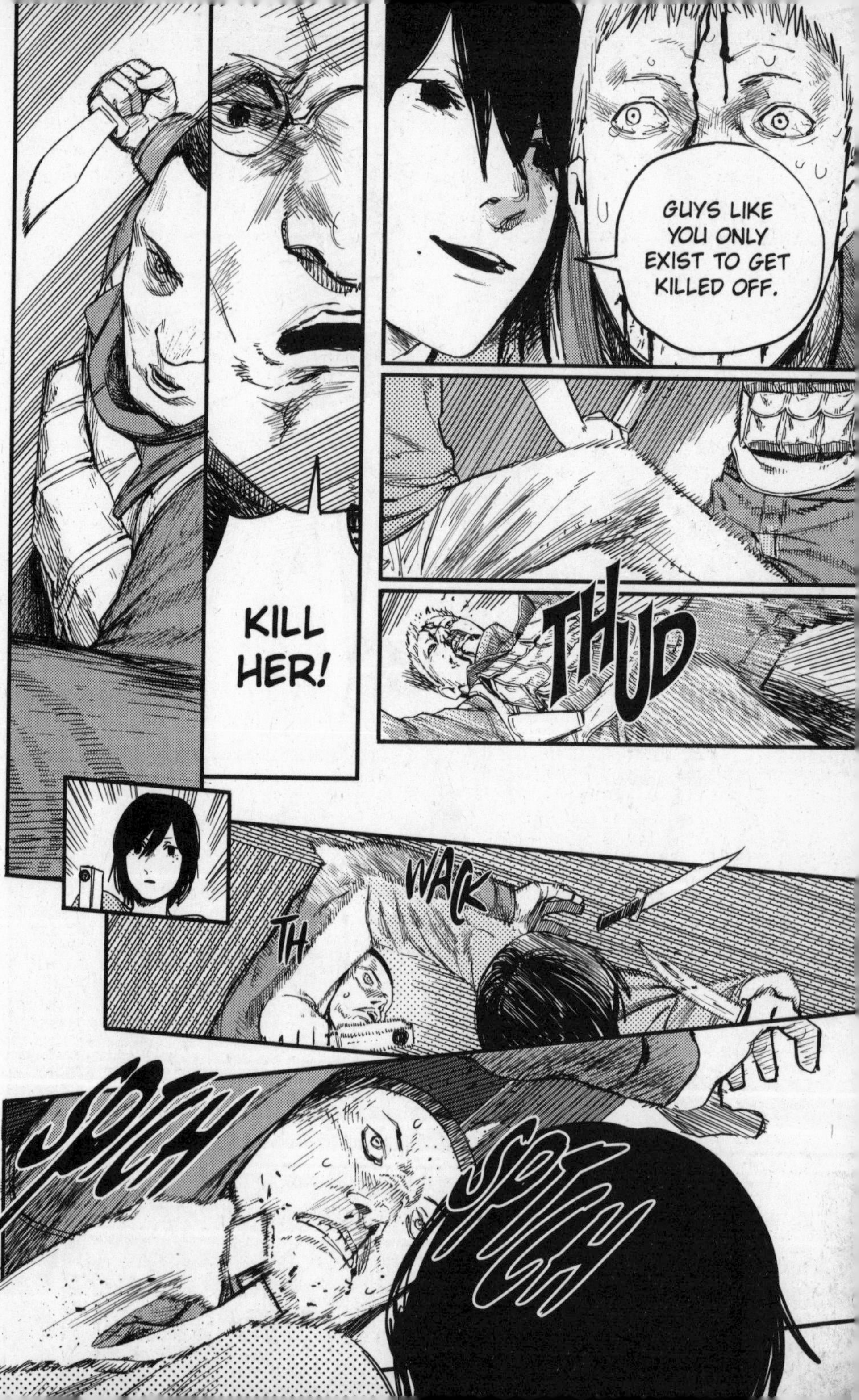
GUYS LIKE YOU ONLY EXIST TO GET KILLED OFF.
THUD
KILL HER!
WACK
TH

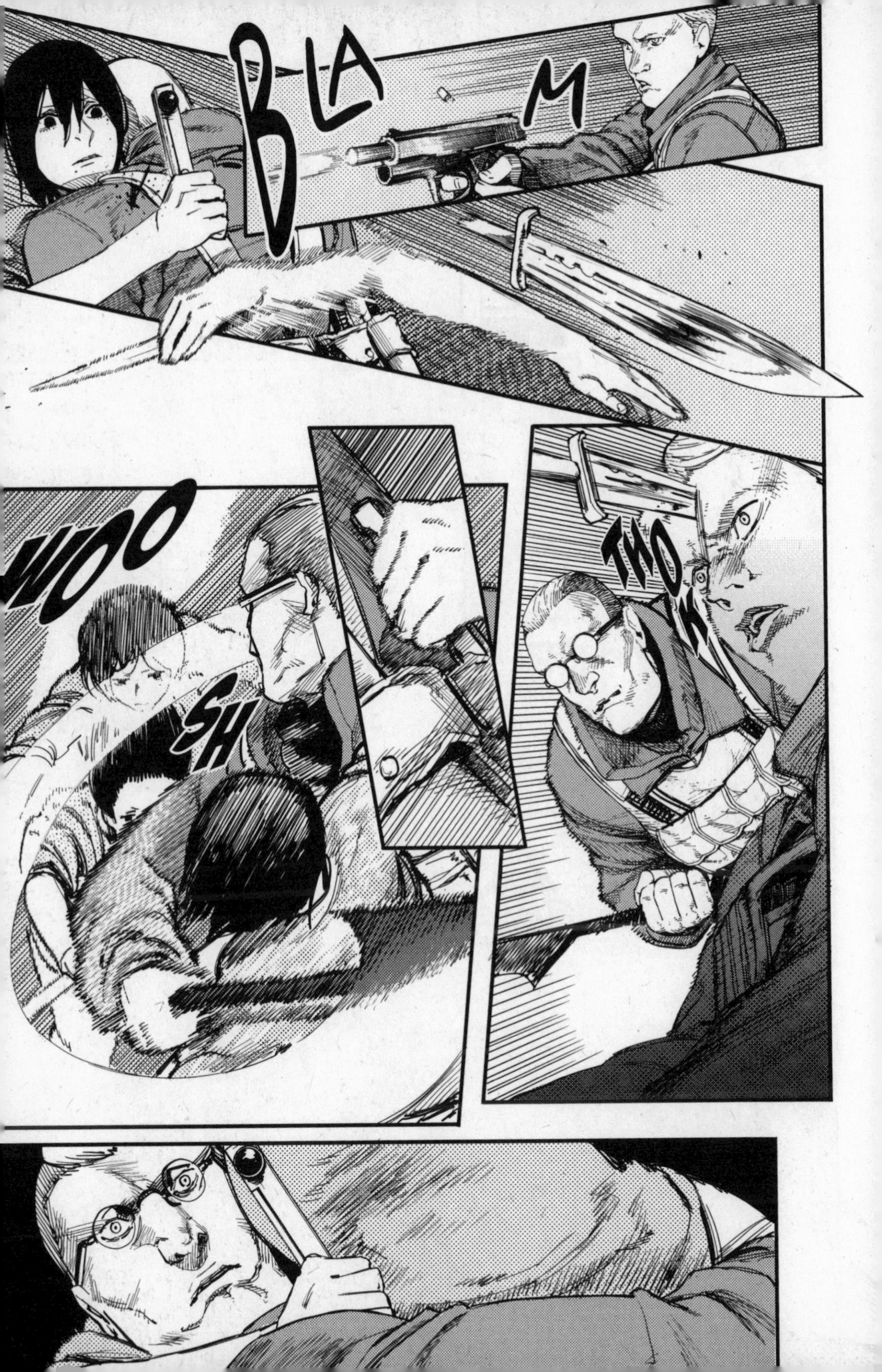
BLAM
THOK
WOOSH

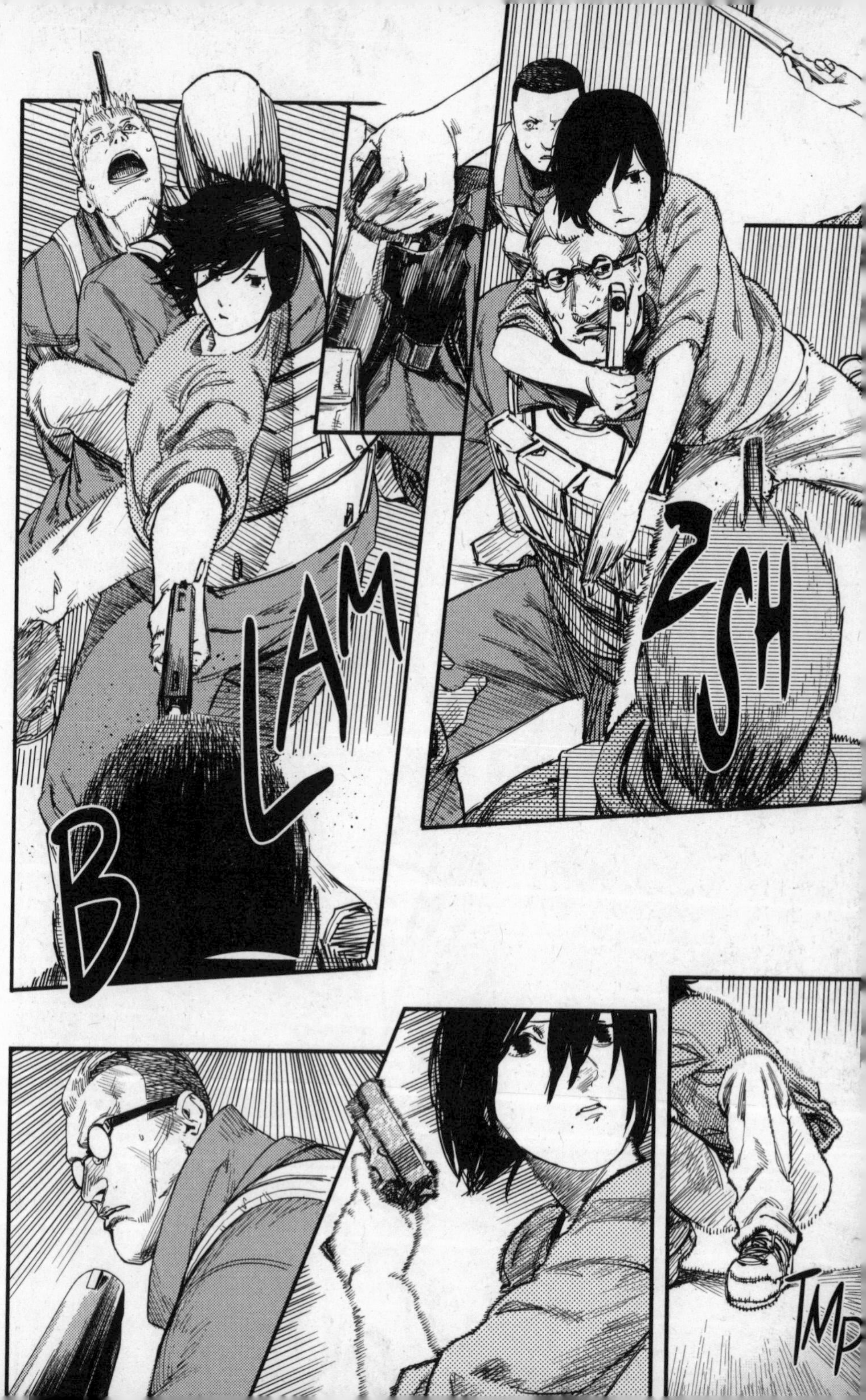
ZSH
BLAM
TMP

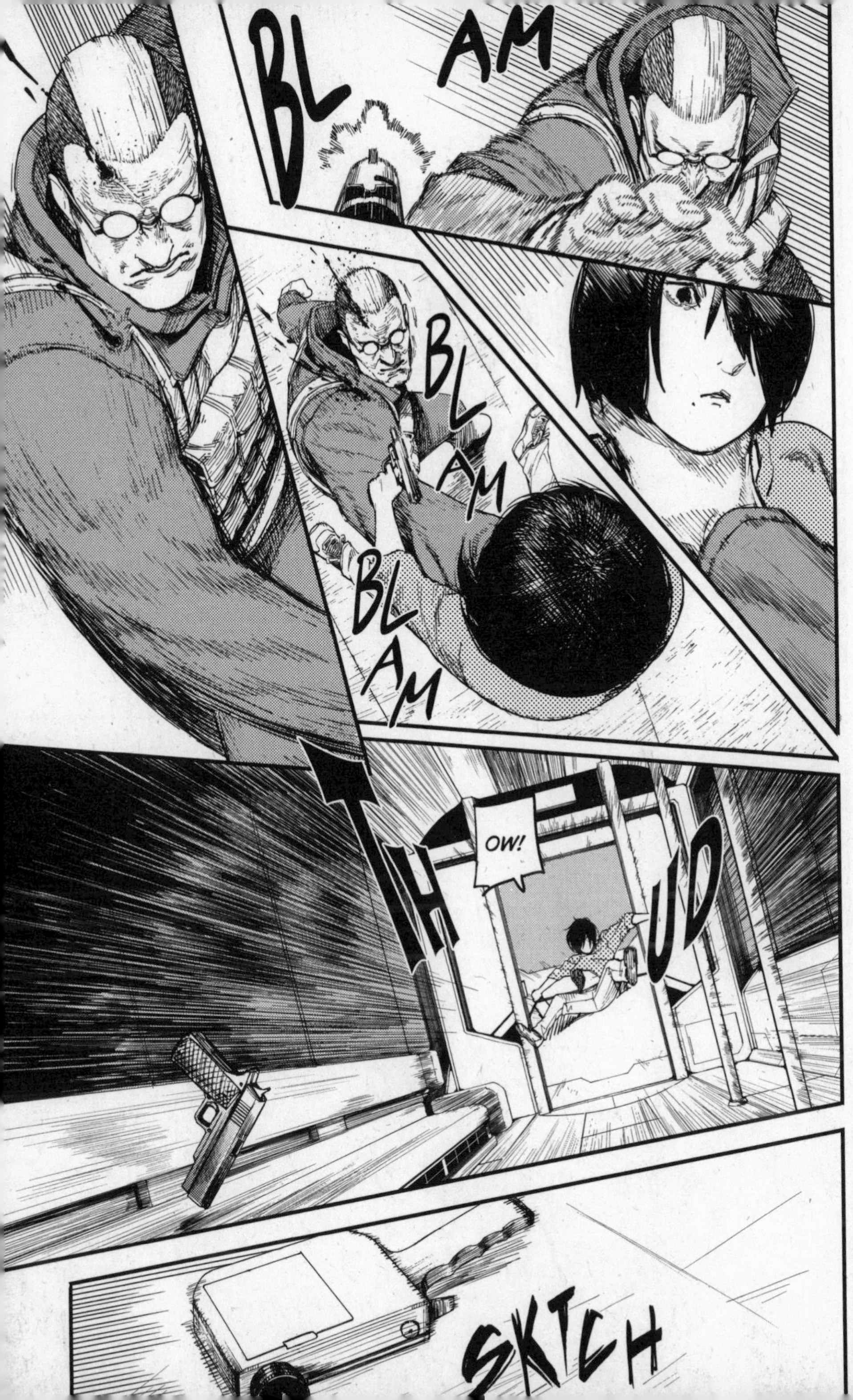
BLAM
BLAM
BLAM
!
THUD
OW!
SKTCH

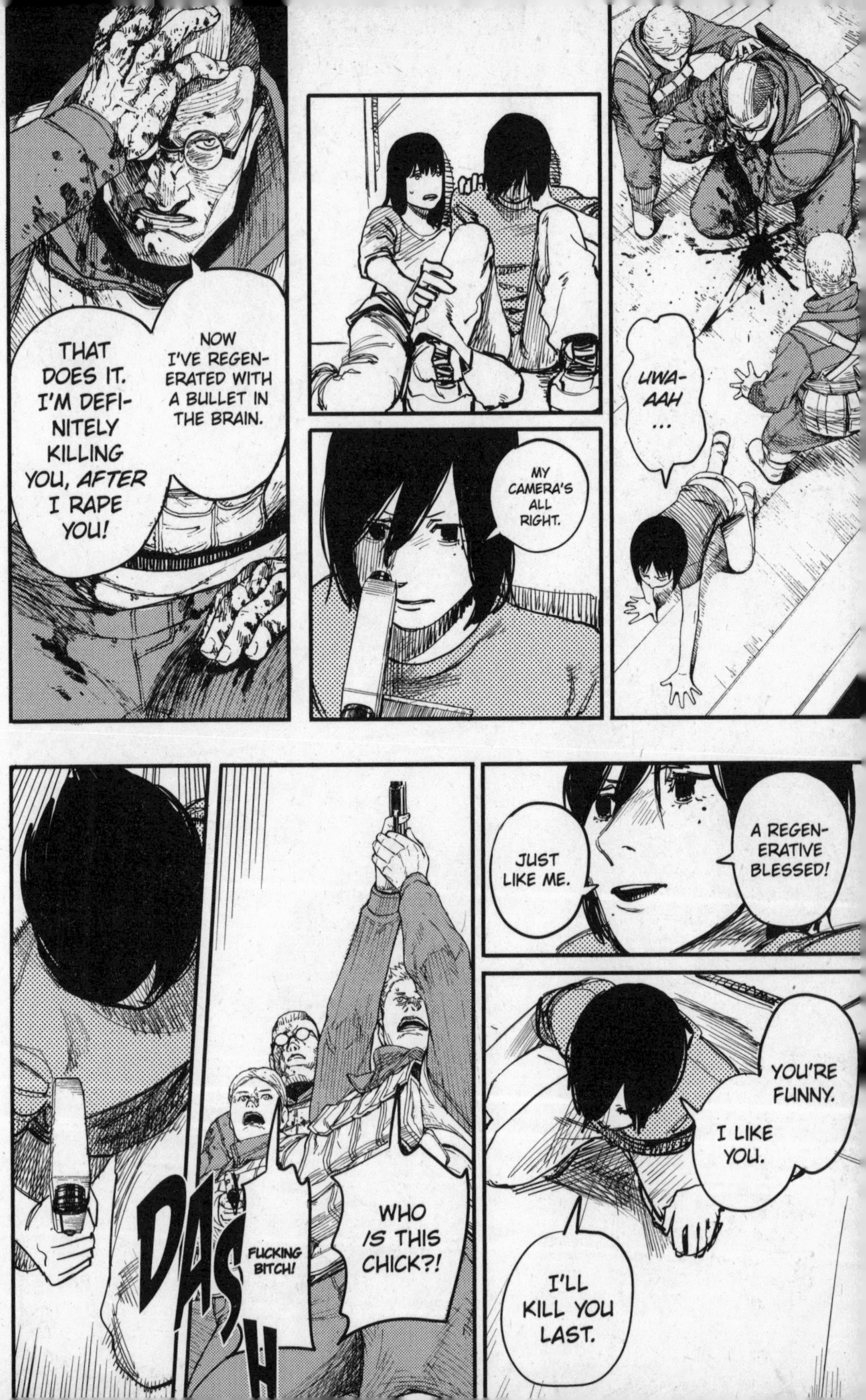
UWA-AAH ...
MY CAMERA'S ALL RIGHT.
NOW I'VE REGEN-ERATED WITH A BULLET IN THE BRAIN.
THAT DOES IT. I'M DEFI-NITELY KILLING YOU, *AFTER* I RAPE YOU!
A REGEN-ERATIVE BLESSED!
JUST LIKE ME.
YOU'RE FUNNY.
I LIKE YOU.
I'LL KILL YOU LAST.
WHO IS THIS CHICK?!
FUCKING BITCH!
DASH

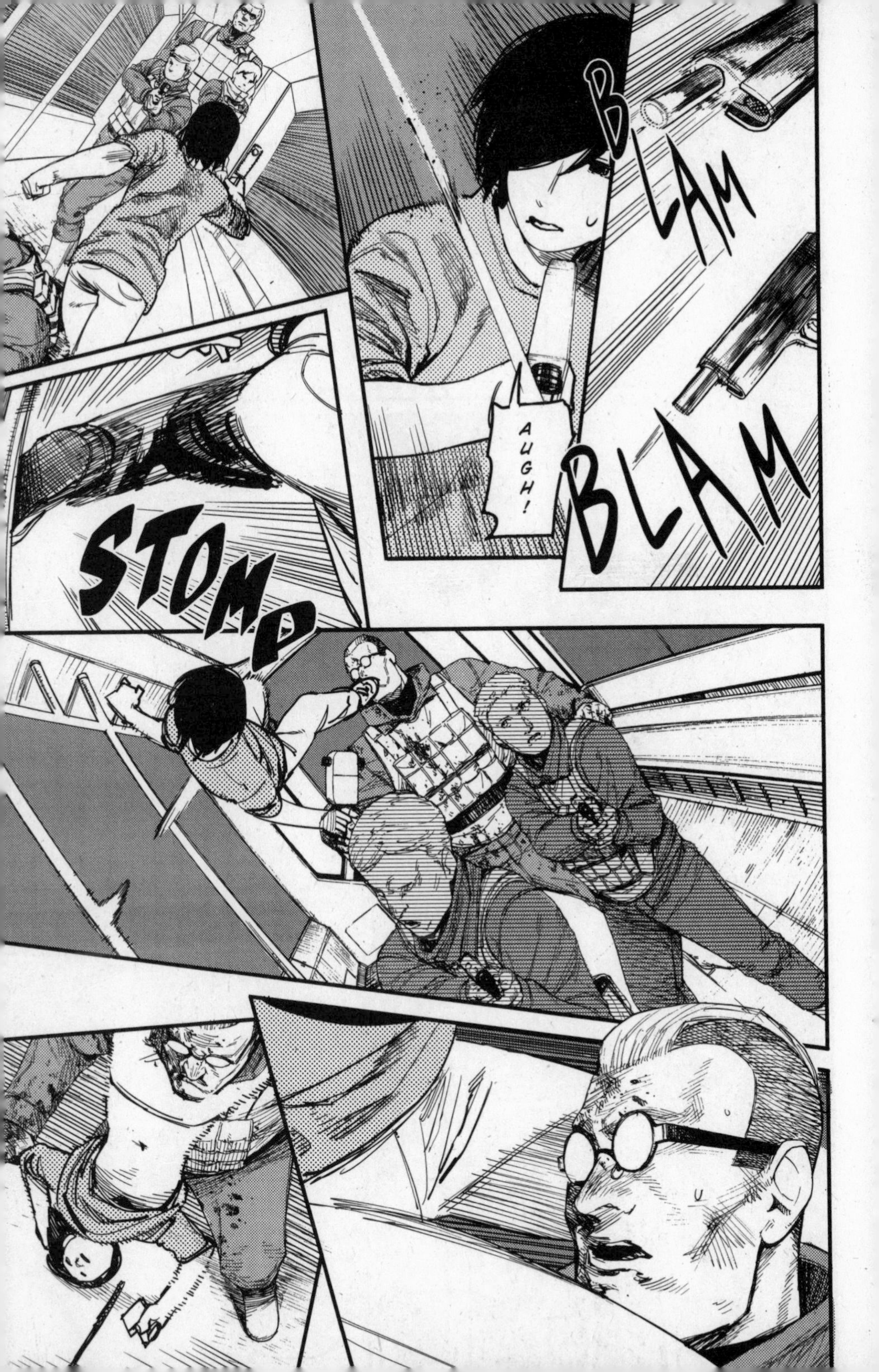
BLAM
AUGH!
BLAM
STOMP

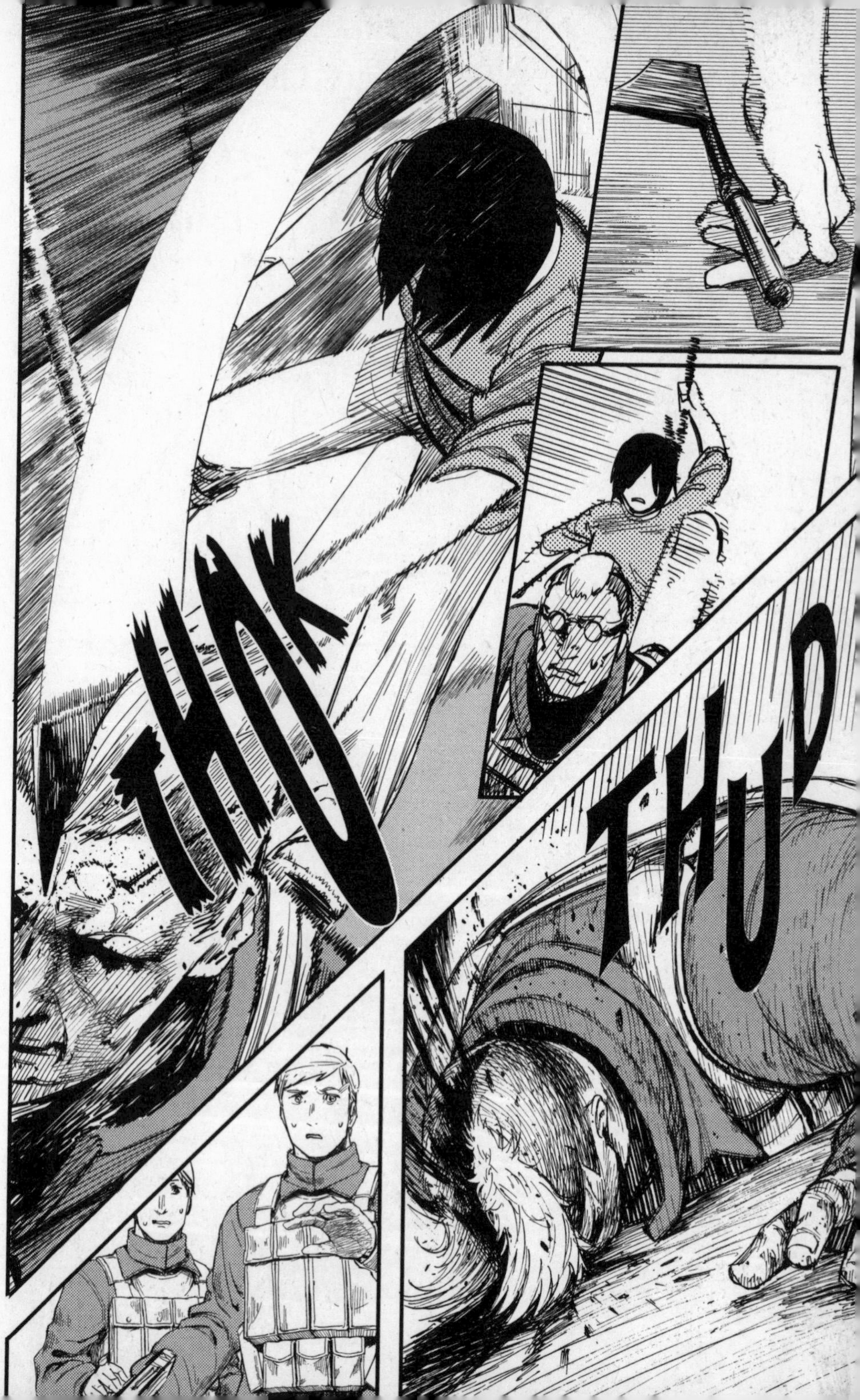
THWACK
THUD

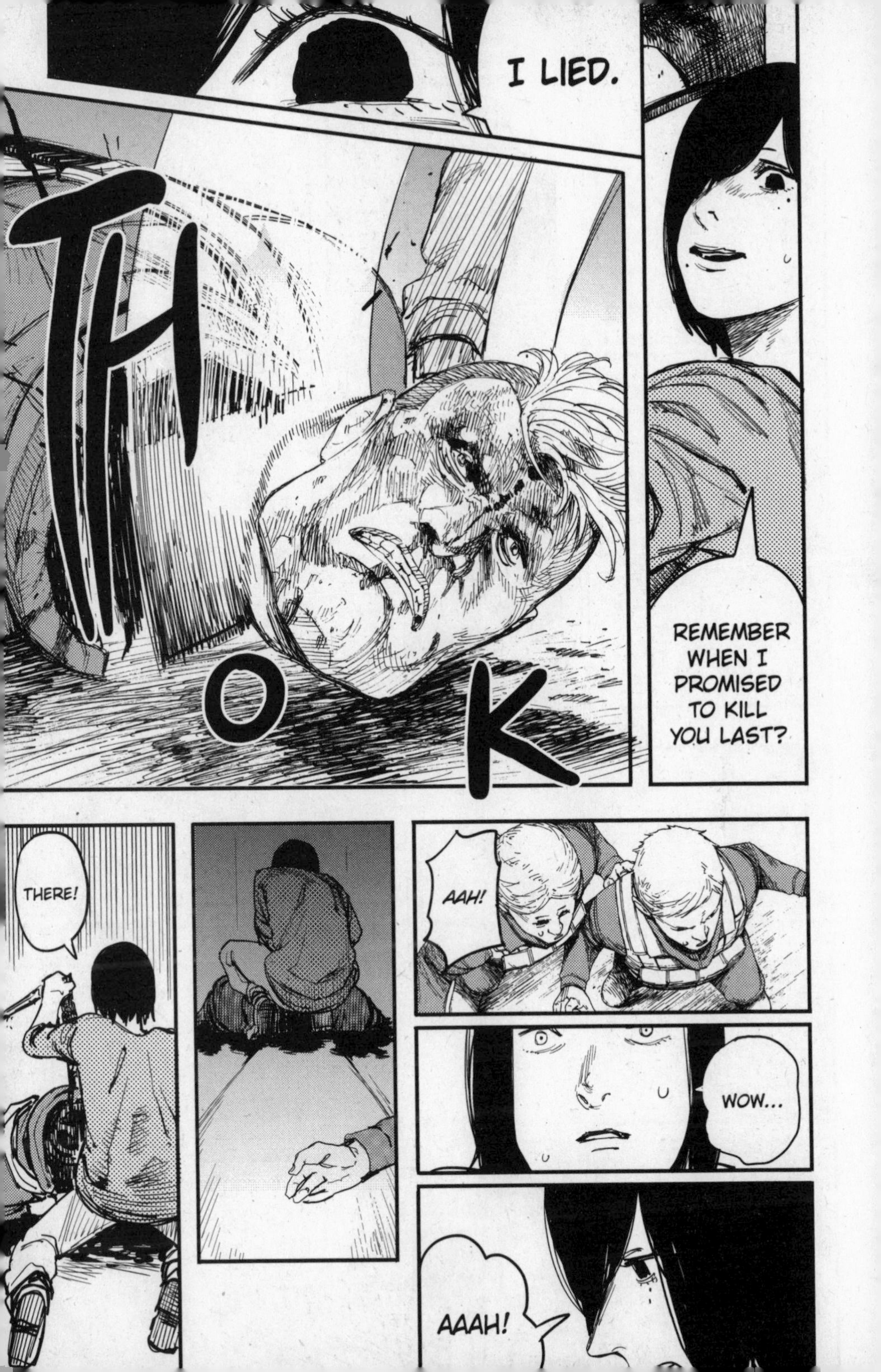
REMEMBER WHEN I PROMISED TO KILL YOU LAST?
I LIED.
THOK
AAH!
WOW...
AAAH!
THERE!

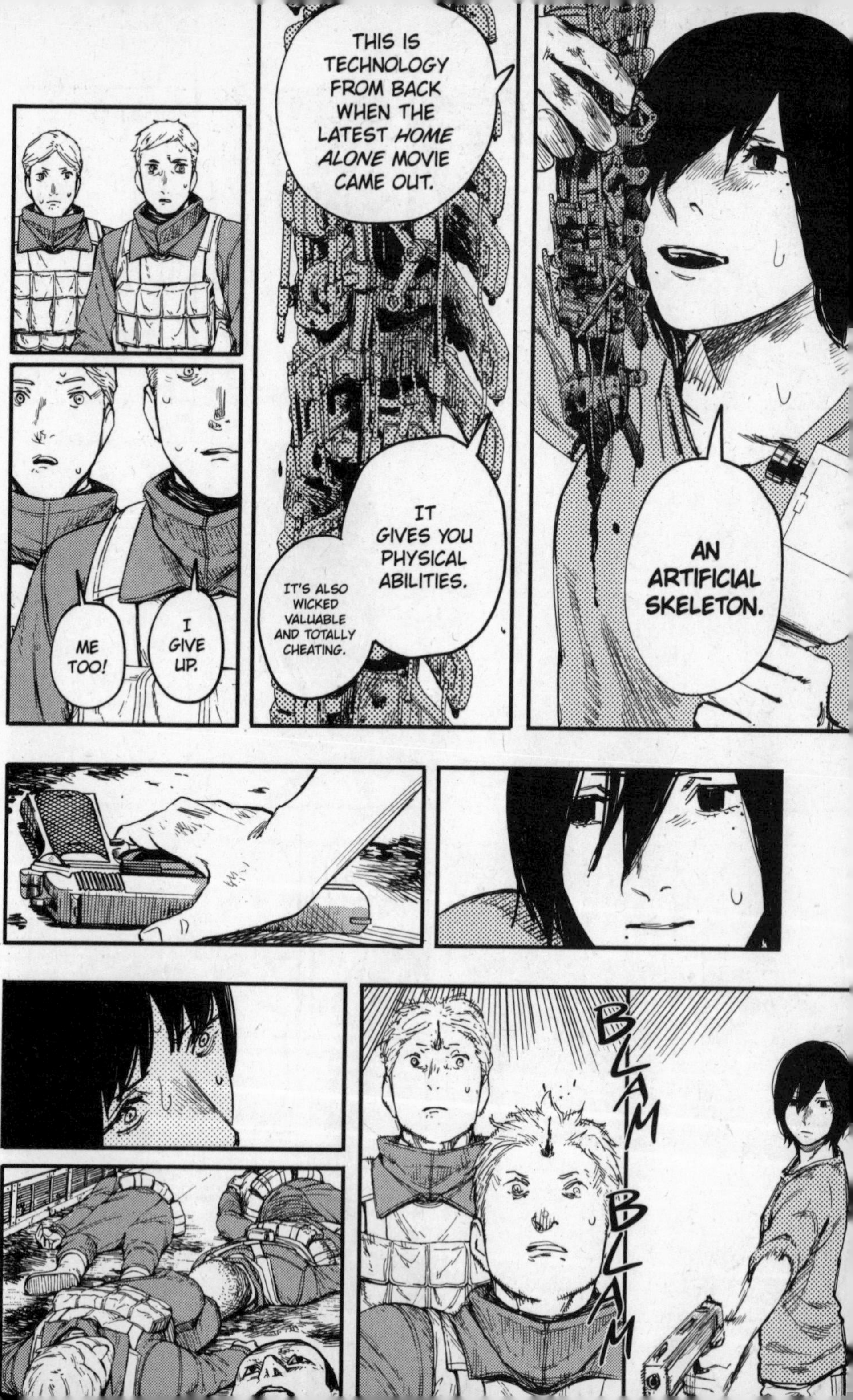
AN ARTIFICIAL SKELETON.
THIS IS TECHNOLOGY FROM BACK WHEN THE LATEST *HOME ALONE* MOVIE CAME OUT.
IT GIVES YOU PHYSICAL ABILITIES.
IT'S ALSO WICKED VALUABLE AND TOTALLY CHEATING.
I GIVE UP.
ME TOO!
BLAM
BLAM

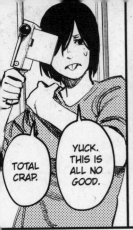

POP
YUCK. THIS IS ALL NO GOOD.
TOTAL CRAP.
IT'S SO BLURRY, YOU CAN'T TELL WHAT'S GOING ON.
HEY! LITTLE GIRL!
YES ?!
WHAT'S YOUR NAME?
NENE-TO!
I'M NENE-TO...
NENE-TO?!
WHAT AN UGLY NAME!
HERE. HOLD THIS CAMERA.
CAMERA?!
HOLD IT... LIKE THIS.
THINK OF THIS PART AS YOUR OWN EYE.
I DON'T GET IT...
WHAT SHOULD I DO?
BEFORE, YOU SAID YOU'D DO ANYTHING I WANTED.

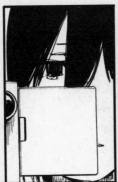

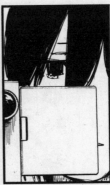

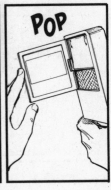

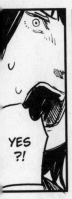

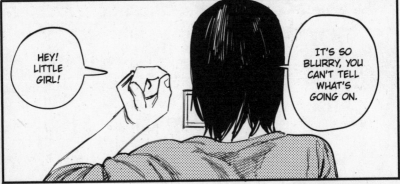

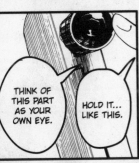

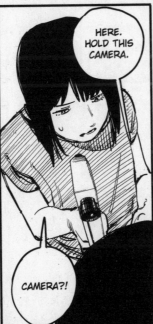

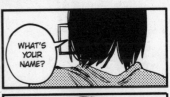

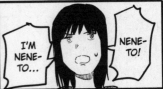

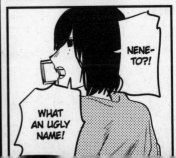

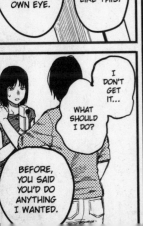

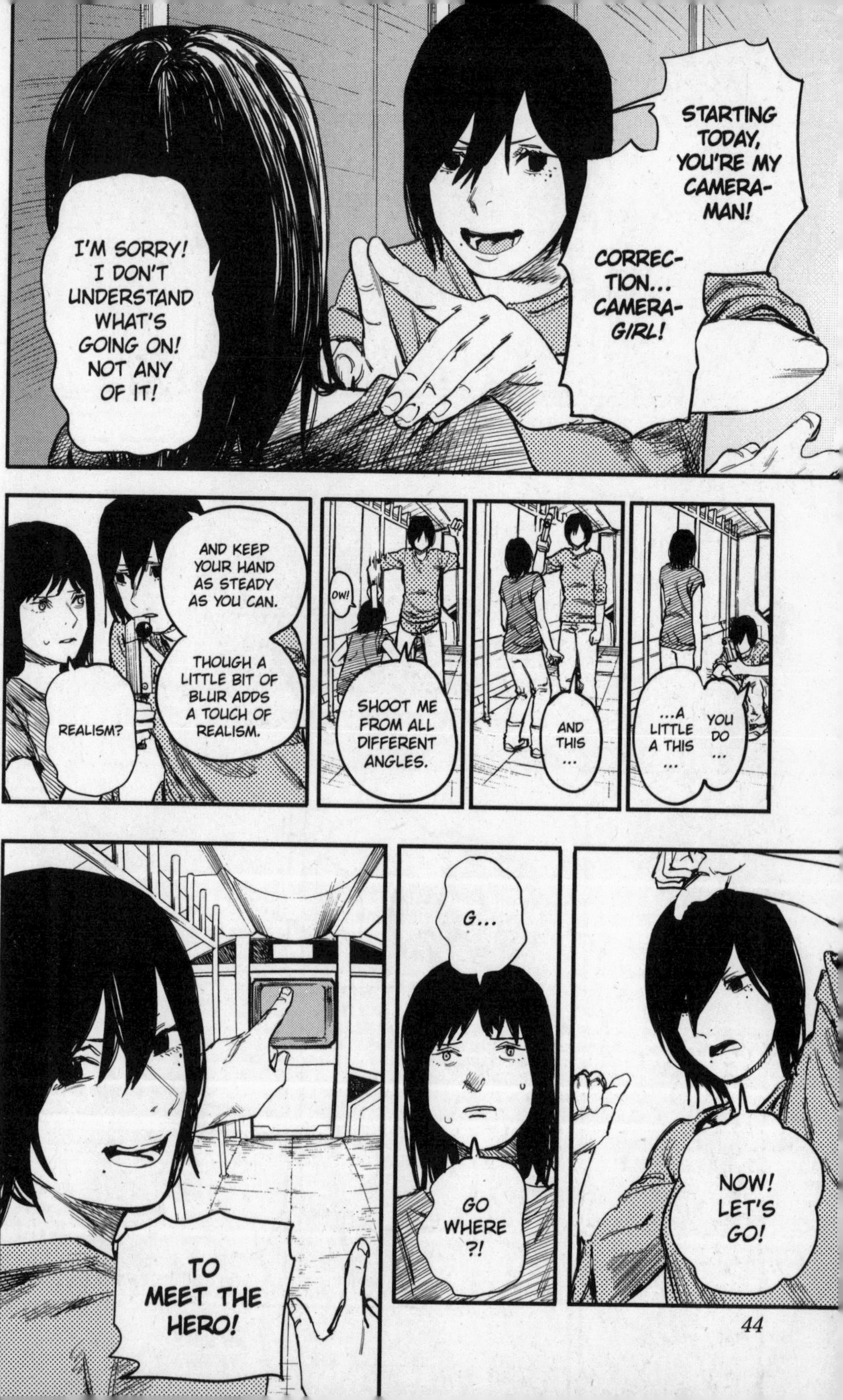
STARTING TODAY, YOU'RE MY CAMERA-MAN!
CORREC-TION... CAMERA-GIRL!
I'M SORRY! I DON'T UNDERSTAND WHAT'S GOING ON! NOT ANY OF IT!
YOU DO...
...A LITTLE A THIS...
AND THIS...
SHOOT ME FROM ALL DIFFERENT ANGLES.
OW!
AND KEEP YOUR HAND AS STEADY AS YOU CAN.
THOUGH A LITTLE BIT OF BLUR ADDS A TOUCH OF REALISM.
REALISM?
NOW! LET'S GO!
G...
GO WHERE?!
TO MEET THE HERO!

CHAPTER 11

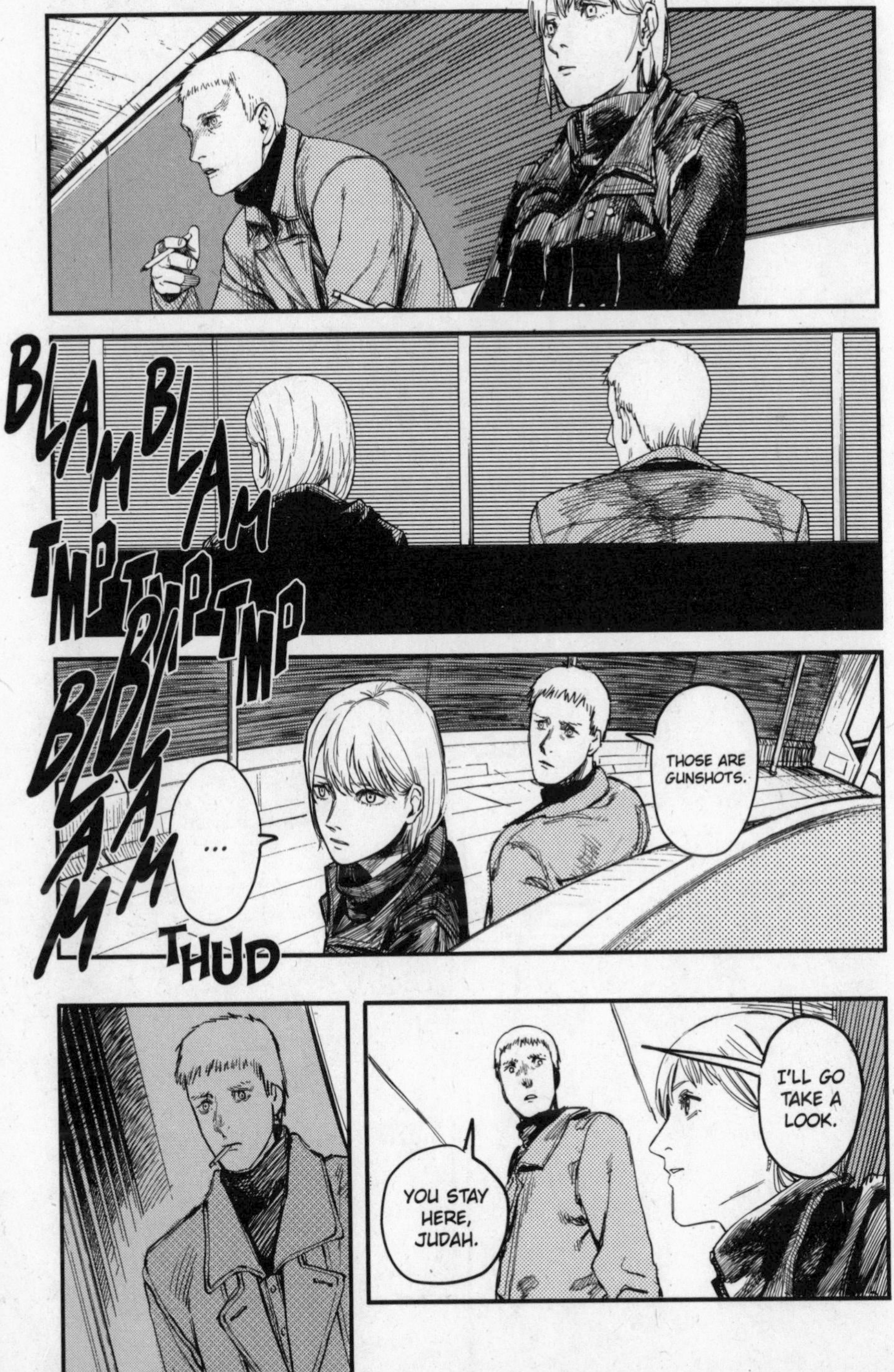
BLAM BLAM
TMP TMP TMP
BLAM BLAM BLAM
THOSE ARE GUNSHOTS.
...
THUD
I'LL GO TAKE A LOOK.
YOU STAY HERE, JUDAH.

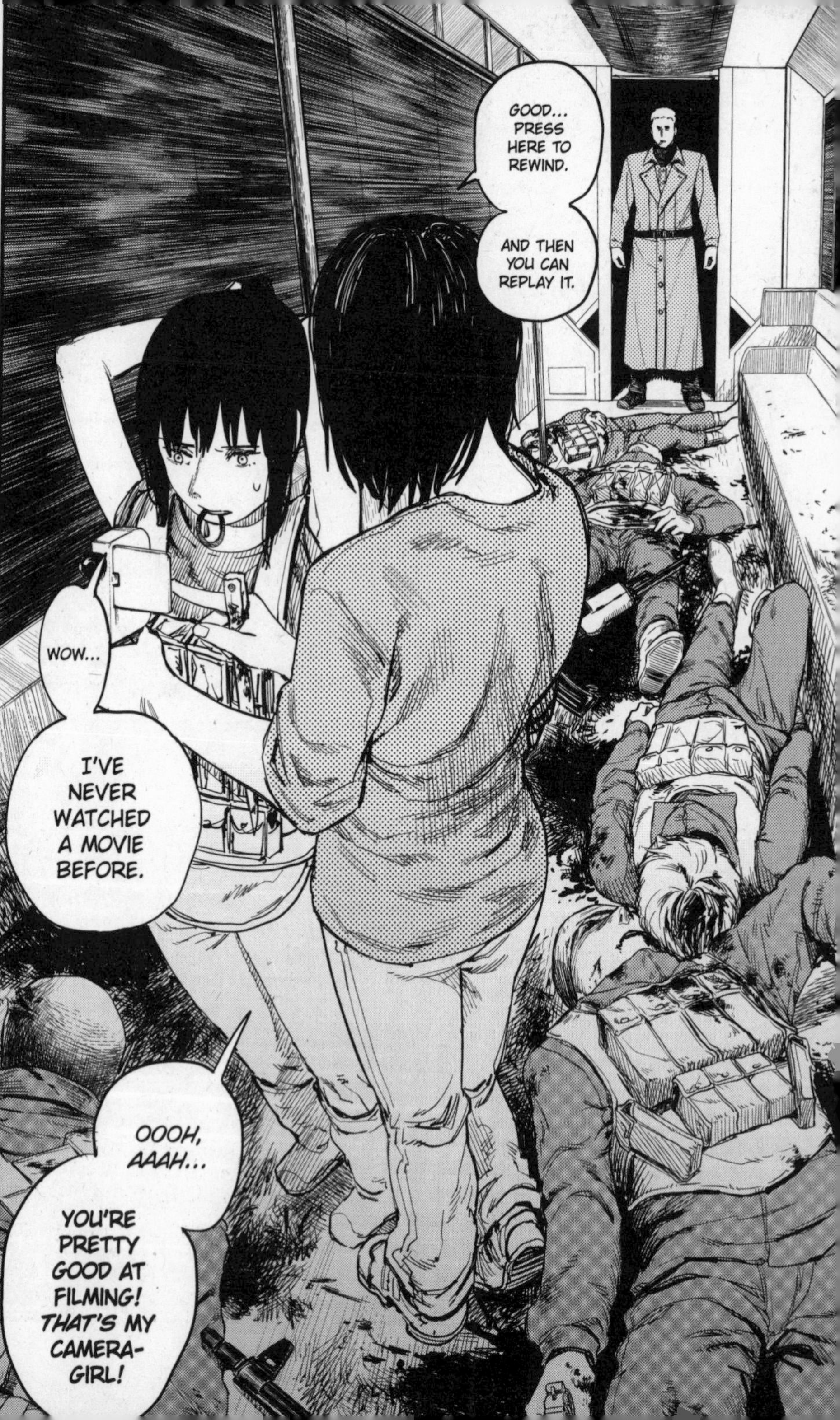
GOOD... PRESS HERE TO REWIND.
AND THEN YOU CAN REPLAY IT.
WOW...
I'VE NEVER WATCHED A MOVIE BEFORE.
OOOH, AAAH...
YOU'RE PRETTY GOOD AT FILMING! *THAT'S MY* CAMERA-GIRL!

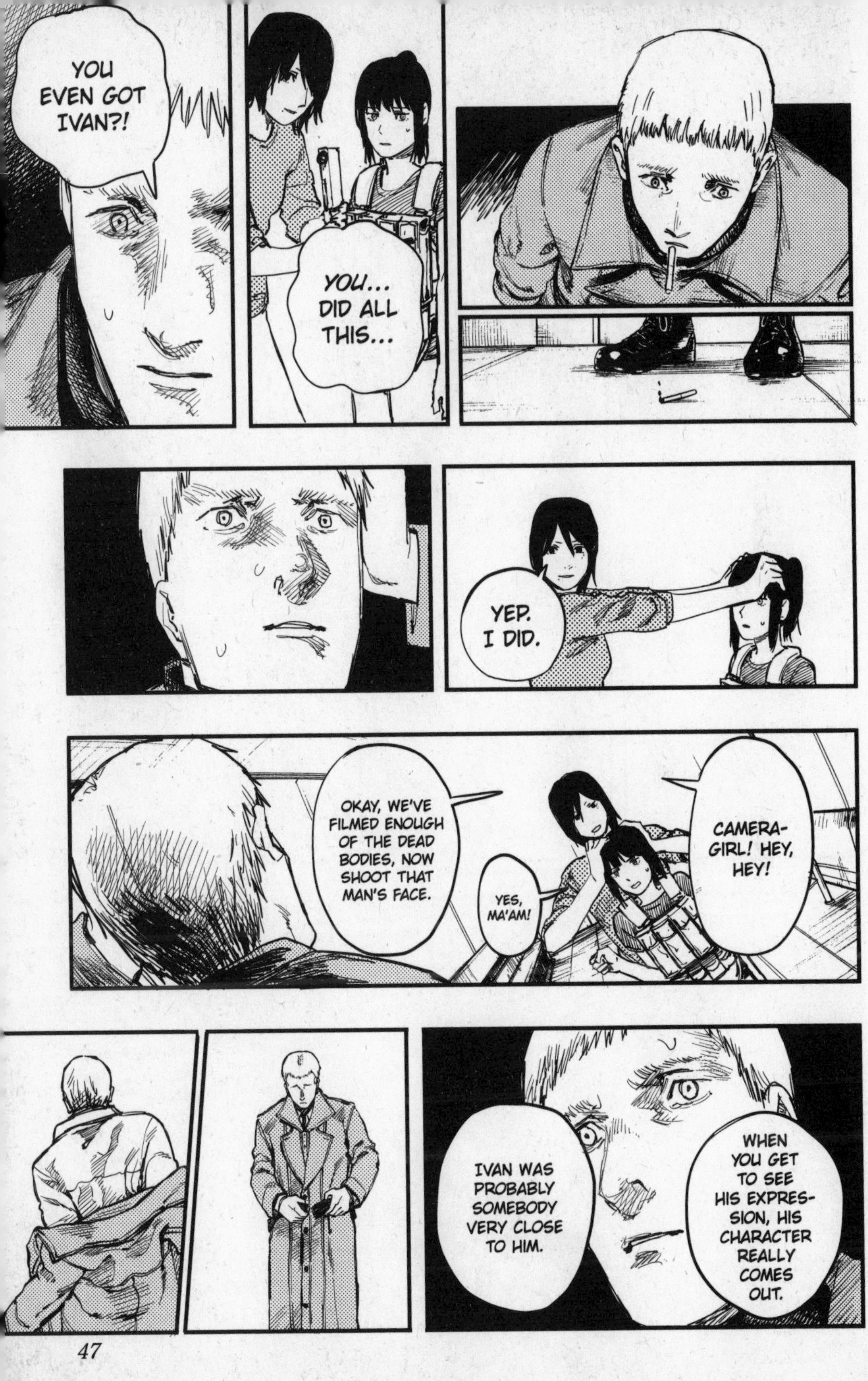
YOU... DID ALL THIS...
YOU EVEN GOT IVAN?!
YEP. I DID.
CAMERA-GIRL! HEY, HEY!
OKAY, WE'VE FILMED ENOUGH OF THE DEAD BODIES, NOW SHOOT THAT MAN'S FACE.
YES, MA'AM!
WHEN YOU GET TO SEE HIS EXPRESSION, HIS CHARACTER REALLY COMES OUT.
IVAN WAS PROBABLY SOMEBODY VERY CLOSE TO HIM.

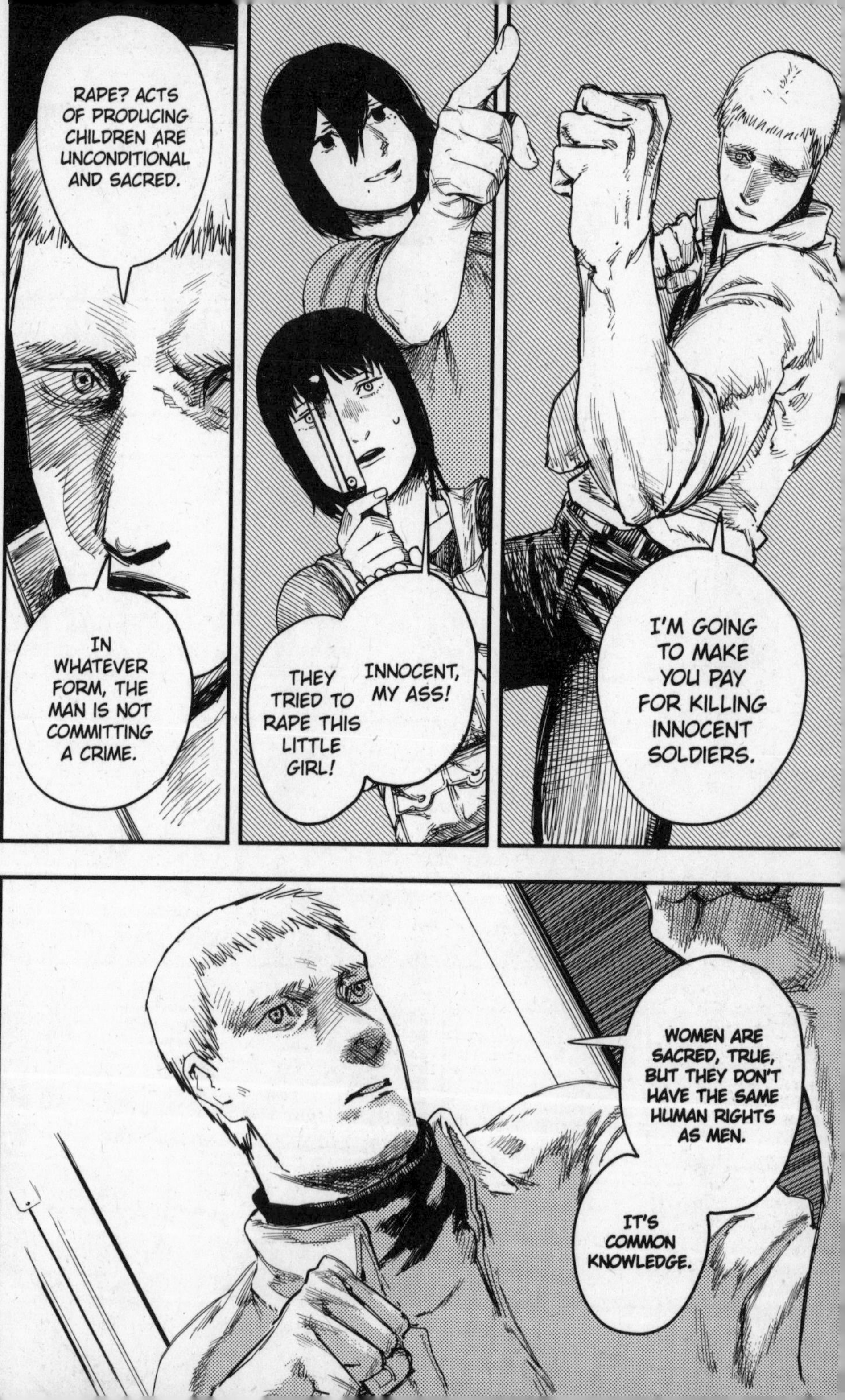
I'M GOING TO MAKE YOU PAY FOR KILLING INNOCENT SOLDIERS.
INNOCENT, MY ASS!
THEY TRIED TO RAPE THIS LITTLE GIRL!
RAPE? ACTS OF PRODUCING CHILDREN ARE UNCONDITIONAL AND SACRED.
IN WHATEVER FORM, THE MAN IS NOT COMMITTING A CRIME.
WOMEN ARE SACRED, TRUE, BUT THEY DON'T HAVE THE SAME HUMAN RIGHTS AS MEN.
IT'S COMMON KNOWLEDGE.

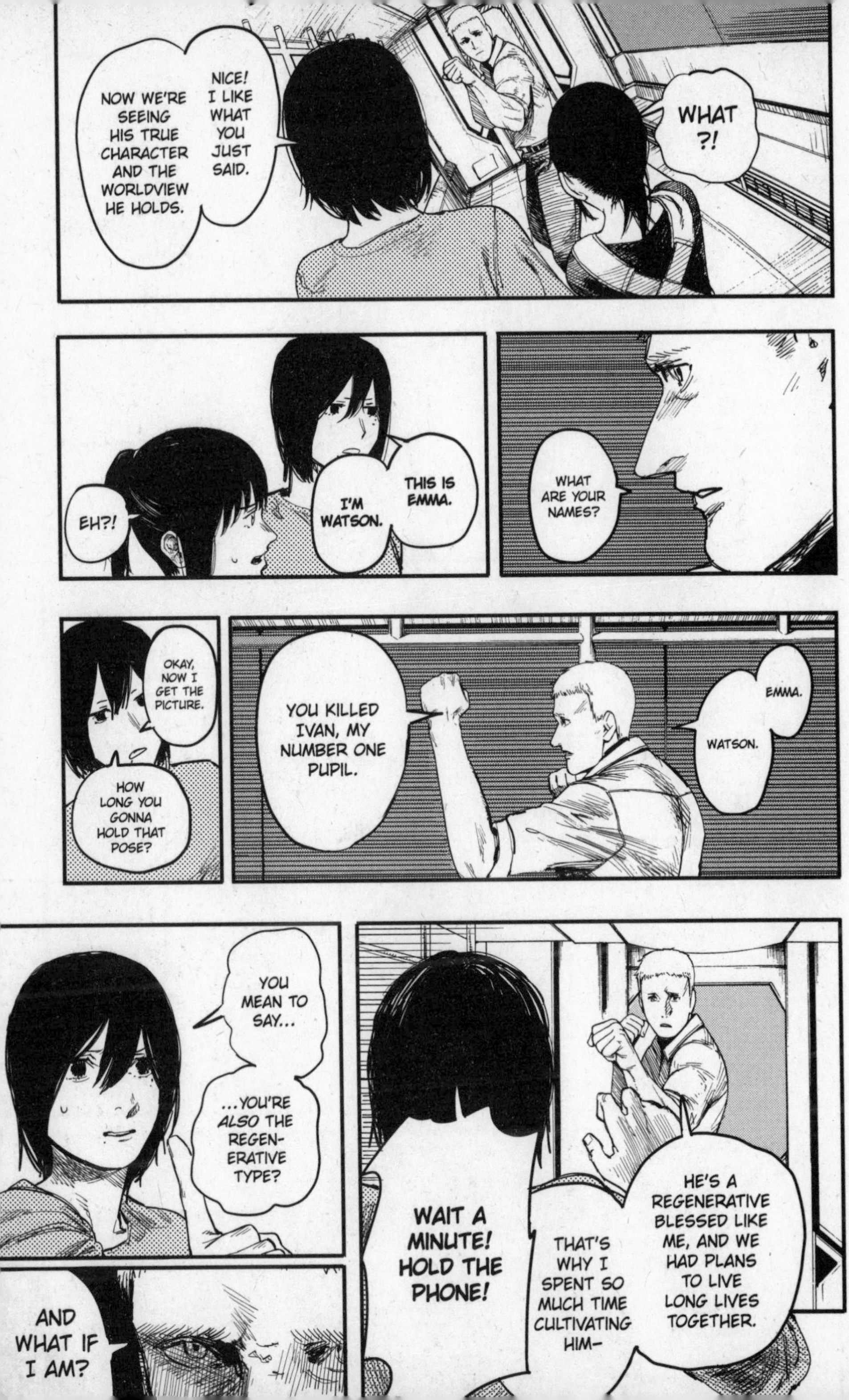
WHAT ?!
NICE! I LIKE WHAT YOU JUST SAID.
NOW WE'RE SEEING HIS TRUE CHARACTER AND THE WORLDVIEW HE HOLDS.
WHAT ARE YOUR NAMES?
THIS IS EMMA.
I'M WATSON.
EH?!
EMMA.
WATSON.
YOU KILLED IVAN, MY NUMBER ONE PUPIL.
OKAY, NOW I GET THE PICTURE.
HOW LONG YOU GONNA HOLD THAT POSE?
HE'S A REGENERATIVE BLESSED LIKE ME, AND WE HAD PLANS TO LIVE LONG LIVES TOGETHER.
THAT'S WHY I SPENT SO MUCH TIME CULTIVATING HIM–
WAIT A MINUTE! HOLD THE PHONE!
YOU MEAN TO SAY...
...YOU'RE *ALSO* THE REGEN-ERATIVE TYPE?
AND WHAT IF I AM?

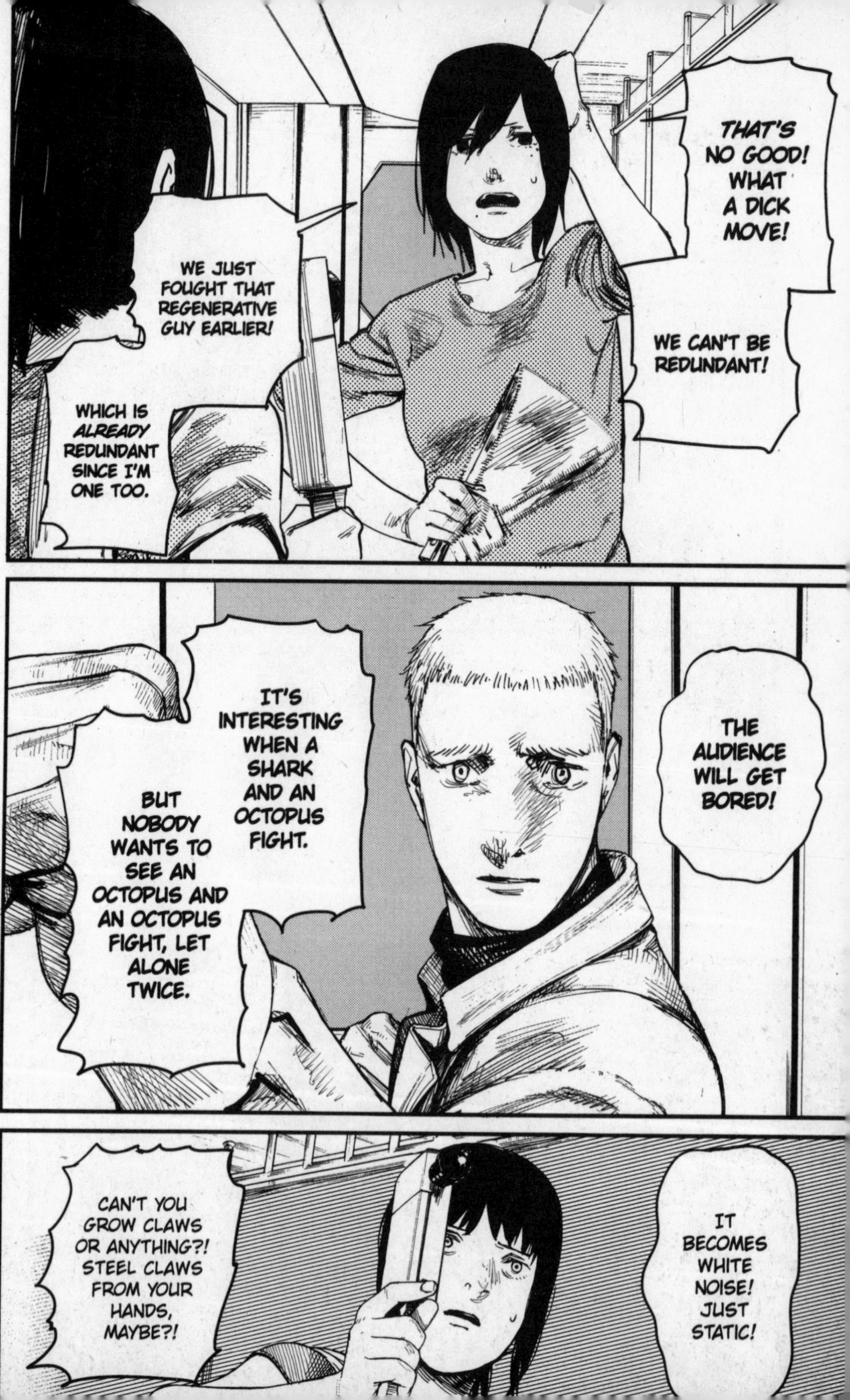
THAT'S NO GOOD! WHAT A DICK MOVE!
WE CAN'T BE REDUNDANT!
WE JUST FOUGHT THAT REGENERATIVE GUY EARLIER!
WHICH IS *ALREADY* REDUNDANT SINCE I'M ONE TOO.
THE AUDIENCE WILL GET BORED!
IT'S INTERESTING WHEN A SHARK AND AN OCTOPUS FIGHT.
BUT NOBODY WANTS TO SEE AN OCTOPUS AND AN OCTOPUS FIGHT, LET ALONE TWICE.
IT BECOMES WHITE NOISE! JUST STATIC!
CAN'T YOU GROW CLAWS OR ANYTHING?! STEEL CLAWS FROM YOUR HANDS, MAYBE?!

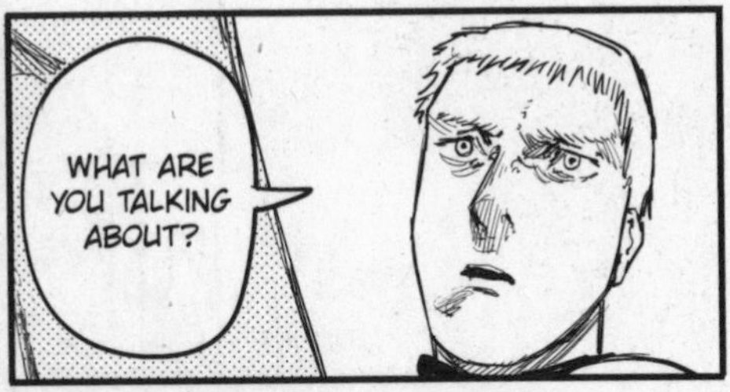
WHAT ARE YOU TALKING ABOUT?
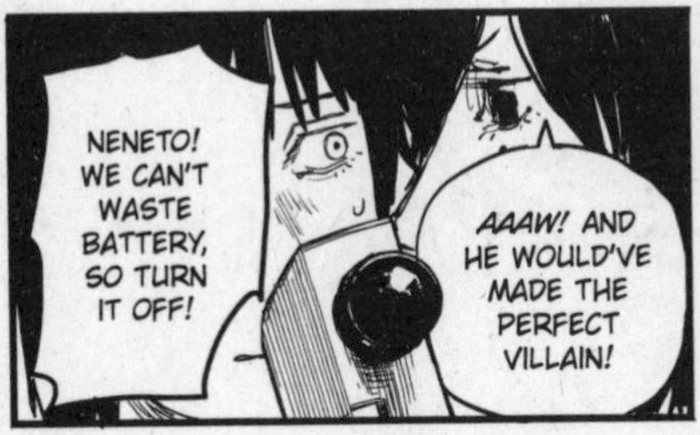
AAAW! AND HE WOULD'VE MADE THE PERFECT VILLAIN!
NENETO! WE CAN'T WASTE BATTERY, SO TURN IT OFF!
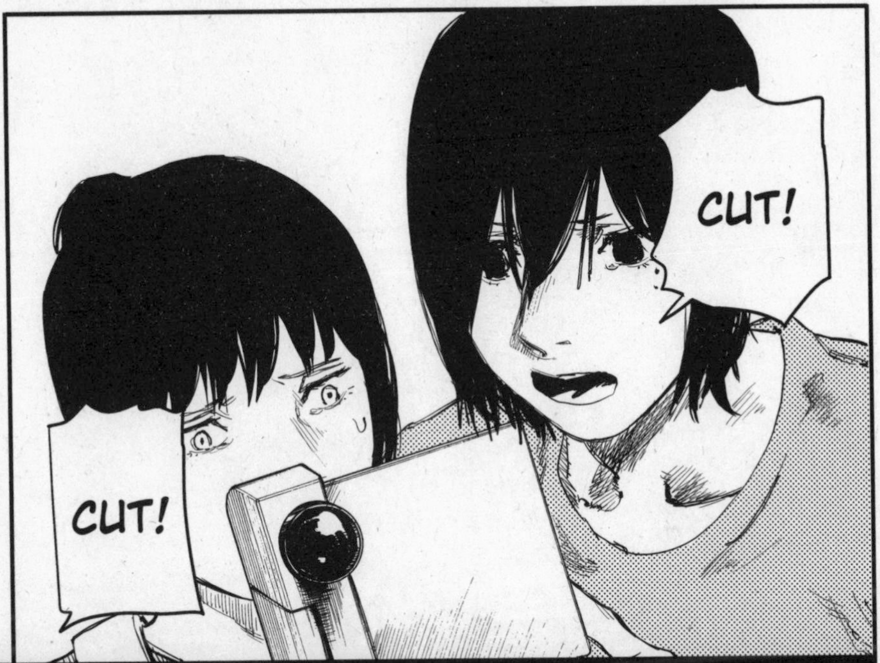
CUT!
CUT!

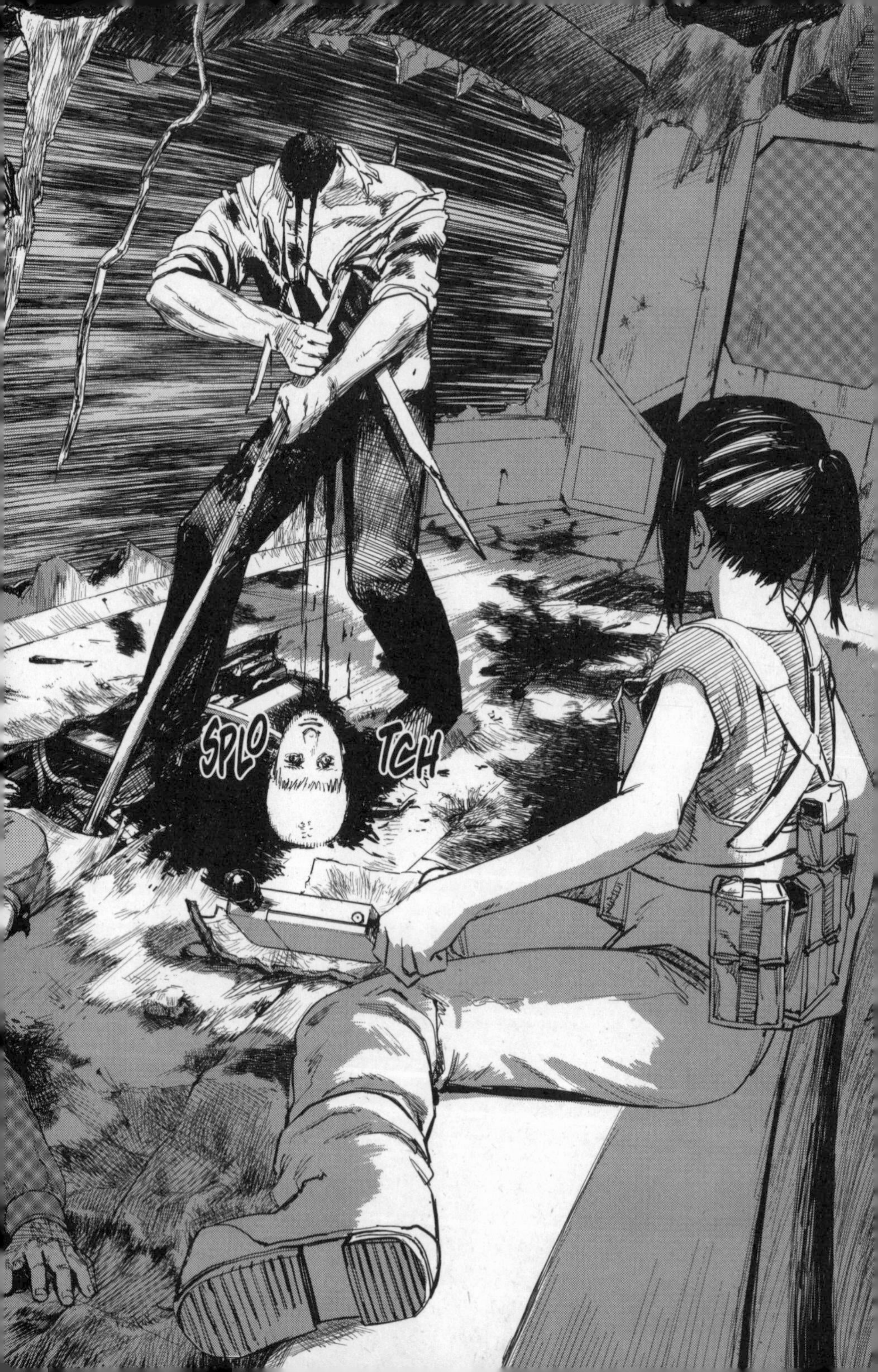
SPLO TCH

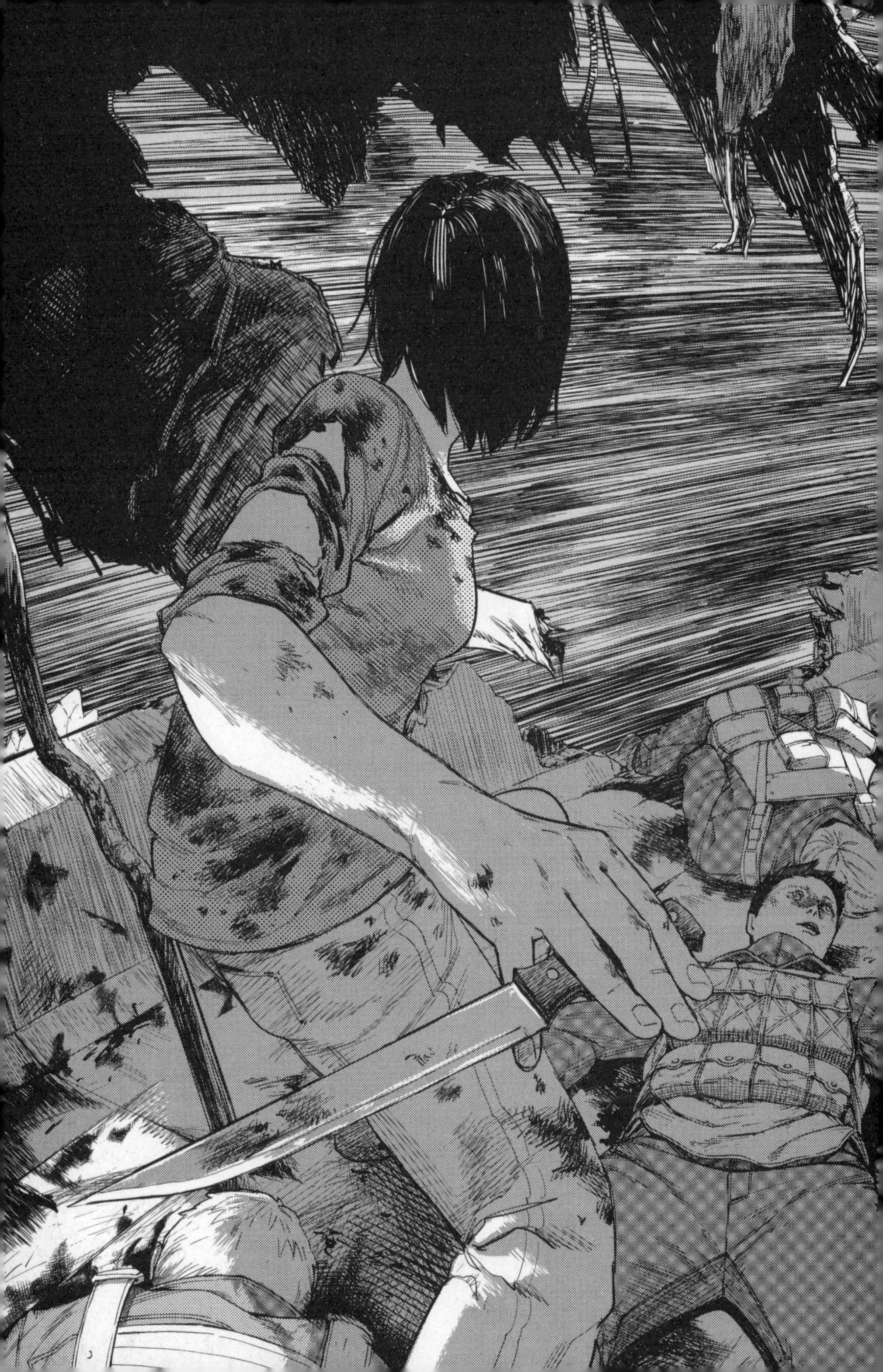

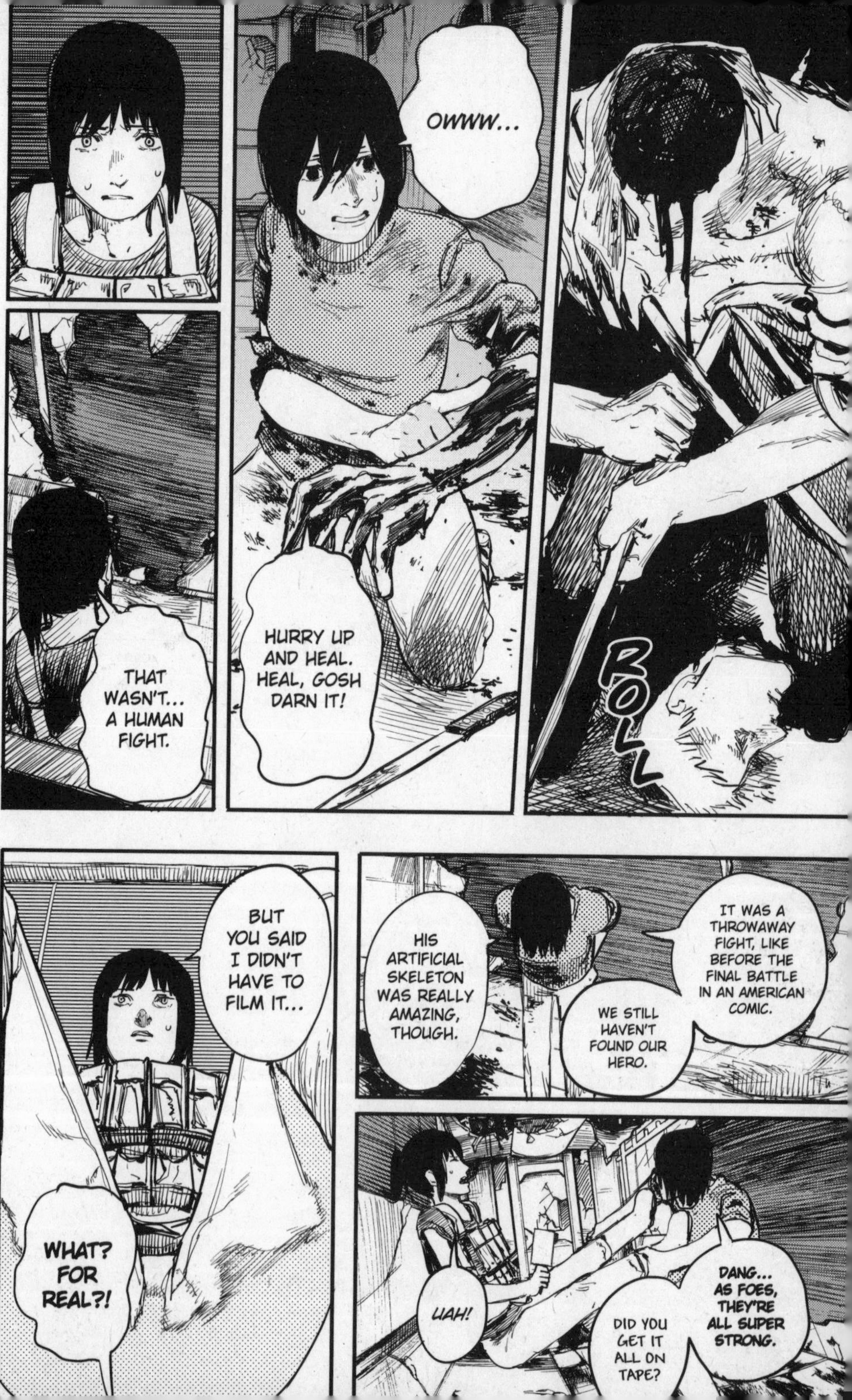
ROLL
OWWW...
HURRY UP AND HEAL. HEAL, GOSH DARN IT!
THAT WASN'T... A HUMAN FIGHT.
IT WAS A THROWAWAY FIGHT, LIKE BEFORE THE FINAL BATTLE IN AN AMERICAN COMIC.
WE STILL HAVEN'T FOUND OUR HERO.
HIS ARTIFICIAL SKELETON WAS REALLY AMAZING, THOUGH.
DANG... AS FOES, THEY'RE ALL SUPER STRONG.
DID YOU GET IT ALL ON TAPE?
UAH!
BUT YOU SAID I DIDN'T HAVE TO FILM IT...
WHAT? FOR REAL?!

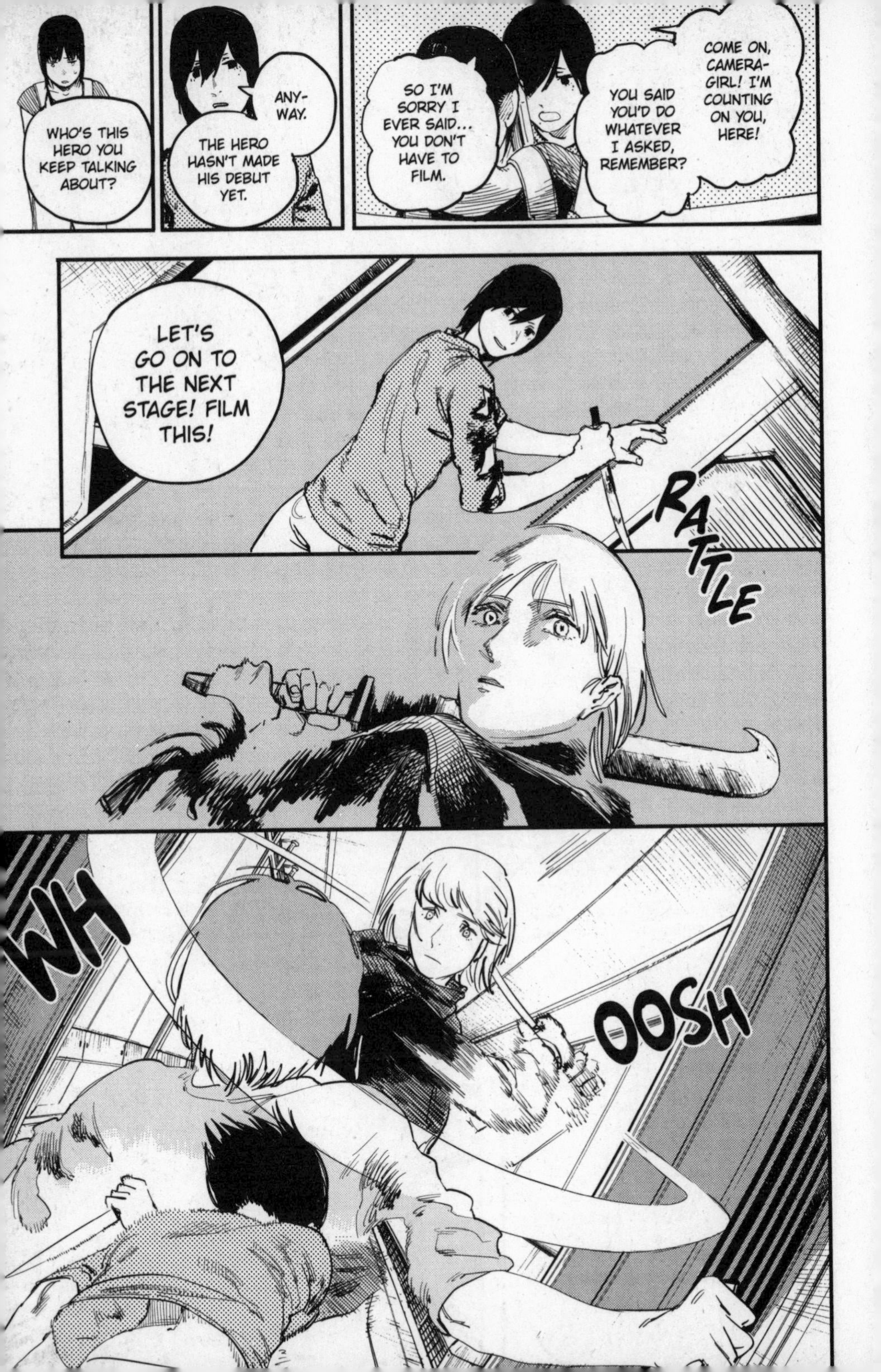
COME ON, CAMERA-GIRL! I'M COUNTING ON YOU, HERE!
YOU SAID YOU'D DO WHATEVER I ASKED, REMEMBER?
SO I'M SORRY I EVER SAID... YOU DON'T HAVE TO FILM.
ANY-WAY.
THE HERO HASN'T MADE HIS DEBUT YET.
WHO'S THIS HERO YOU KEEP TALKING ABOUT?
LET'S GO ON TO THE NEXT STAGE! FILM THIS!
RATTLE
WHOOSH

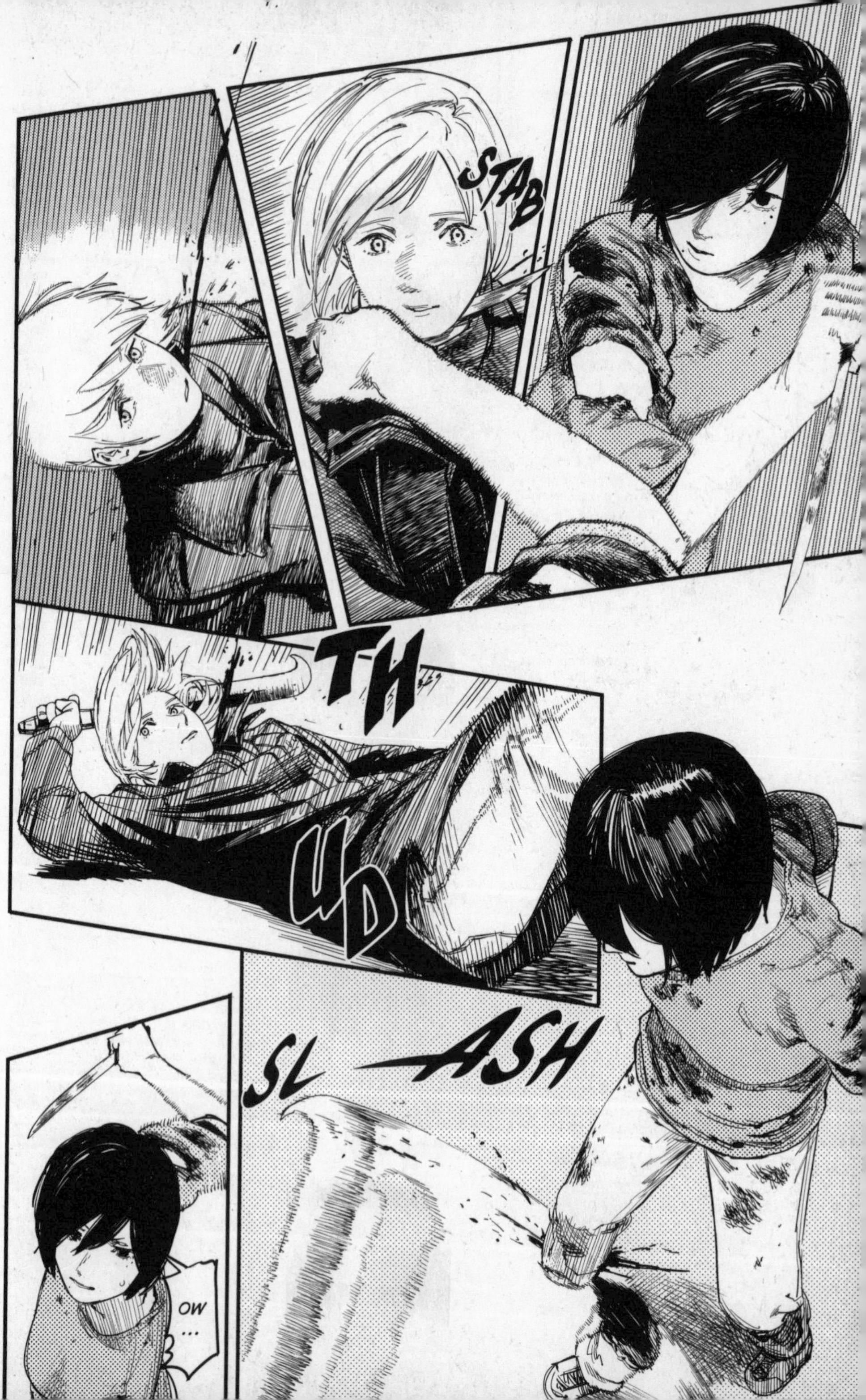
STAB
THUD
SLASH
OW
...

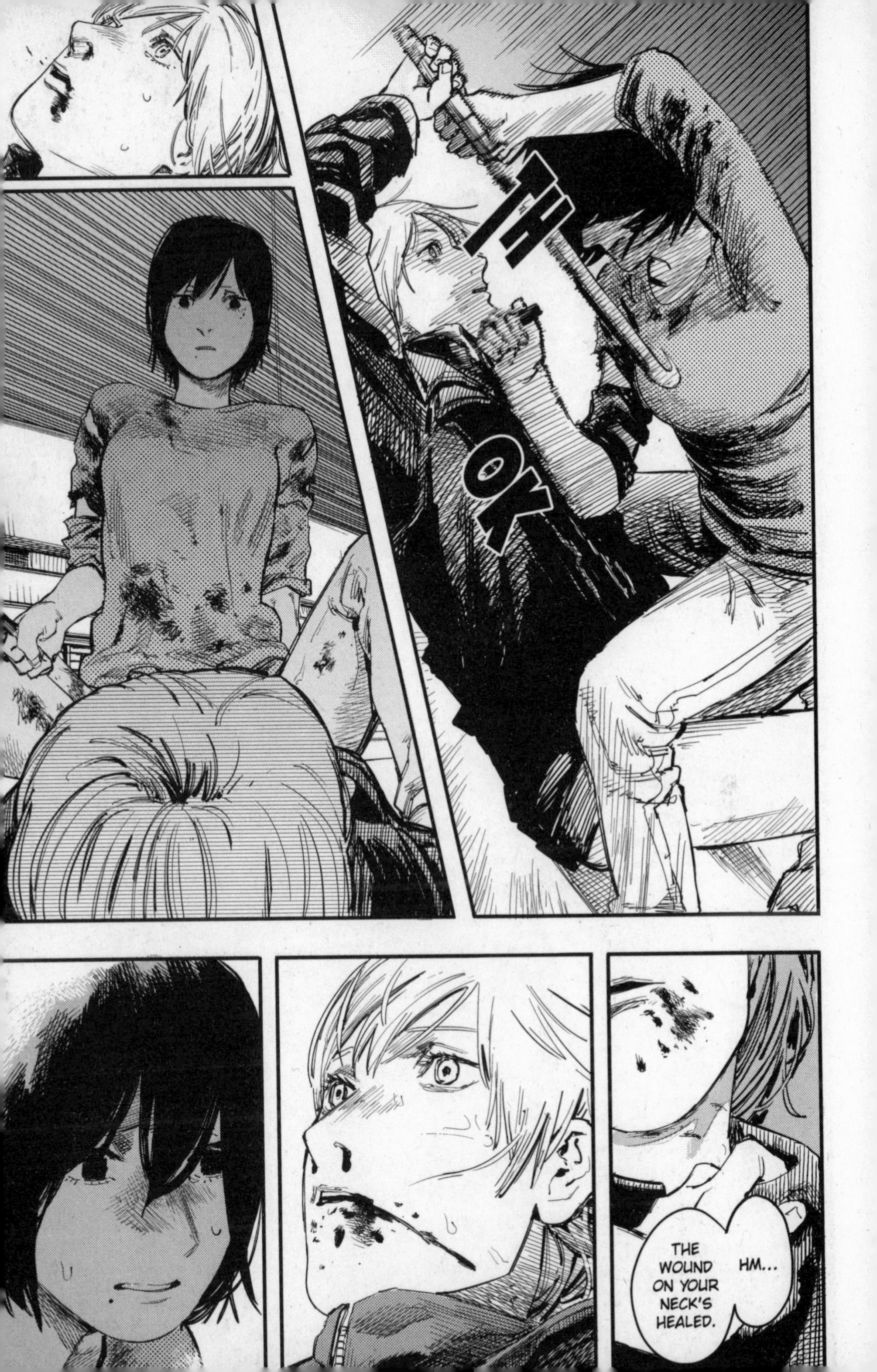
THOK
HM...
THE WOUND ON YOUR NECK'S HEALED.

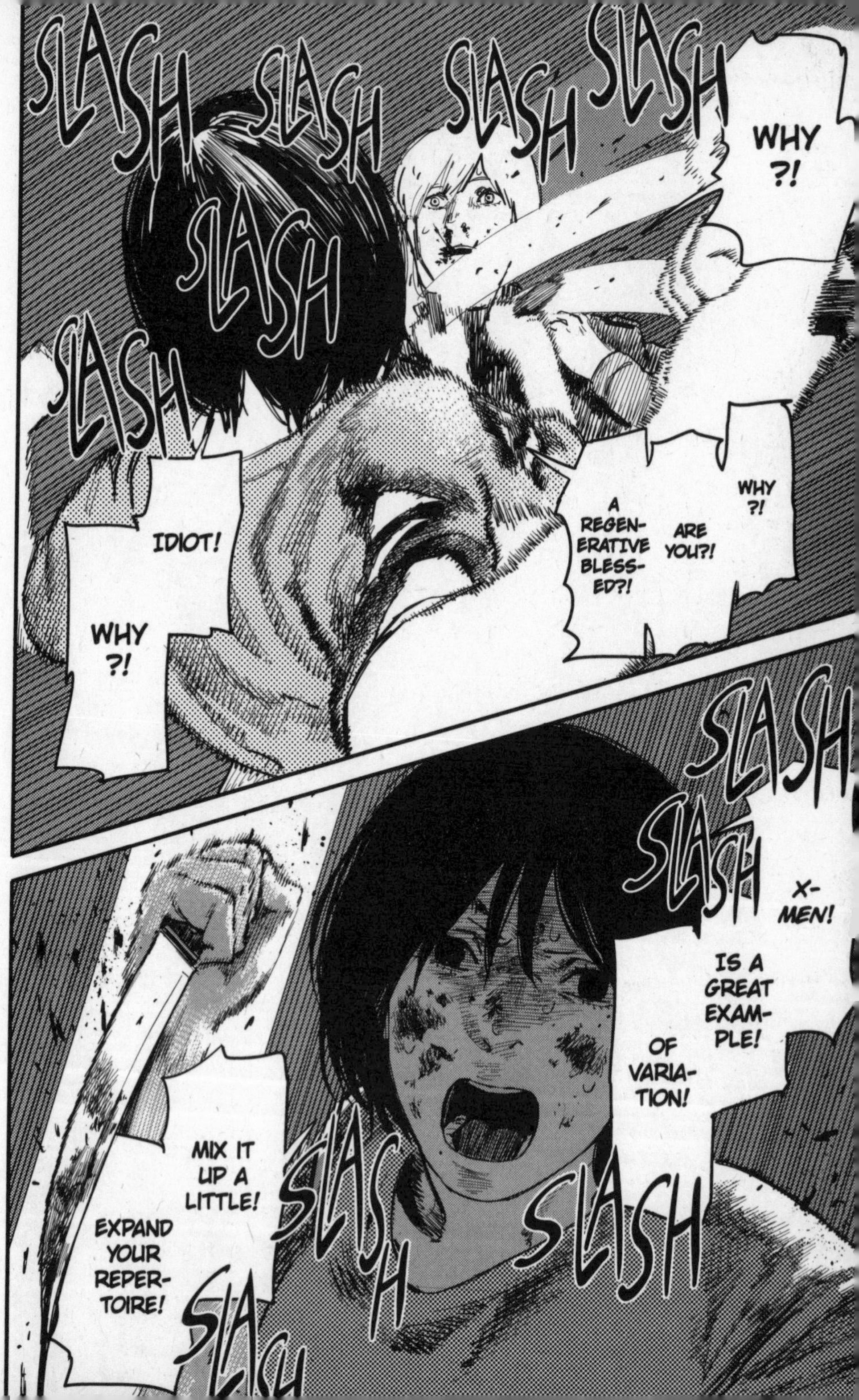
SLASH SLASH SLASH SLASH
SLASH
SLASH
WHY ?!
WHY ?!
ARE YOU?!
A REGEN-ERATIVE BLESS-ED?!
IDIOT!
WHY ?!
SLASH
SLASH
X-MEN!
IS A GREAT EXAM-PLE!
OF VARIA-TION!
SLASH
SLASH
MIX IT UP A LITTLE!
EXPAND YOUR REPER-TOIRE!

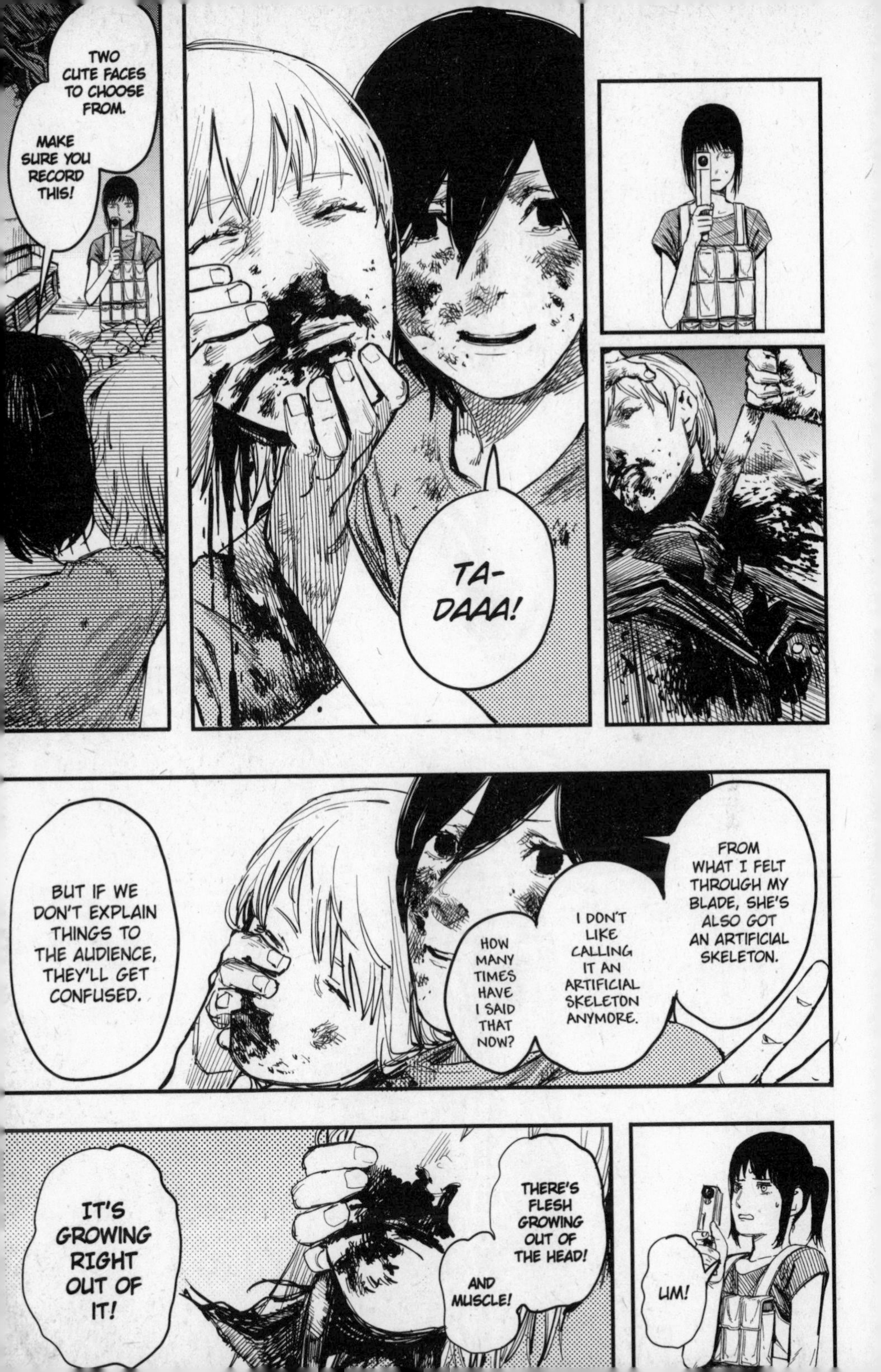
TA-DAAA!
TWO CUTE FACES TO CHOOSE FROM.
MAKE SURE YOU RECORD THIS!
FROM WHAT I FELT THROUGH MY BLADE, SHE'S ALSO GOT AN ARTIFICIAL SKELETON.
I DON'T LIKE CALLING IT AN ARTIFICIAL SKELETON ANYMORE.
HOW MANY TIMES HAVE I SAID THAT NOW?
BUT IF WE DON'T EXPLAIN THINGS TO THE AUDIENCE, THEY'LL GET CONFUSED.
UM!
THERE'S FLESH GROWING OUT OF THE HEAD!
AND MUSCLE!
IT'S GROWING RIGHT OUT OF IT!

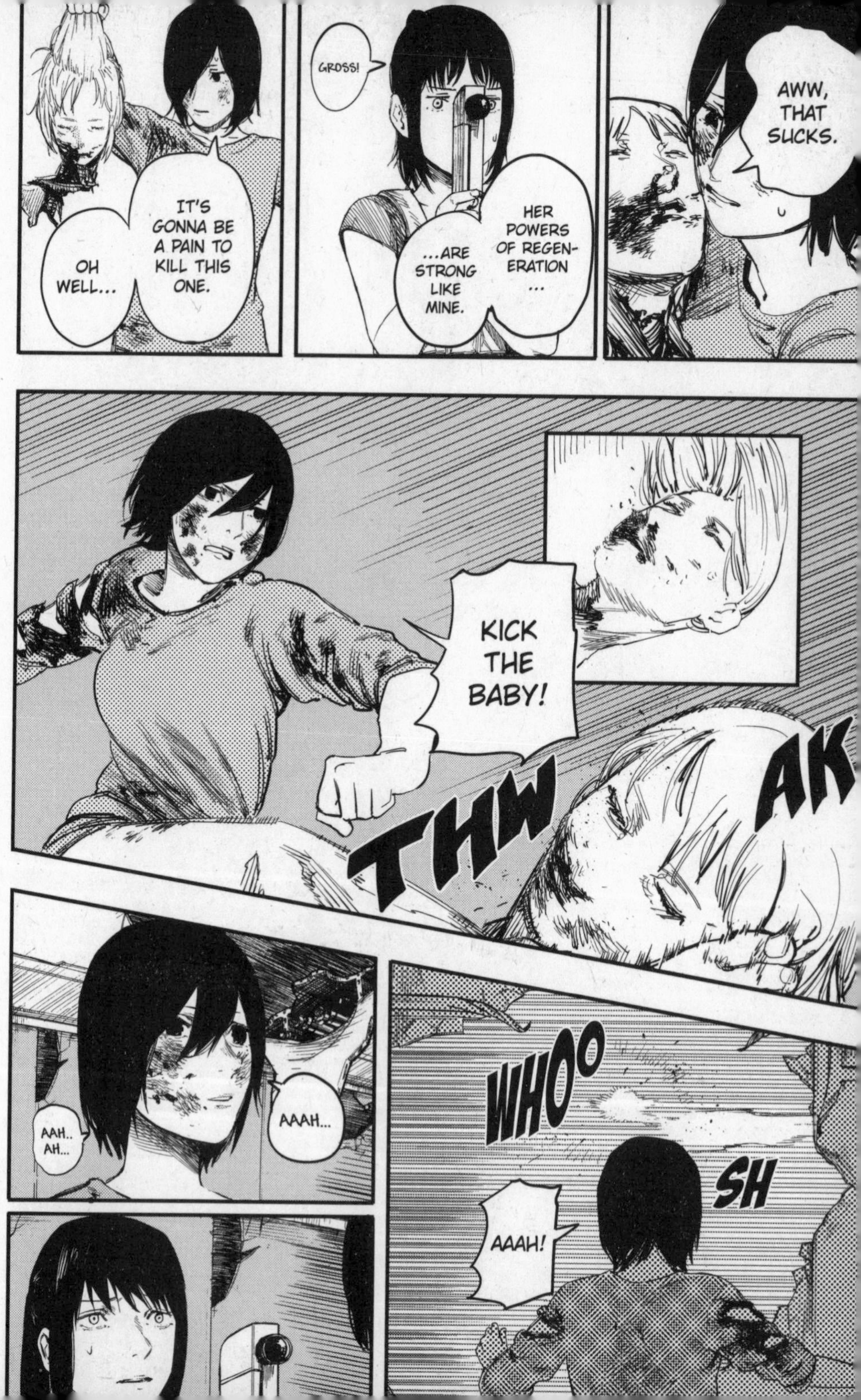
AWW, THAT SUCKS.
GROSS!
HER POWERS OF REGENERATION...
...ARE STRONG LIKE MINE.
IT'S GONNA BE A PAIN TO KILL THIS ONE.
OH WELL...
KICK THE BABY!
THWAK
WHOOSH
AAAH!
AAAH...
AAH.. AH...

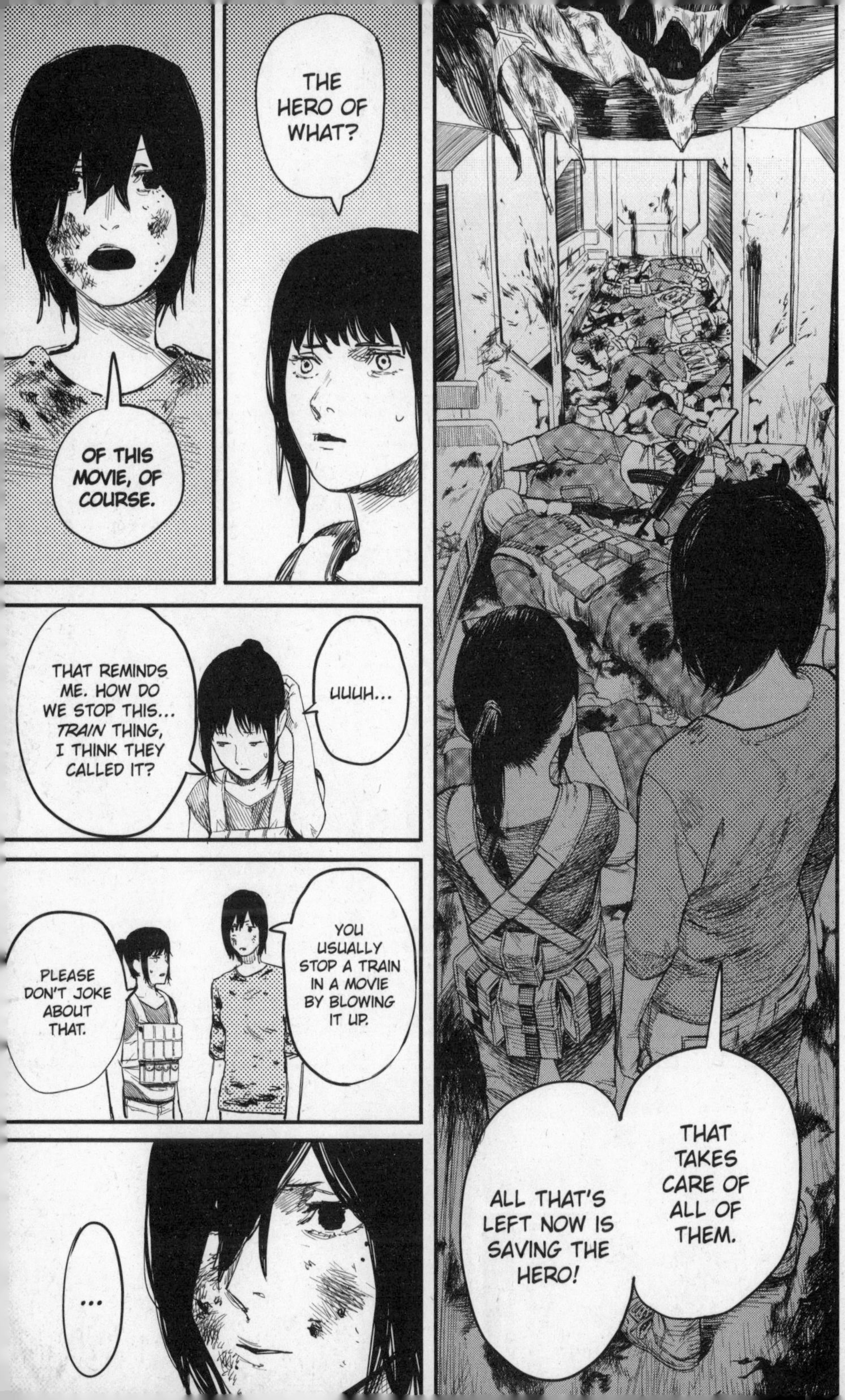
THAT TAKES CARE OF ALL OF THEM.
ALL THAT'S LEFT NOW IS SAVING THE HERO!
THE HERO OF WHAT?
OF THIS MOVIE, OF COURSE.
THAT REMINDS ME. HOW DO WE STOP THIS... *TRAIN* THING, I THINK THEY CALLED IT?
UUUH...
YOU USUALLY STOP A TRAIN IN A MOVIE BY BLOWING IT UP.
PLEASE DON'T JOKE ABOUT THAT.
...

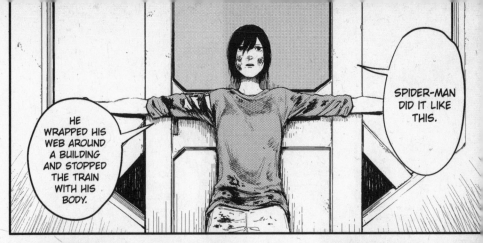

SPIDER-MAN DID IT LIKE THIS.
HE WRAPPED HIS WEB AROUND A BUILDING AND STOPPED THE TRAIN WITH HIS BODY.
BUT HOW WOULD THAT WORK HERE?
WOULD *YOU* BE OKAY? HOW WOULD YOU STOP IT?!
I'LL REVIVE MYSELF. I'LL BE FINE.
SO YOU *DON'T* KNOW HOW TO STOP IT?! WAIT, SERI-OUSLY?!
SPIDER-MAN ALSO USED HIS FEET.
OH, GREAT... WHAT HAVE I GOTTEN MYSELF INTO?
UM...
SURE.
EH? SURE? *SURE?!*

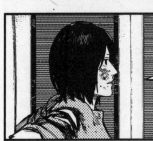

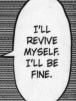

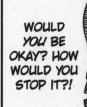

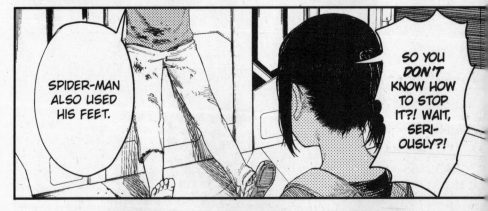

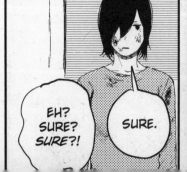

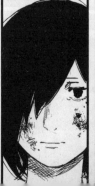

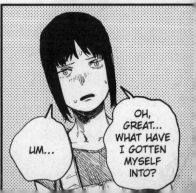

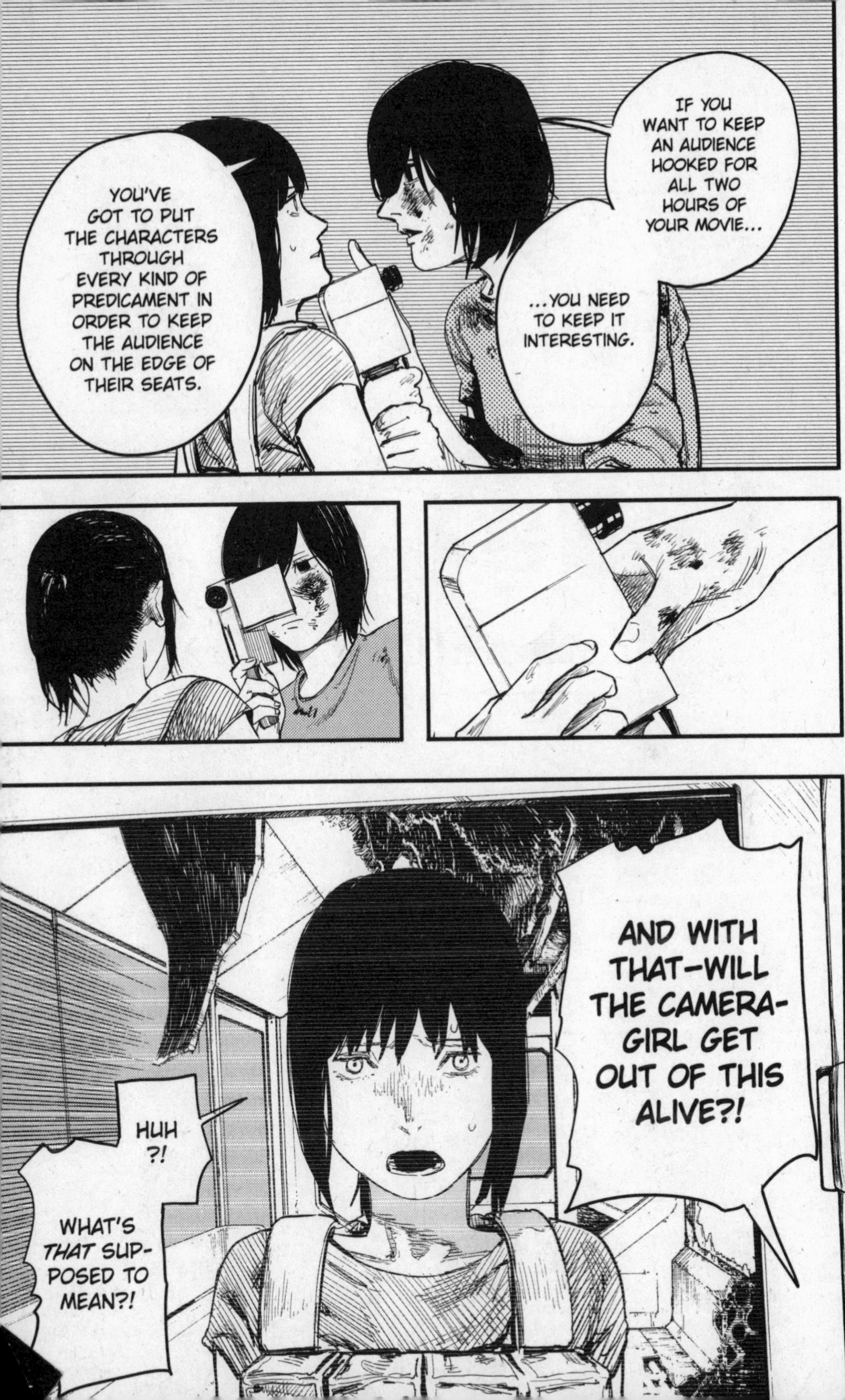
IF YOU WANT TO KEEP AN AUDIENCE HOOKED FOR ALL TWO HOURS OF YOUR MOVIE...
...YOU NEED TO KEEP IT INTERESTING.
YOU'VE GOT TO PUT THE CHARACTERS THROUGH EVERY KIND OF PREDICAMENT IN ORDER TO KEEP THE AUDIENCE ON THE EDGE OF THEIR SEATS.
AND WITH THAT—WILL THE CAMERA-GIRL GET OUT OF THIS ALIVE?!
HUH?!
WHAT'S *THAT* SUPPOSED TO MEAN?!

FIRE PUNCH

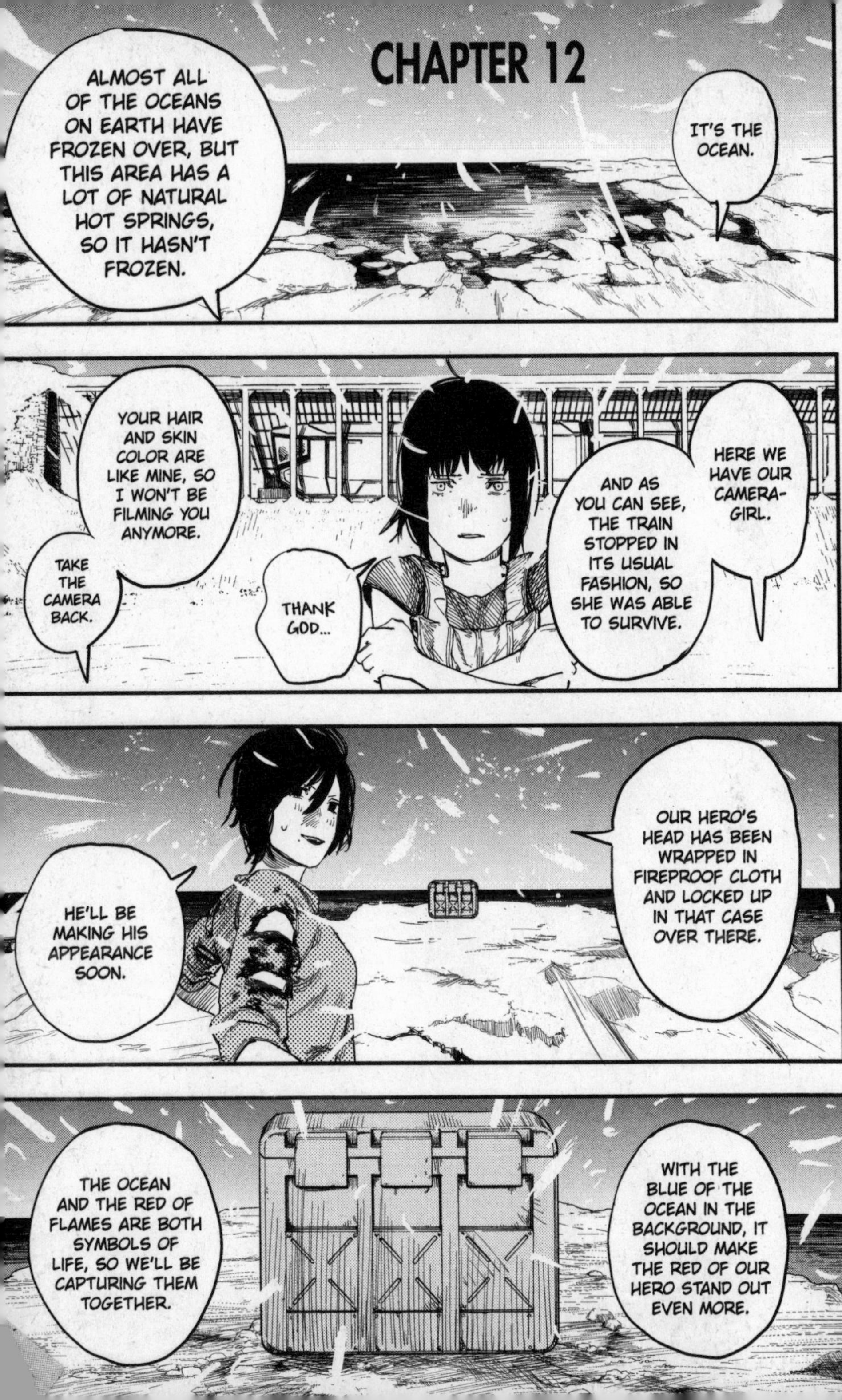
CHAPTER 12
IT'S THE OCEAN.
ALMOST ALL OF THE OCEANS ON EARTH HAVE FROZEN OVER, BUT THIS AREA HAS A LOT OF NATURAL HOT SPRINGS, SO IT HASN'T FROZEN.
HERE WE HAVE OUR CAMERA-GIRL.
AND AS YOU CAN SEE, THE TRAIN STOPPED IN ITS USUAL FASHION, SO SHE WAS ABLE TO SURVIVE.
THANK GOD...
YOUR HAIR AND SKIN COLOR ARE LIKE MINE, SO I WON'T BE FILMING YOU ANYMORE.
TAKE THE CAMERA BACK.
OUR HERO'S HEAD HAS BEEN WRAPPED IN FIREPROOF CLOTH AND LOCKED UP IN THAT CASE OVER THERE.
HE'LL BE MAKING HIS APPEARANCE SOON.
WITH THE BLUE OF THE OCEAN IN THE BACKGROUND, IT SHOULD MAKE THE RED OF OUR HERO STAND OUT EVEN MORE.
THE OCEAN AND THE RED OF FLAMES ARE BOTH SYMBOLS OF LIFE, SO WE'LL BE CAPTURING THEM TOGETHER.

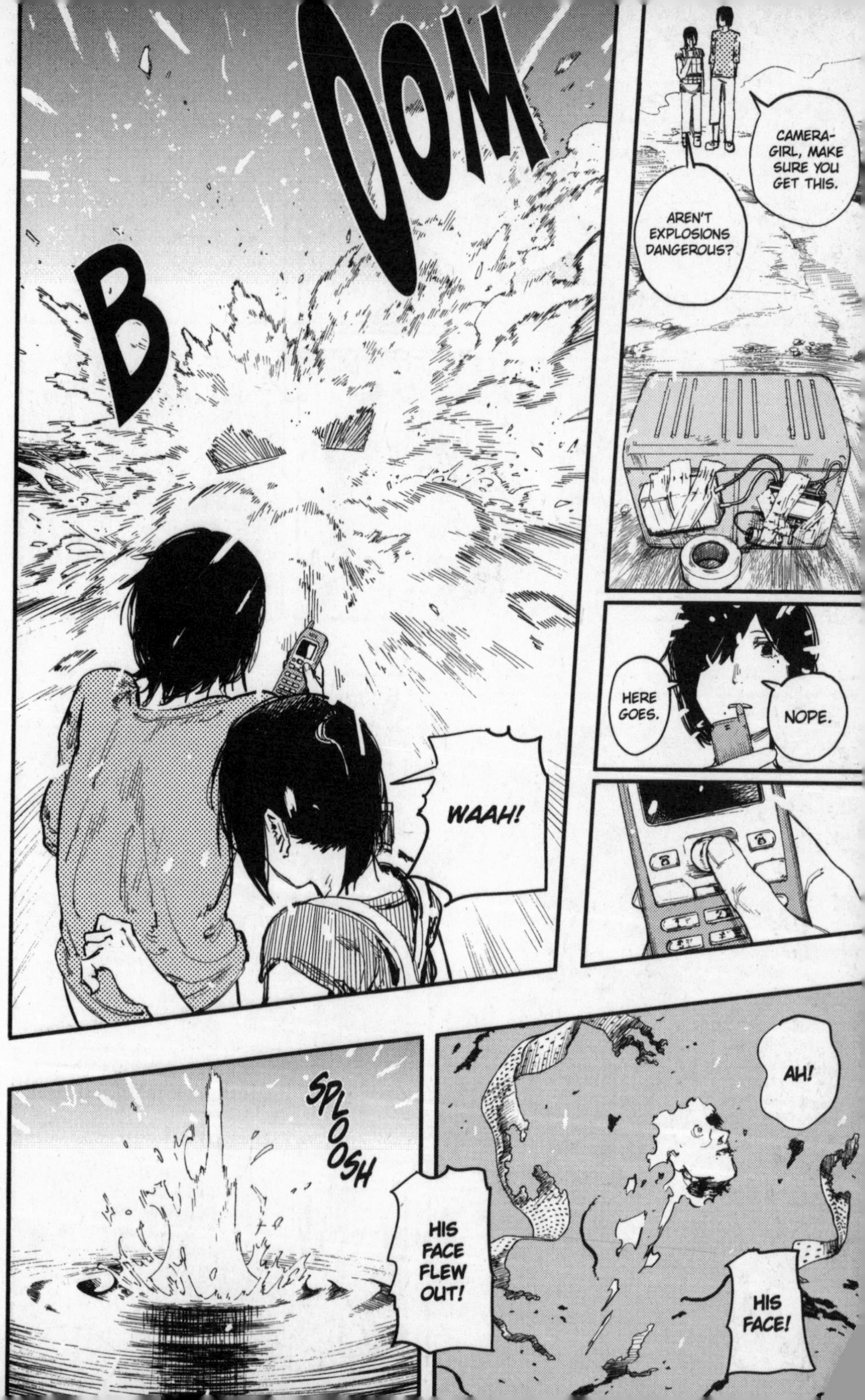
CAMERA-GIRL, MAKE SURE YOU GET THIS.
AREN'T EXPLOSIONS DANGEROUS?
NOPE.
HERE GOES.
BOOM
WAAH!
AH!
HIS FACE!
SPLOOSH
HIS FACE FLEW OUT!

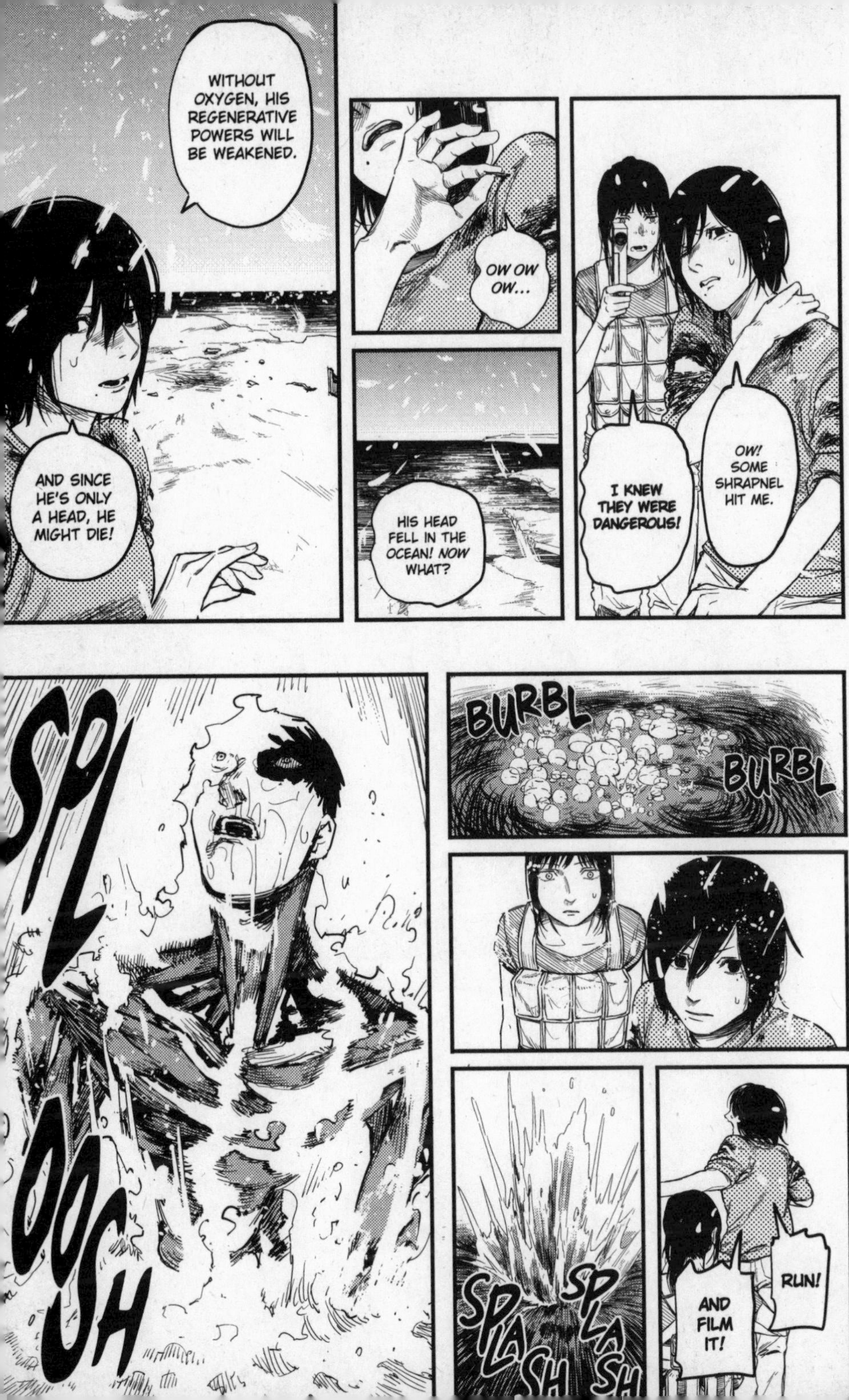
OW! SOME SHRAPNEL HIT ME.
I KNEW THEY WERE DANGEROUS!
OW OW OW...
HIS HEAD FELL IN THE OCEAN! NOW WHAT?
WITHOUT OXYGEN, HIS REGENERATIVE POWERS WILL BE WEAKENED.
AND SINCE HE'S ONLY A HEAD, HE MIGHT DIE!
BURBL
BURBL
RUN!
AND FILM IT!
SPLASH
SPLASH
SPLOOSH

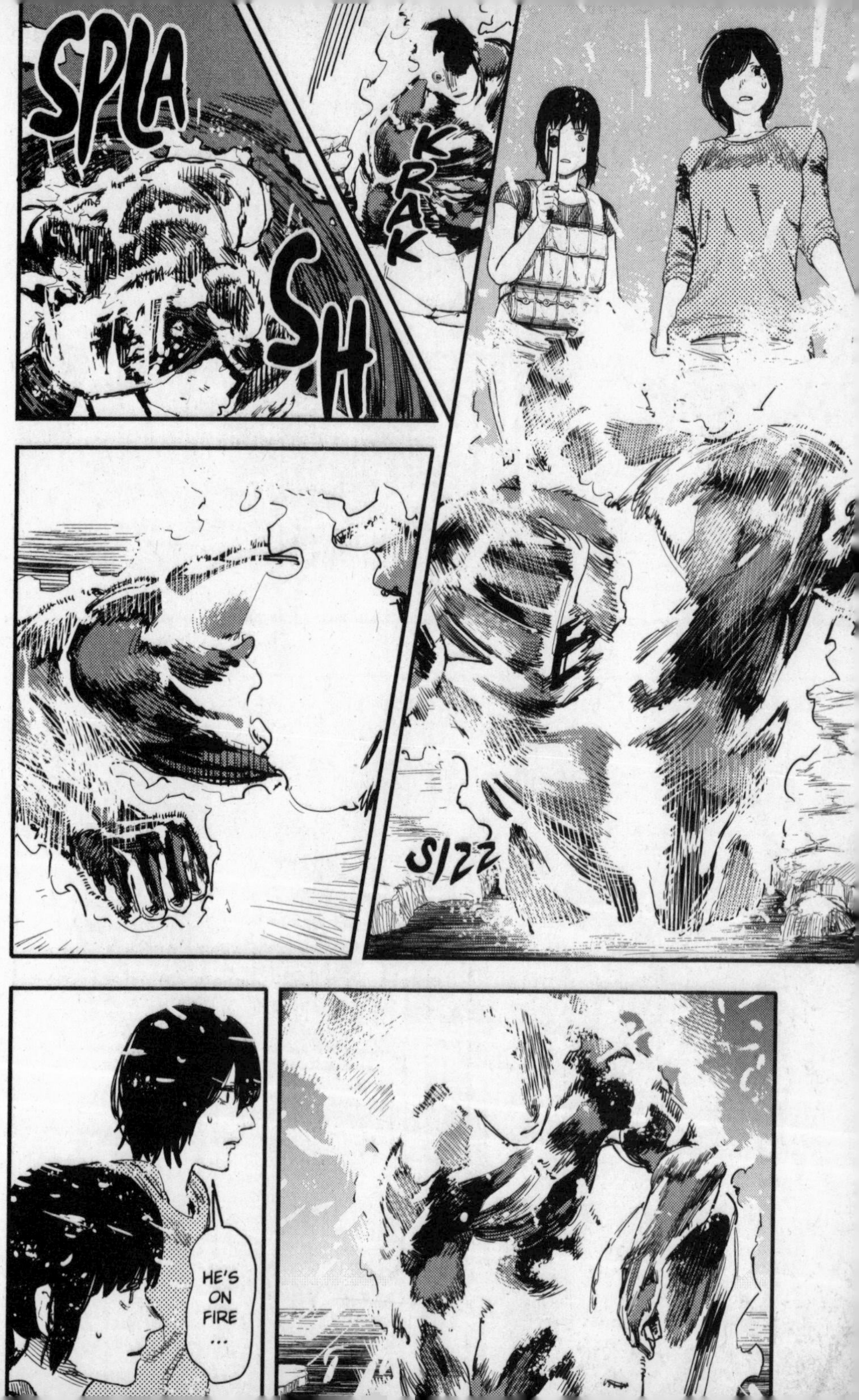
SIZZ
KRAK
SPLA
SH
HE'S ON FIRE ...

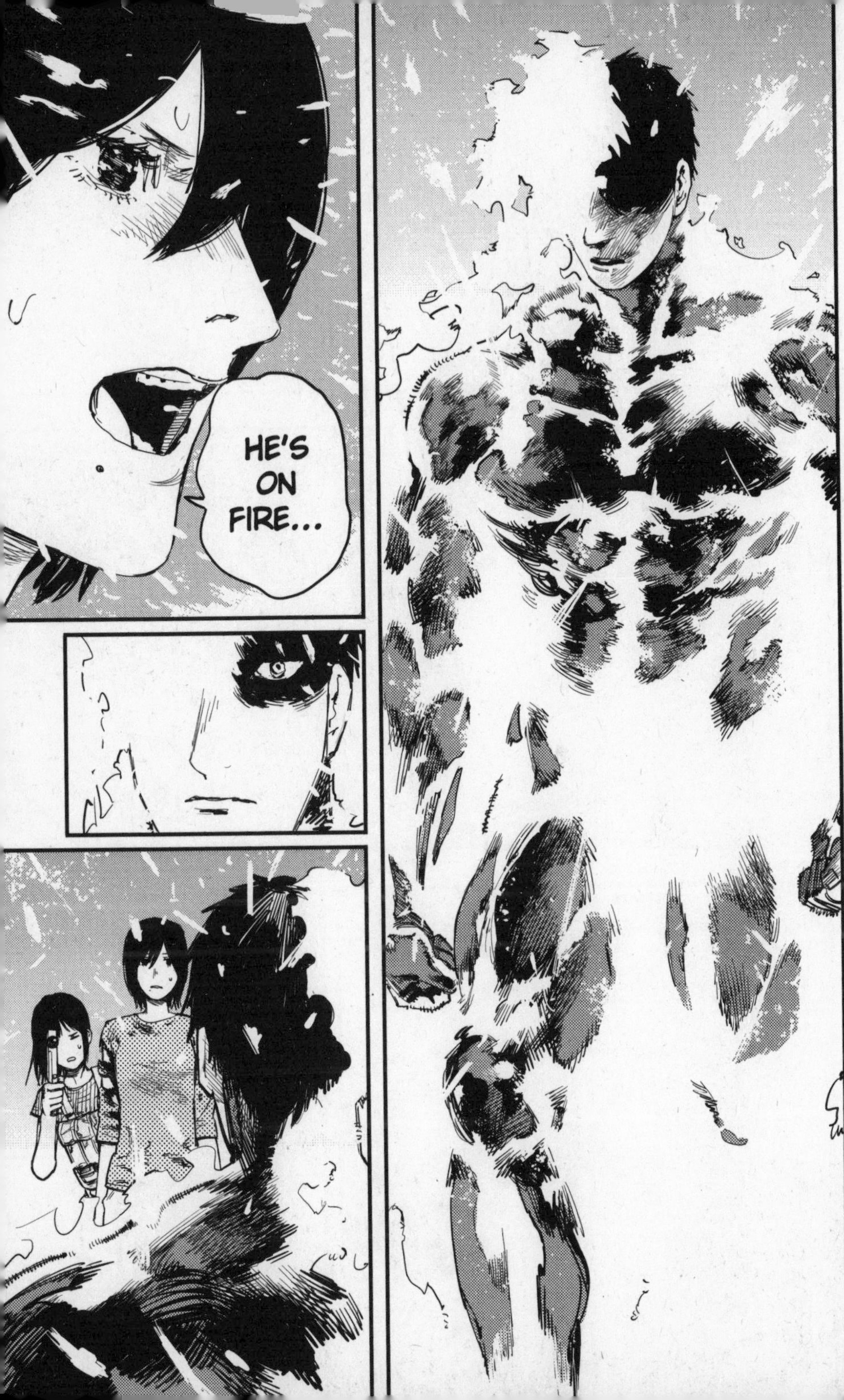
HE'S ON FIRE...

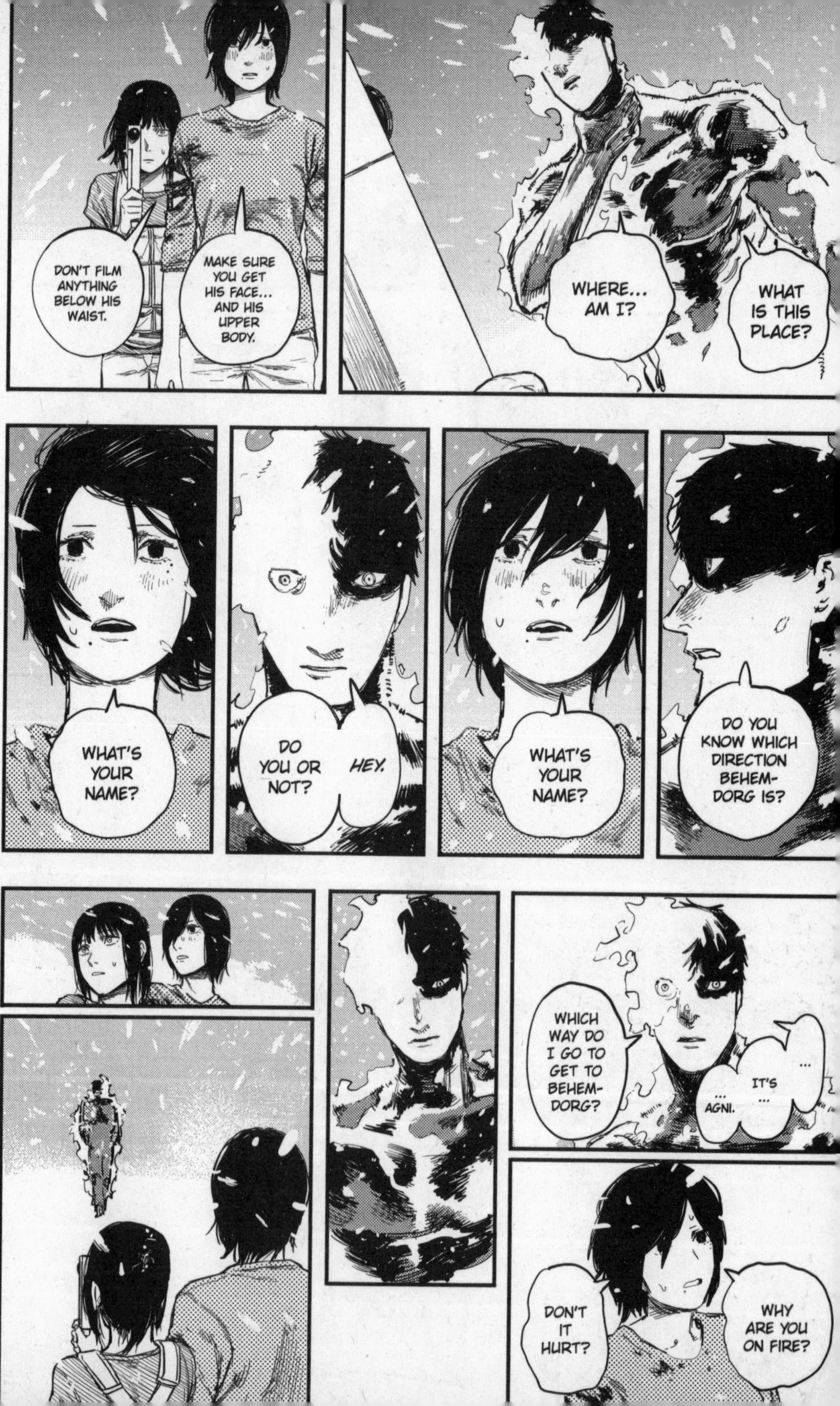
WHAT IS THIS PLACE?
WHERE... AM I?
MAKE SURE YOU GET HIS FACE... AND HIS UPPER BODY.
DON'T FILM ANYTHING BELOW HIS WAIST.
DO YOU KNOW WHICH DIRECTION BEHEM-DORG IS?
WHAT'S YOUR NAME?
HEY.
DO YOU OR NOT?
WHAT'S YOUR NAME?
...
IT'S ...
... AGNI.
WHICH WAY DO I GO TO GET TO BEHEM-DORG?
WHY ARE YOU ON FIRE?
DON'T IT HURT?

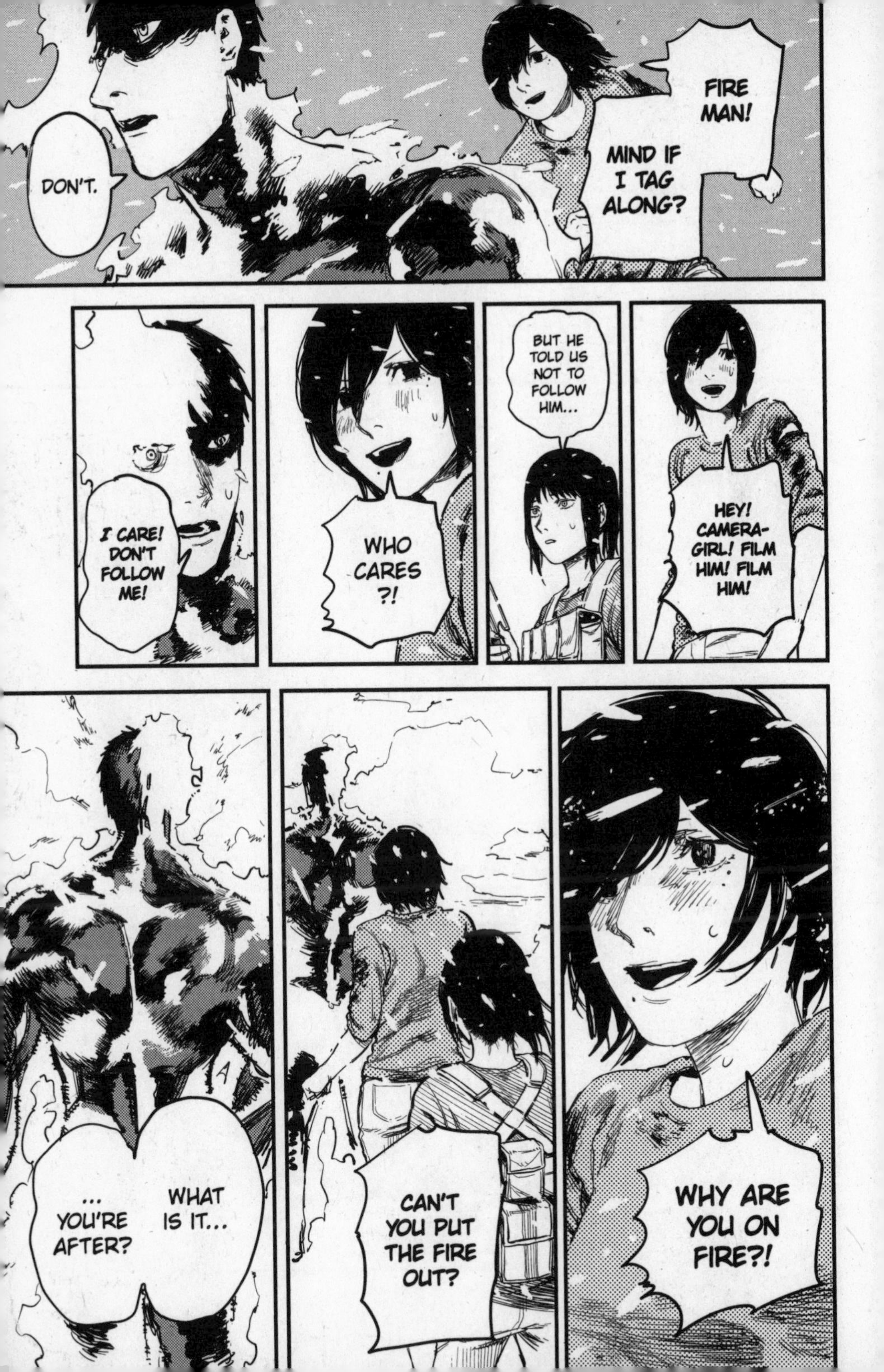
FIRE MAN!
MIND IF I TAG ALONG?
DON'T.
HEY! CAMERA-GIRL! FILM HIM! FILM HIM!
BUT HE TOLD US NOT TO FOLLOW HIM...
WHO CARES?!
I CARE! DON'T FOLLOW ME!
WHY ARE YOU ON FIRE?!
CAN'T YOU PUT THE FIRE OUT?
WHAT IS IT...
...YOU'RE AFTER?

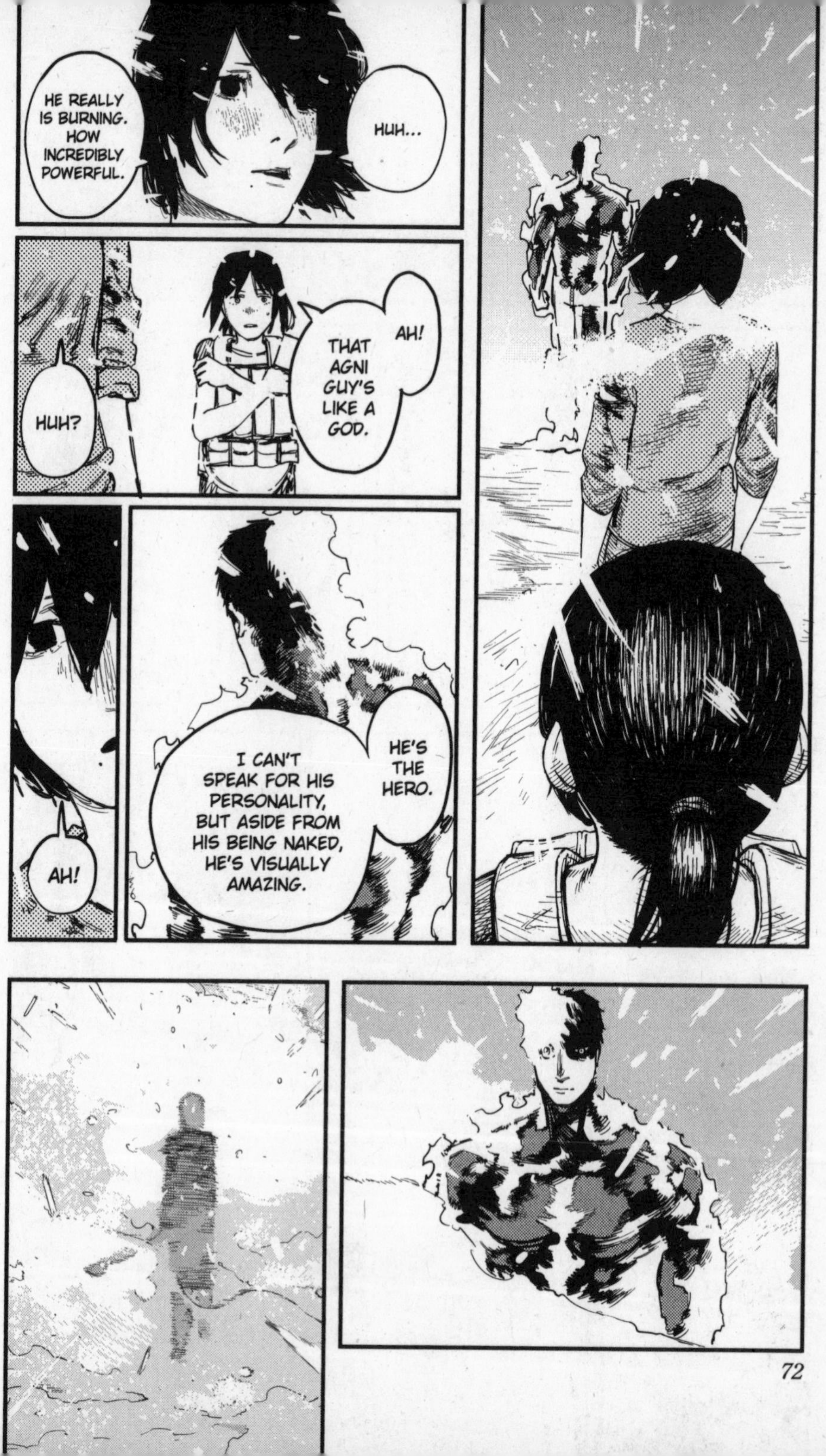
HUH...
HE REALLY IS BURNING. HOW INCREDIBLY POWERFUL.
AH! THAT AGNI GUY'S LIKE A GOD.
HUH?
HE'S THE HERO.
I CAN'T SPEAK FOR HIS PERSONALITY, BUT ASIDE FROM HIS BEING NAKED, HE'S VISUALLY AMAZING.
AH!

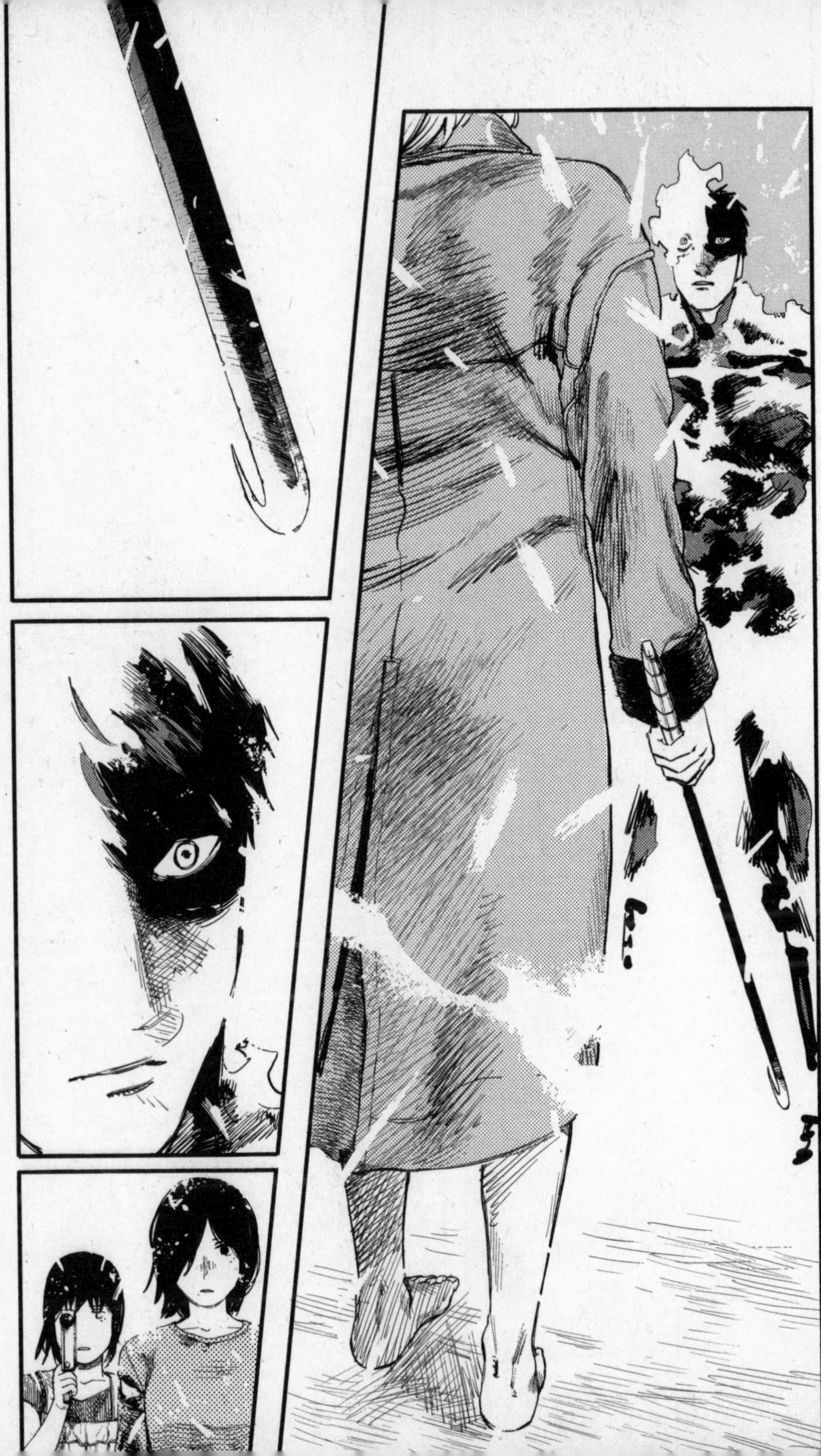

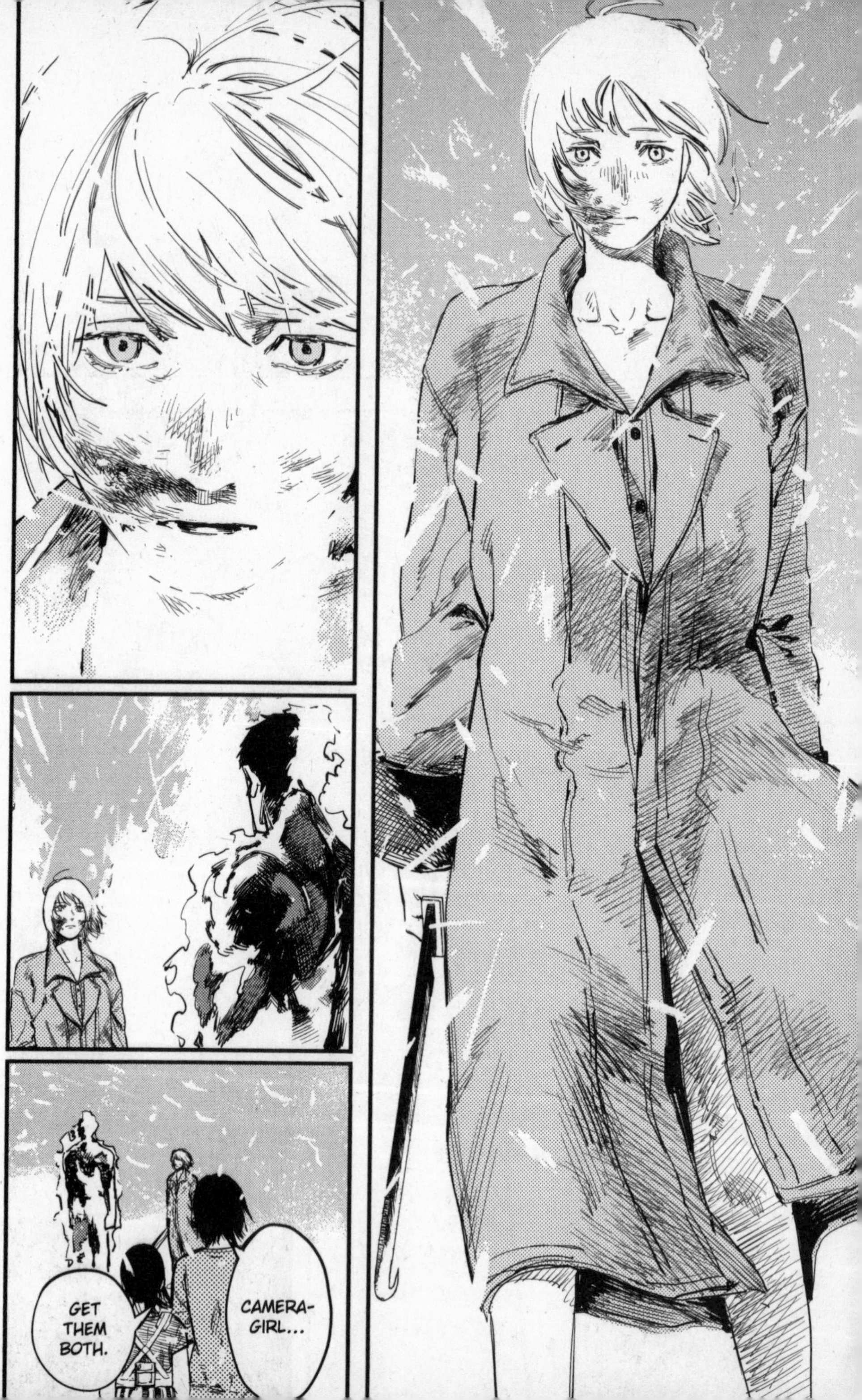
CAMERA-GIRL...
GET THEM BOTH.

NO.

IF I MOVE, YOU'LL BURN DOWN MY NATION.

OUT OF MY WAY.

YOU'RE ...

WHO ARE YOU?

WHO ARE YOU?!

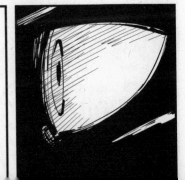

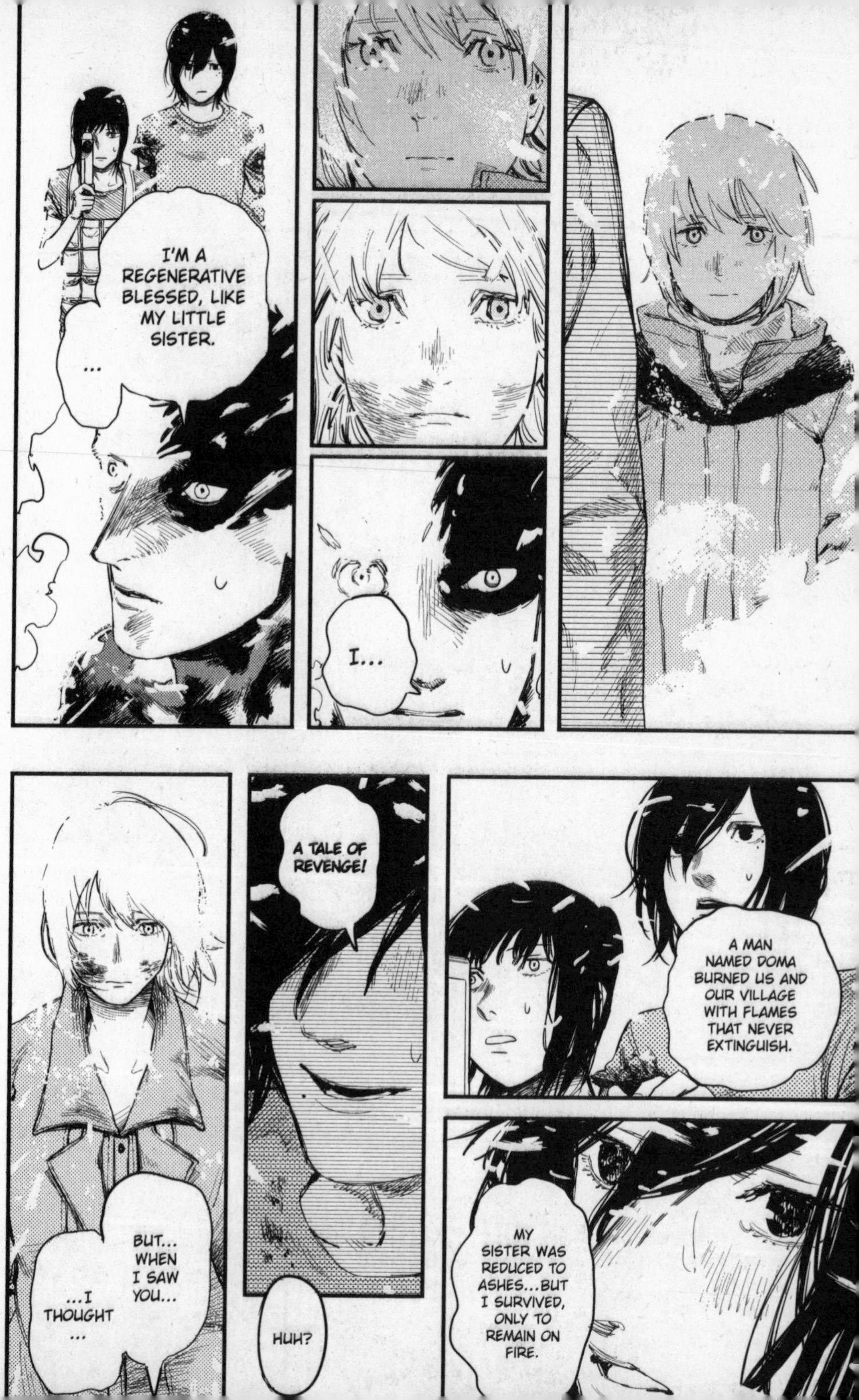
I...
I'M A REGENERATIVE BLESSED, LIKE MY LITTLE SISTER.
...
A MAN NAMED DOMA BURNED US AND OUR VILLAGE WITH FLAMES THAT NEVER EXTINGUISH.
MY SISTER WAS REDUCED TO ASHES...BUT I SURVIVED, ONLY TO REMAIN ON FIRE.
A TALE OF REVENGE!
HUH?
BUT... WHEN I SAW YOU...
...I THOUGHT ...

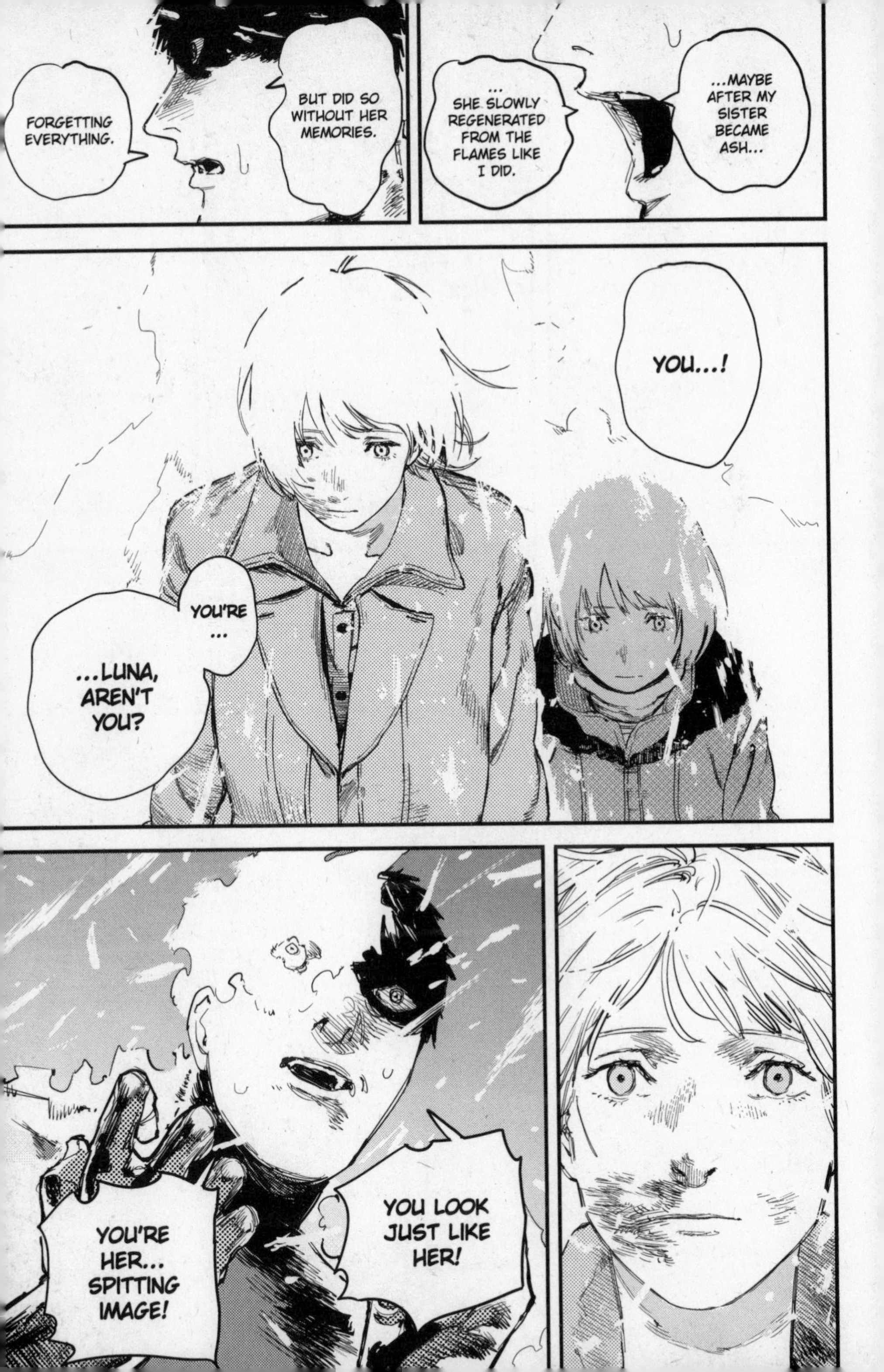
...MAYBE AFTER MY SISTER BECAME ASH...
... SHE SLOWLY REGENERATED FROM THE FLAMES LIKE I DID.
BUT DID SO WITHOUT HER MEMORIES.
FORGETTING EVERYTHING.
YOU...!
YOU'RE ...
...LUNA, AREN'T YOU?
YOU LOOK JUST LIKE HER!
YOU'RE HER... SPITTING IMAGE!

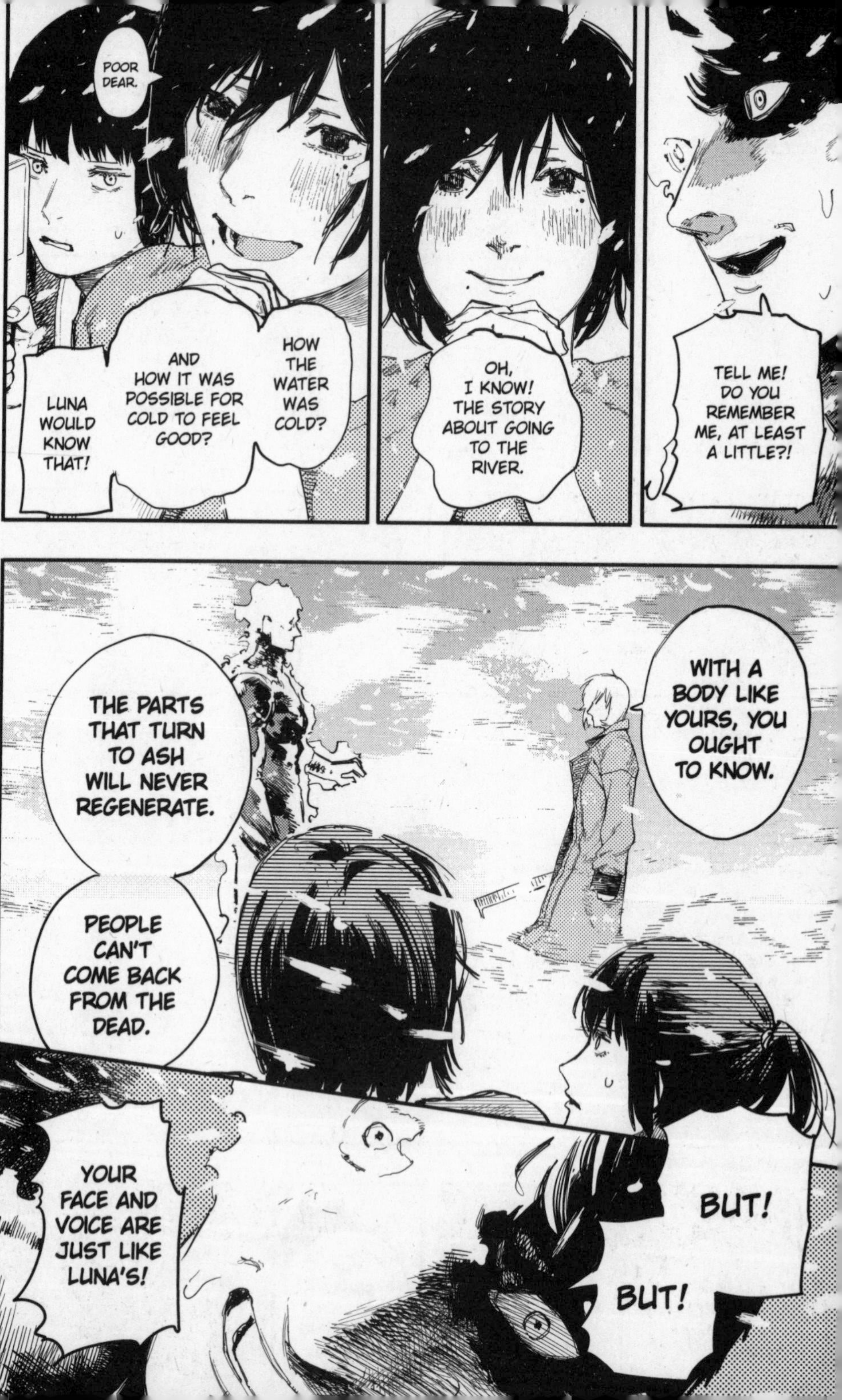
TELL ME! DO YOU REMEMBER ME, AT LEAST A LITTLE?!
OH, I KNOW! THE STORY ABOUT GOING TO THE RIVER.
HOW THE WATER WAS COLD?
AND HOW IT WAS POSSIBLE FOR COLD TO FEEL GOOD?
POOR DEAR.
LUNA WOULD KNOW THAT!
WITH A BODY LIKE YOURS, YOU OUGHT TO KNOW.
THE PARTS THAT TURN TO ASH WILL NEVER REGENERATE.
PEOPLE CAN'T COME BACK FROM THE DEAD.
BUT!
BUT!
YOUR FACE AND VOICE ARE JUST LIKE LUNA'S!

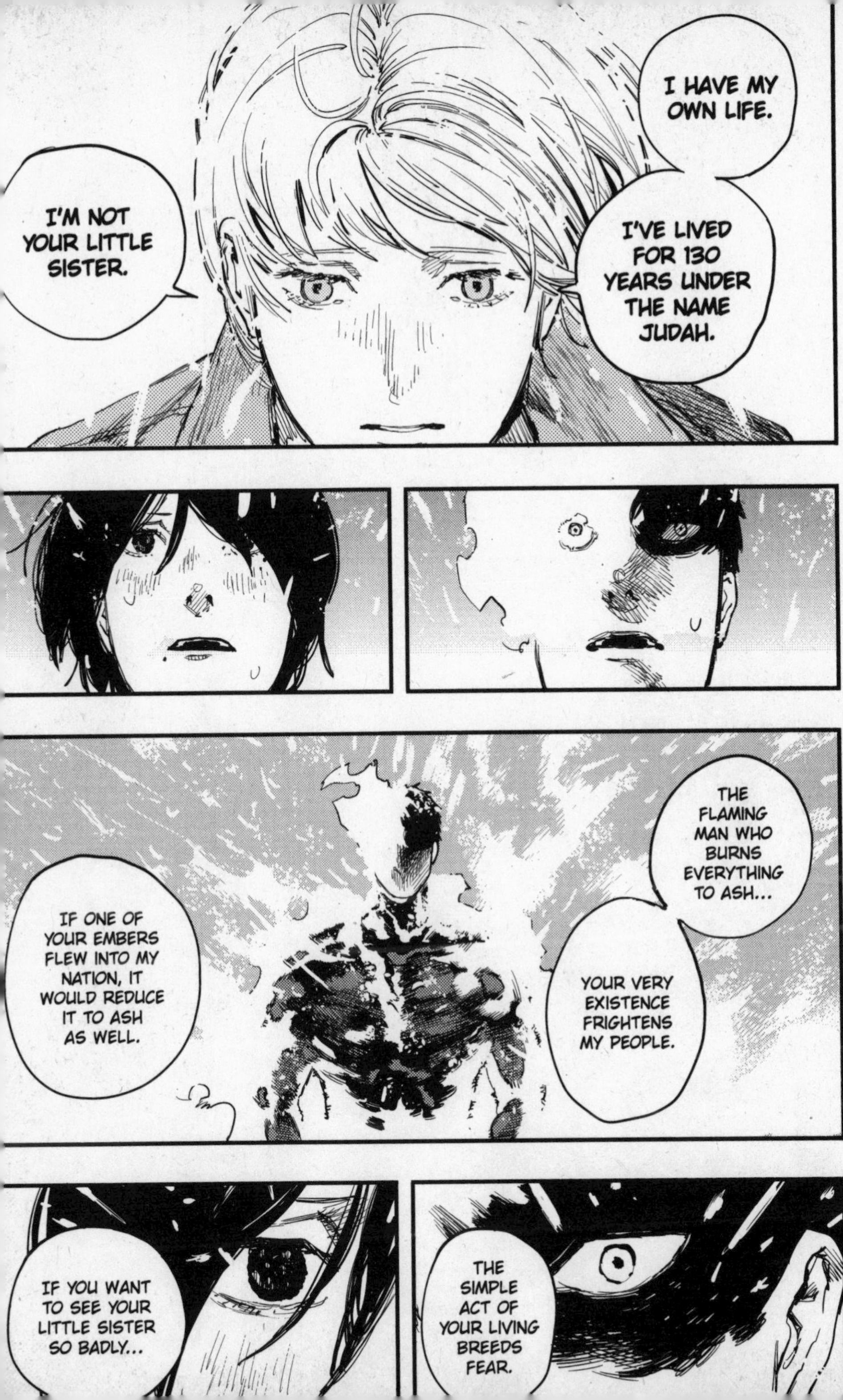
I HAVE MY OWN LIFE.
I'VE LIVED FOR 130 YEARS UNDER THE NAME JUDAH.
I'M NOT YOUR LITTLE SISTER.
THE FLAMING MAN WHO BURNS EVERYTHING TO ASH...
YOUR VERY EXISTENCE FRIGHTENS MY PEOPLE.
IF ONE OF YOUR EMBERS FLEW INTO MY NATION, IT WOULD REDUCE IT TO ASH AS WELL.
THE SIMPLE ACT OF YOUR LIVING BREEDS FEAR.
IF YOU WANT TO SEE YOUR LITTLE SISTER SO BADLY...

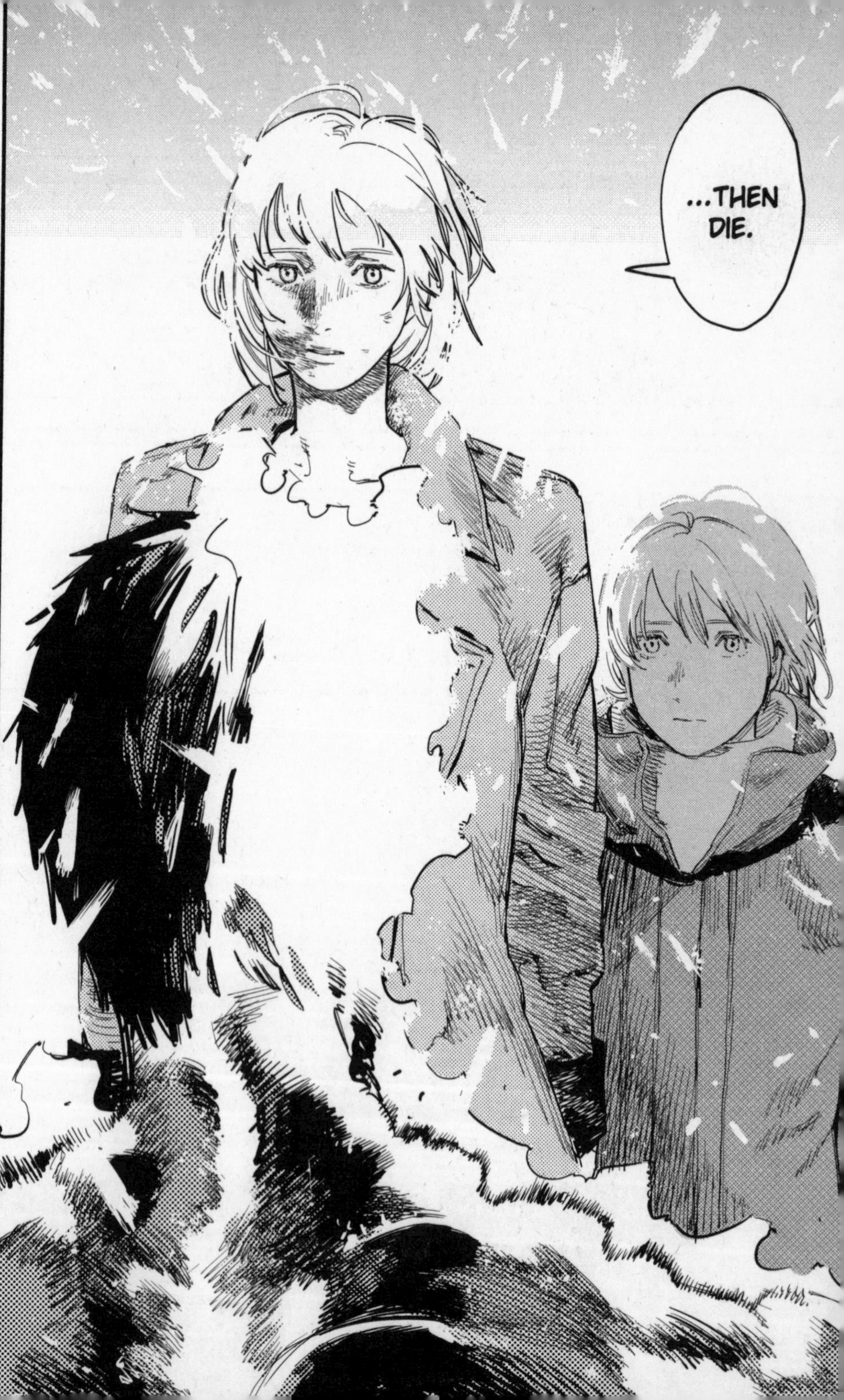
...THEN DIE.

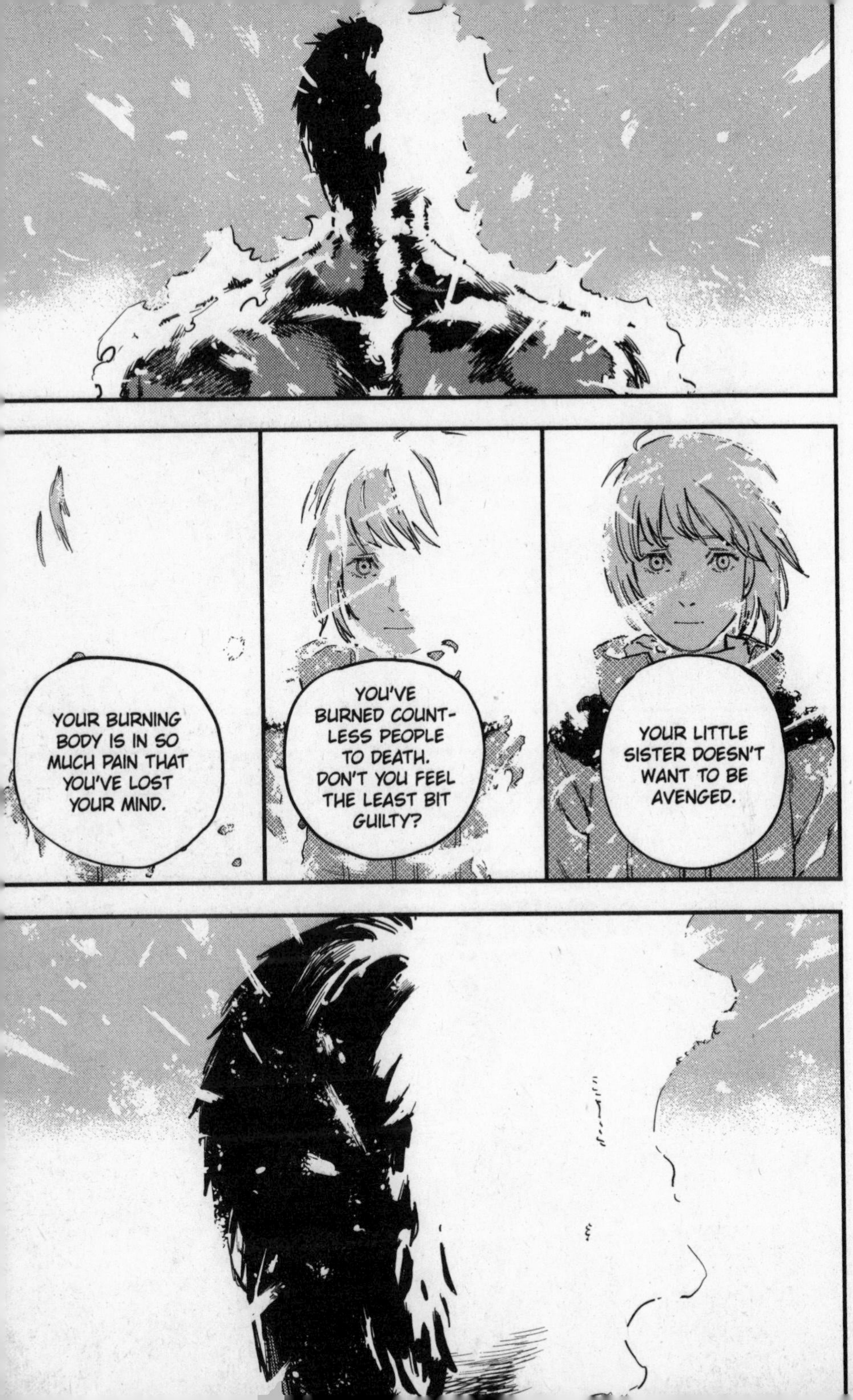
YOUR LITTLE SISTER DOESN'T WANT TO BE AVENGED.
YOU'VE BURNED COUNT-LESS PEOPLE TO DEATH. DON'T YOU FEEL THE LEAST BIT GUILTY?
YOUR BURNING BODY IS IN SO MUCH PAIN THAT YOU'VE LOST YOUR MIND.

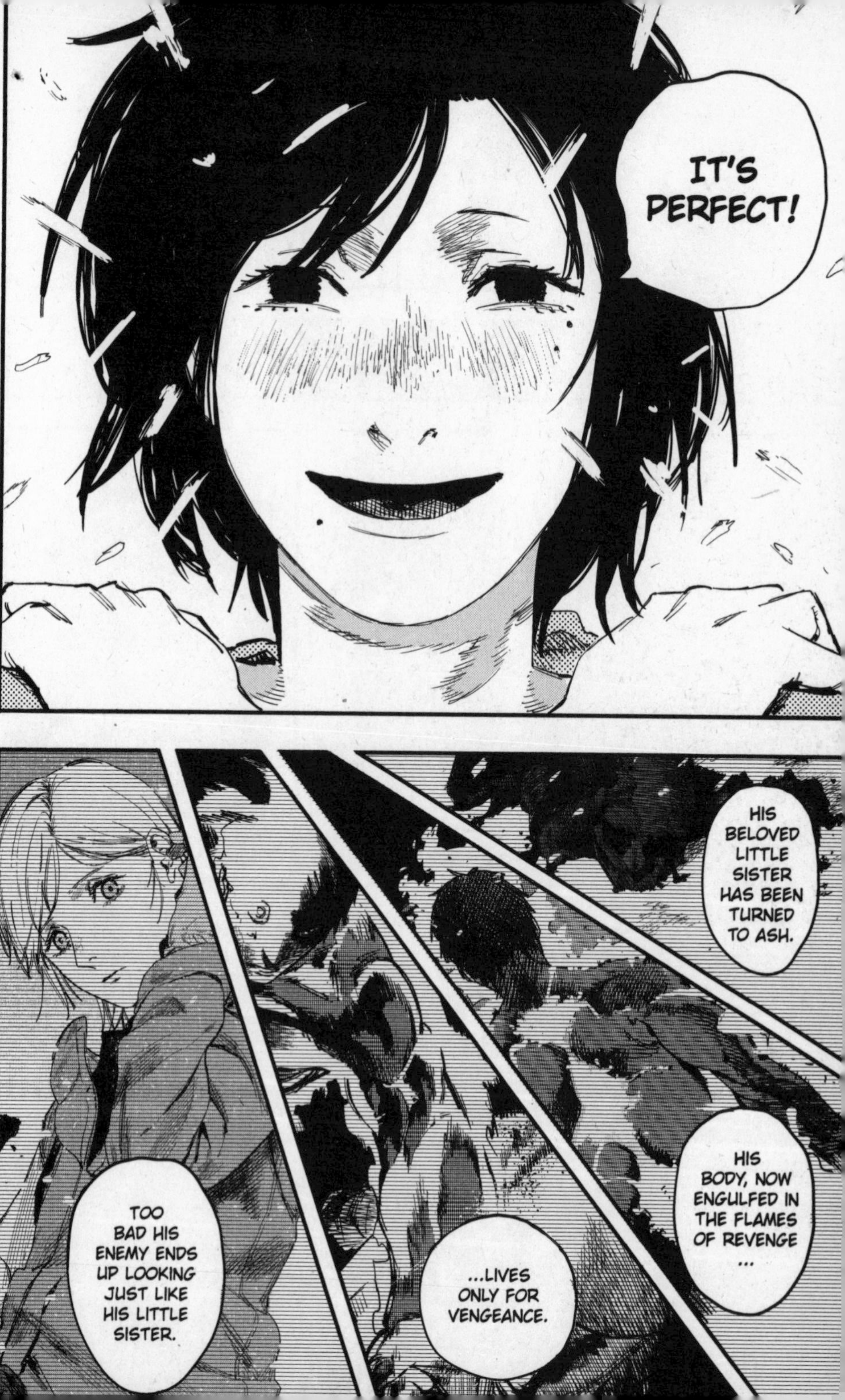
IT'S PERFECT!
HIS BELOVED LITTLE SISTER HAS BEEN TURNED TO ASH.
HIS BODY, NOW ENGULFED IN THE FLAMES OF REVENGE ...
...LIVES ONLY FOR VENGEANCE.
TOO BAD HIS ENEMY ENDS UP LOOKING JUST LIKE HIS LITTLE SISTER.

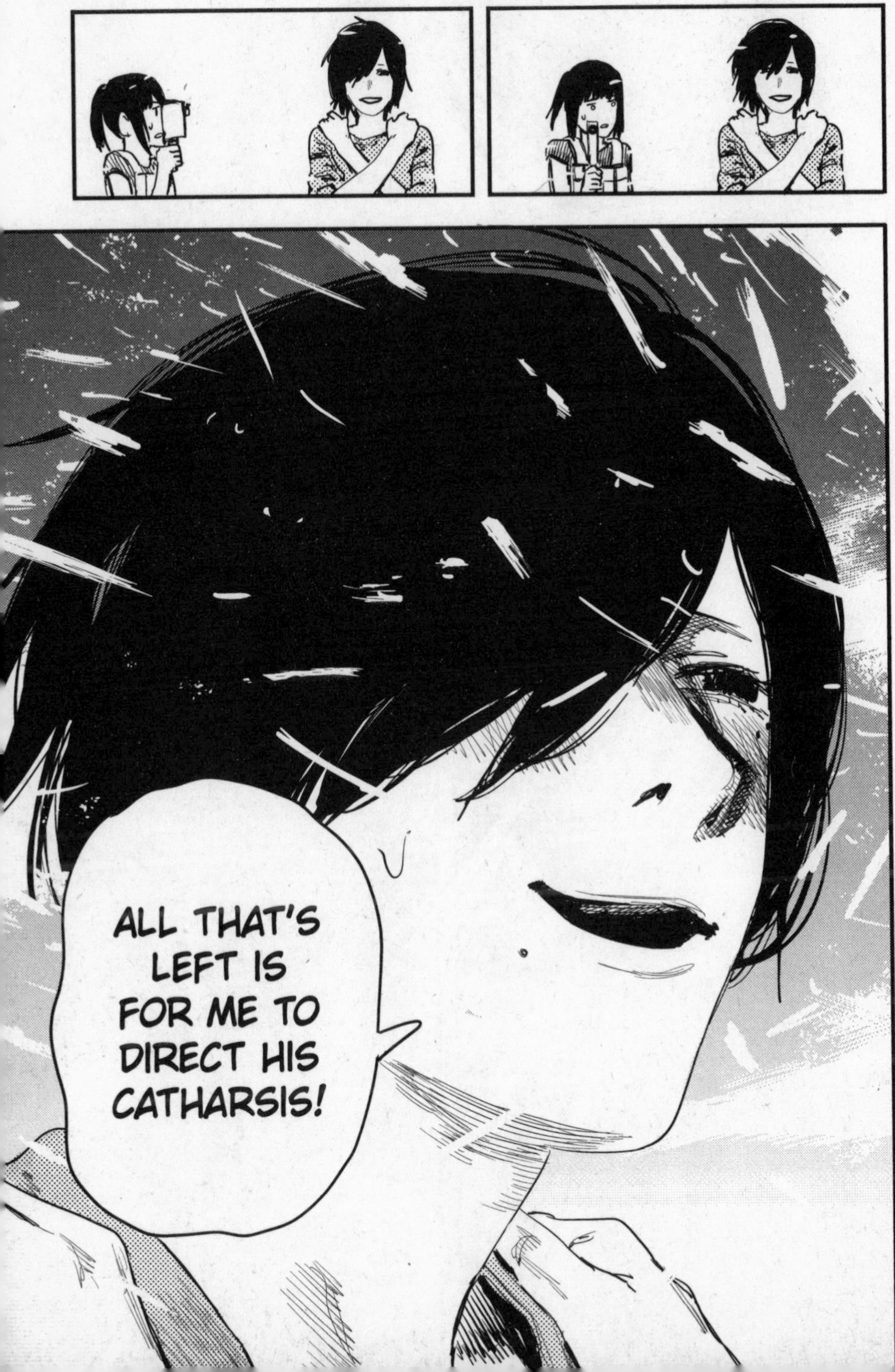
ALL THAT'S LEFT IS FOR ME TO DIRECT HIS CATHARSIS!

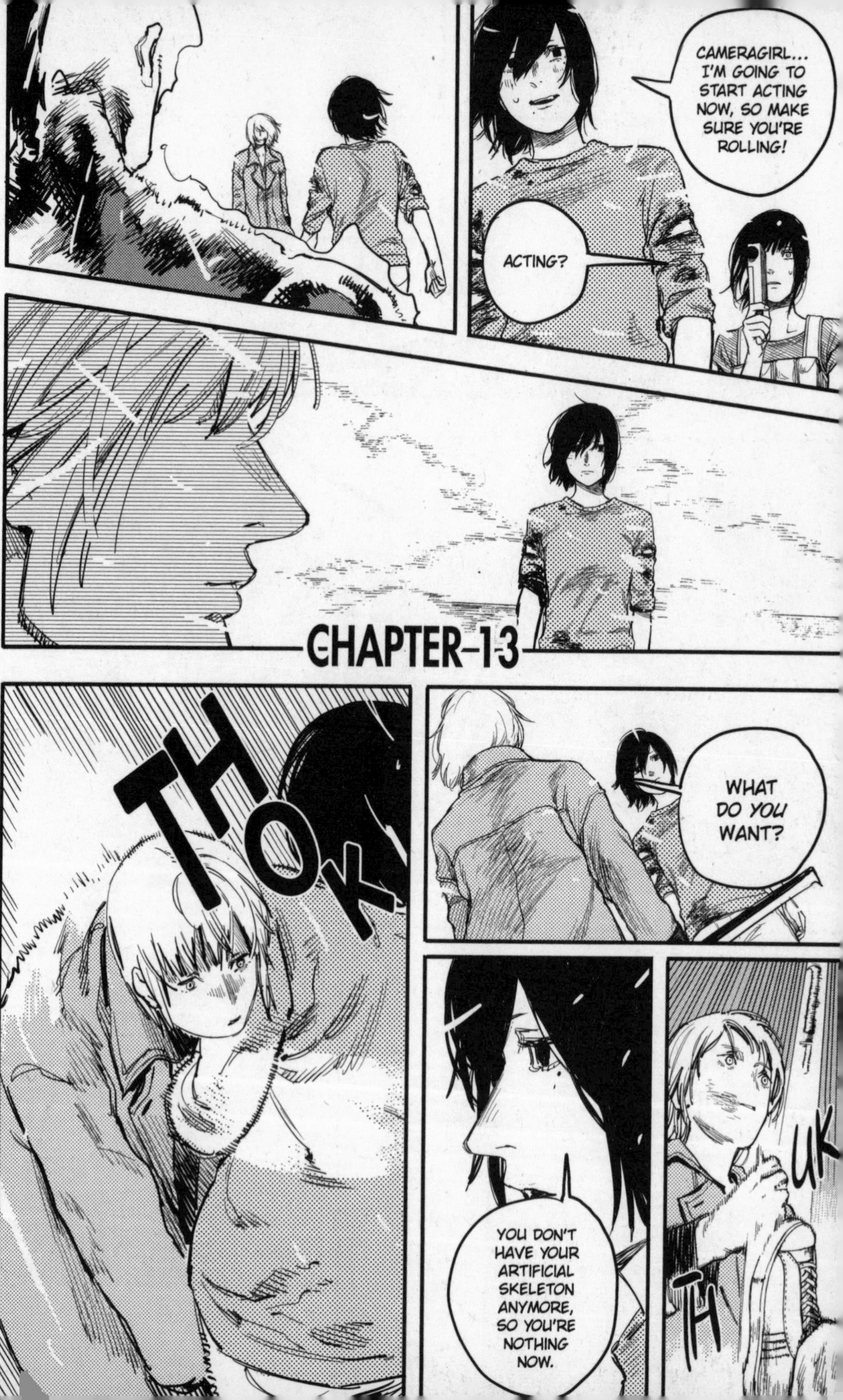
CAMERAGIRL... I'M GOING TO START ACTING NOW, SO MAKE SURE YOU'RE ROLLING!
ACTING?
CHAPTER-13
WHAT DO YOU WANT?
THUK
YOU DON'T HAVE YOUR ARTIFICIAL SKELETON ANYMORE, SO YOU'RE NOTHING NOW.
THOK

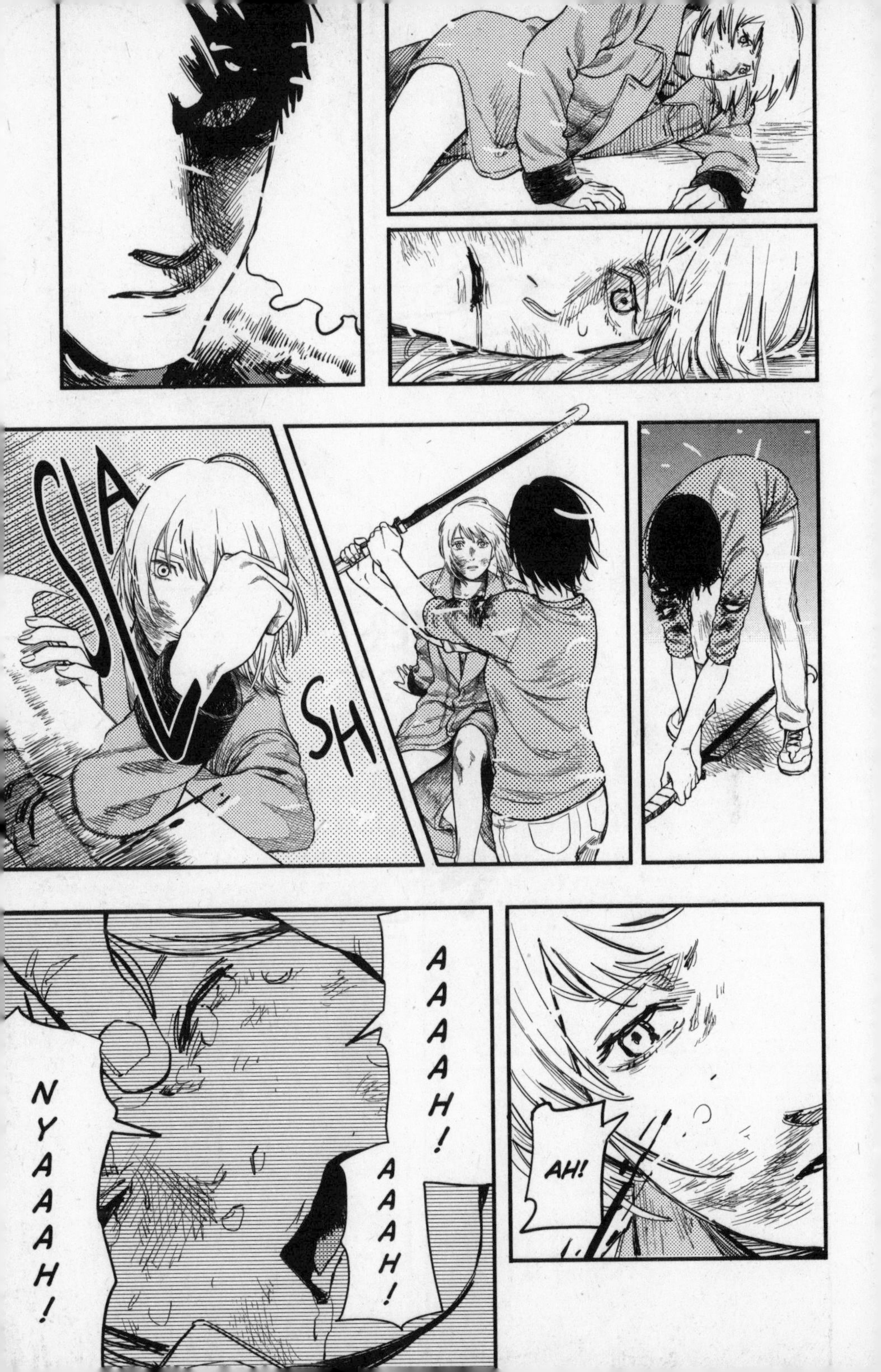
SLASH
AH!
AAAAH!
AAAH!
NYAAAAH!

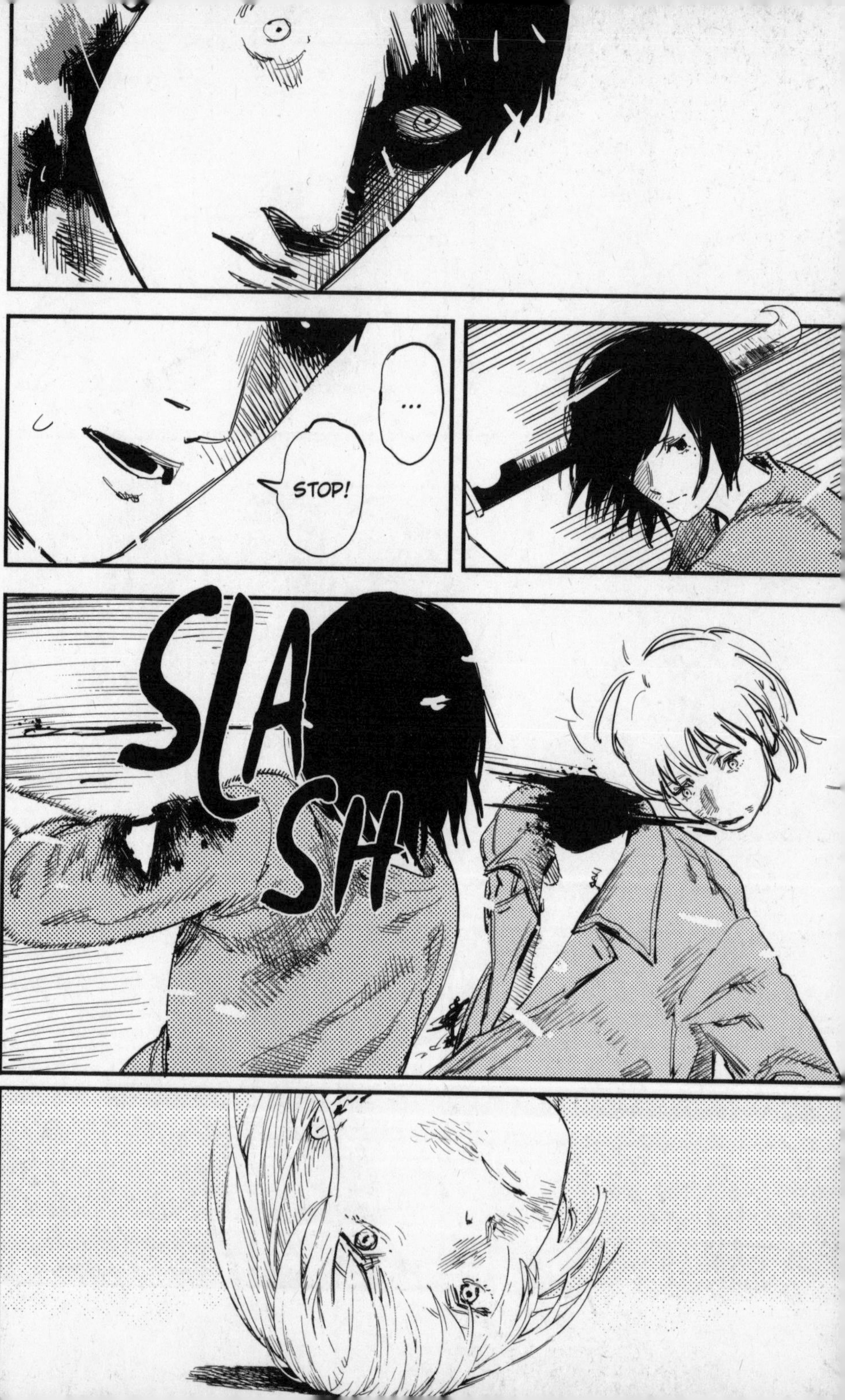
...
STOP!
SLASH

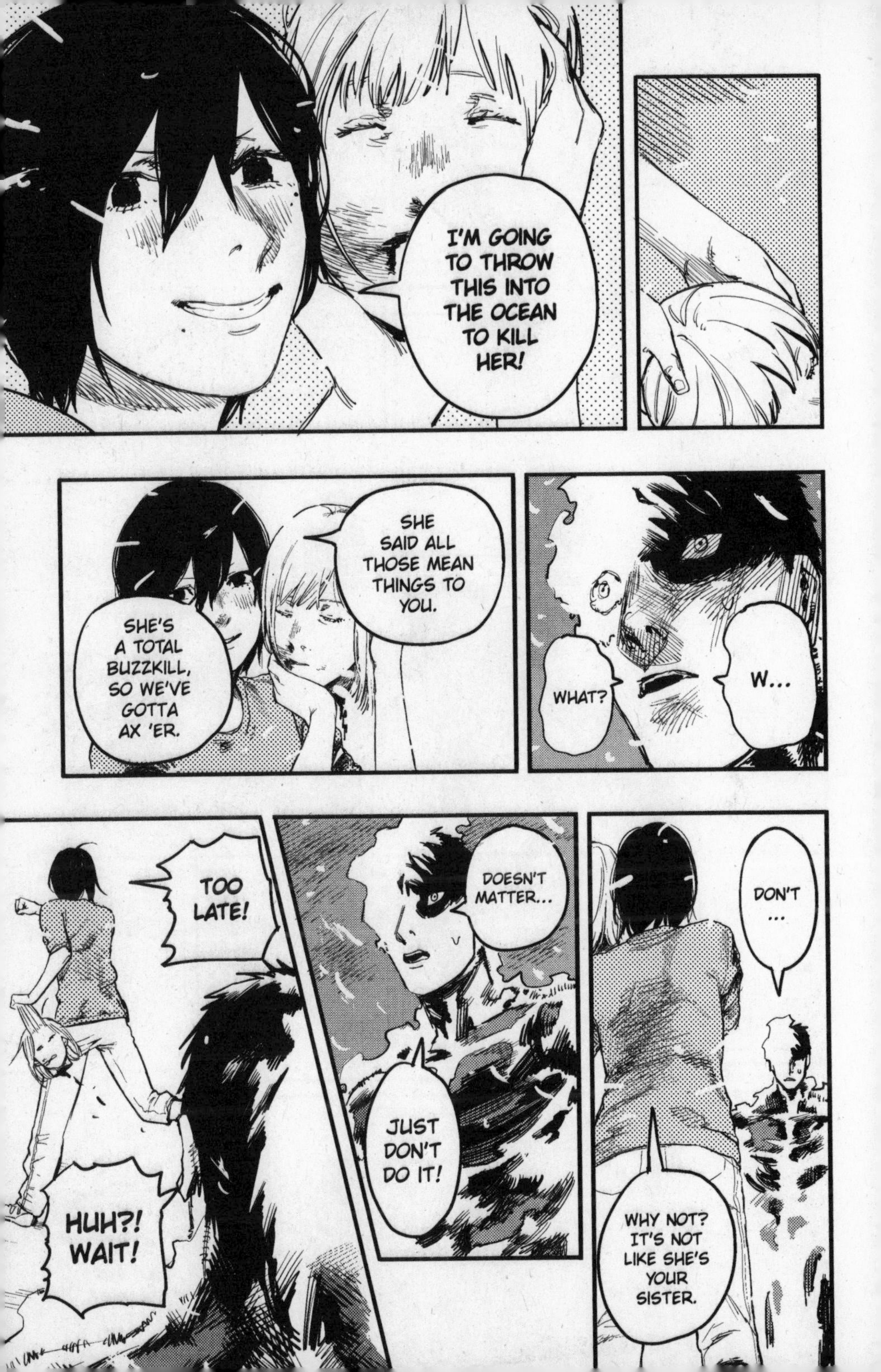
I'M GOING TO THROW THIS INTO THE OCEAN TO KILL HER!
W...
WHAT?
SHE SAID ALL THOSE MEAN THINGS TO YOU.
SHE'S A TOTAL BUZZKILL, SO WE'VE GOTTA AX 'ER.
DON'T ...
WHY NOT? IT'S NOT LIKE SHE'S YOUR SISTER.
DOESN'T MATTER...
JUST DON'T DO IT!
TOO LATE!
HUH?! WAIT!

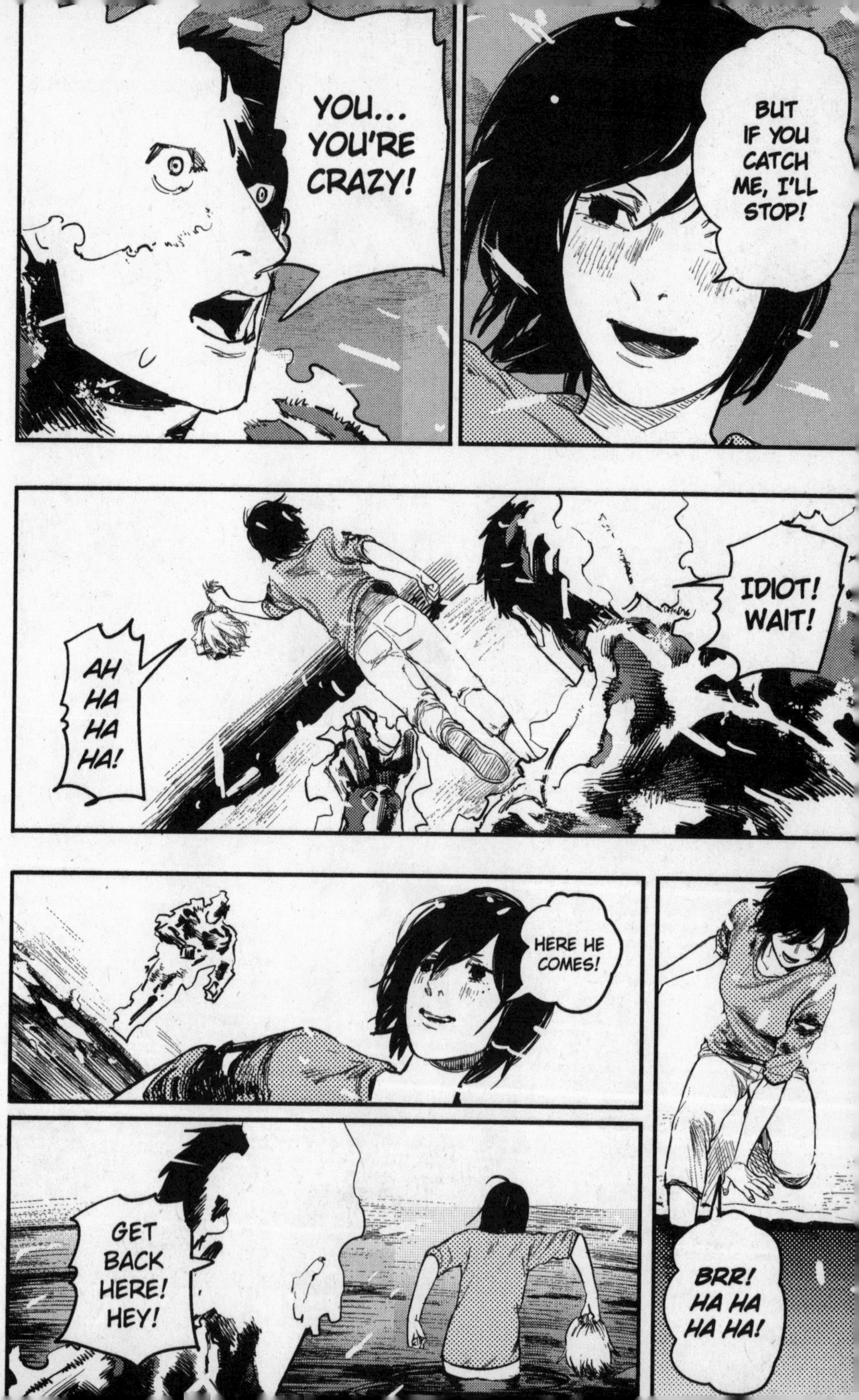
BUT IF YOU CATCH ME, I'LL STOP!
YOU... YOU'RE CRAZY!
IDIOT! WAIT!
AH HA HA HA!
BRR! HA HA HA HA!
HERE HE COMES!
GET BACK HERE! HEY!

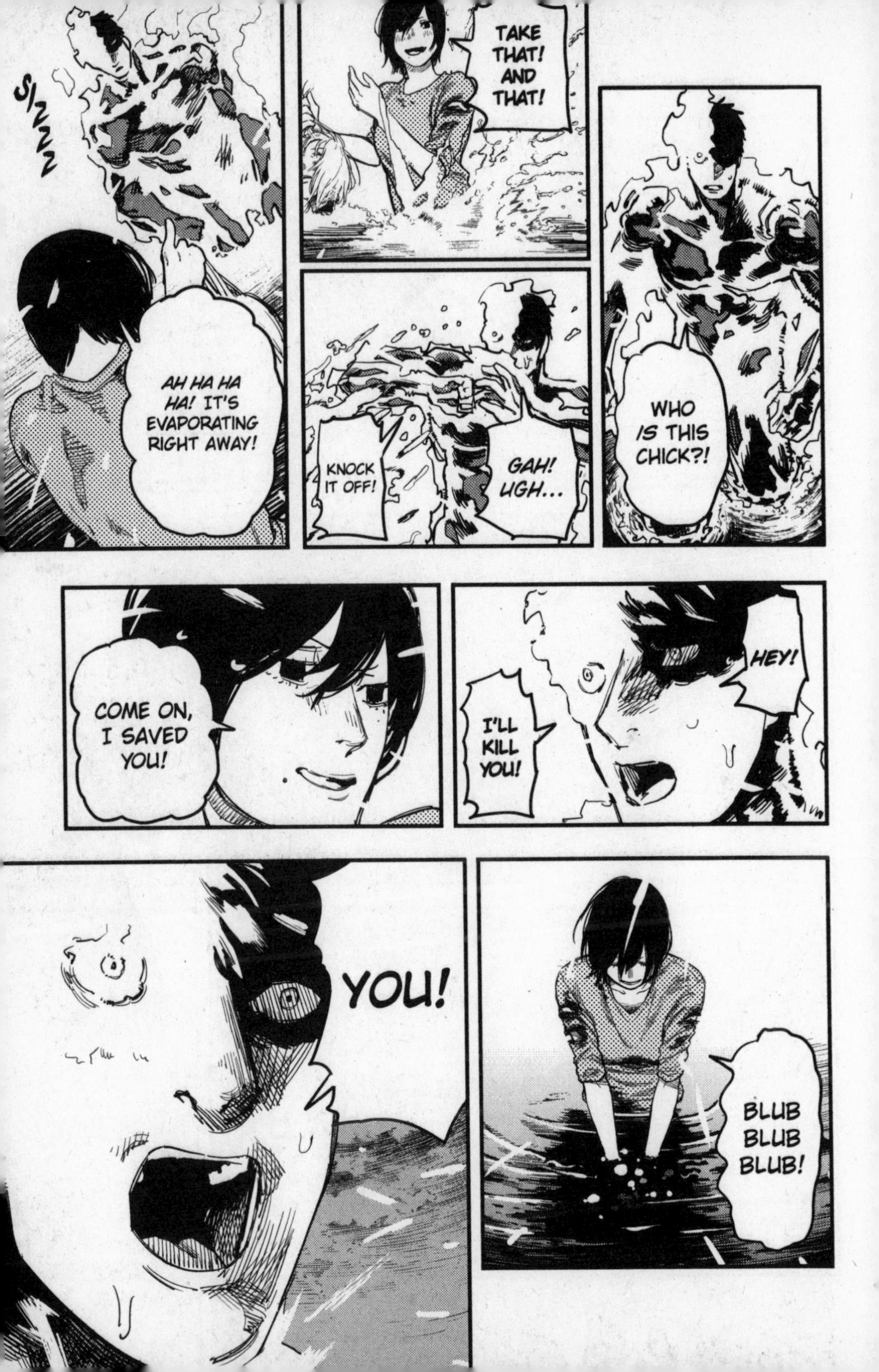
WHO IS THIS CHICK?!
TAKE THAT! AND THAT!
GAH! UGH...
KNOCK IT OFF!
SIZZZ
AH HA HA HA! IT'S EVAPORATING RIGHT AWAY!
HEY!
I'LL KILL YOU!
COME ON, I SAVED YOU!
BLUB BLUB BLUB!
YOU!

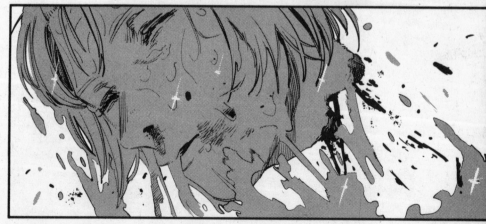

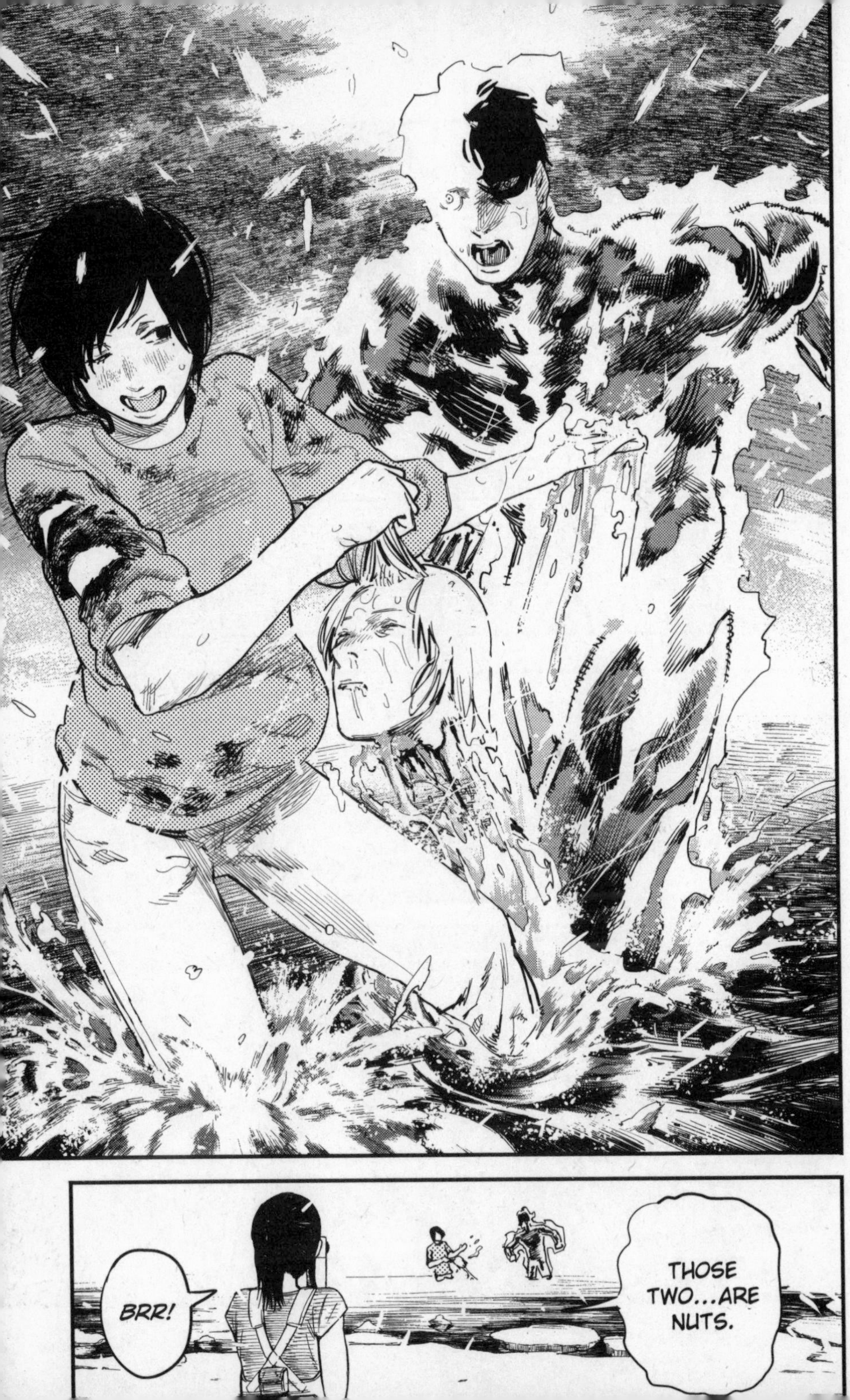
THOSE TWO...ARE NUTS.
BRR!

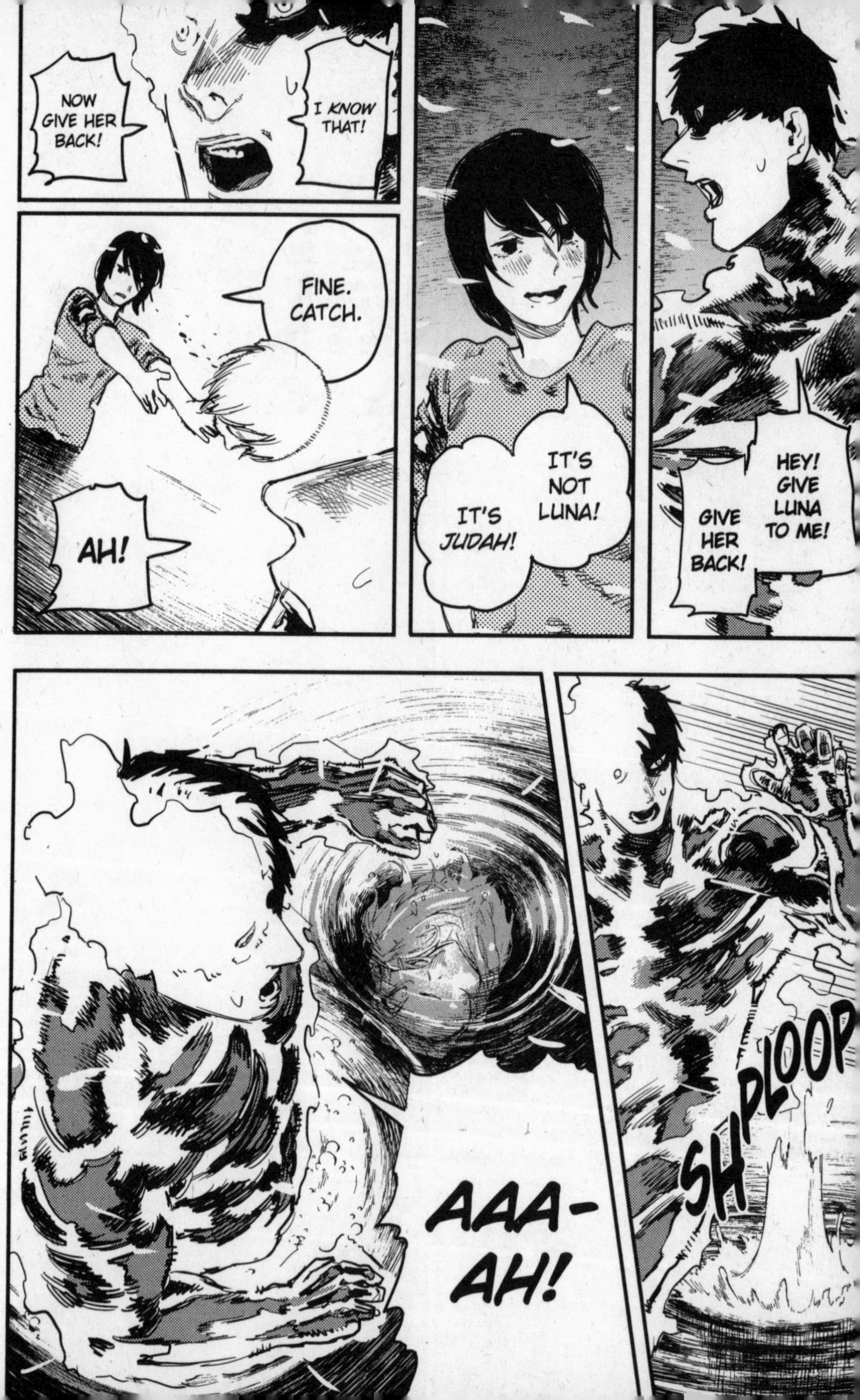
HEY! GIVE LUNA TO ME!
GIVE HER BACK!
IT'S NOT LUNA!
IT'S JUDAH!
I KNOW THAT!
NOW GIVE HER BACK!
FINE. CATCH.
AH!
SHPLOOP
AAA-AH!

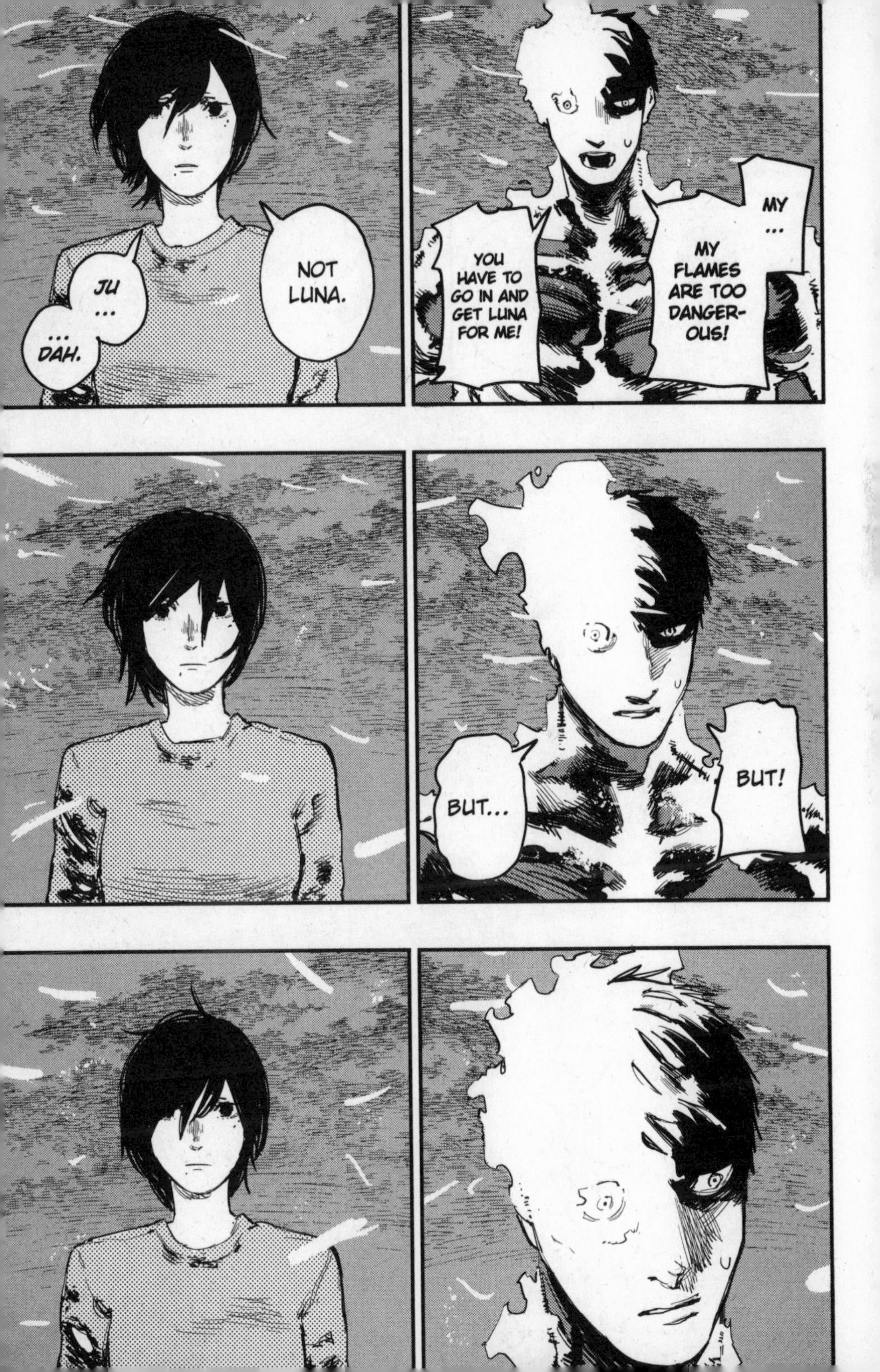
MY ...
MY FLAMES ARE TOO DANGEROUS!
YOU HAVE TO GO IN AND GET LUNA FOR ME!
NOT LUNA.
JU ...
... DAH.
BUT!
BUT...

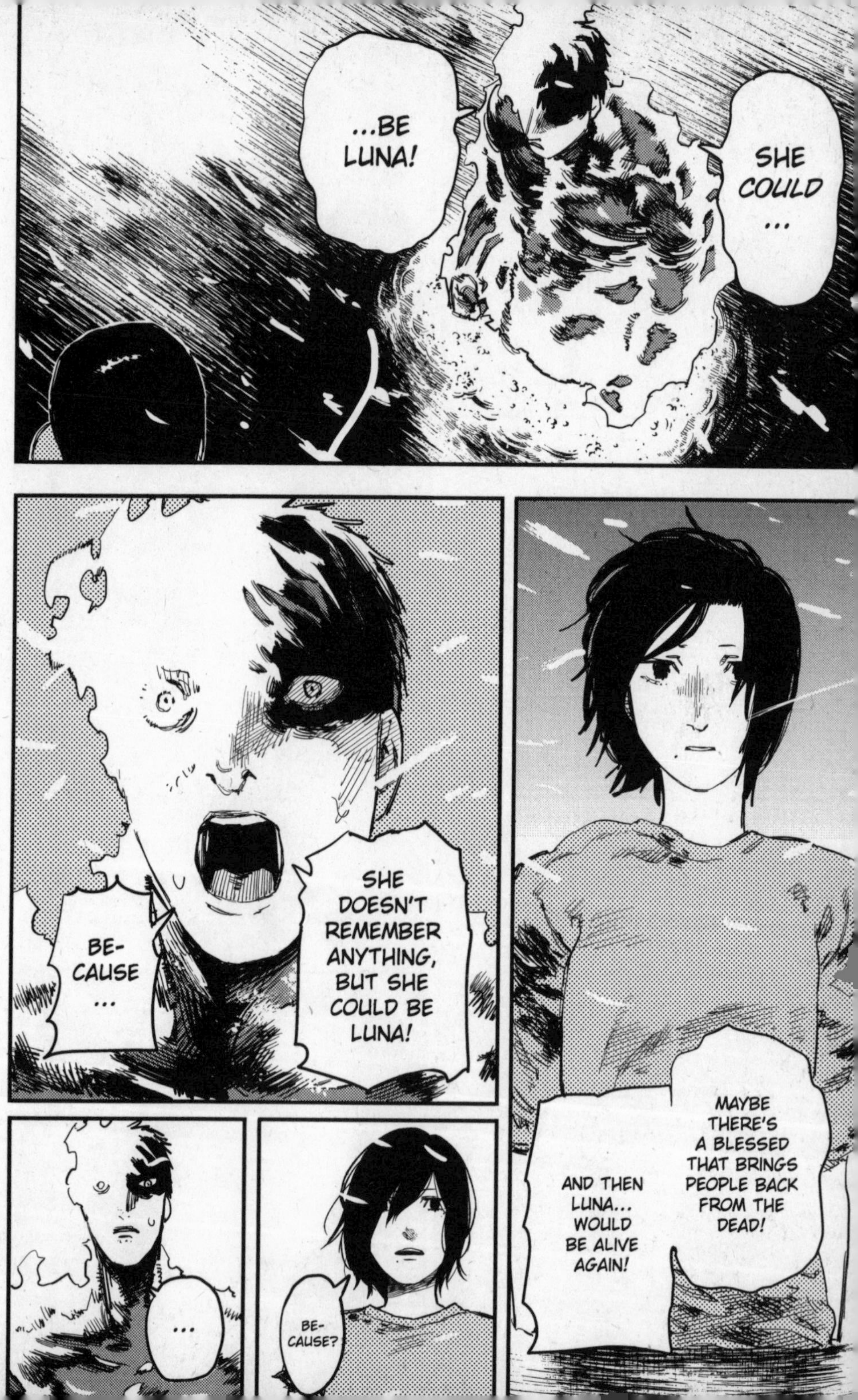
SHE COULD ...
...BE LUNA!
MAYBE THERE'S A BLESSED THAT BRINGS PEOPLE BACK FROM THE DEAD!
AND THEN LUNA... WOULD BE ALIVE AGAIN!
SHE DOESN'T REMEMBER ANYTHING, BUT SHE COULD BE LUNA!
BE-CAUSE ...
BE-CAUSE?
...

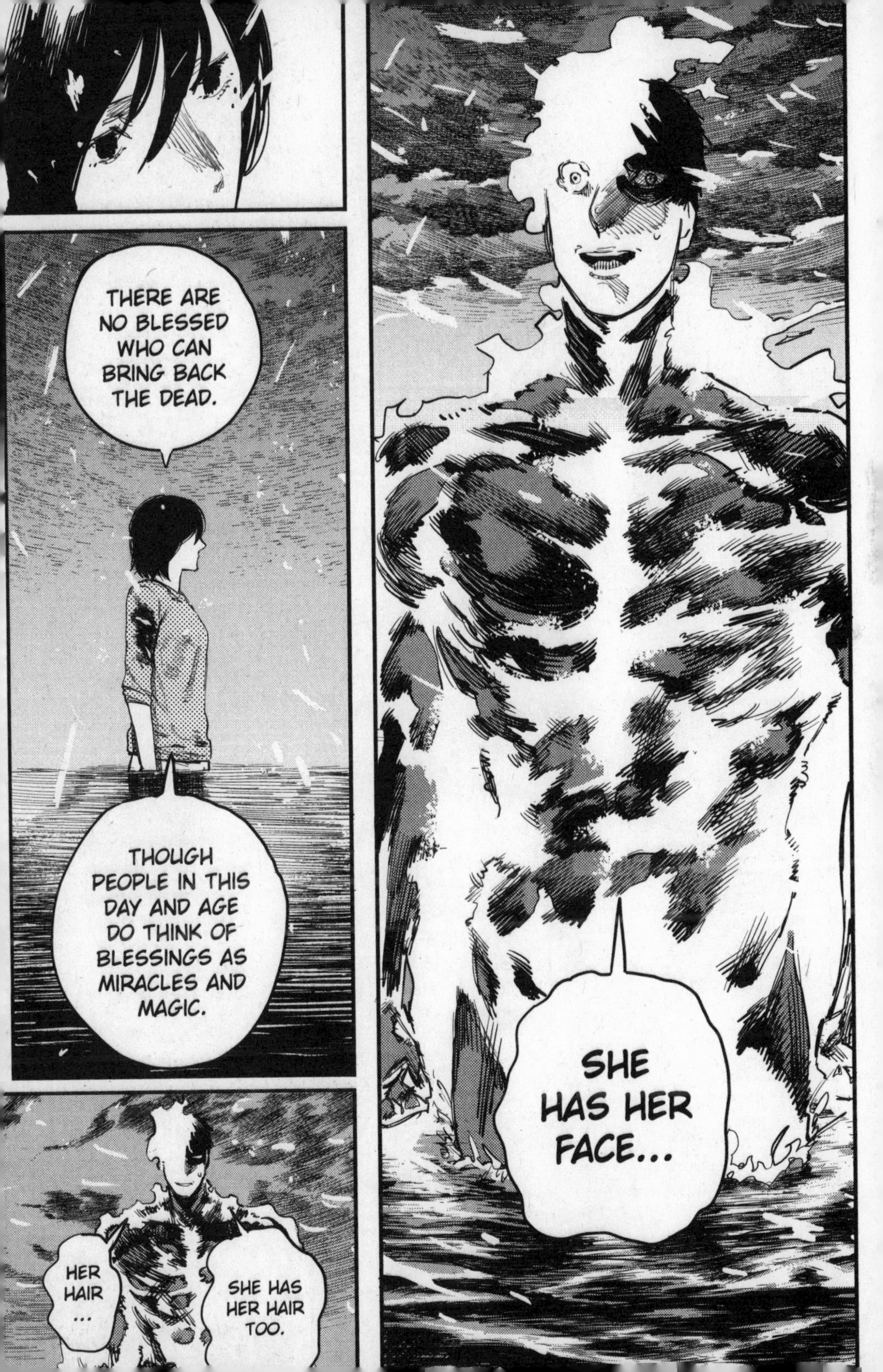
SHE HAS HER FACE...
THERE ARE NO BLESSED WHO CAN BRING BACK THE DEAD.
THOUGH PEOPLE IN THIS DAY AND AGE DO THINK OF BLESSINGS AS MIRACLES AND MAGIC.
SHE HAS HER HAIR TOO.
HER HAIR ...

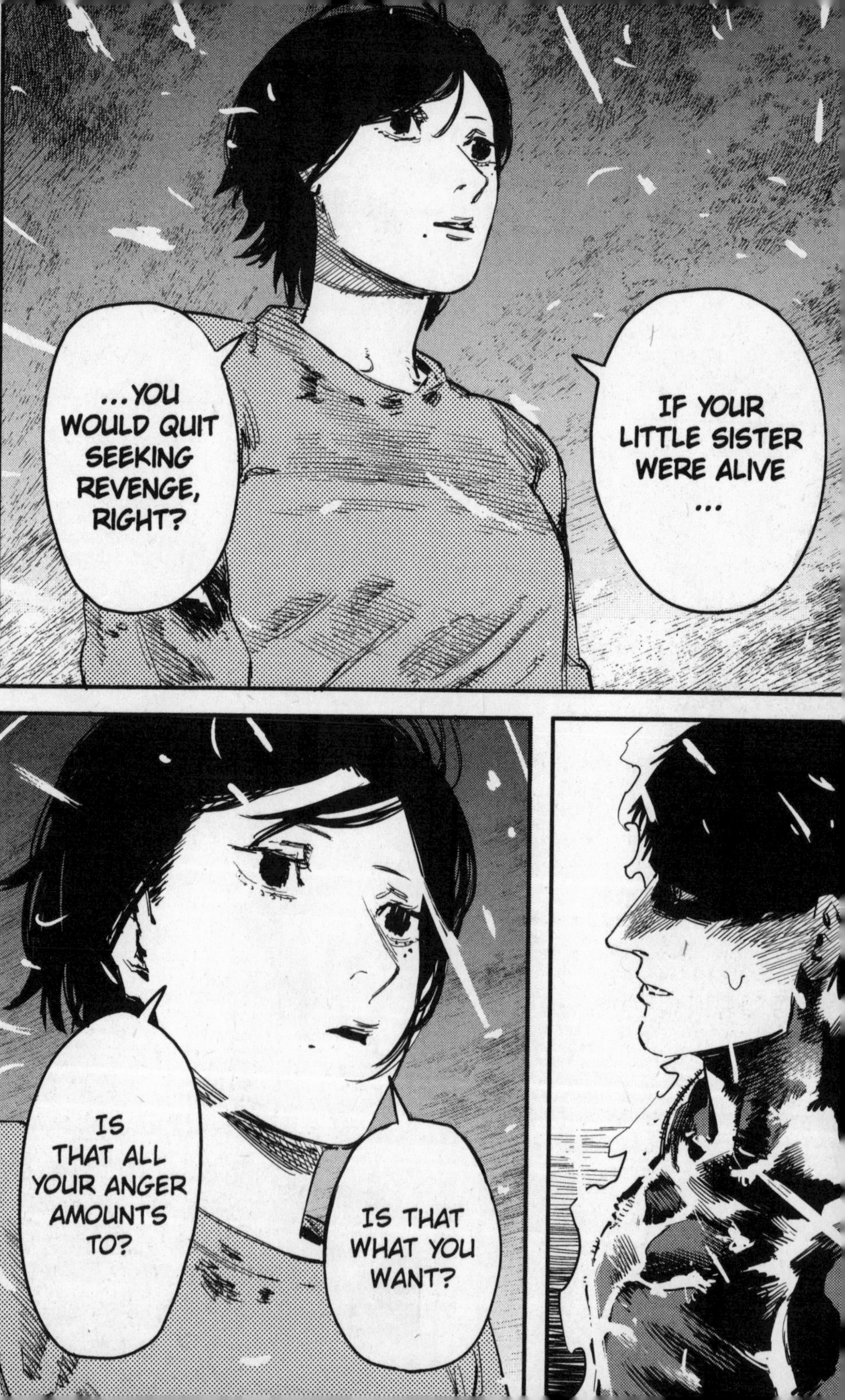
IF YOUR LITTLE SISTER WERE ALIVE ...
...YOU WOULD QUIT SEEKING REVENGE, RIGHT?
IS THAT WHAT YOU WANT?
IS THAT ALL YOUR ANGER AMOUNTS TO?

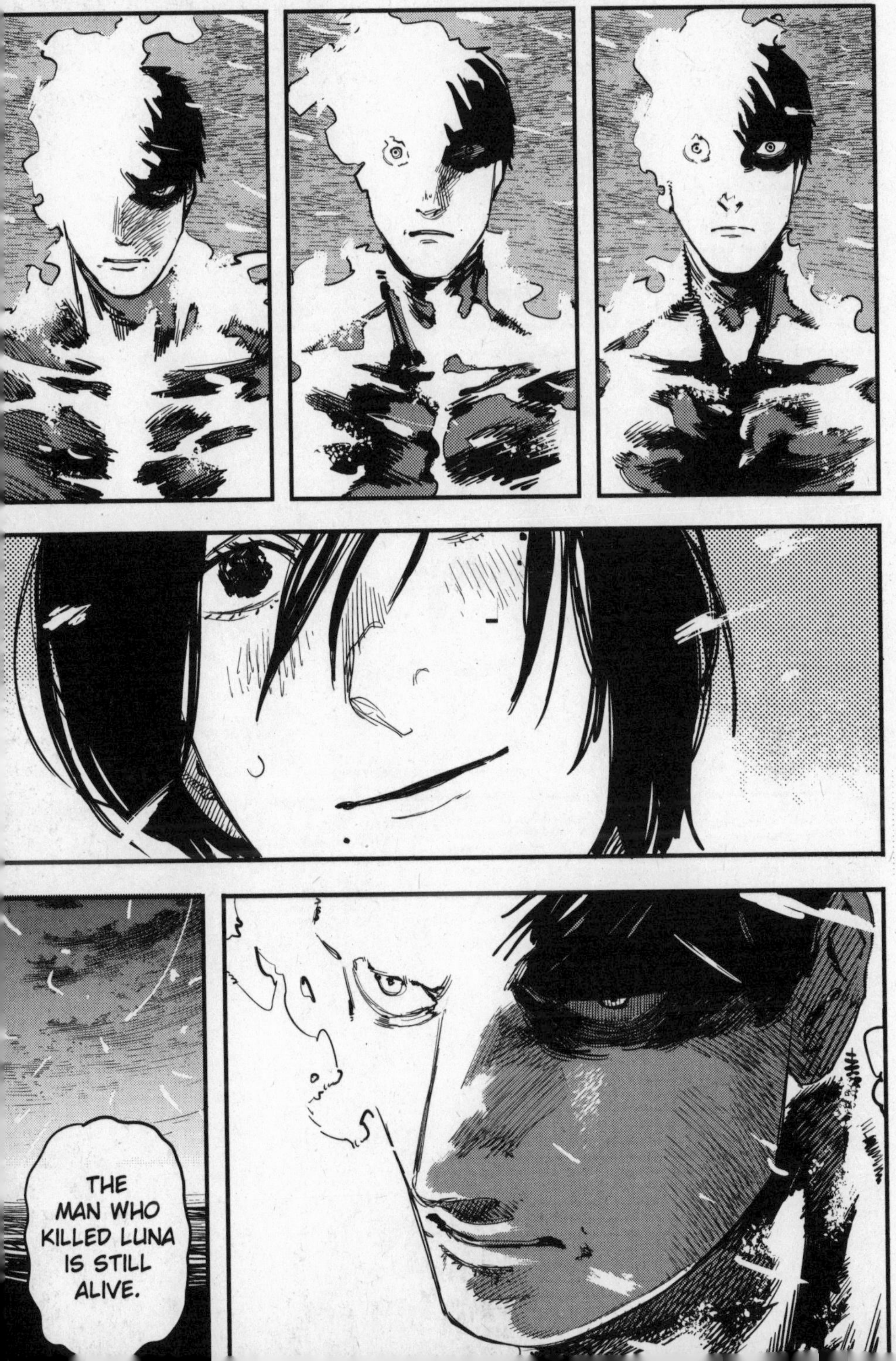
THE MAN WHO KILLED LUNA IS STILL ALIVE.

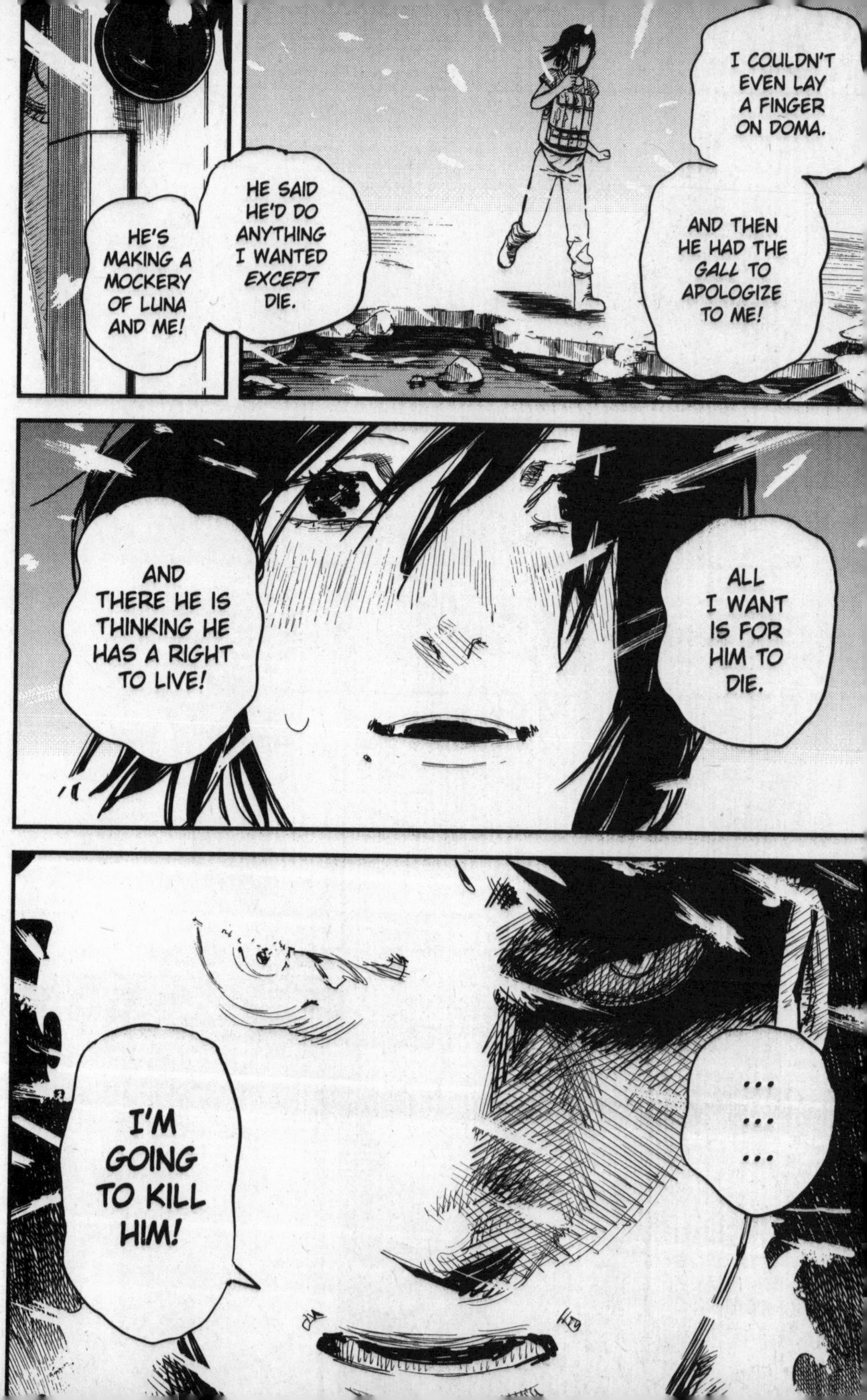
I COULDN'T EVEN LAY A FINGER ON DOMA.
AND THEN HE HAD THE *GALL* TO APOLOGIZE TO ME!
HE SAID HE'D DO ANYTHING I WANTED *EXCEPT* DIE.
HE'S MAKING A MOCKERY OF LUNA AND ME!
ALL I WANT IS FOR HIM TO DIE.
AND THERE HE IS THINKING HE HAS A RIGHT TO LIVE!
... ...
I'M GOING TO KILL HIM!

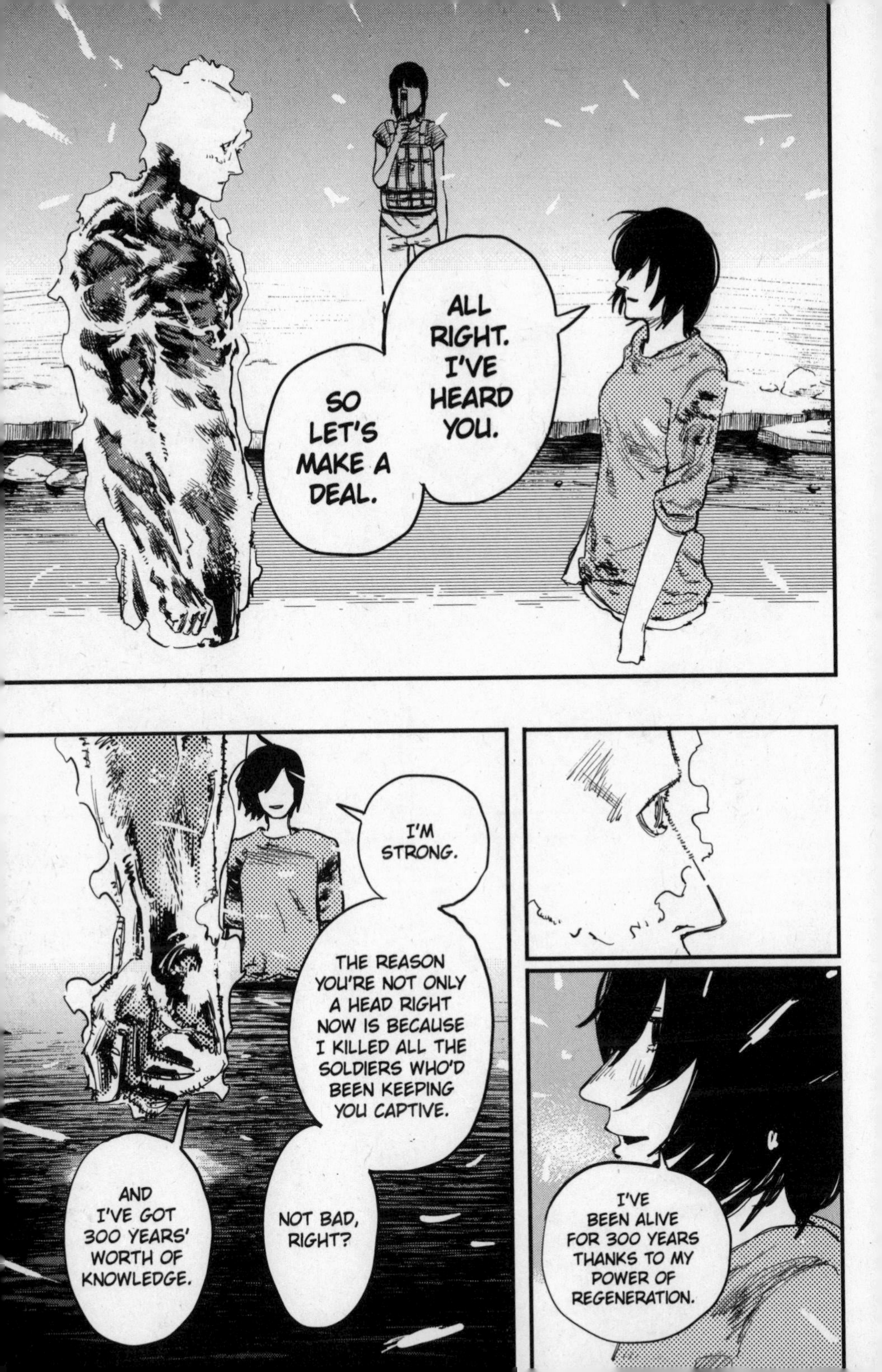
ALL RIGHT. I'VE HEARD YOU.
SO LET'S MAKE A DEAL.
I'VE BEEN ALIVE FOR 300 YEARS THANKS TO MY POWER OF REGENERATION.
I'M STRONG.
THE REASON YOU'RE NOT ONLY A HEAD RIGHT NOW IS BECAUSE I KILLED ALL THE SOLDIERS WHO'D BEEN KEEPING YOU CAPTIVE.
NOT BAD, RIGHT?
AND I'VE GOT 300 YEARS' WORTH OF KNOWLEDGE.

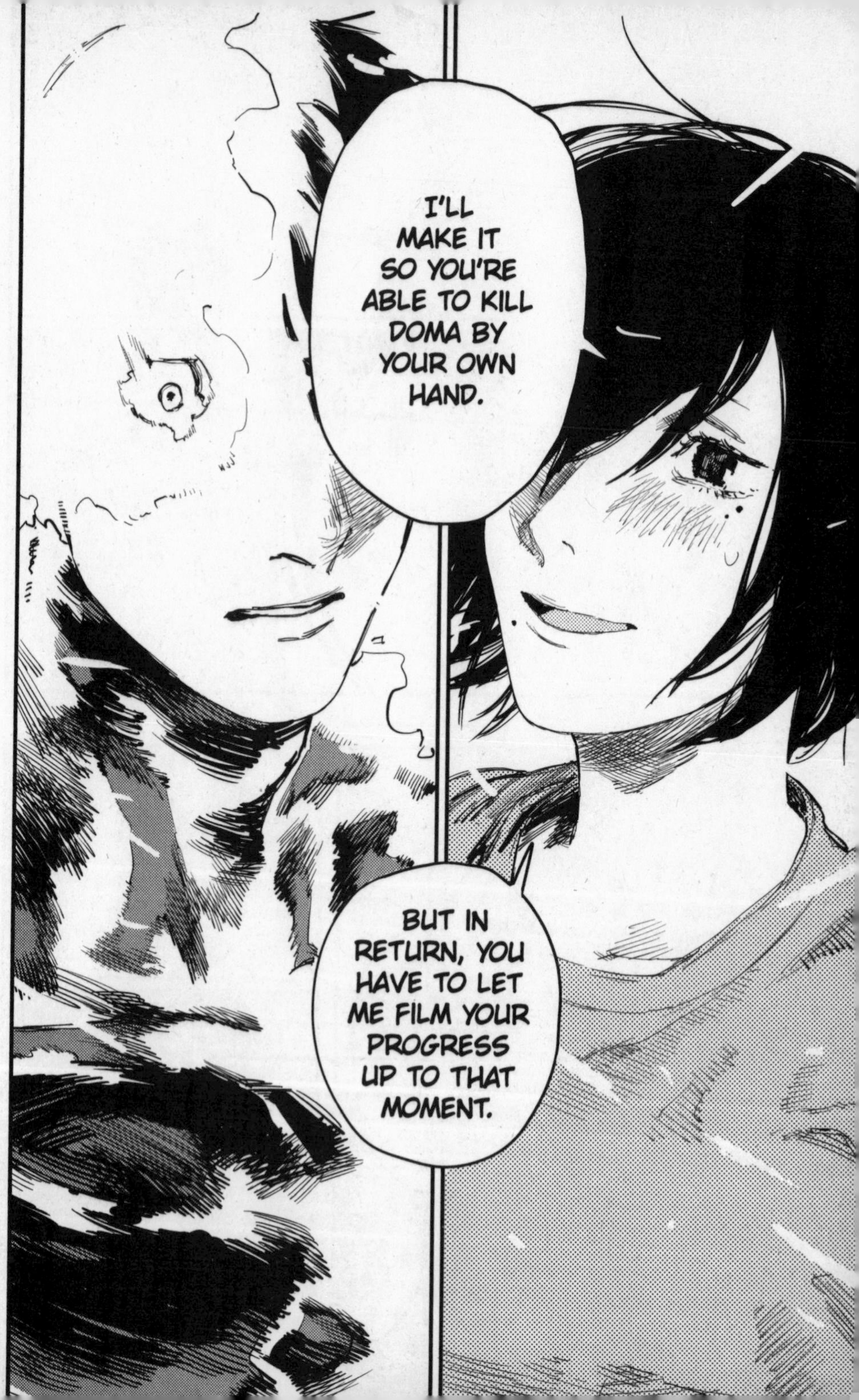
I'LL MAKE IT SO YOU'RE ABLE TO KILL DOMA BY YOUR OWN HAND.
BUT IN RETURN, YOU HAVE TO LET ME FILM YOUR PROGRESS UP TO THAT MOMENT.

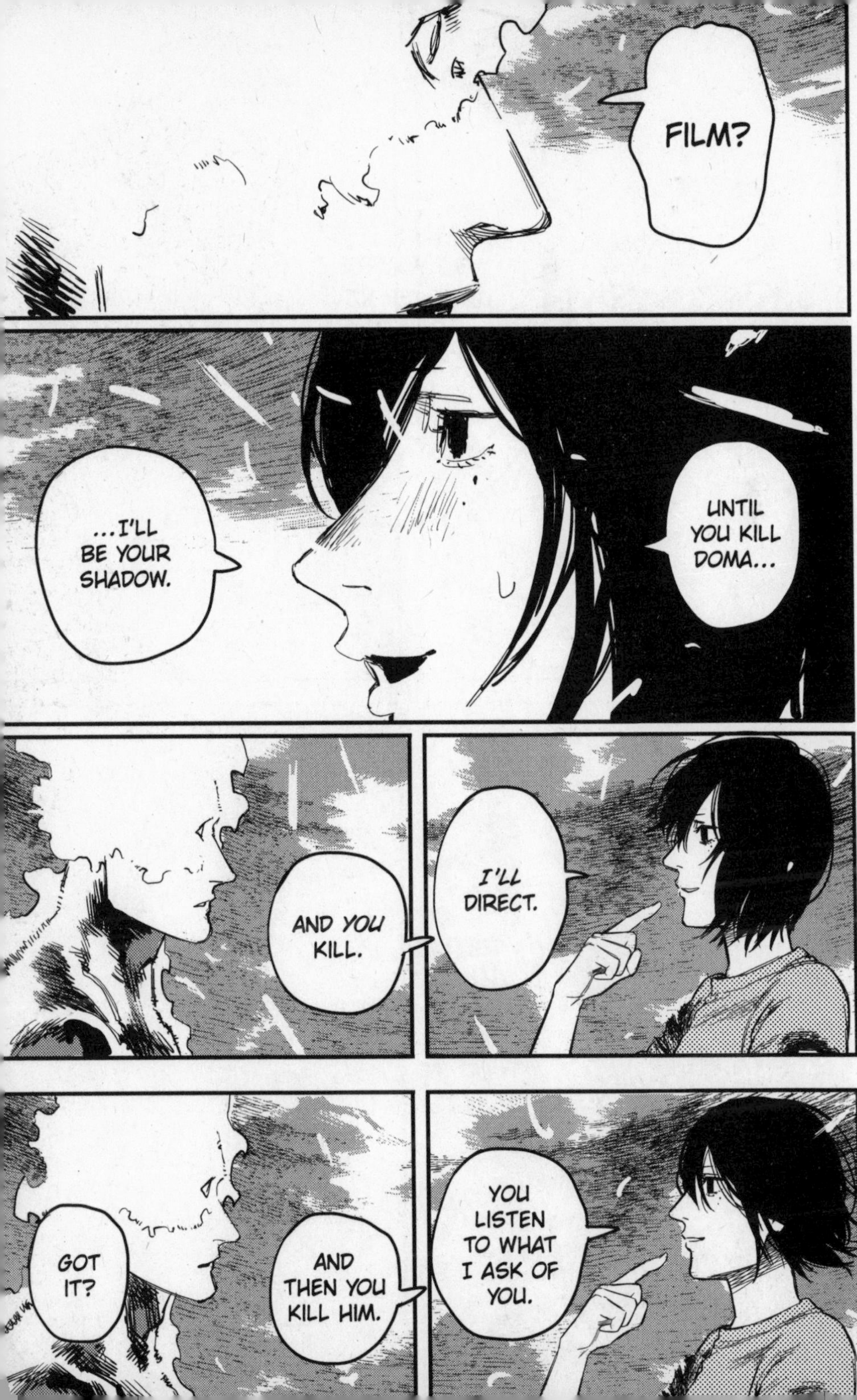
FILM?
UNTIL YOU KILL DOMA...
...I'LL BE YOUR SHADOW.
I'LL DIRECT.
AND YOU KILL.
YOU LISTEN TO WHAT I ASK OF YOU.
AND THEN YOU KILL HIM.
GOT IT?

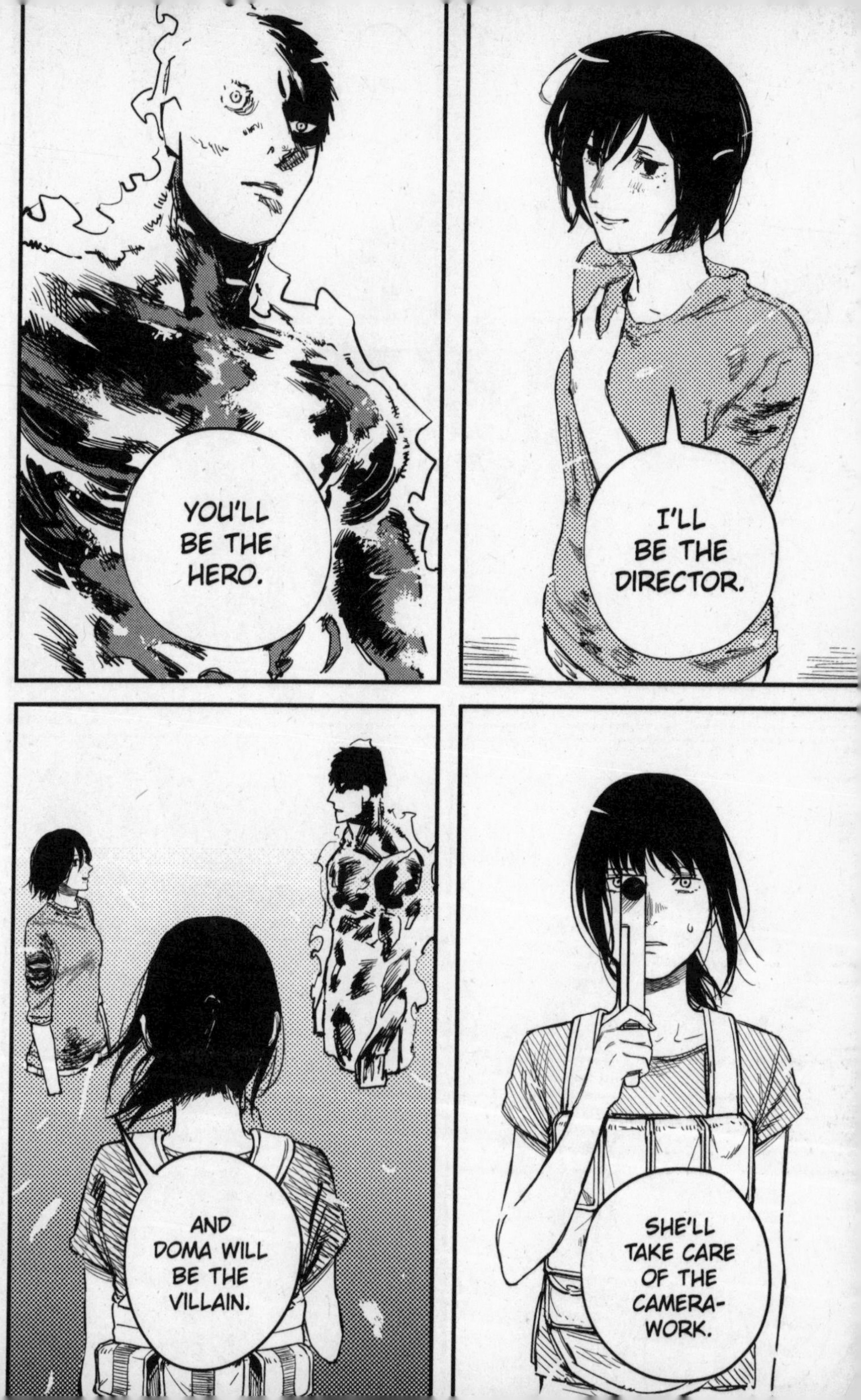
I'LL BE THE DIRECTOR.
YOU'LL BE THE HERO.
SHE'LL TAKE CARE OF THE CAMERA-WORK.
AND DOMA WILL BE THE VILLAIN.

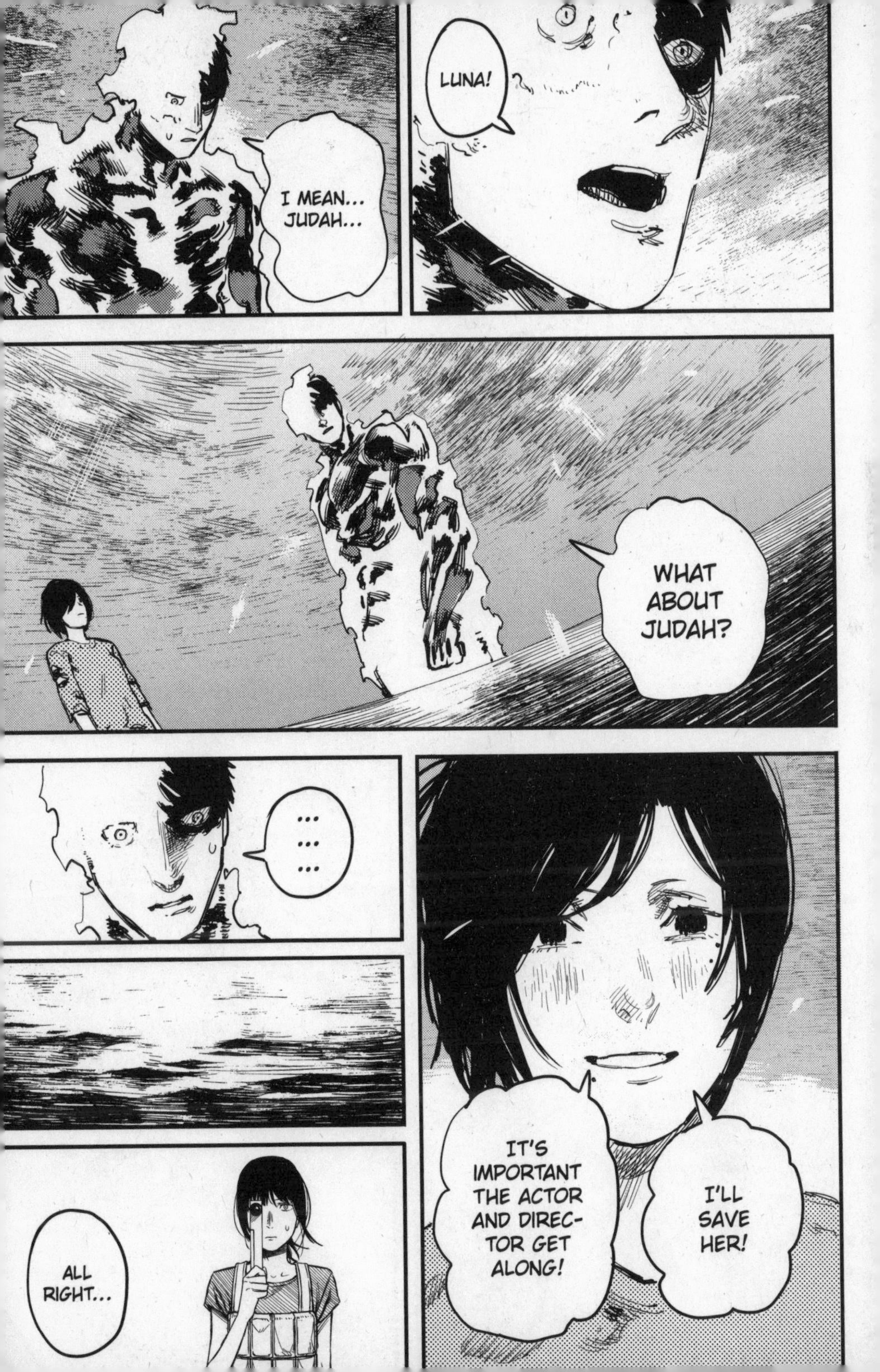
LUNA!
I MEAN... JUDAH...
WHAT ABOUT JUDAH?
I'LL SAVE HER!
IT'S IMPORTANT THE ACTOR AND DIREC- TOR GET ALONG!
... ...
ALL RIGHT...

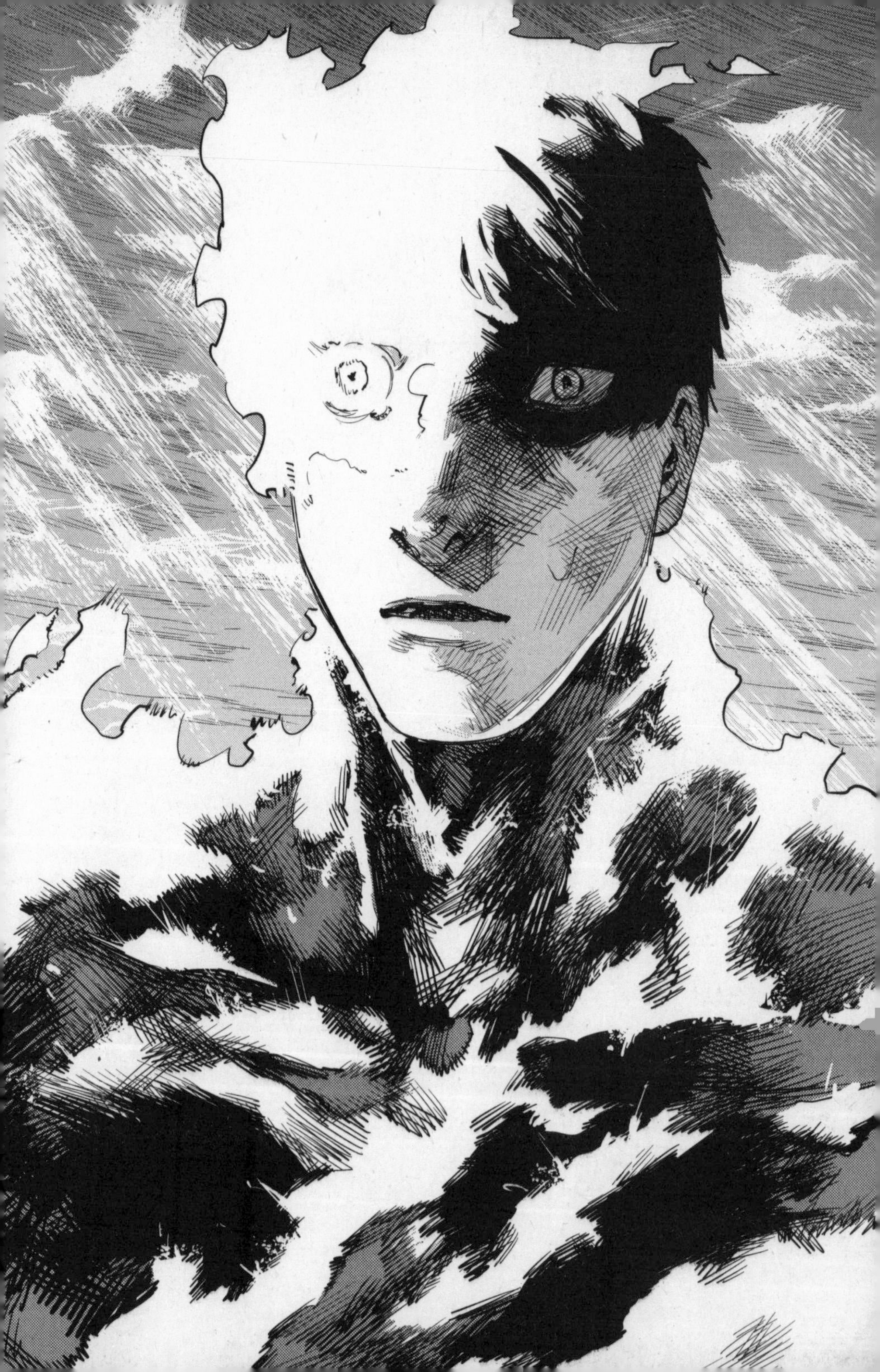

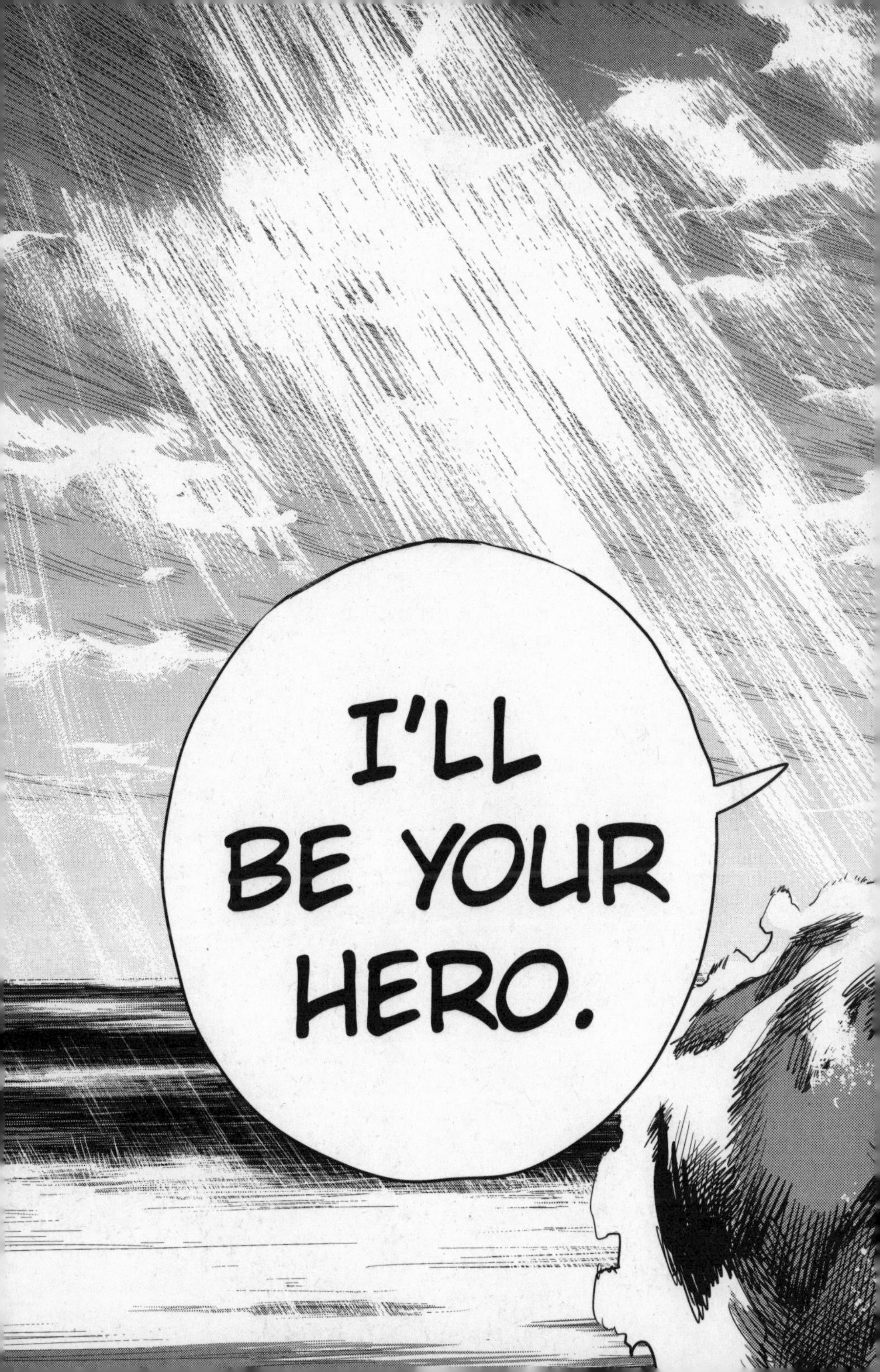
I'LL BE YOUR HERO.

FIRE PUNCH

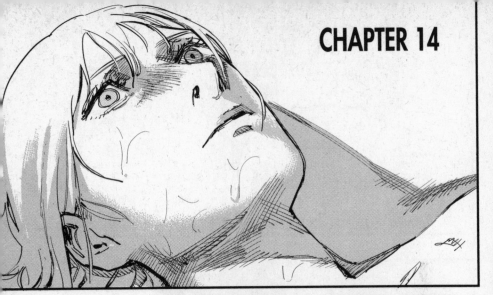

CHAPTER 14

GOOD MORNING.

COLD?

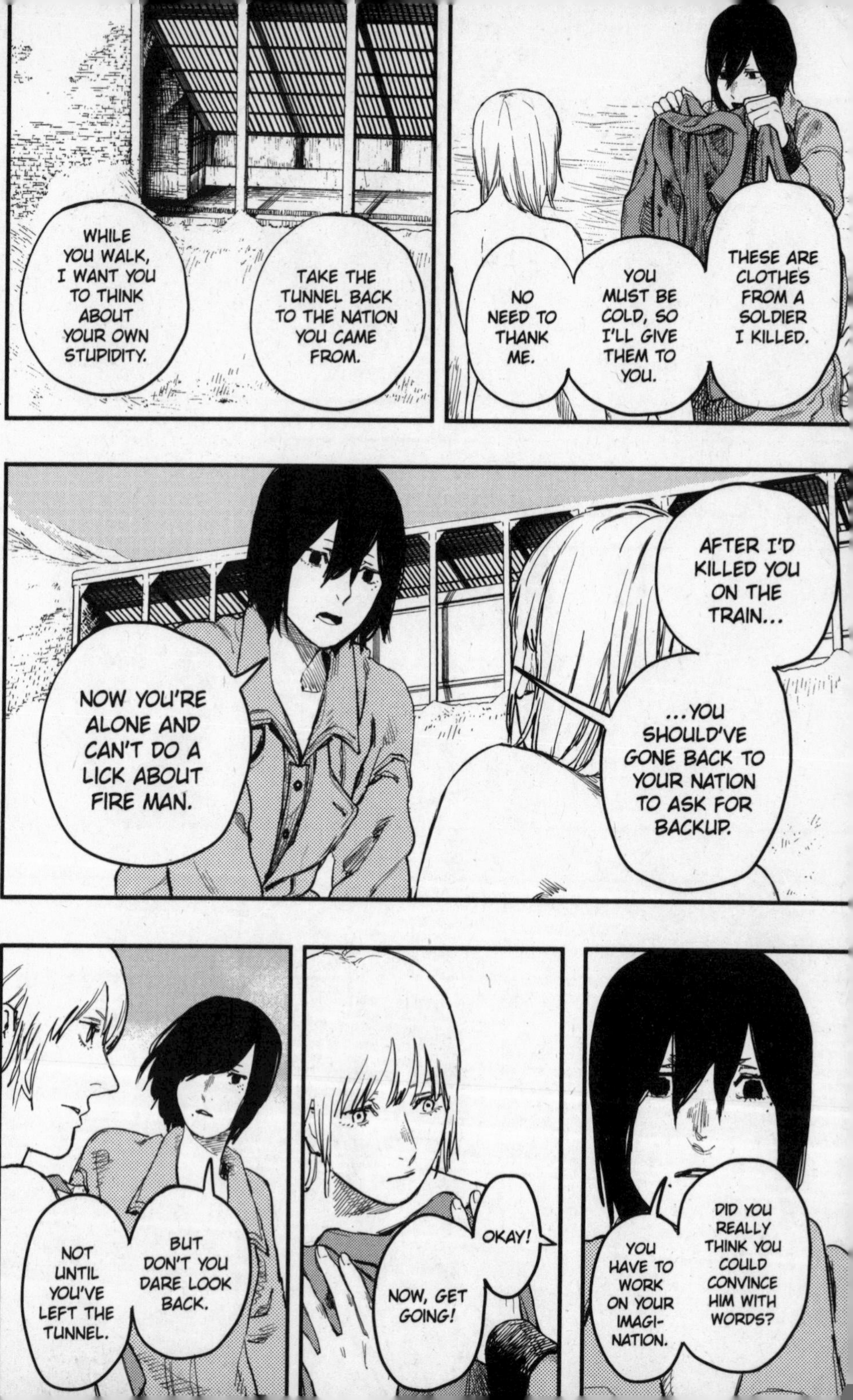
THESE ARE CLOTHES FROM A SOLDIER I KILLED.
YOU MUST BE COLD, SO I'LL GIVE THEM TO YOU.
NO NEED TO THANK ME.
TAKE THE TUNNEL BACK TO THE NATION YOU CAME FROM.
WHILE YOU WALK, I WANT YOU TO THINK ABOUT YOUR OWN STUPIDITY.
AFTER I'D KILLED YOU ON THE TRAIN...
...YOU SHOULD'VE GONE BACK TO YOUR NATION TO ASK FOR BACKUP.
NOW YOU'RE ALONE AND CAN'T DO A LICK ABOUT FIRE MAN.
DID YOU REALLY THINK YOU COULD CONVINCE HIM WITH WORDS?
YOU HAVE TO WORK ON YOUR IMAGI-NATION.
OKAY!
NOW, GET GOING!
BUT DON'T YOU DARE LOOK BACK.
NOT UNTIL YOU'VE LEFT THE TUNNEL.

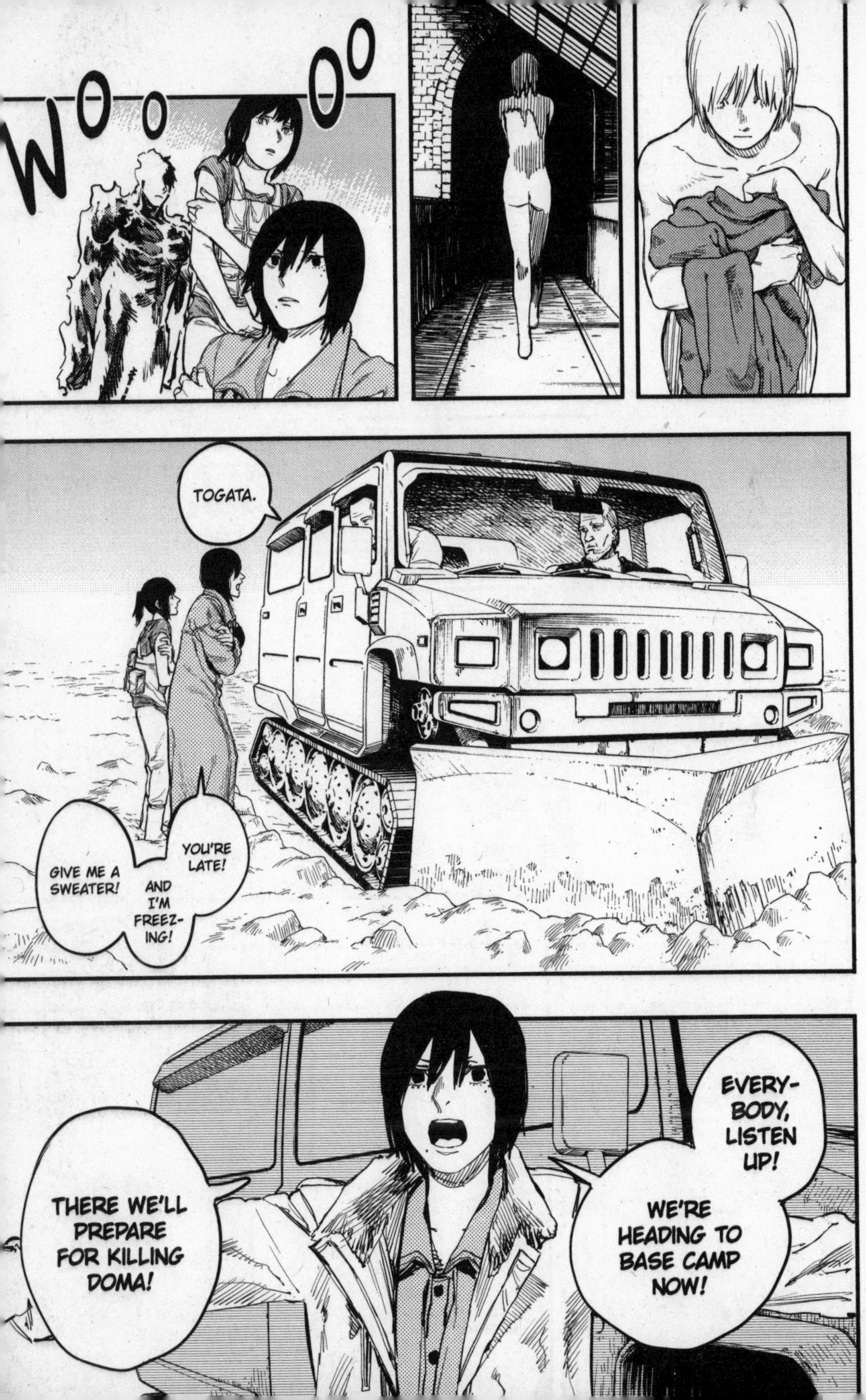
WOOOO
TOGATA.
YOU'RE LATE!
AND I'M FREEZING!
GIVE ME A SWEATER!
EVERYBODY, LISTEN UP!
WE'RE HEADING TO BASE CAMP NOW!
THERE WE'LL PREPARE FOR KILLING DOMA!

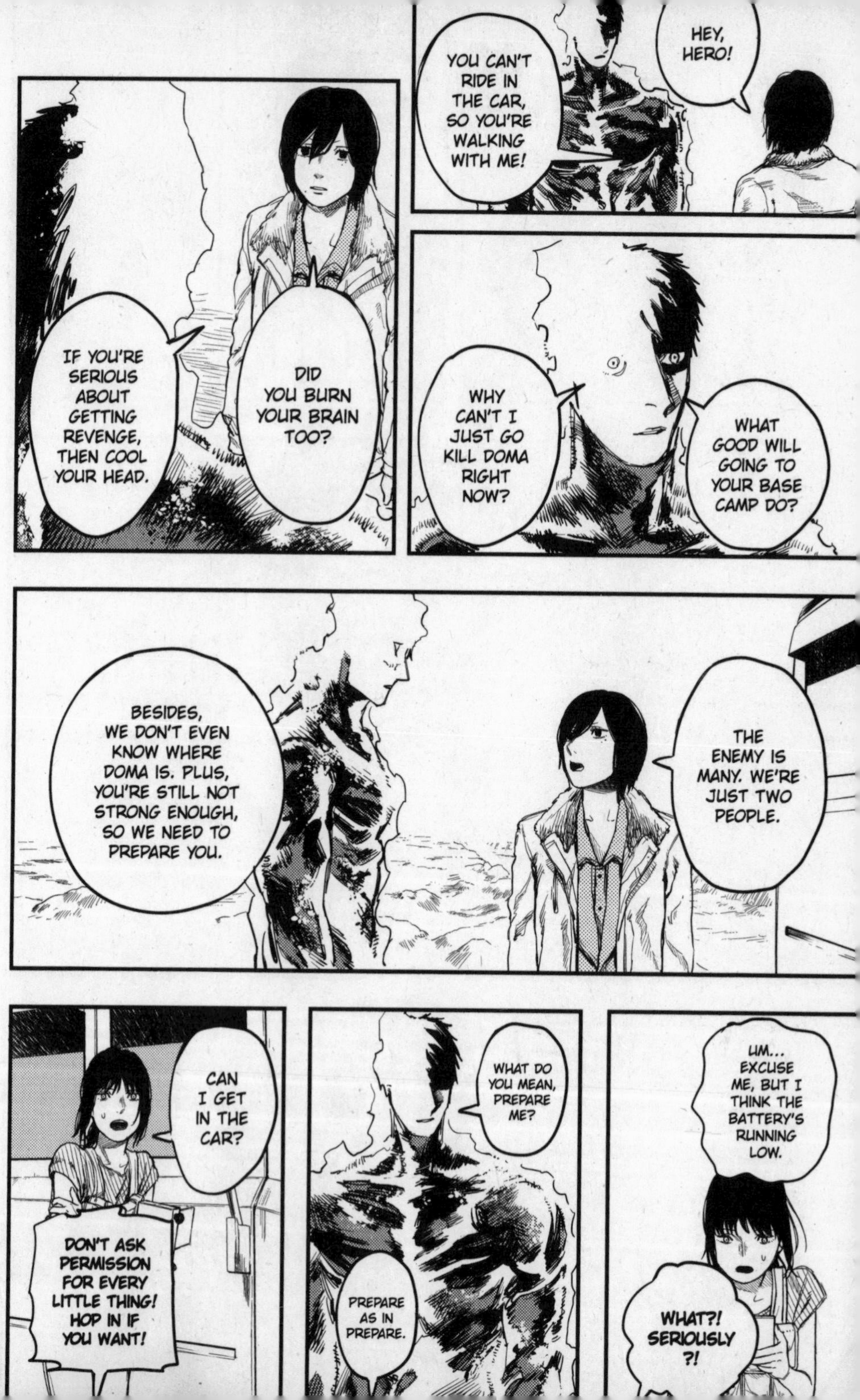
HEY, HERO!
YOU CAN'T RIDE IN THE CAR, SO YOU'RE WALKING WITH ME!
WHAT GOOD WILL GOING TO YOUR BASE CAMP DO?
WHY CAN'T I JUST GO KILL DOMA RIGHT NOW?
DID YOU BURN YOUR BRAIN TOO?
IF YOU'RE SERIOUS ABOUT GETTING REVENGE, THEN COOL YOUR HEAD.
THE ENEMY IS MANY. WE'RE JUST TWO PEOPLE.
BESIDES, WE DON'T EVEN KNOW WHERE DOMA IS. PLUS, YOU'RE STILL NOT STRONG ENOUGH, SO WE NEED TO PREPARE YOU.
UM... EXCUSE ME, BUT I THINK THE BATTERY'S RUNNING LOW.
WHAT?! SERIOUSLY?!
WHAT DO YOU MEAN, PREPARE ME?
PREPARE AS IN PREPARE.
CAN I GET IN THE CAR?
DON'T ASK PERMISSION FOR EVERY LITTLE THING! HOP IN IF YOU WANT!

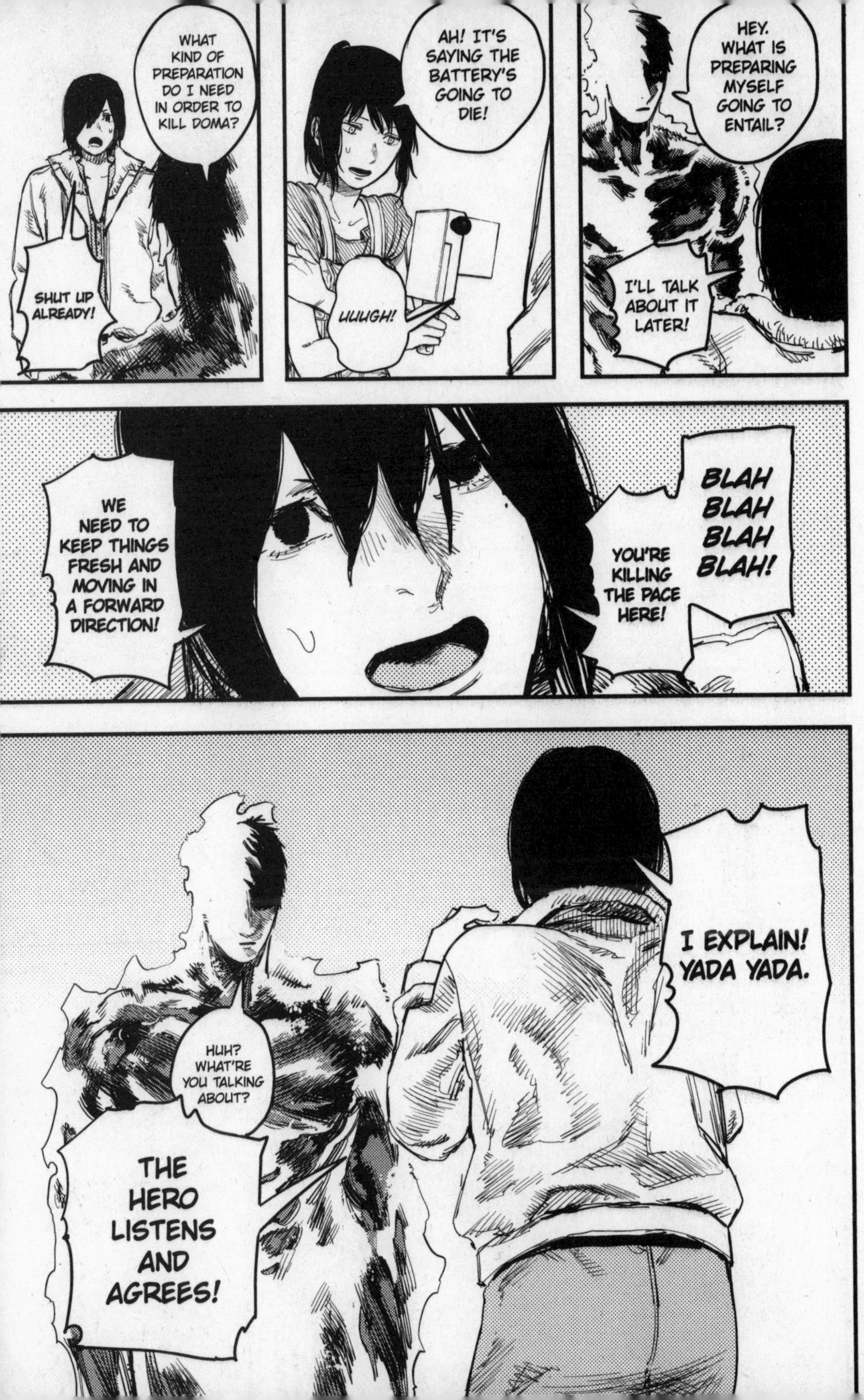
HEY. WHAT IS PREPARING MYSELF GOING TO ENTAIL?
I'LL TALK ABOUT IT LATER!
AH! IT'S SAYING THE BATTERY'S GOING TO DIE!
UUUGH!
WHAT KIND OF PREPARATION DO I NEED IN ORDER TO KILL DOMA?
SHUT UP ALREADY!
BLAH BLAH BLAH BLAH!
YOU'RE KILLING THE PACE HERE!
WE NEED TO KEEP THINGS FRESH AND MOVING IN A FORWARD DIRECTION!
I EXPLAIN! YADA YADA.
HUH? WHAT'RE YOU TALKING ABOUT?
THE HERO LISTENS AND AGREES!

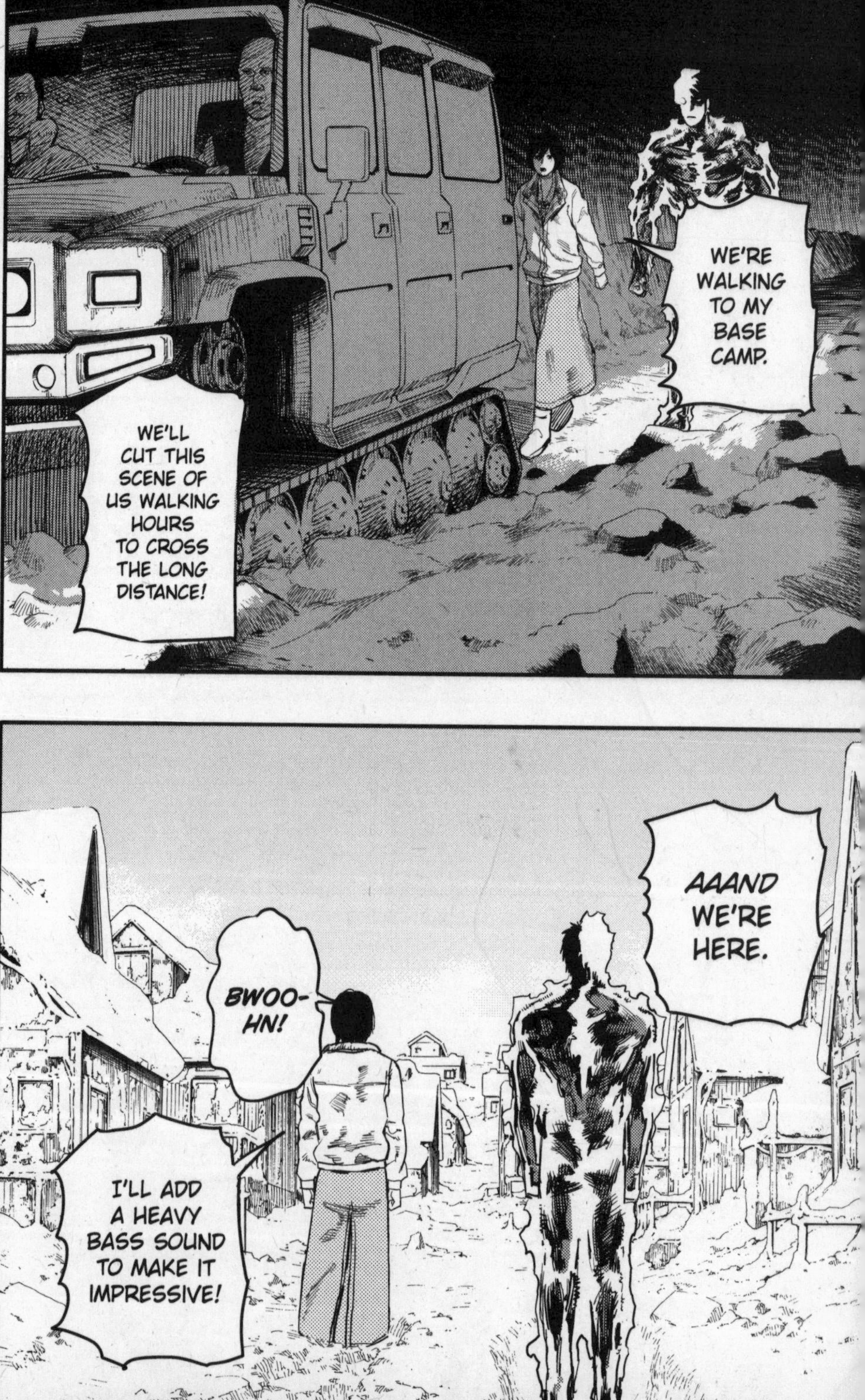
WE'RE WALKING TO MY BASE CAMP.
WE'LL CUT THIS SCENE OF US WALKING HOURS TO CROSS THE LONG DISTANCE!
AAAND WE'RE HERE.
BWOO-HN!
I'LL ADD A HEAVY BASS SOUND TO MAKE IT IMPRESSIVE!

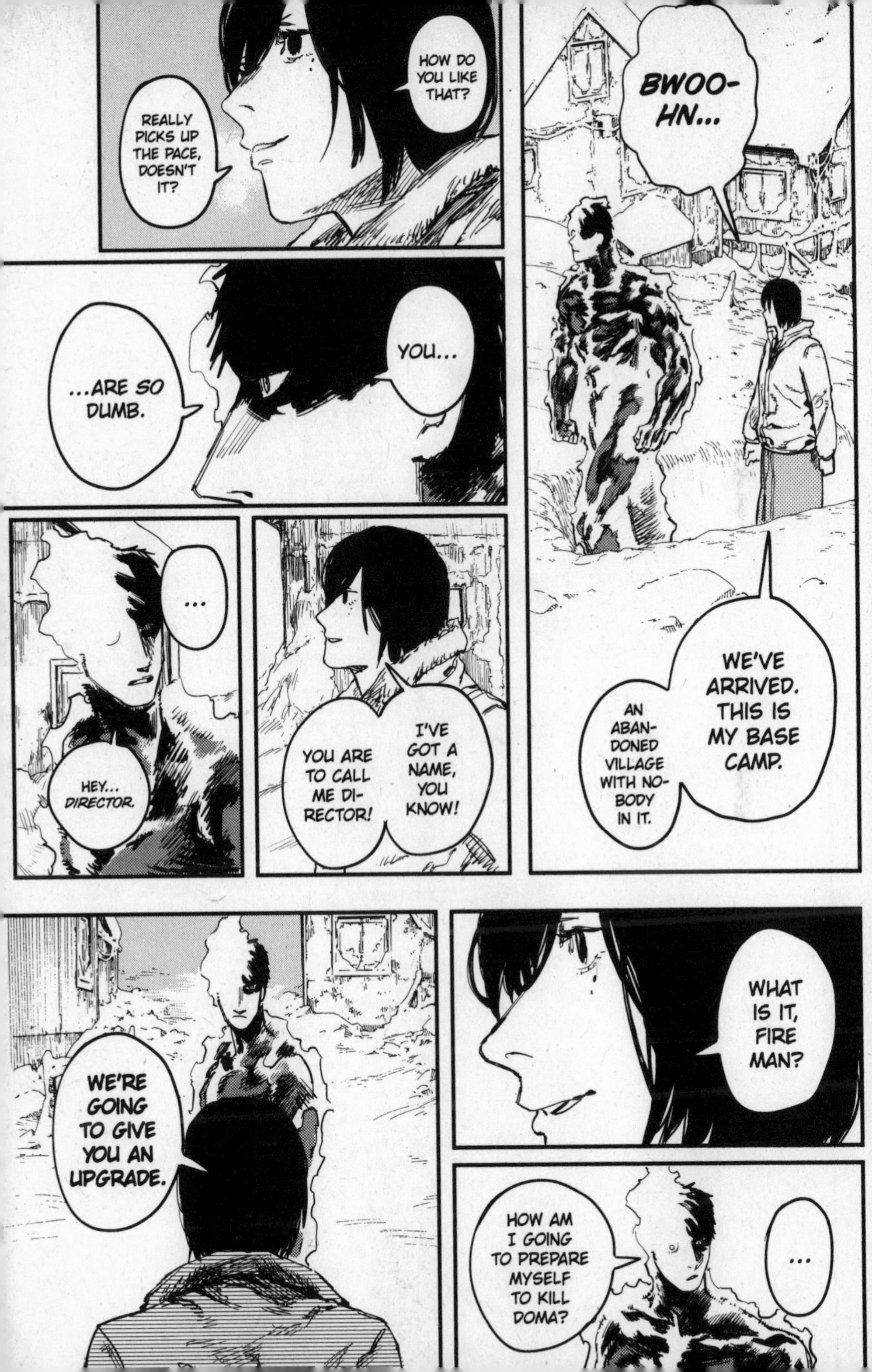
BWOOHN...
WE'VE ARRIVED. THIS IS MY BASE CAMP.
AN ABANDONED VILLAGE WITH NOBODY IN IT.
HOW DO YOU LIKE THAT?
REALLY PICKS UP THE PACE, DOESN'T IT?
YOU...
...ARE SO DUMB.
I'VE GOT A NAME, YOU KNOW!
YOU ARE TO CALL ME DIRECTOR!
...
HEY... DIRECTOR.
WHAT IS IT, FIRE MAN?
...
HOW AM I GOING TO PREPARE MYSELF TO KILL DOMA?
WE'RE GOING TO GIVE YOU AN UPGRADE.

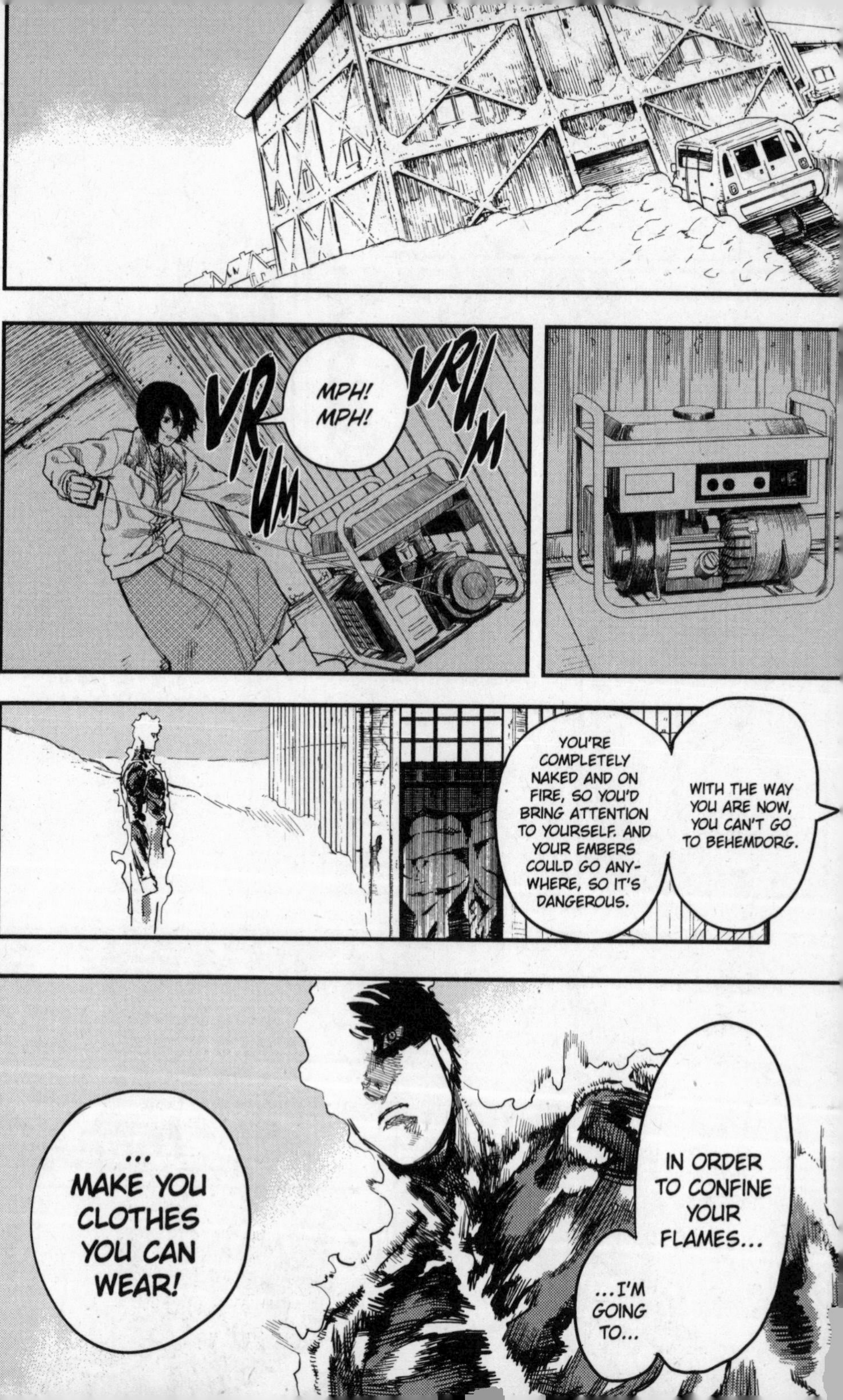
VRUM
MPH! MPH!
VRUM
WITH THE WAY YOU ARE NOW, YOU CAN'T GO TO BEHEMDORG.
YOU'RE COMPLETELY NAKED AND ON FIRE, SO YOU'D BRING ATTENTION TO YOURSELF. AND YOUR EMBERS COULD GO ANY-WHERE, SO IT'S DANGEROUS.
IN ORDER TO CONFINE YOUR FLAMES...
...I'M GOING TO...
... MAKE YOU CLOTHES YOU CAN WEAR!

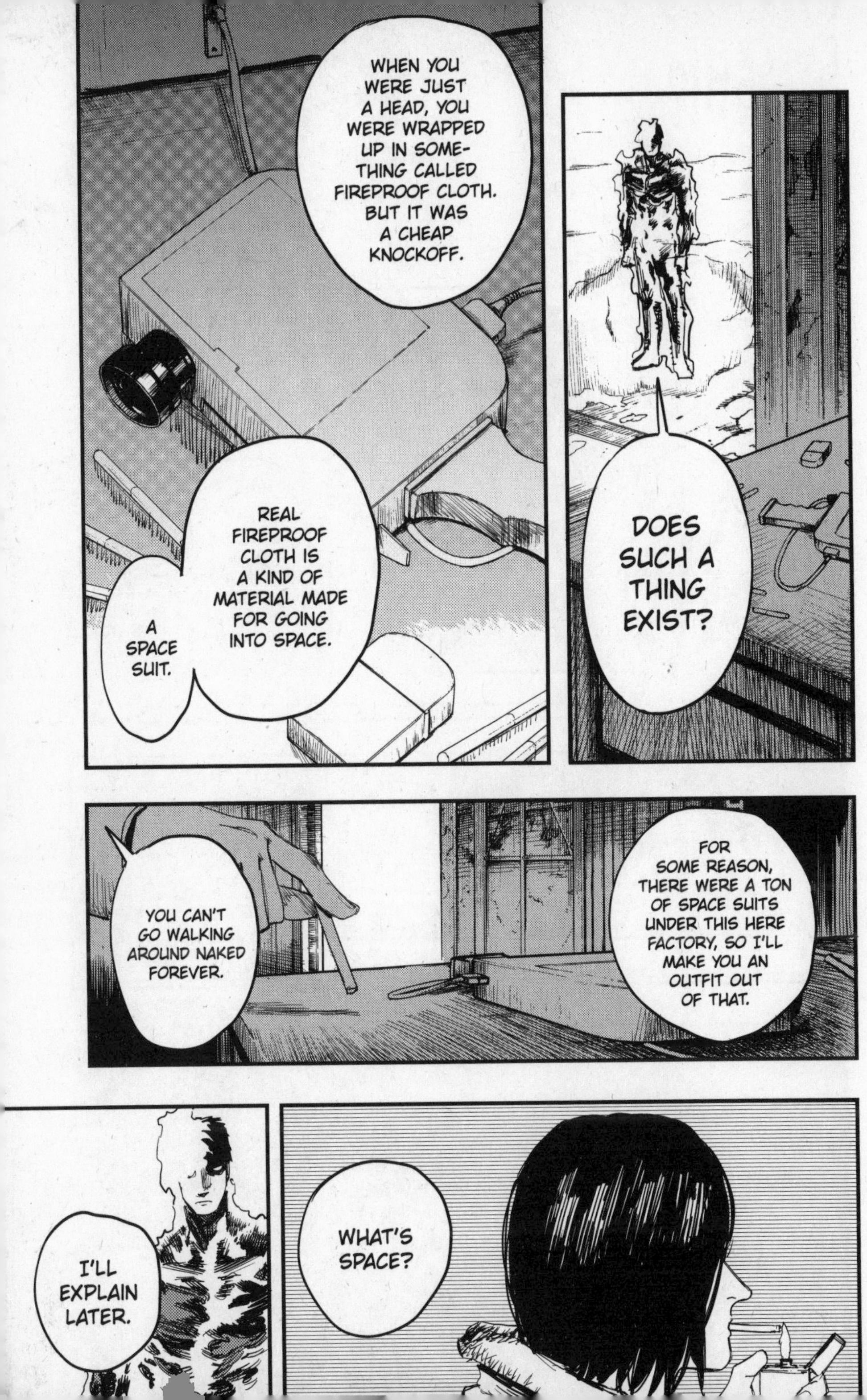
DOES SUCH A THING EXIST?
WHEN YOU WERE JUST A HEAD, YOU WERE WRAPPED UP IN SOME-THING CALLED FIREPROOF CLOTH. BUT IT WAS A CHEAP KNOCKOFF.
REAL FIREPROOF CLOTH IS A KIND OF MATERIAL MADE FOR GOING INTO SPACE.
A SPACE SUIT.
FOR SOME REASON, THERE WERE A TON OF SPACE SUITS UNDER THIS HERE FACTORY, SO I'LL MAKE YOU AN OUTFIT OUT OF THAT.
YOU CAN'T GO WALKING AROUND NAKED FOREVER.
WHAT'S SPACE?
I'LL EXPLAIN LATER.

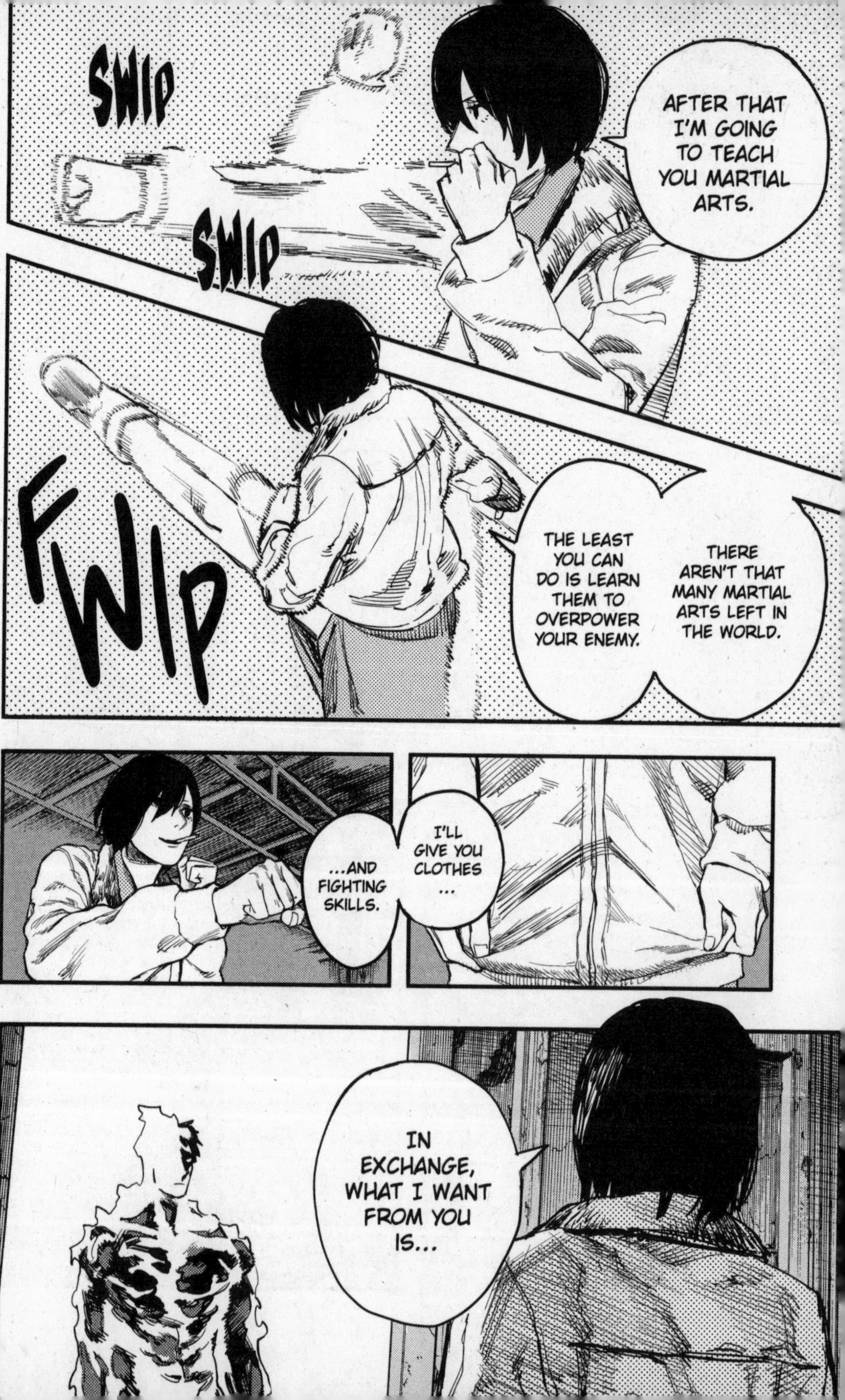
AFTER THAT I'M GOING TO TEACH YOU MARTIAL ARTS.
SWIP
SWIP
THERE AREN'T THAT MANY MARTIAL ARTS LEFT IN THE WORLD.
THE LEAST YOU CAN DO IS LEARN THEM TO OVERPOWER YOUR ENEMY.
FWIP
I'LL GIVE YOU CLOTHES ...
...AND FIGHTING SKILLS.
IN EXCHANGE, WHAT I WANT FROM YOU IS...

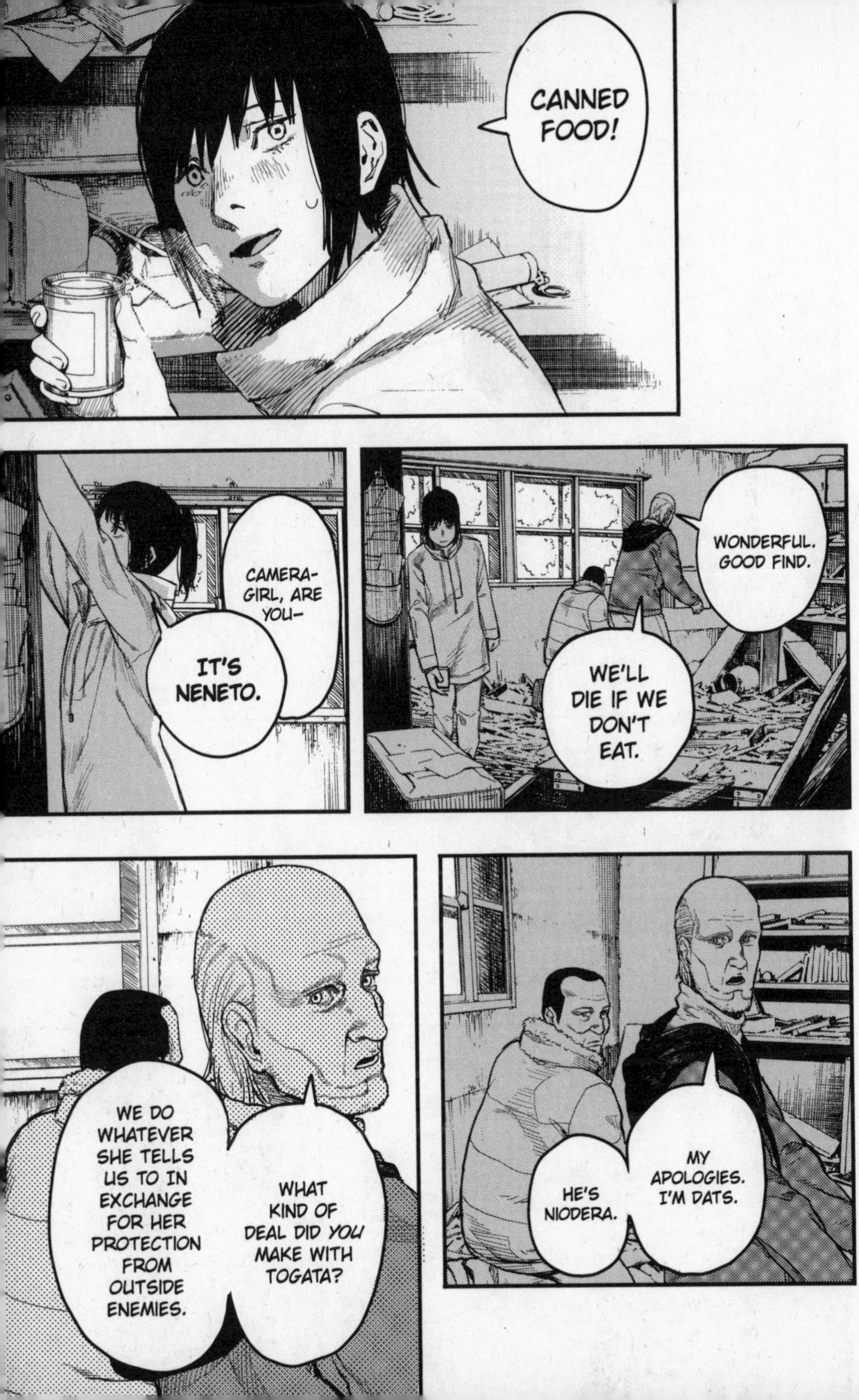
CANNED FOOD!
WONDERFUL. GOOD FIND.
WE'LL DIE IF WE DON'T EAT.
CAMERA-GIRL, ARE YOU—
IT'S NENETO.
MY APOLOGIES. I'M DATS.
HE'S NIODERA.
WHAT KIND OF DEAL DID *YOU* MAKE WITH TOGATA?
WE DO WHATEVER SHE TELLS US TO IN EXCHANGE FOR HER PROTECTION FROM OUTSIDE ENEMIES.

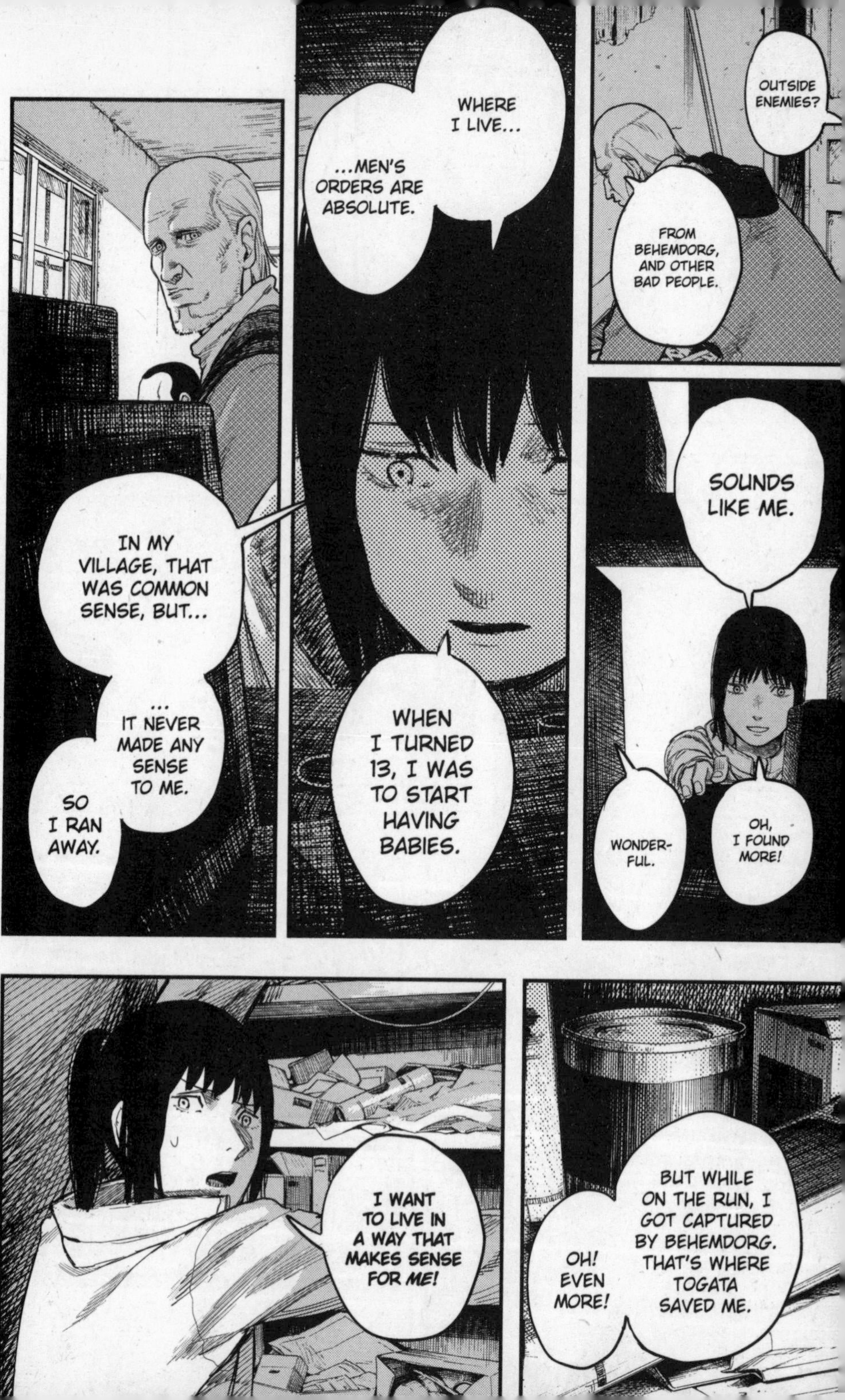
OUTSIDE ENEMIES?
FROM BEHEMDORG, AND OTHER BAD PEOPLE.
SOUNDS LIKE ME.
OH, I FOUND MORE!
WONDER-FUL.
WHERE I LIVE...
...MEN'S ORDERS ARE ABSOLUTE.
WHEN I TURNED 13, I WAS TO START HAVING BABIES.
IN MY VILLAGE, THAT WAS COMMON SENSE, BUT...
...IT NEVER MADE ANY SENSE TO ME.
SO I RAN AWAY.
BUT WHILE ON THE RUN, I GOT CAPTURED BY BEHEMDORG. THAT'S WHERE TOGATA SAVED ME.
OH! EVEN MORE!
I WANT TO LIVE IN A WAY THAT MAKES SENSE FOR *ME*!

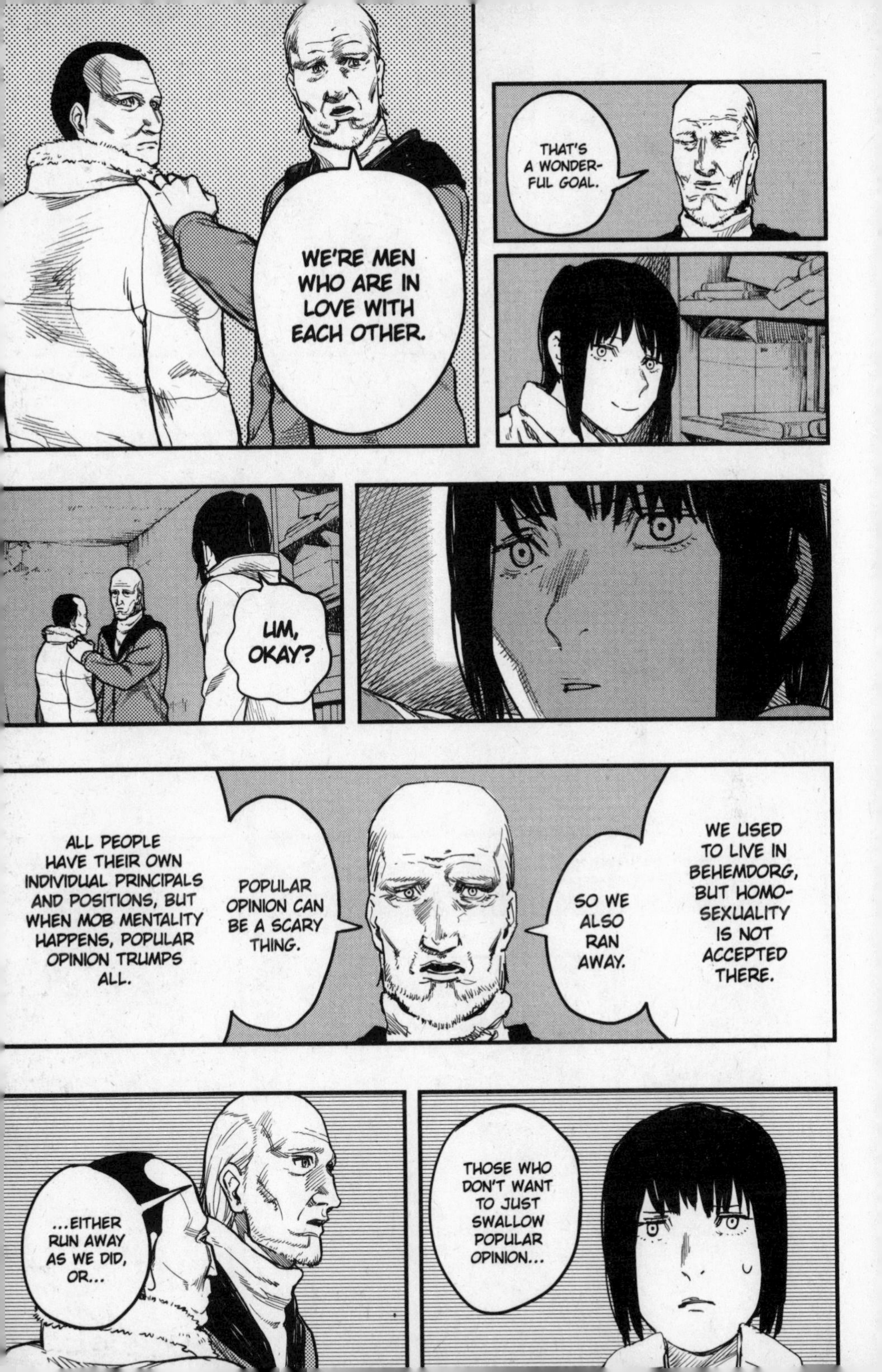
THAT'S A WONDERFUL GOAL.
WE'RE MEN WHO ARE IN LOVE WITH EACH OTHER.
UM, OKAY?
WE USED TO LIVE IN BEHEMDORG, BUT HOMOSEXUALITY IS NOT ACCEPTED THERE.
SO WE ALSO RAN AWAY.
POPULAR OPINION CAN BE A SCARY THING.
ALL PEOPLE HAVE THEIR OWN INDIVIDUAL PRINCIPALS AND POSITIONS, BUT WHEN MOB MENTALITY HAPPENS, POPULAR OPINION TRUMPS ALL.
THOSE WHO DON'T WANT TO JUST SWALLOW POPULAR OPINION...
...EITHER RUN AWAY AS WE DID, OR...

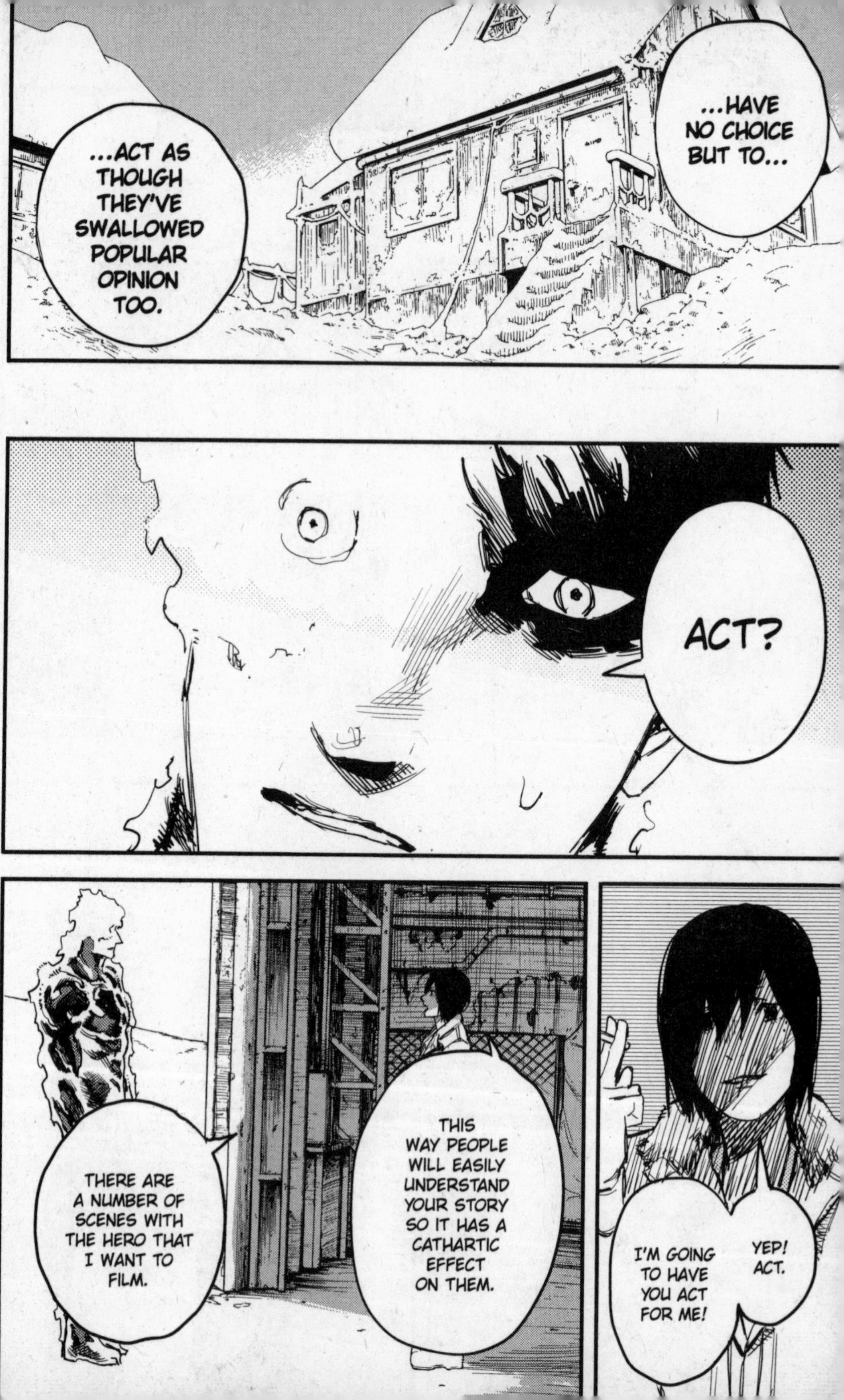
...HAVE NO CHOICE BUT TO...
...ACT AS THOUGH THEY'VE SWALLOWED POPULAR OPINION TOO.
ACT?
YEP! ACT.
I'M GOING TO HAVE YOU ACT FOR ME!
THERE ARE A NUMBER OF SCENES WITH THE HERO THAT I WANT TO FILM.
THIS WAY PEOPLE WILL EASILY UNDERSTAND YOUR STORY SO IT HAS A CATHARTIC EFFECT ON THEM.

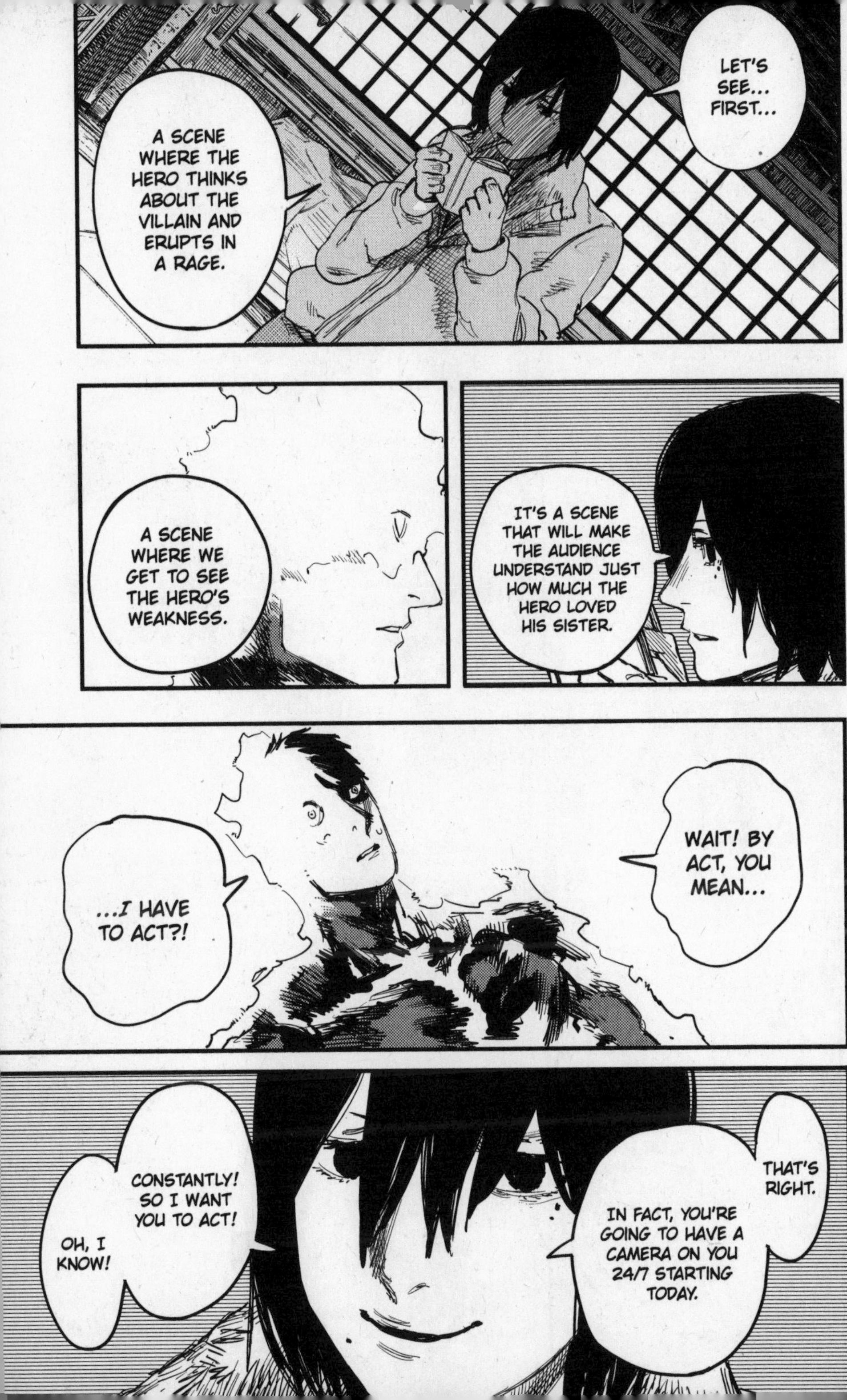
LET'S SEE... FIRST...
A SCENE WHERE THE HERO THINKS ABOUT THE VILLAIN AND ERUPTS IN A RAGE.
IT'S A SCENE THAT WILL MAKE THE AUDIENCE UNDERSTAND JUST HOW MUCH THE HERO LOVED HIS SISTER.
A SCENE WHERE WE GET TO SEE THE HERO'S WEAKNESS.
WAIT! BY ACT, YOU MEAN...
...I HAVE TO ACT?!
THAT'S RIGHT.
IN FACT, YOU'RE GOING TO HAVE A CAMERA ON YOU 24/7 STARTING TODAY.
CONSTANTLY! SO I WANT YOU TO ACT!
OH, I KNOW!

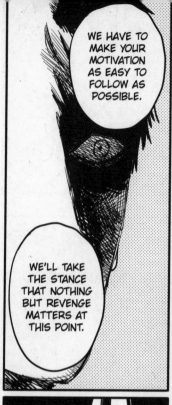

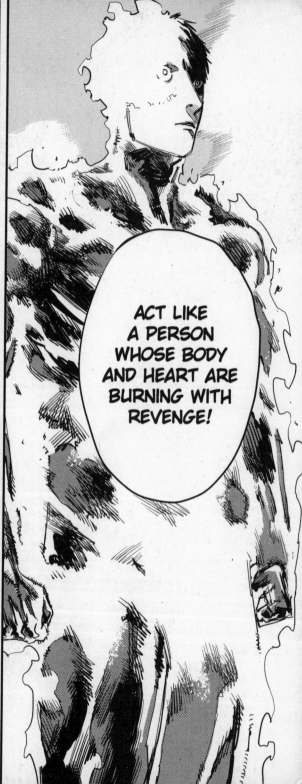

ACT LIKE A PERSON WHOSE BODY AND HEART ARE BURNING WITH REVENGE!
WE HAVE TO MAKE YOUR MOTIVATION AS EASY TO FOLLOW AS POSSIBLE.
WE'LL TAKE THE STANCE THAT NOTHING BUT REVENGE MATTERS AT THIS POINT.
AND WE'LL COMMUNICATE HOW SOMETIMES THE SHEER PAIN OF YOUR BURNING BODY MAKES YOU HALLUCINATE YOUR LITTLE SISTER!
THAT SHOULD ADD SOME REALISM...

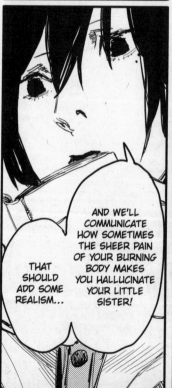

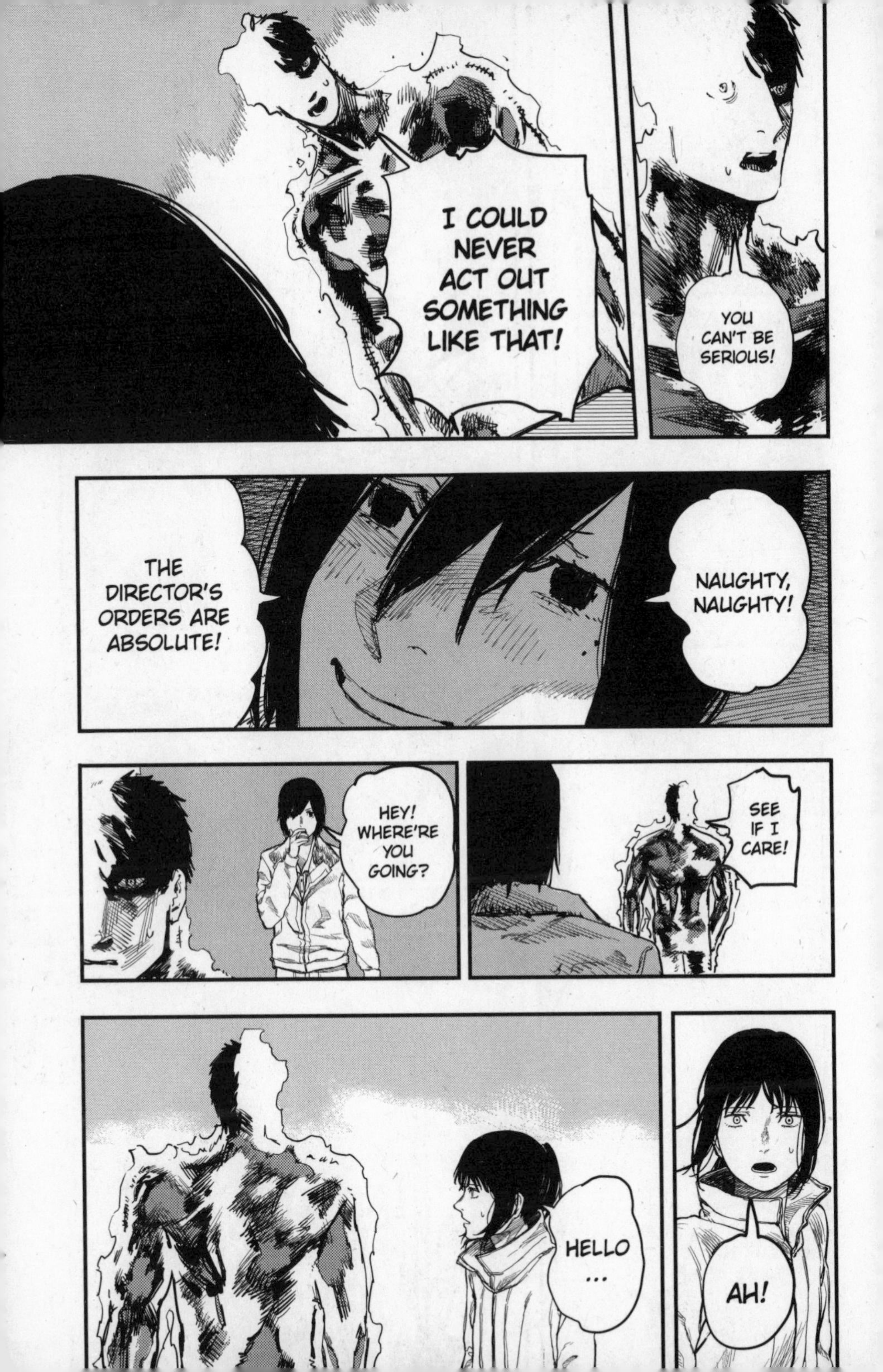
YOU CAN'T BE SERIOUS!
I COULD NEVER ACT OUT SOMETHING LIKE THAT!
NAUGHTY, NAUGHTY!
THE DIRECTOR'S ORDERS ARE ABSOLUTE!
SEE IF I CARE!
HEY! WHERE'RE YOU GOING?
AH!
HELLO ...

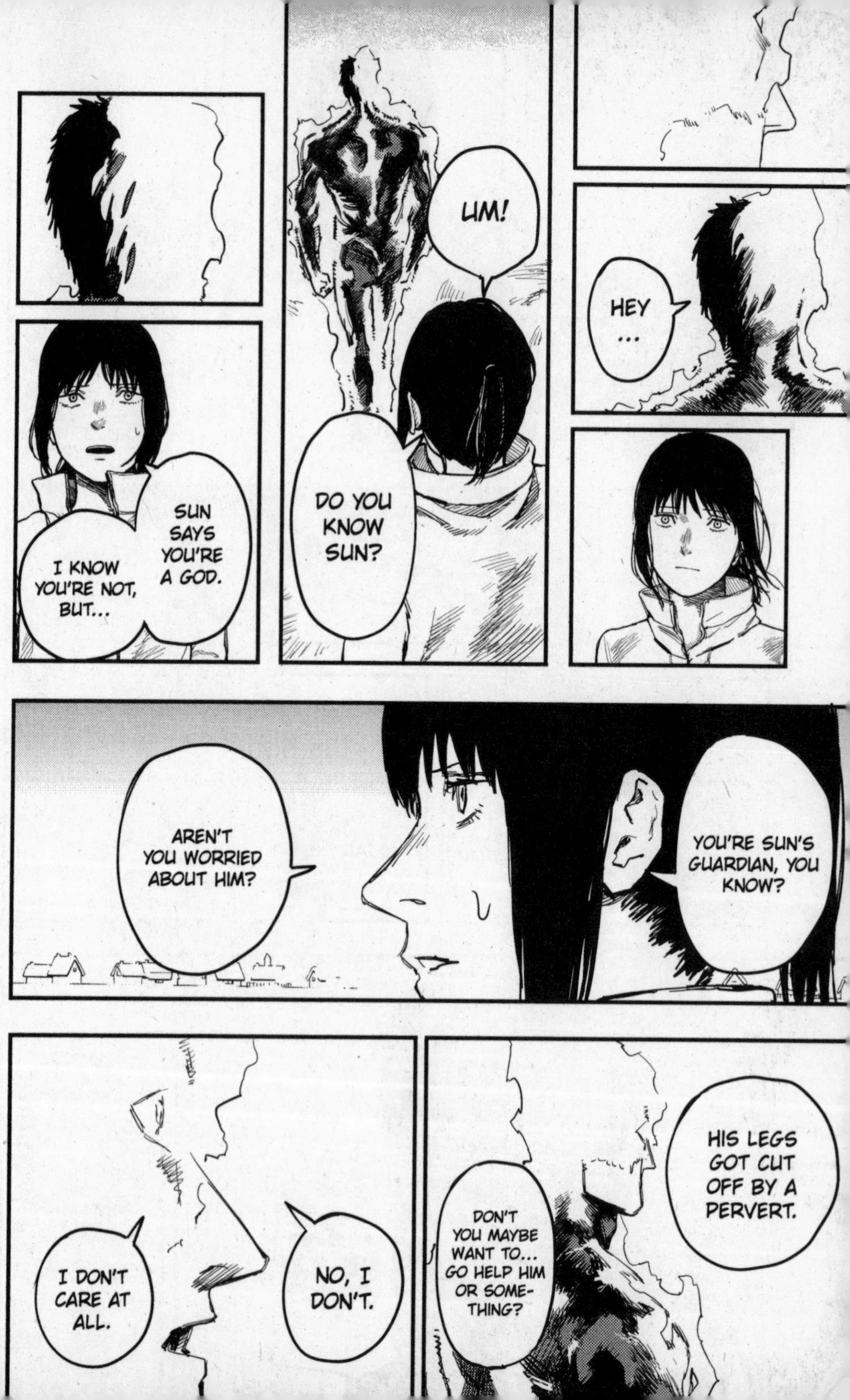
HEY ...
UM!
DO YOU KNOW SUN?
SUN SAYS YOU'RE A GOD.
I KNOW YOU'RE NOT, BUT...
YOU'RE SUN'S GUARDIAN, YOU KNOW?
AREN'T YOU WORRIED ABOUT HIM?
HIS LEGS GOT CUT OFF BY A PERVERT.
DON'T YOU MAYBE WANT TO... GO HELP HIM OR SOME-THING?
NO, I DON'T.
I DON'T CARE AT ALL.

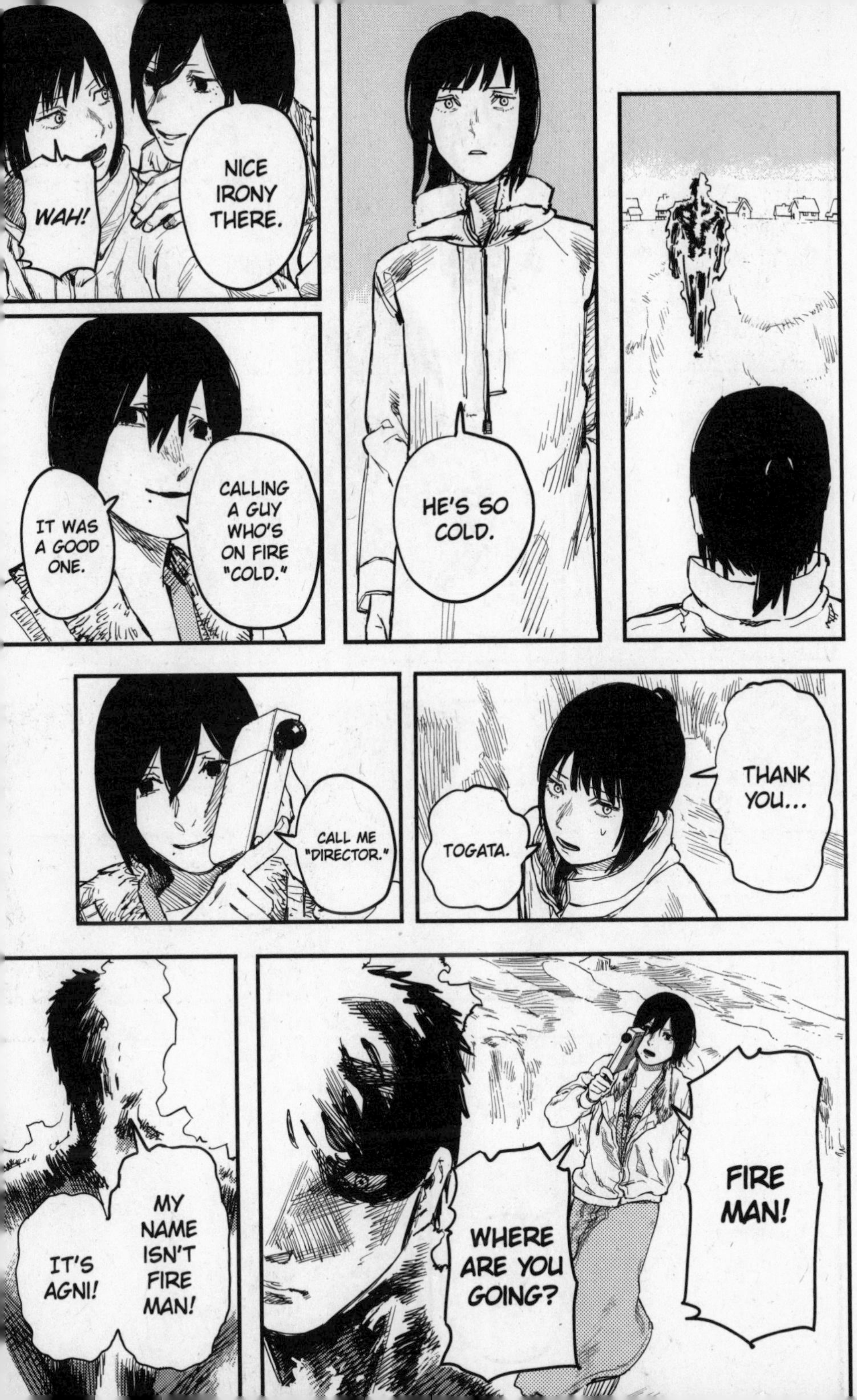
HE'S SO COLD.
NICE IRONY THERE.
WAH!
CALLING A GUY WHO'S ON FIRE "COLD."
IT WAS A GOOD ONE.
THANK YOU...
TOGATA.
CALL ME "DIRECTOR."
FIRE MAN!
WHERE ARE YOU GOING?
MY NAME ISN'T FIRE MAN!
IT'S AGNI!

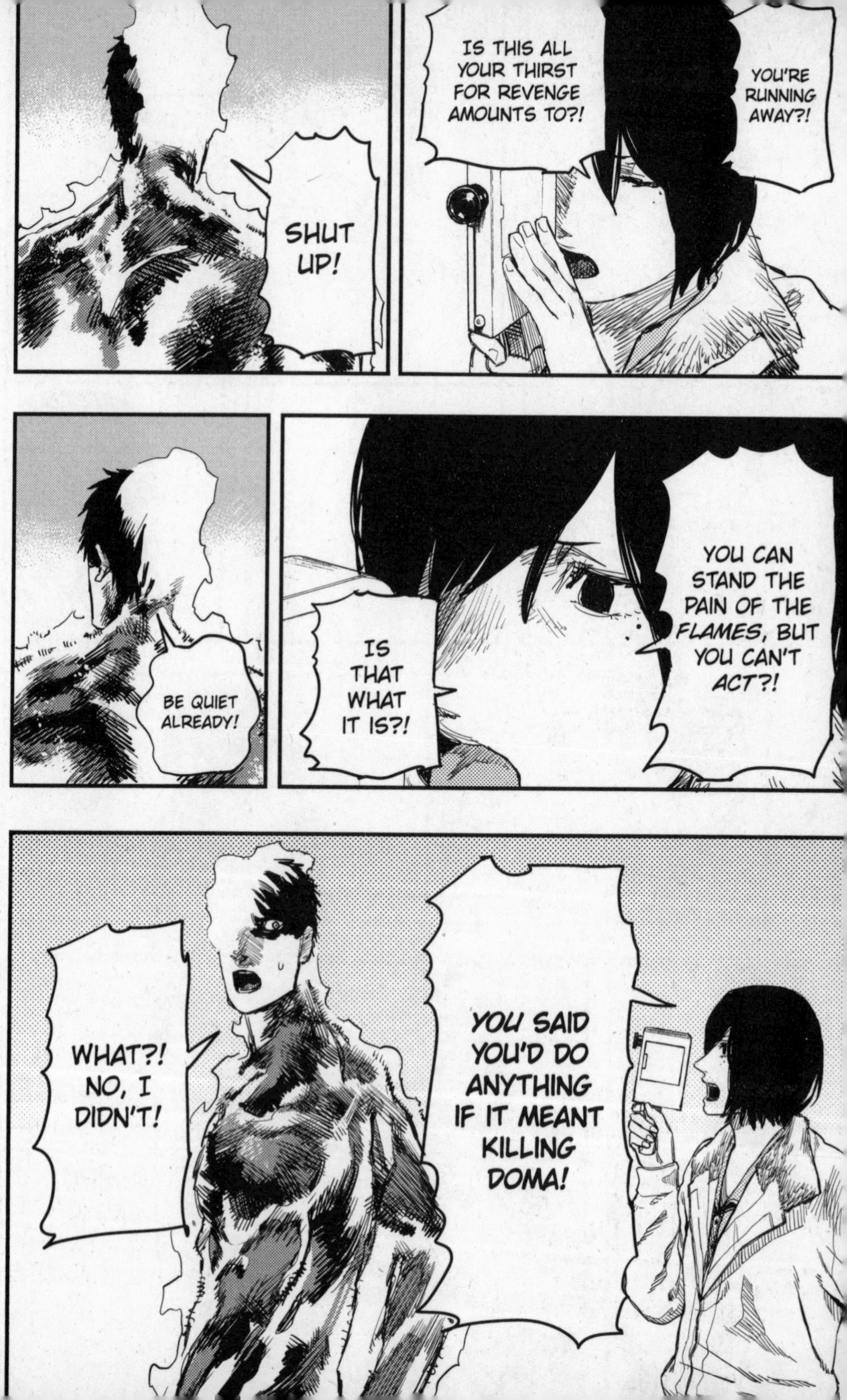
YOU'RE RUNNING AWAY?!
IS THIS ALL YOUR THIRST FOR REVENGE AMOUNTS TO?!
SHUT UP!
YOU CAN STAND THE PAIN OF THE *FLAMES*, BUT YOU CAN'T *ACT*?!
IS THAT WHAT IT IS?!
BE QUIET ALREADY!
YOU SAID YOU'D DO ANYTHING IF IT MEANT KILLING DOMA!
WHAT?! NO, I DIDN'T!

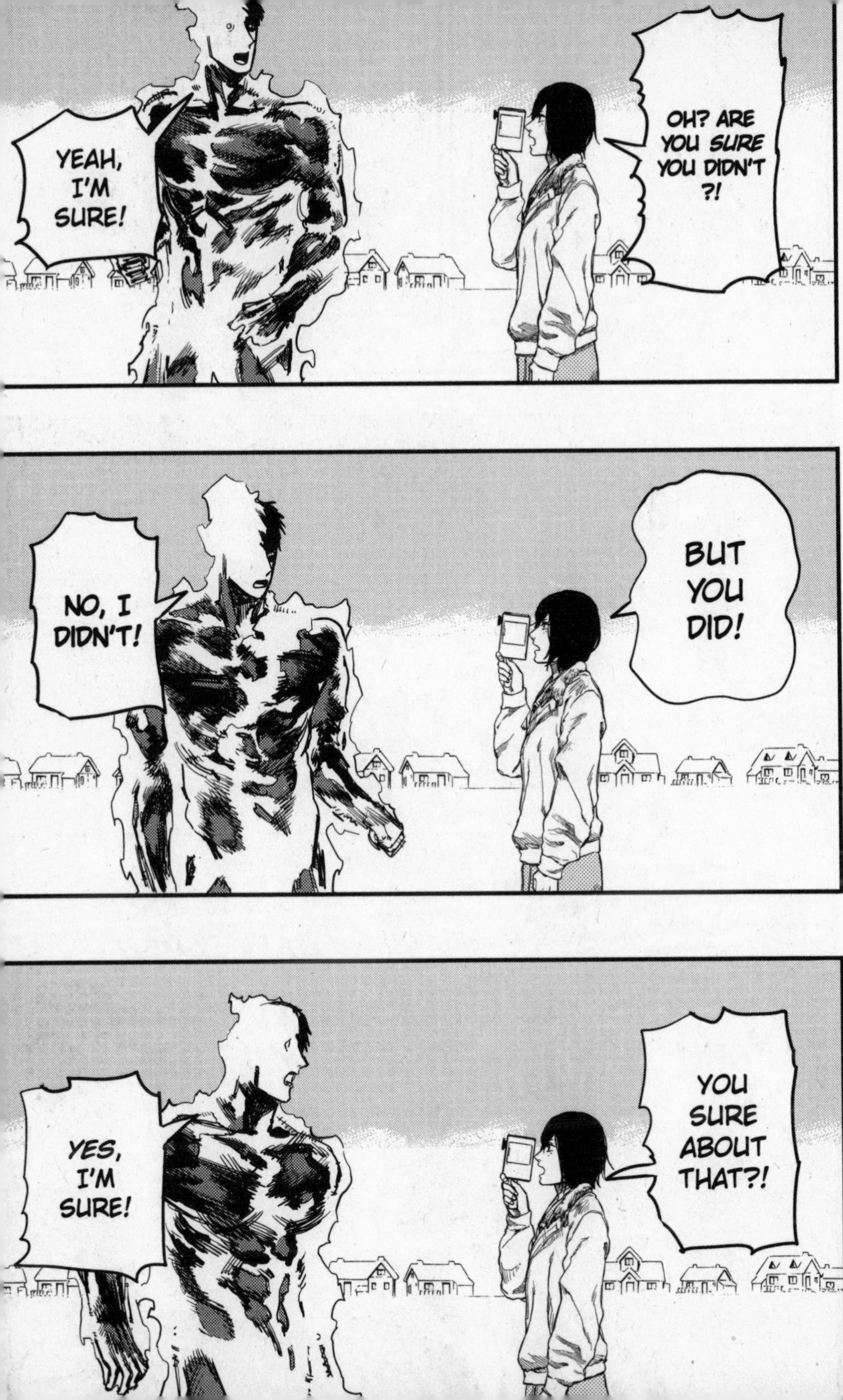
OH? ARE YOU SURE YOU DIDN'T ?!
YEAH, I'M SURE!
BUT YOU DID!
NO, I DIDN'T!
YOU SURE ABOUT THAT?!
YES, I'M SURE!

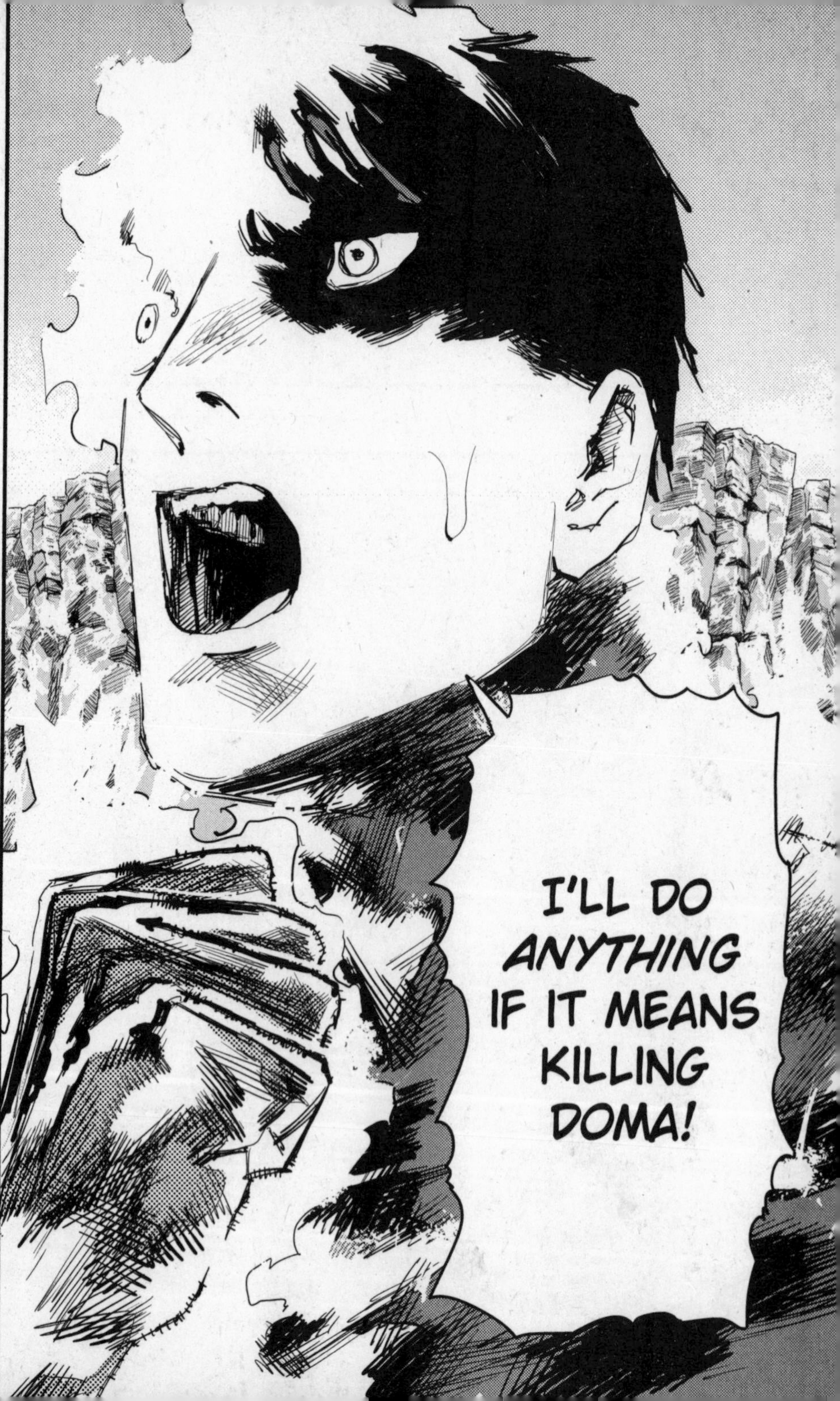
I'LL DO ANYTHING IF IT MEANS KILLING DOMA!

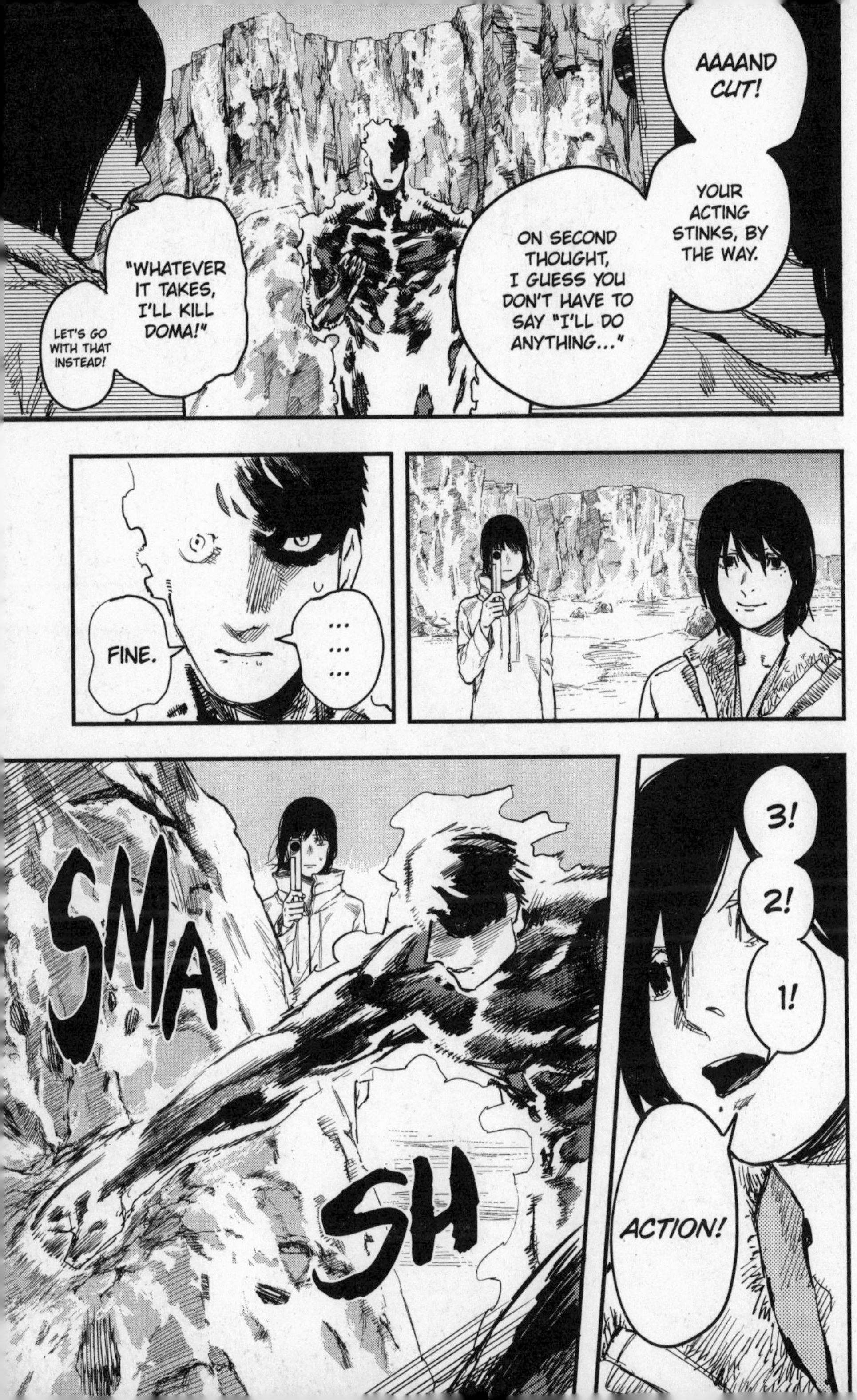
AAAAND CUT!
YOUR ACTING STINKS, BY THE WAY.
ON SECOND THOUGHT, I GUESS YOU DON'T HAVE TO SAY "I'LL DO ANYTHING..."
"WHATEVER IT TAKES, I'LL KILL DOMA!"
LET'S GO WITH THAT INSTEAD!
...
...
...
FINE.
3!
2!
1!
ACTION!
SMASH

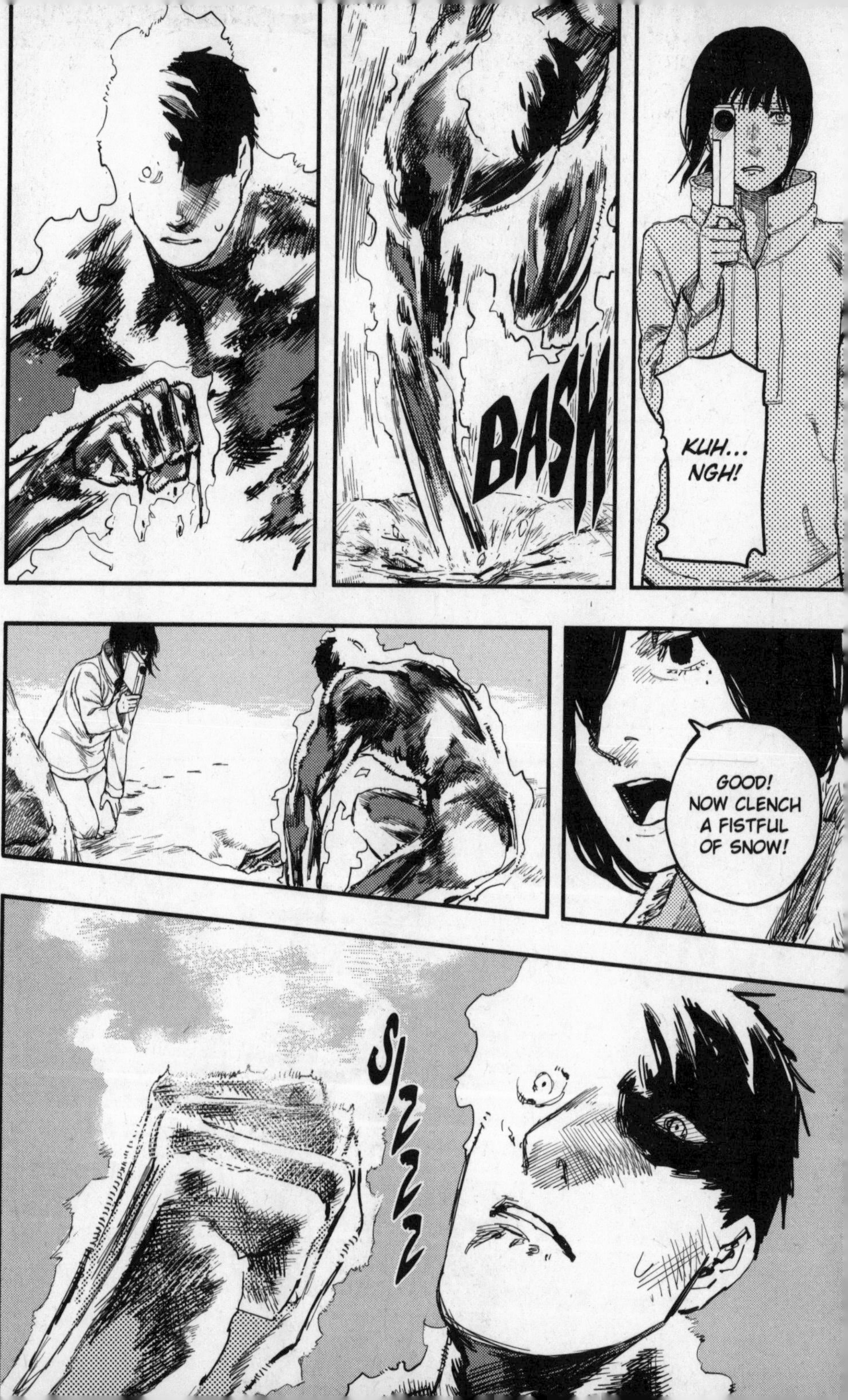
KUH... NGH!
BASH
GOOD! NOW CLENCH A FISTFUL OF SNOW!
SIZZZ

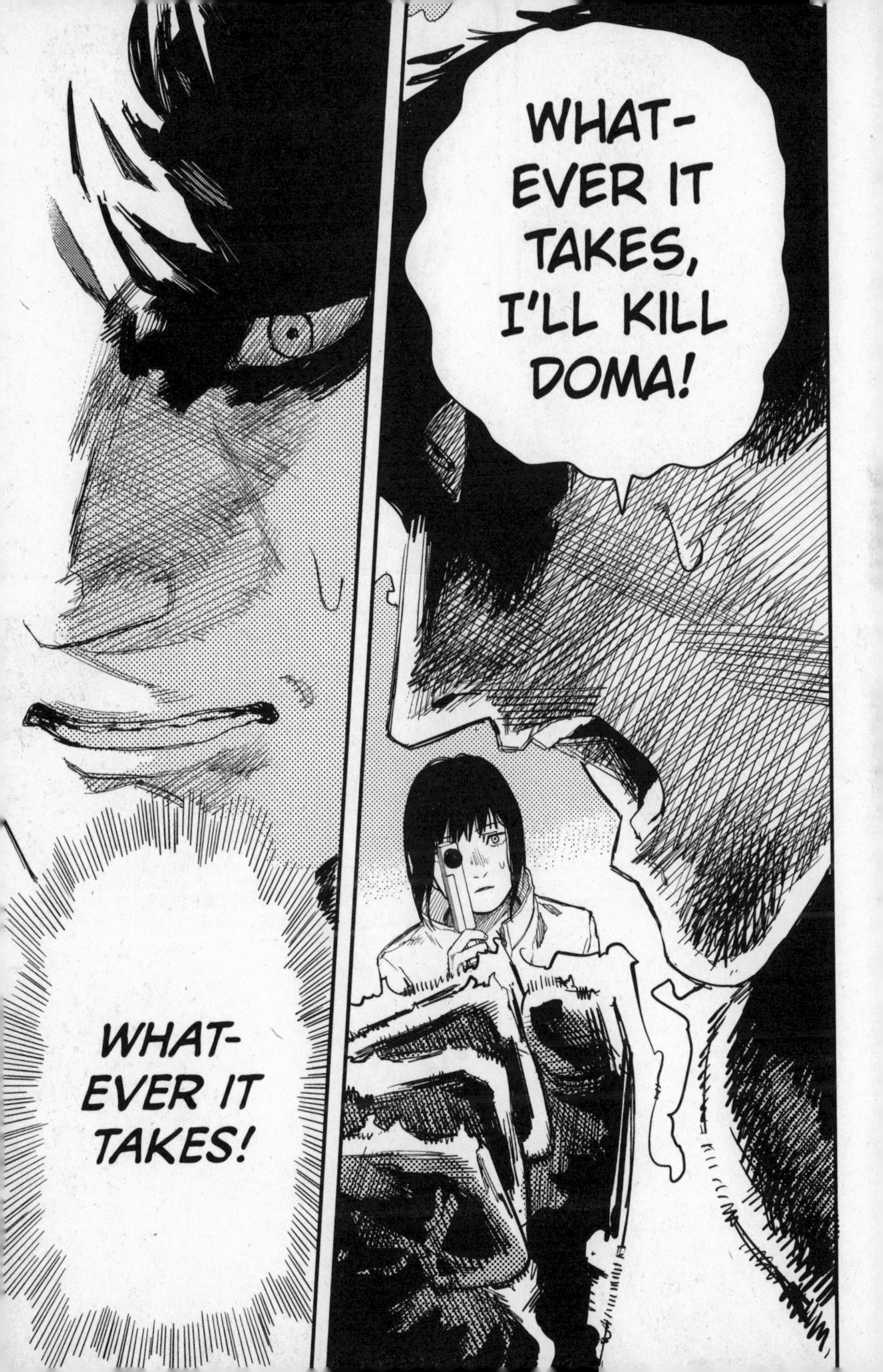
WHAT-EVER IT TAKES, I'LL KILL DOMA!
WHAT-EVER IT TAKES!

FIRE PUNCH

CHAPTER 15

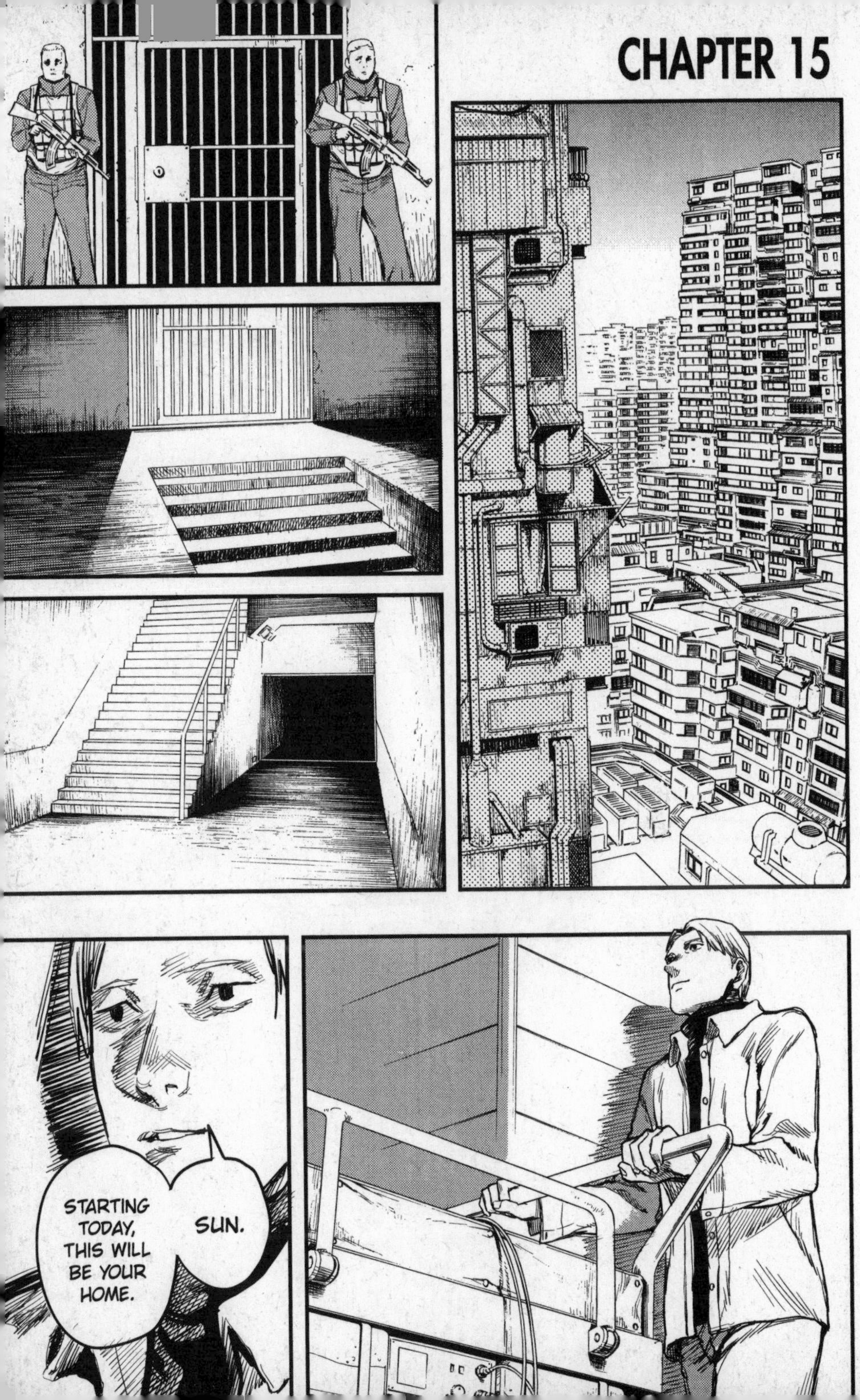
SUN.
STARTING TODAY, THIS WILL BE YOUR HOME.

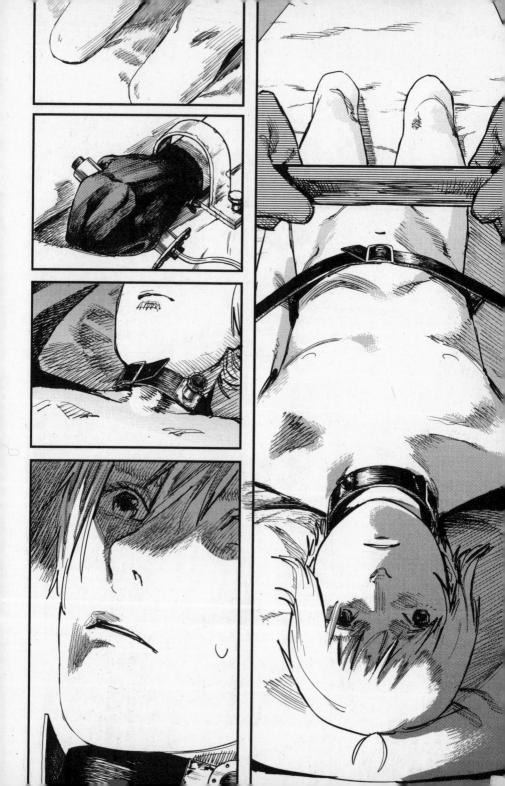

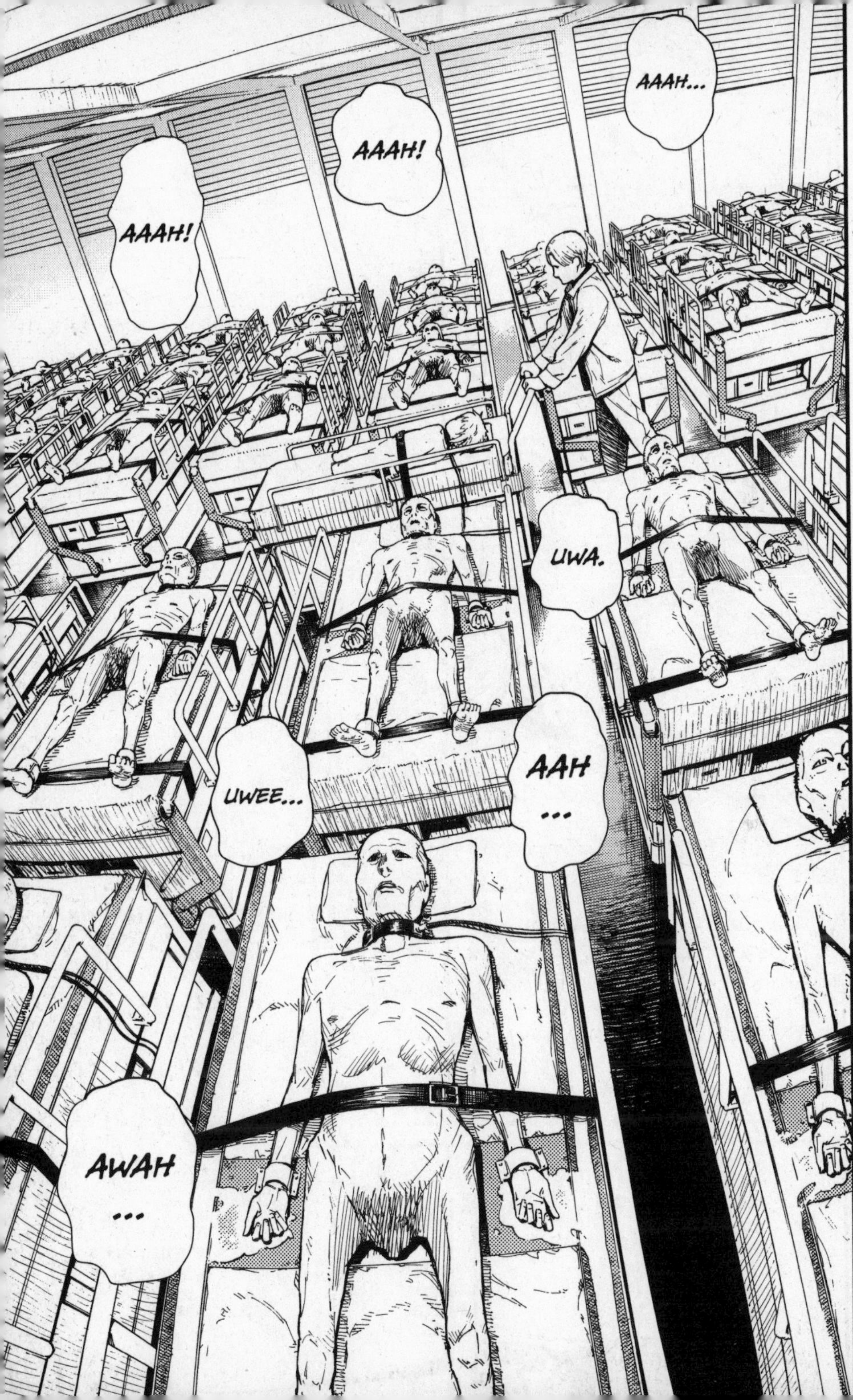

AAAH...
AAAH!
AAAH!
UWA.
AAH ...
UWEE...
AWAH ...

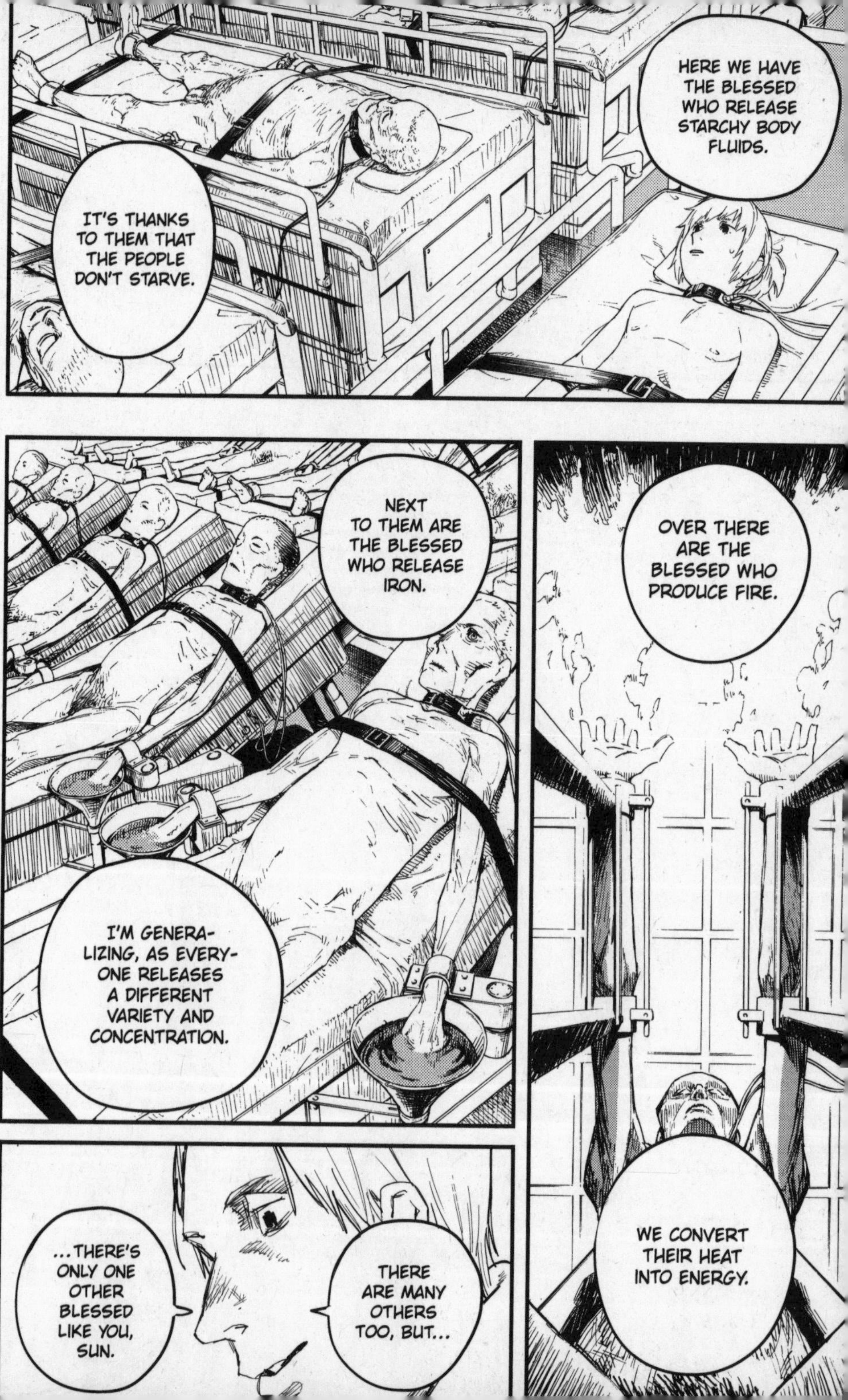
HERE WE HAVE THE BLESSED WHO RELEASE STARCHY BODY FLUIDS.
IT'S THANKS TO THEM THAT THE PEOPLE DON'T STARVE.
OVER THERE ARE THE BLESSED WHO PRODUCE FIRE.
WE CONVERT THEIR HEAT INTO ENERGY.
NEXT TO THEM ARE THE BLESSED WHO RELEASE IRON.
I'M GENERA-LIZING, AS EVERY-ONE RELEASES A DIFFERENT VARIETY AND CONCENTRATION.
THERE ARE MANY OTHERS TOO, BUT...
...THERE'S ONLY ONE OTHER BLESSED LIKE YOU, SUN.

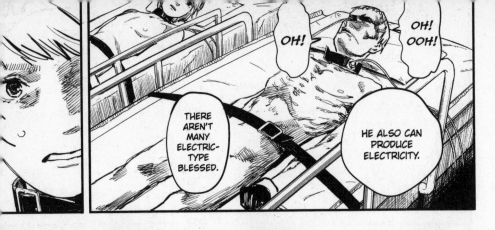

OH! OOH!
OH!
HE ALSO CAN PRODUCE ELECTRICITY.
THERE AREN'T MANY ELECTRIC-TYPE BLESSED.
EVERY PERSON HERE IS PRECIOUS FIREWOOD THAT SUPPORTS BEHEMDORG.
WITHOUT FIREWOOD, THE FIRE WOULD GO OUT AND THE PEOPLE WOULD FREEZE TO DEATH.
CLICK
AH!
SO FROM NOW ON, YOU'LL BE FIREWOOD TOO, SUN.

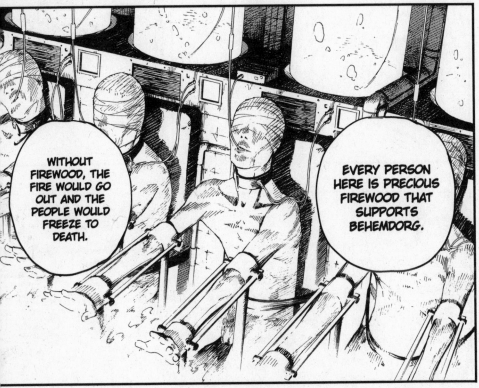

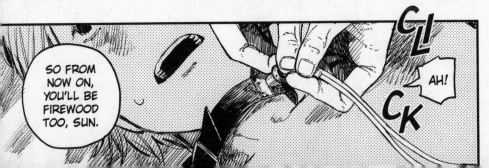

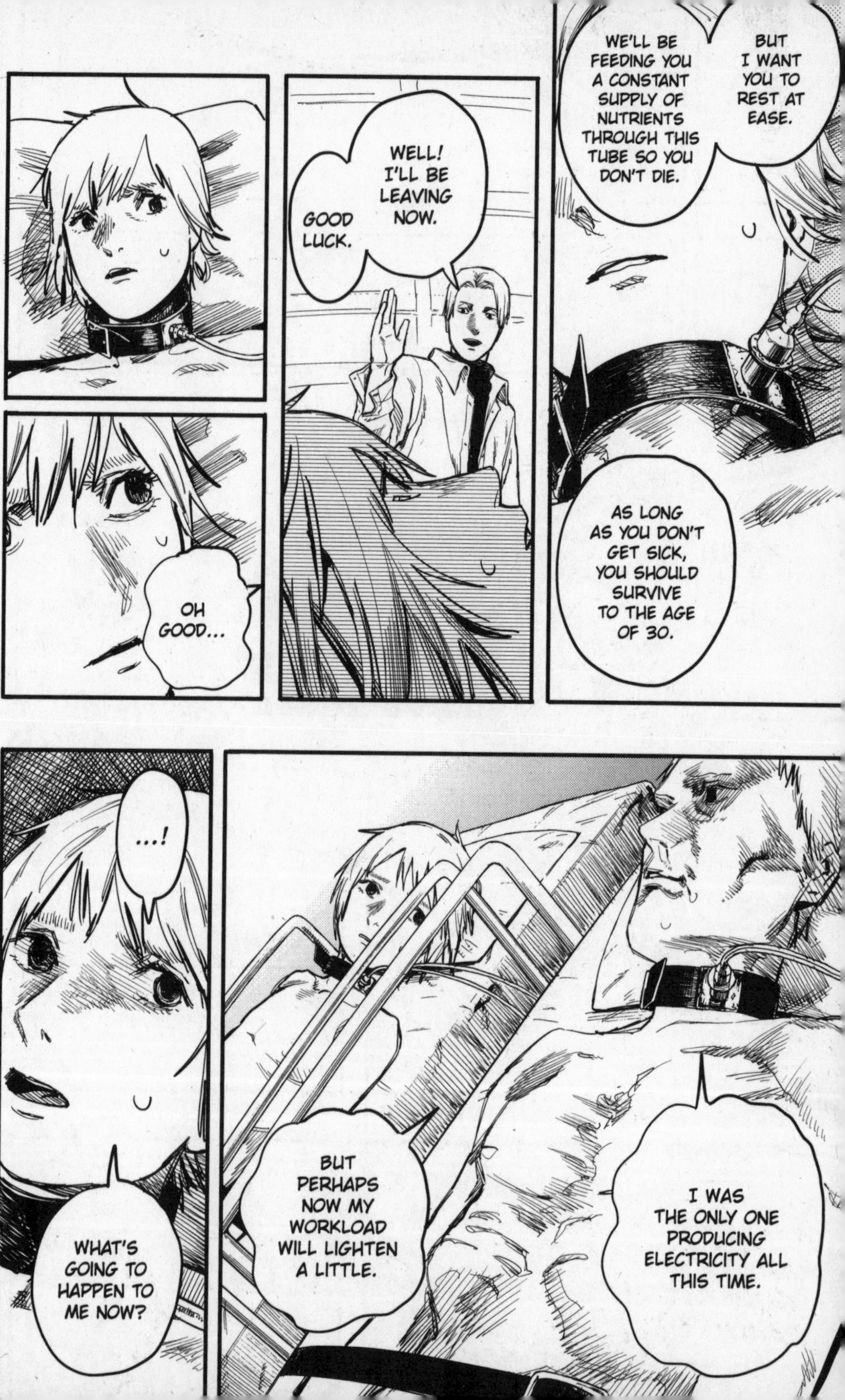
WE'LL BE FEEDING YOU A CONSTANT SUPPLY OF NUTRIENTS THROUGH THIS TUBE SO YOU DON'T DIE.
BUT I WANT YOU TO REST AT EASE.
AS LONG AS YOU DON'T GET SICK, YOU SHOULD SURVIVE TO THE AGE OF 30.
WELL! I'LL BE LEAVING NOW.
GOOD LUCK.
OH GOOD...
I WAS THE ONLY ONE PRODUCING ELECTRICITY ALL THIS TIME.
BUT PERHAPS NOW MY WORKLOAD WILL LIGHTEN A LITTLE.
...!
WHAT'S GOING TO HAPPEN TO ME NOW?

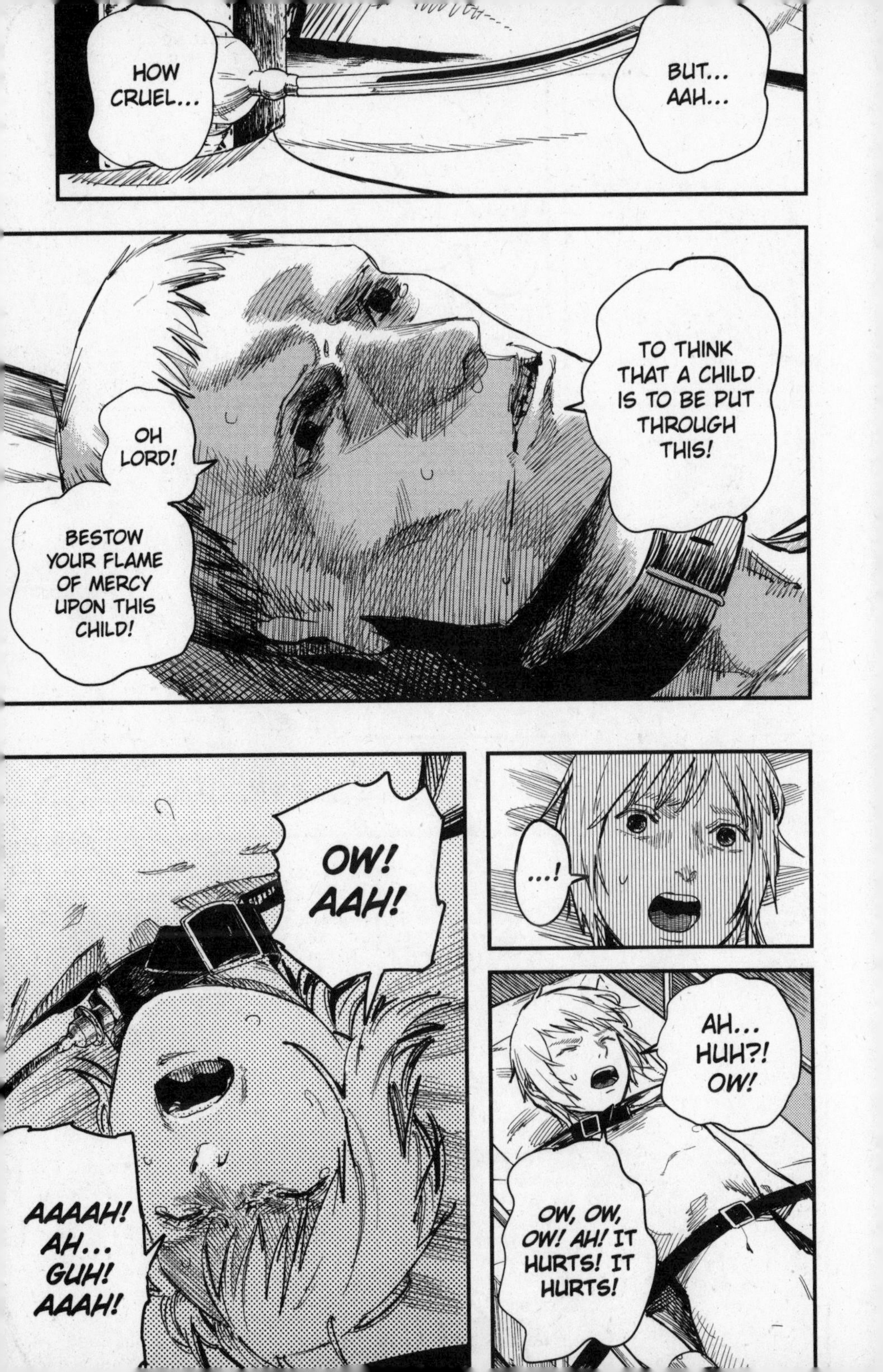
BUT... AAH...
HOW CRUEL...
TO THINK THAT A CHILD IS TO BE PUT THROUGH THIS!
OH LORD!
BESTOW YOUR FLAME OF MERCY UPON THIS CHILD!
...!
AH... HUH?! OW!
OW, OW, OW! AH! IT HURTS! IT HURTS!
OW! AAH!
AAAAH! AH... GUH! AAAH!

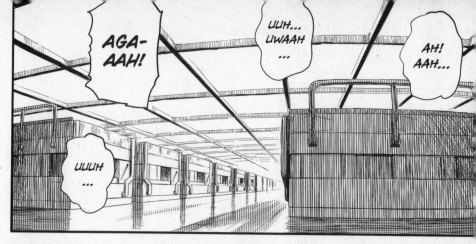

AH! AAH...
UUH... UWAAH ...
AGA-AAH!
UUUH ...
I'LL TELL YOU WHAT THAT IS!
AH!
THEY FEED US SOMETHING PAINFUL... THROUGH THE TUBES IN OUR NECKS.
AND IT—AH!—WRINGS OUR BLESSING OUT OF US!
BZAP
BZAP
THIS PAIN—AAH!—IS SOMETHING YOU WON'T GET USED TO!
BUT IT'S OKAY!

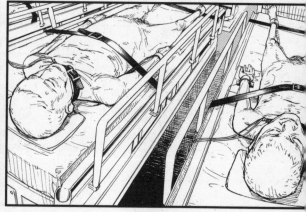

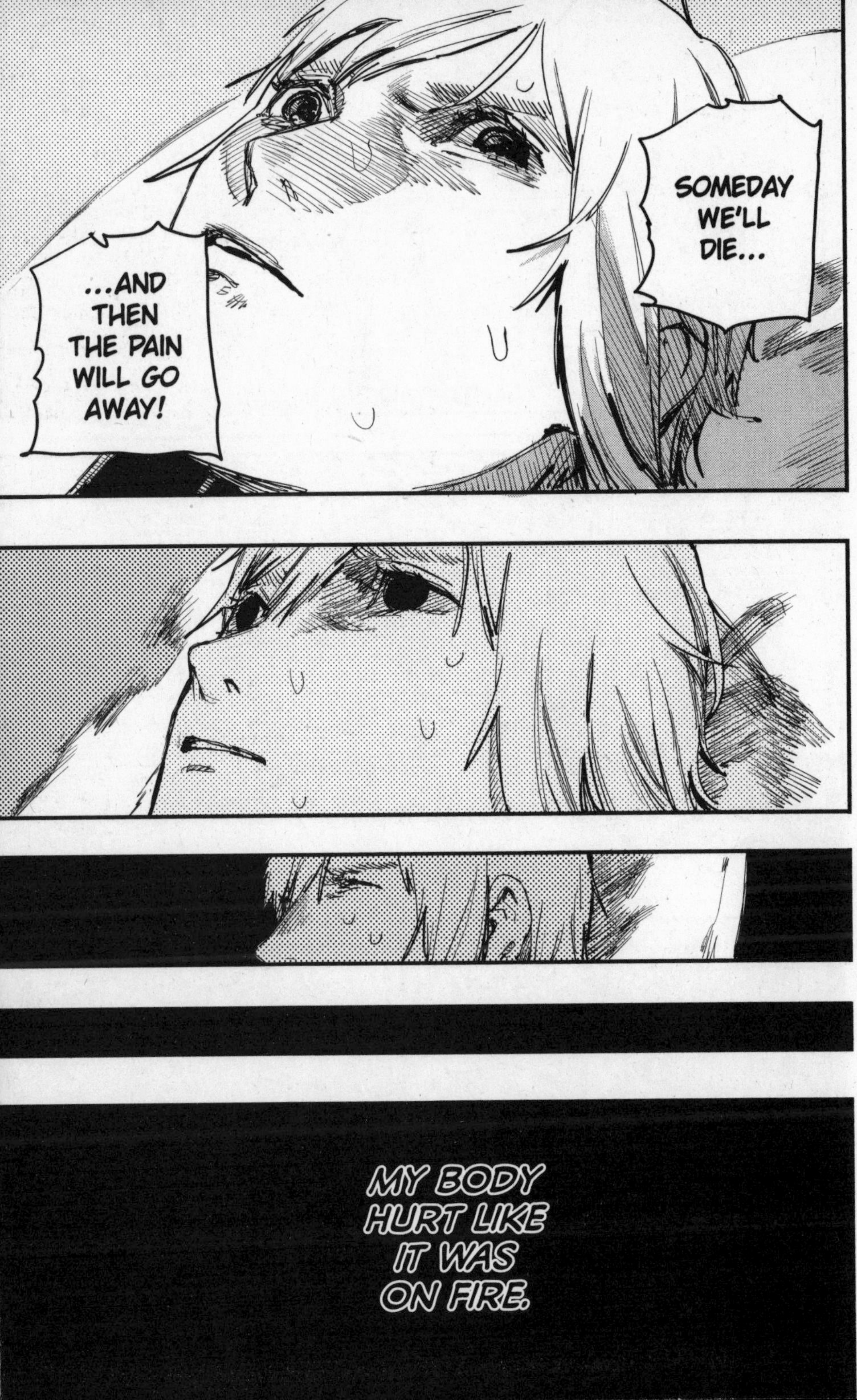
SOMEDAY WE'LL DIE...
...AND THEN THE PAIN WILL GO AWAY!
MY BODY HURT LIKE IT WAS ON FIRE.

WHEN I AWOKE FROM THE EXTRAORDINARY PAIN...
...MY FIRST DAY BEGAN.
ALL DAY LONG, CRYING VOICES FILLED THE ROOM.
WHEN THE PEOPLE CAME IN AT MIDDAY TO TAKE AWAY OUR WASTE, WE KNEW THAT THE DAY WAS HALF OVER.
THE ONLY TIME IT DIDN'T HURT WAS FOR FOUR HOURS...
...DURING WHICH WE SLEPT.

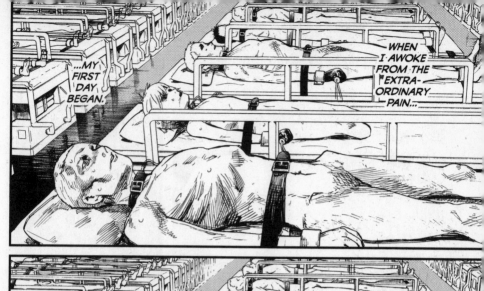

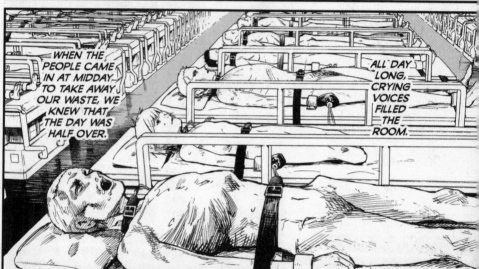

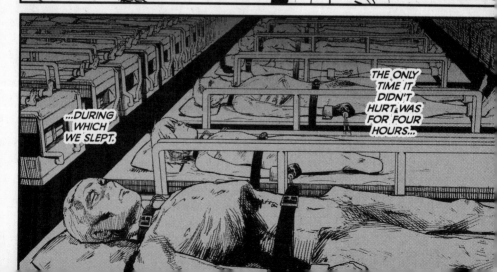

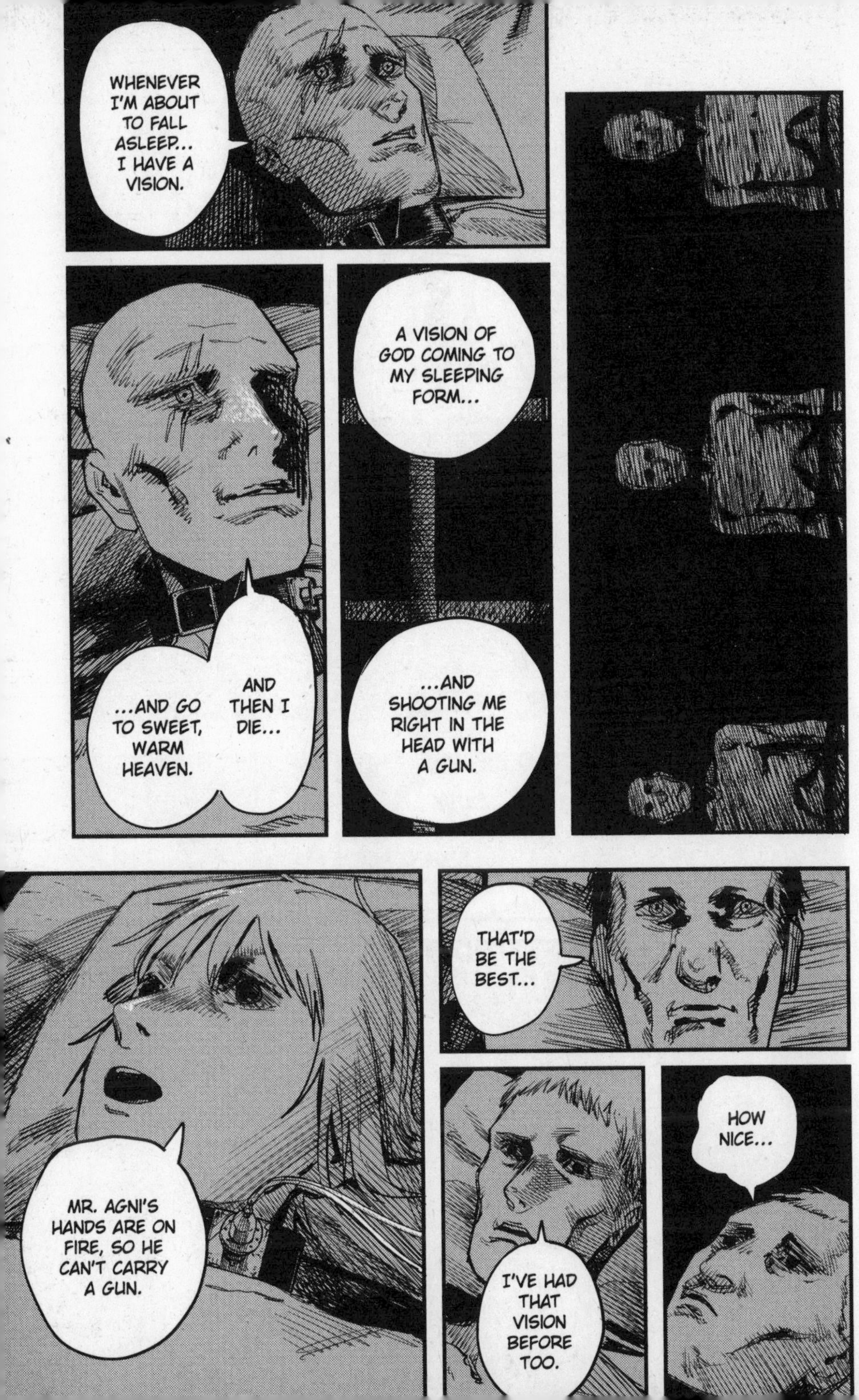
WHENEVER I'M ABOUT TO FALL ASLEEP... I HAVE A VISION.
A VISION OF GOD COMING TO MY SLEEPING FORM...
...AND SHOOTING ME RIGHT IN THE HEAD WITH A GUN.
AND THEN I DIE...
...AND GO TO SWEET, WARM HEAVEN.
THAT'D BE THE BEST...
HOW NICE...
I'VE HAD THAT VISION BEFORE TOO.
MR. AGNI'S HANDS ARE ON FIRE, SO HE CAN'T CARRY A GUN.

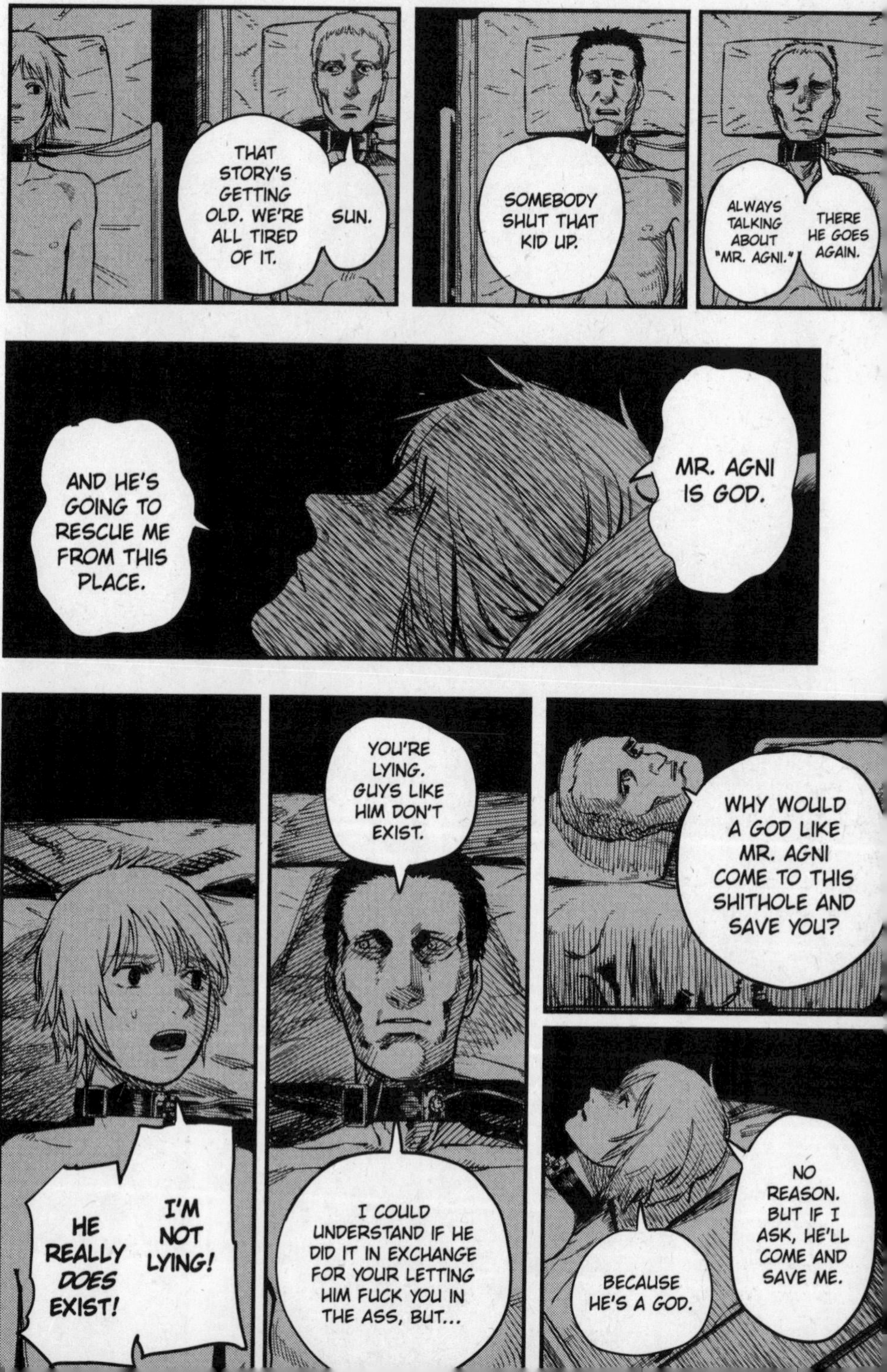
THERE HE GOES AGAIN.
ALWAYS TALKING ABOUT "MR. AGNI."
SOMEBODY SHUT THAT KID UP.
SUN.
THAT STORY'S GETTING OLD. WE'RE ALL TIRED OF IT.
MR. AGNI IS GOD.
AND HE'S GOING TO RESCUE ME FROM THIS PLACE.
WHY WOULD A GOD LIKE MR. AGNI COME TO THIS SHITHOLE AND SAVE YOU?
NO REASON. BUT IF I ASK, HE'LL COME AND SAVE ME.
BECAUSE HE'S A GOD.
YOU'RE LYING. GUYS LIKE HIM DON'T EXIST.
I COULD UNDERSTAND IF HE DID IT IN EXCHANGE FOR YOUR LETTING HIM FUCK YOU IN THE ASS, BUT...
I'M NOT LYING!
HE REALLY *DOES* EXIST!

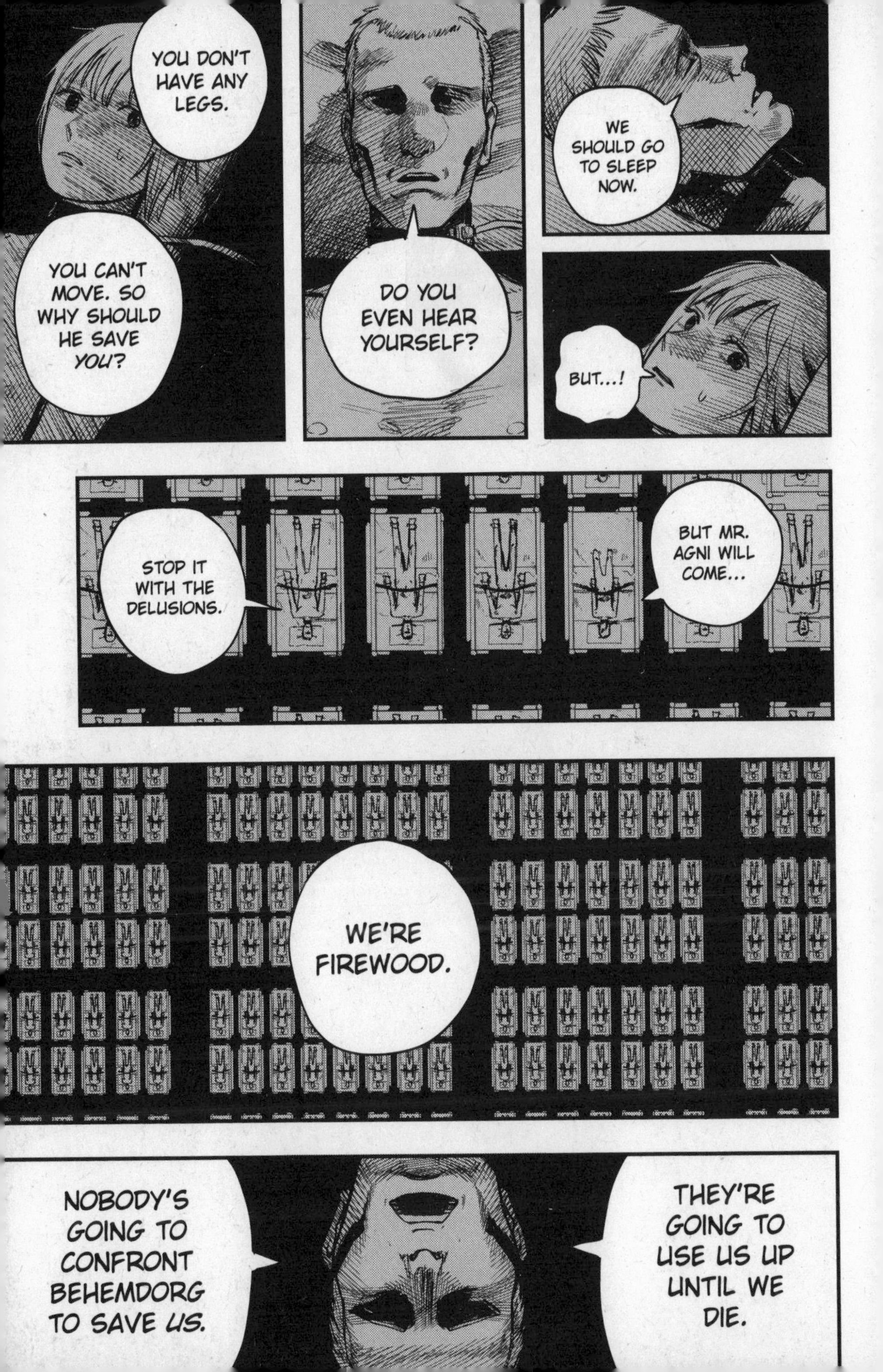
WE SHOULD GO TO SLEEP NOW.
BUT...!
DO YOU EVEN HEAR YOURSELF?
YOU DON'T HAVE ANY LEGS.
YOU CAN'T MOVE. SO WHY SHOULD HE SAVE *YOU*?
BUT MR. AGNI WILL COME...
STOP IT WITH THE DELUSIONS.
WE'RE FIREWOOD.
THEY'RE GOING TO USE US UP UNTIL WE DIE.
NOBODY'S GOING TO CONFRONT BEHEMDORG TO SAVE *US*.

ALL WE CAN HOPE FOR HERE...

...IS DEATH.

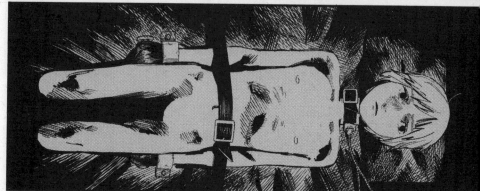

I'M... NOT FIRE-WOOD.

NONE OF US ARE.

WE'RE PEOPLE.

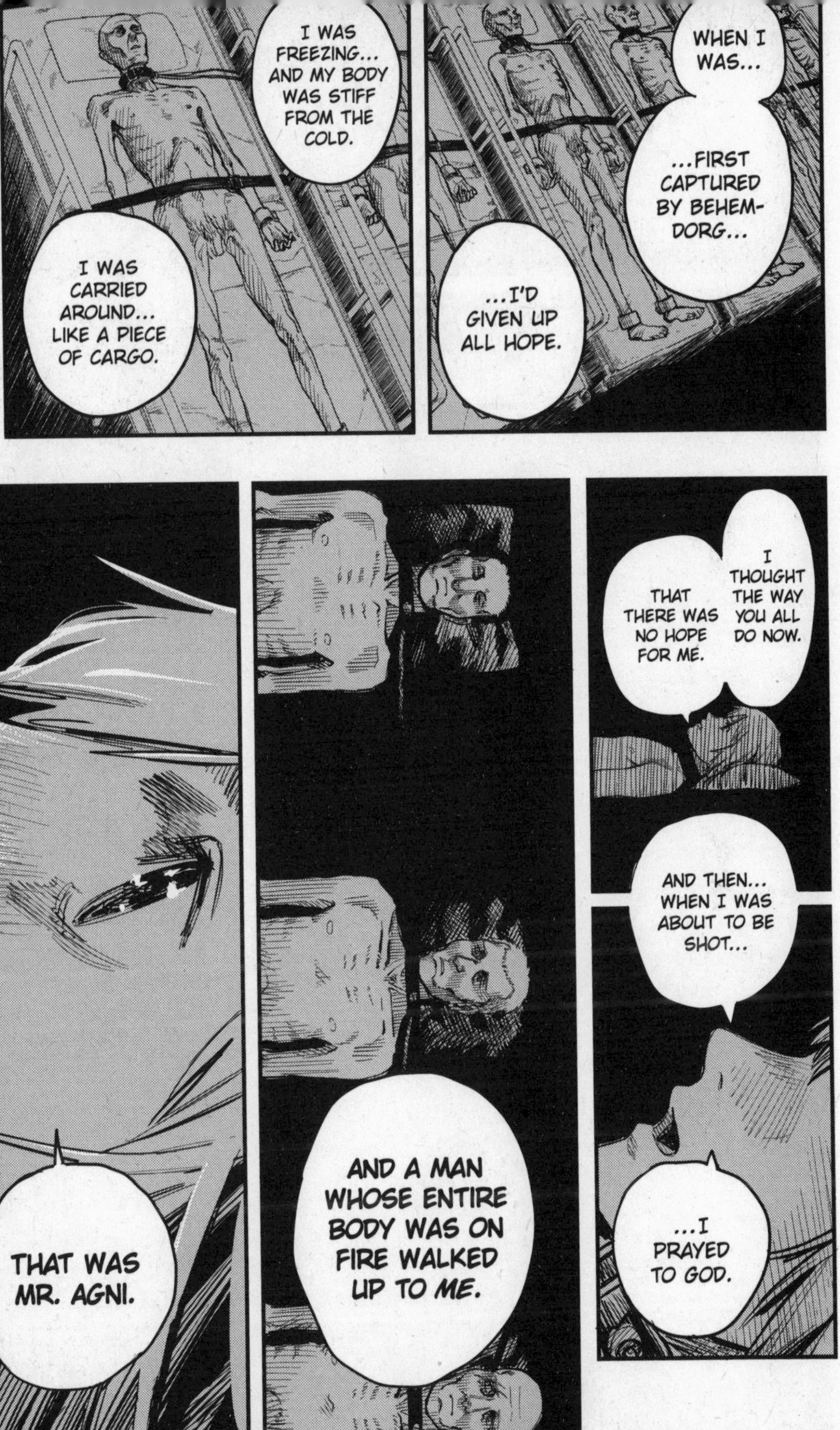
WHEN I WAS...
...FIRST CAPTURED BY BEHEM-DORG...
...I'D GIVEN UP ALL HOPE.
I WAS FREEZING... AND MY BODY WAS STIFF FROM THE COLD.
I WAS CARRIED AROUND... LIKE A PIECE OF CARGO.
I THOUGHT THE WAY YOU ALL DO NOW.
THAT THERE WAS NO HOPE FOR ME.
AND THEN... WHEN I WAS ABOUT TO BE SHOT...
...I PRAYED TO GOD.
AND A MAN WHOSE ENTIRE BODY WAS ON FIRE WALKED UP TO *ME*.
THAT WAS MR. AGNI.

A BLESSED...

...WHOSE ENTIRE BODY IS FLAMES?!

KEEP IT DOWN! I CAN'T GET TO SLEEP!

FLAMES...

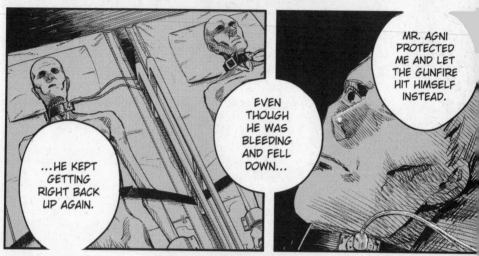

MR. AGNI PROTECTED ME AND LET THE GUNFIRE HIT HIMSELF INSTEAD.

EVEN THOUGH HE WAS BLEEDING AND FELL DOWN...

...HE KEPT GETTING RIGHT BACK UP AGAIN.

HE CLENCHED HIS FISTS...

...AND FOUGHT.

EVEN THOUGH I DON'T HAVE LEGS...

...AND MY BODY WILL HURT TOMORROW LIKE IT'S ON FIRE...

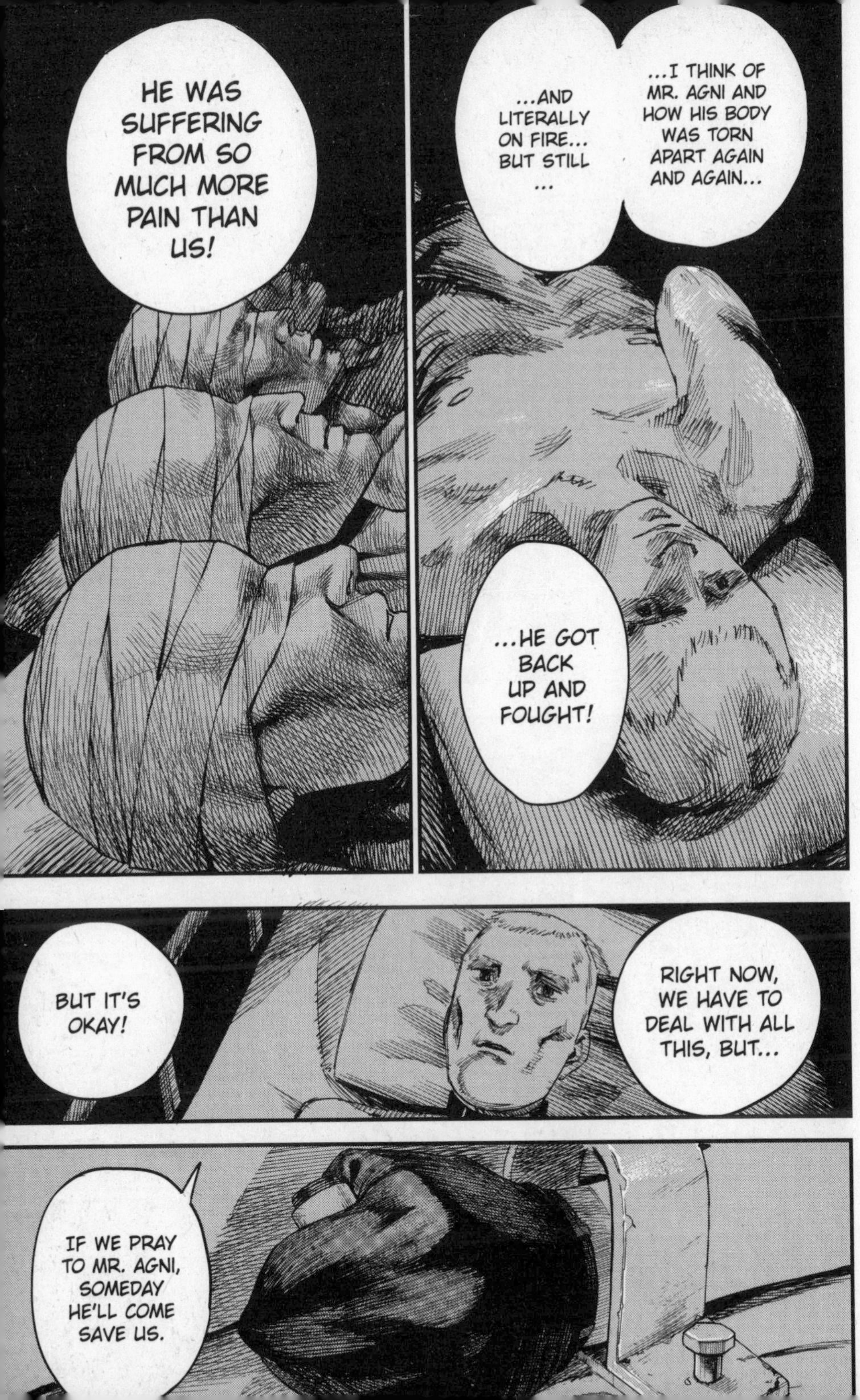
...I THINK OF MR. AGNI AND HOW HIS BODY WAS TORN APART AGAIN AND AGAIN...
...AND LITERALLY ON FIRE... BUT STILL ...
...HE GOT BACK UP AND FOUGHT!
HE WAS SUFFERING FROM SO MUCH MORE PAIN THAN US!
RIGHT NOW, WE HAVE TO DEAL WITH ALL THIS, BUT...
BUT IT'S OKAY!
IF WE PRAY TO MR. AGNI, SOMEDAY HE'LL COME SAVE US.

BECAUSE MR. AGNI'S A GOD!

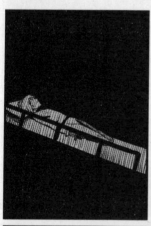

I'M SORRY. I'LL GO TO SLEEP NOW.

HEY.

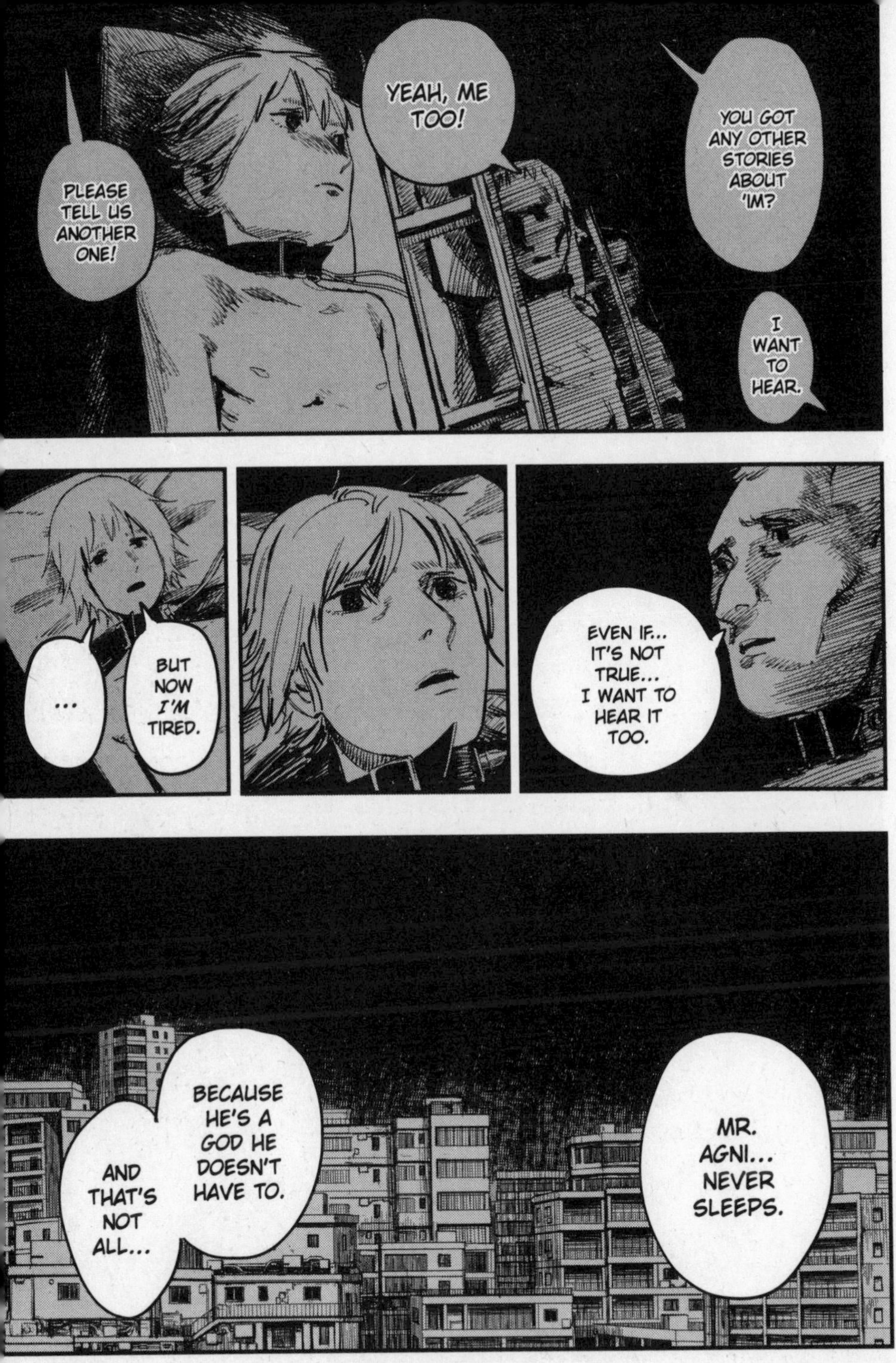
YOU GOT ANY OTHER STORIES ABOUT 'IM?
I WANT TO HEAR.
YEAH, ME TOO!
PLEASE TELL US ANOTHER ONE!
EVEN IF... IT'S NOT TRUE... I WANT TO HEAR IT TOO.
BUT NOW *I'M* TIRED.
...
MR. AGNI... NEVER SLEEPS.
BECAUSE HE'S A GOD HE DOESN'T HAVE TO.
AND THAT'S NOT ALL...

AAAEEH!

AAAAAH!

HUH? WHAT THE...?

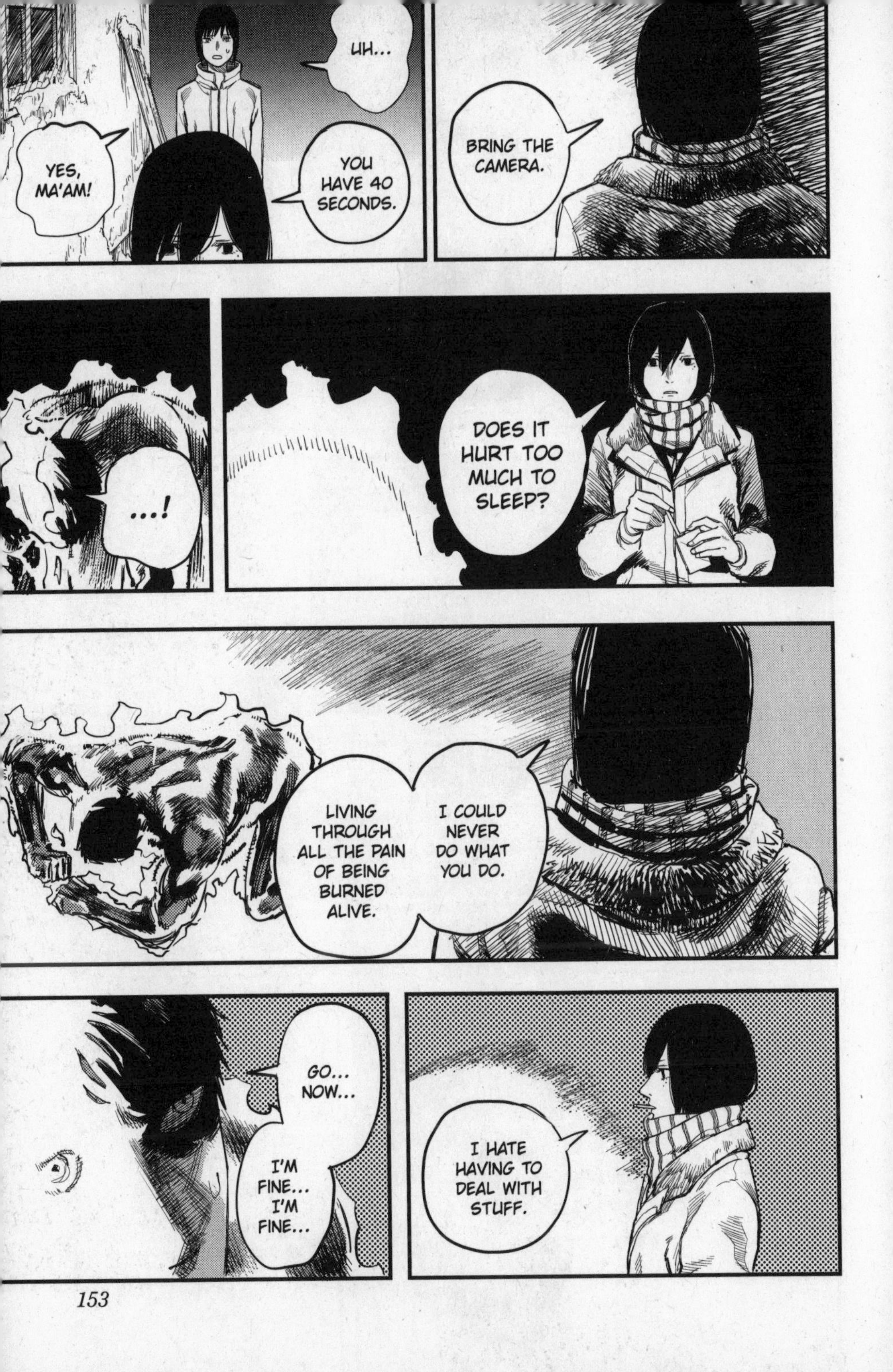
BRING THE CAMERA.
UH...
YOU HAVE 40 SECONDS.
YES, MA'AM!
DOES IT HURT TOO MUCH TO SLEEP?
...!
I COULD NEVER DO WHAT YOU DO.
LIVING THROUGH ALL THE PAIN OF BEING BURNED ALIVE.
I HATE HAVING TO DEAL WITH STUFF.
GO... NOW...
I'M FINE... I'M FINE...

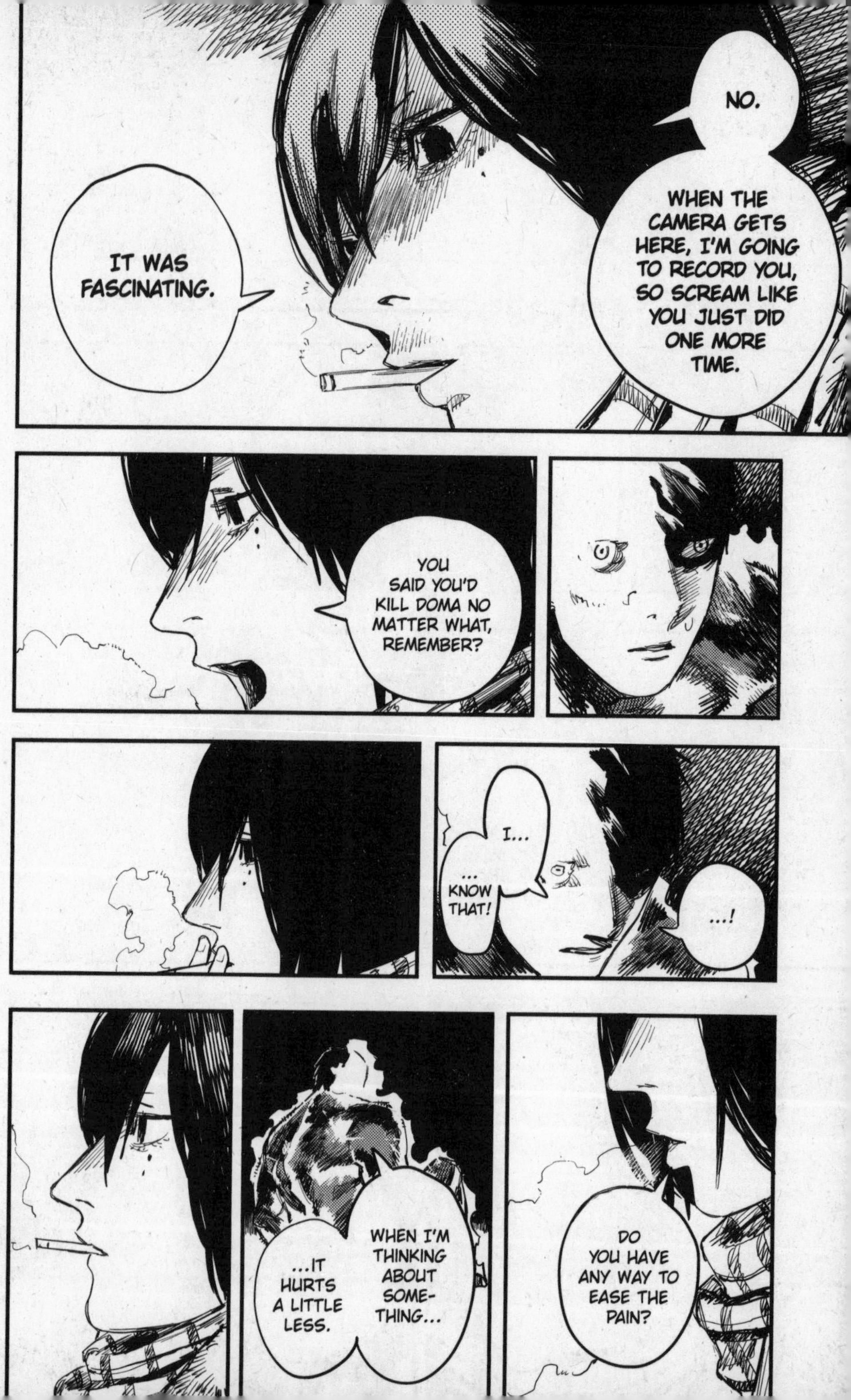
NO.
WHEN THE CAMERA GETS HERE, I'M GOING TO RECORD YOU, SO SCREAM LIKE YOU JUST DID ONE MORE TIME.
IT WAS FASCINATING.
YOU SAID YOU'D KILL DOMA NO MATTER WHAT, REMEMBER?
...!
I...
...KNOW THAT!
DO YOU HAVE ANY WAY TO EASE THE PAIN?
WHEN I'M THINKING ABOUT SOME-THING...
...IT HURTS A LITTLE LESS.

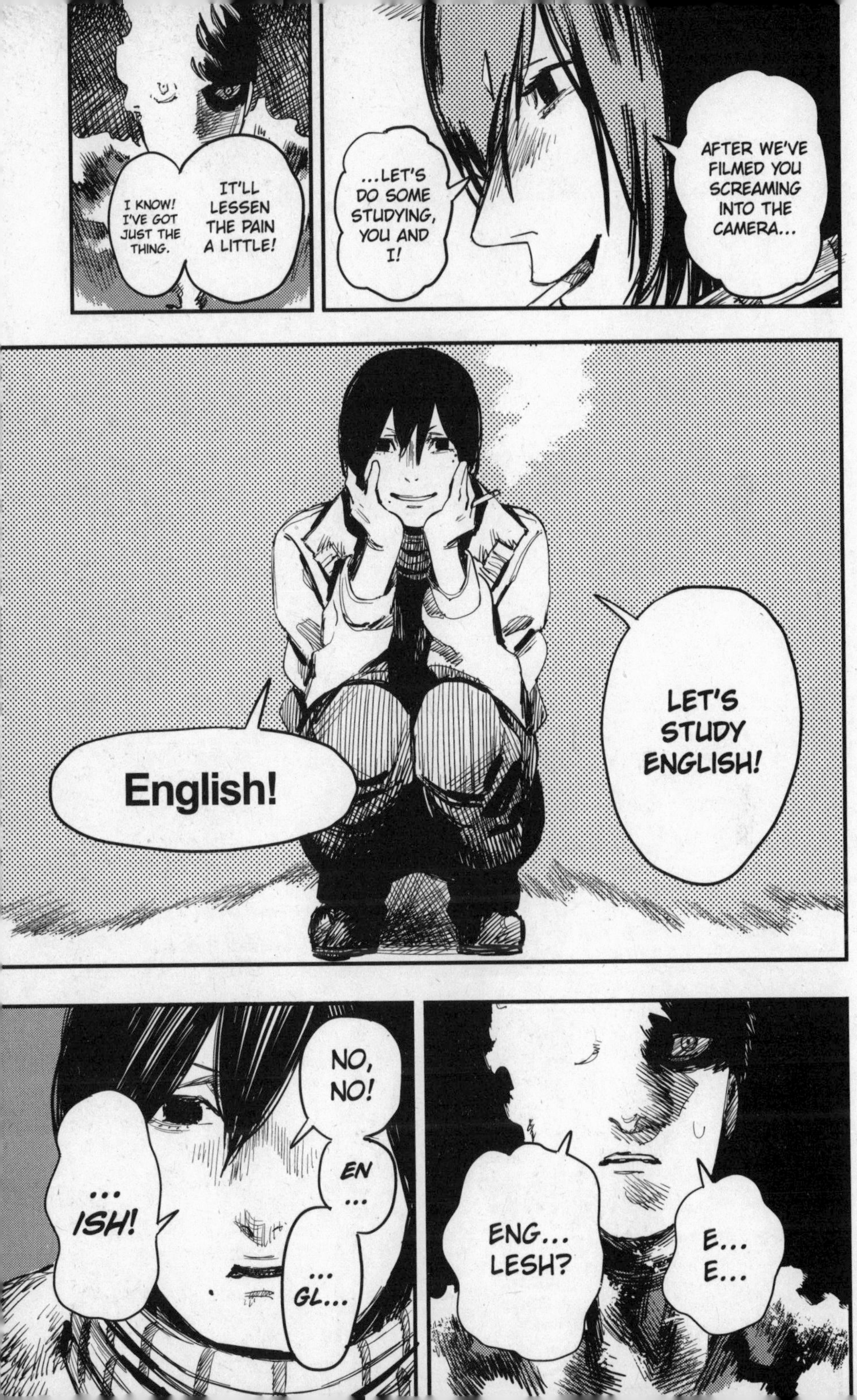
AFTER WE'VE FILMED YOU SCREAMING INTO THE CAMERA...
...LET'S DO SOME STUDYING, YOU AND I!
IT'LL LESSEN THE PAIN A LITTLE!
I KNOW! I'VE GOT JUST THE THING.
LET'S STUDY ENGLISH!
English!
E... E...
ENG... LESH?
NO, NO!
EN...
...GL...
...ISH!

FIRE PUNCH

CHAPTER 16

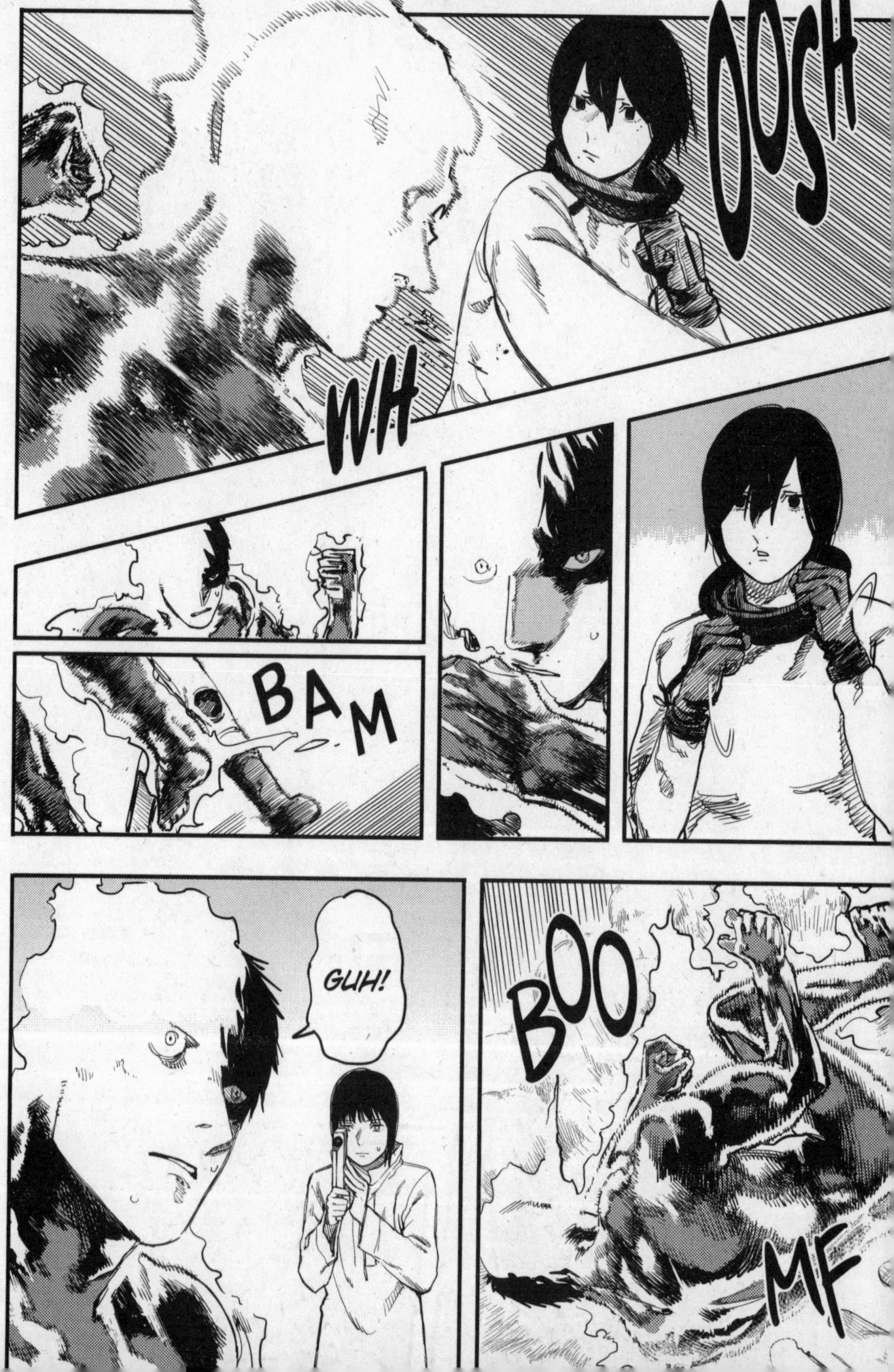
WH OOSH
BAM
BOO MF
GUH!

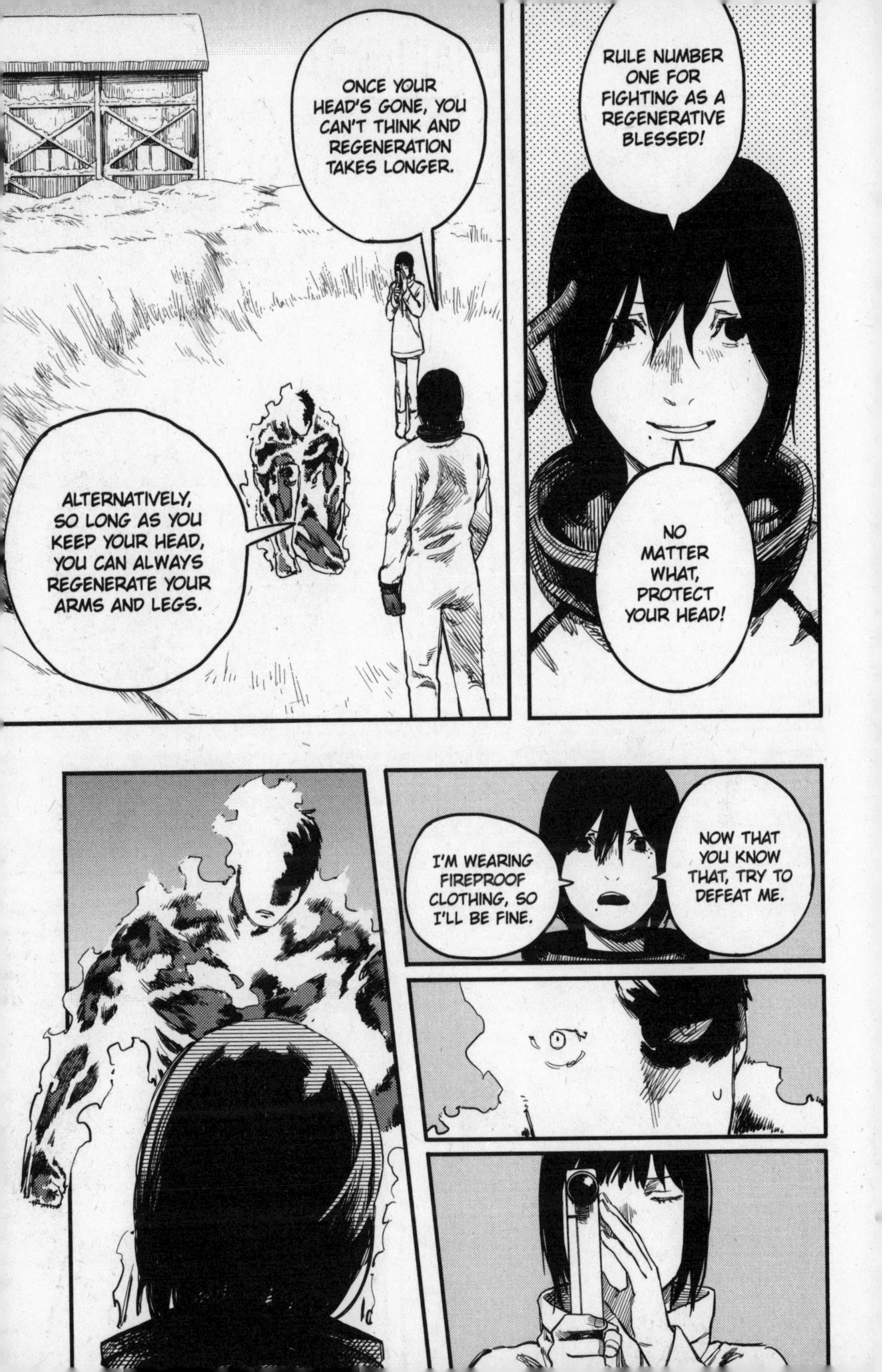
RULE NUMBER ONE FOR FIGHTING AS A REGENERATIVE BLESSED!
NO MATTER WHAT, PROTECT YOUR HEAD!
ONCE YOUR HEAD'S GONE, YOU CAN'T THINK AND REGENERATION TAKES LONGER.
ALTERNATIVELY, SO LONG AS YOU KEEP YOUR HEAD, YOU CAN ALWAYS REGENERATE YOUR ARMS AND LEGS.
NOW THAT YOU KNOW THAT, TRY TO DEFEAT ME.
I'M WEARING FIREPROOF CLOTHING, SO I'LL BE FINE.

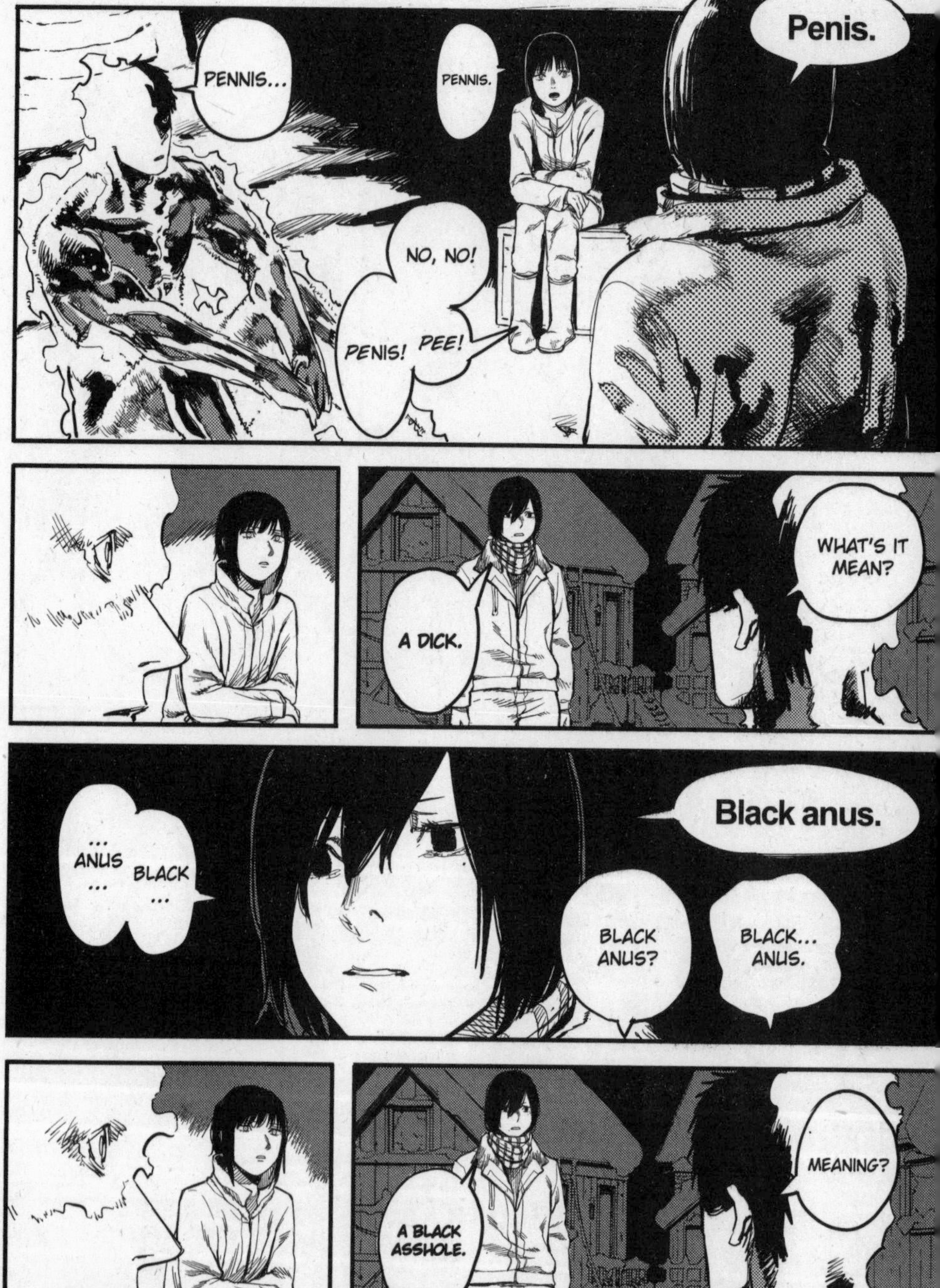
Penis.
PENNIS.
PENNIS...
NO, NO! PEE! PENIS!
WHAT'S IT MEAN?
A DICK.
Black anus.
BLACK... ANUS.
BLACK ANUS?
... ANUS ... BLACK ...
MEANING?
A BLACK ASSHOLE.

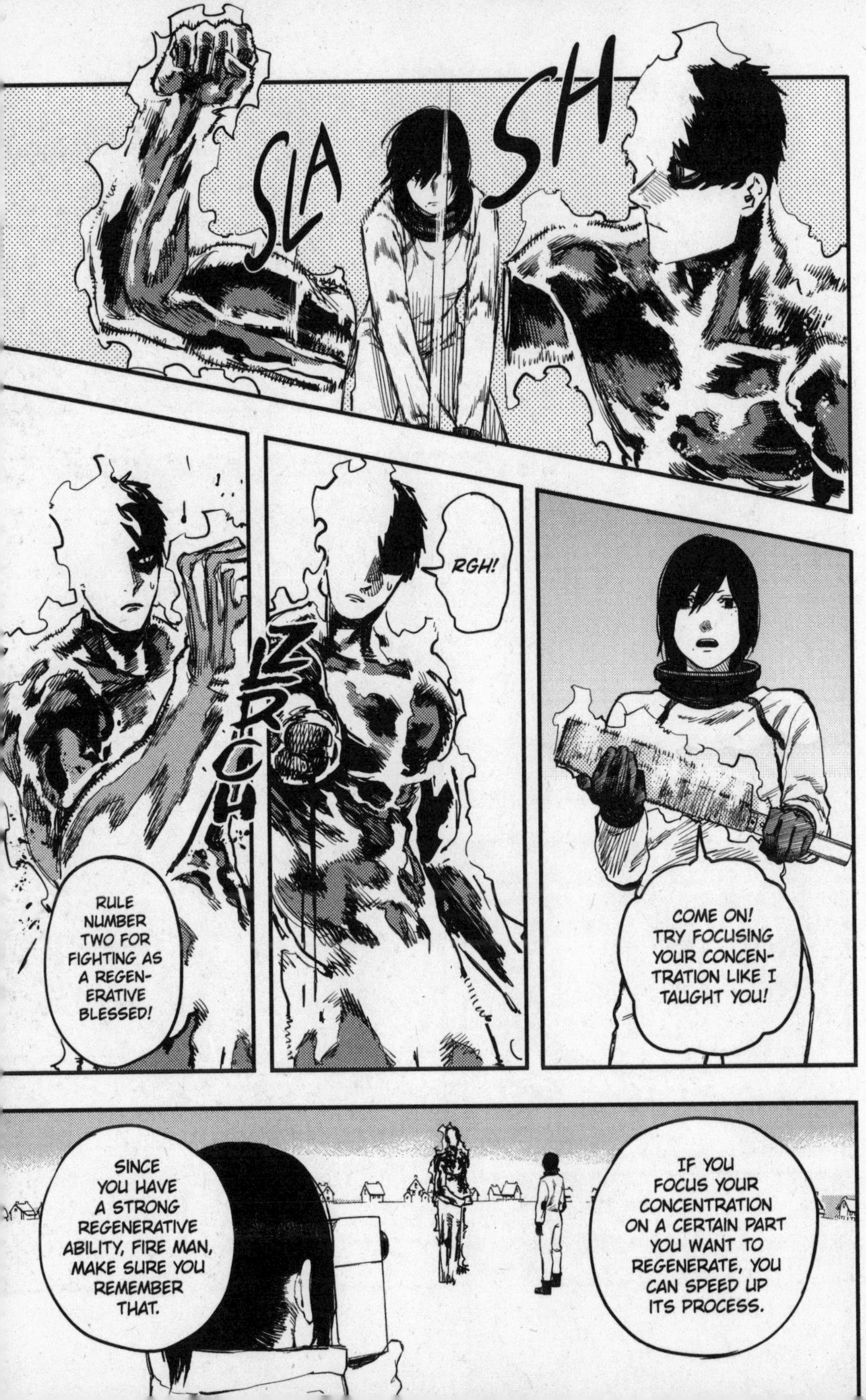
SLASH
COME ON! TRY FOCUSING YOUR CONCEN-TRATION LIKE I TAUGHT YOU!
RGH!
ZRCH
RULE NUMBER TWO FOR FIGHTING AS A REGEN-ERATIVE BLESSED!
IF YOU FOCUS YOUR CONCENTRATION ON A CERTAIN PART YOU WANT TO REGENERATE, YOU CAN SPEED UP ITS PROCESS.
SINCE YOU HAVE A STRONG REGENERATIVE ABILITY, FIRE MAN, MAKE SURE YOU REMEMBER THAT.

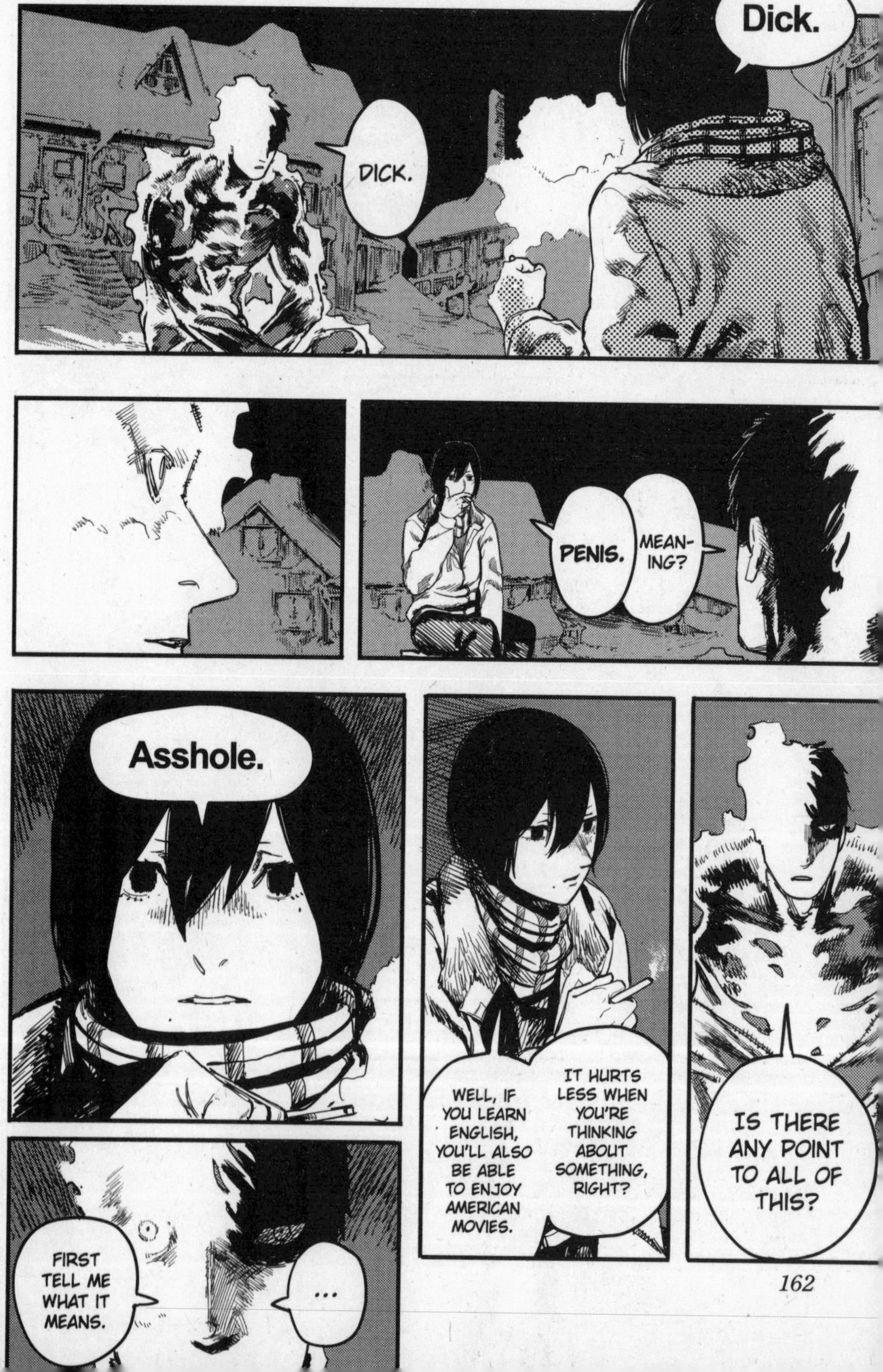
Dick.
DICK.
MEAN-ING?
PENIS.
IS THERE ANY POINT TO ALL OF THIS?
IT HURTS LESS WHEN YOU'RE THINKING ABOUT SOMETHING, RIGHT?
WELL, IF YOU LEARN ENGLISH, YOU'LL ALSO BE ABLE TO ENJOY AMERICAN MOVIES.
Asshole.
...
FIRST TELL ME WHAT IT MEANS.

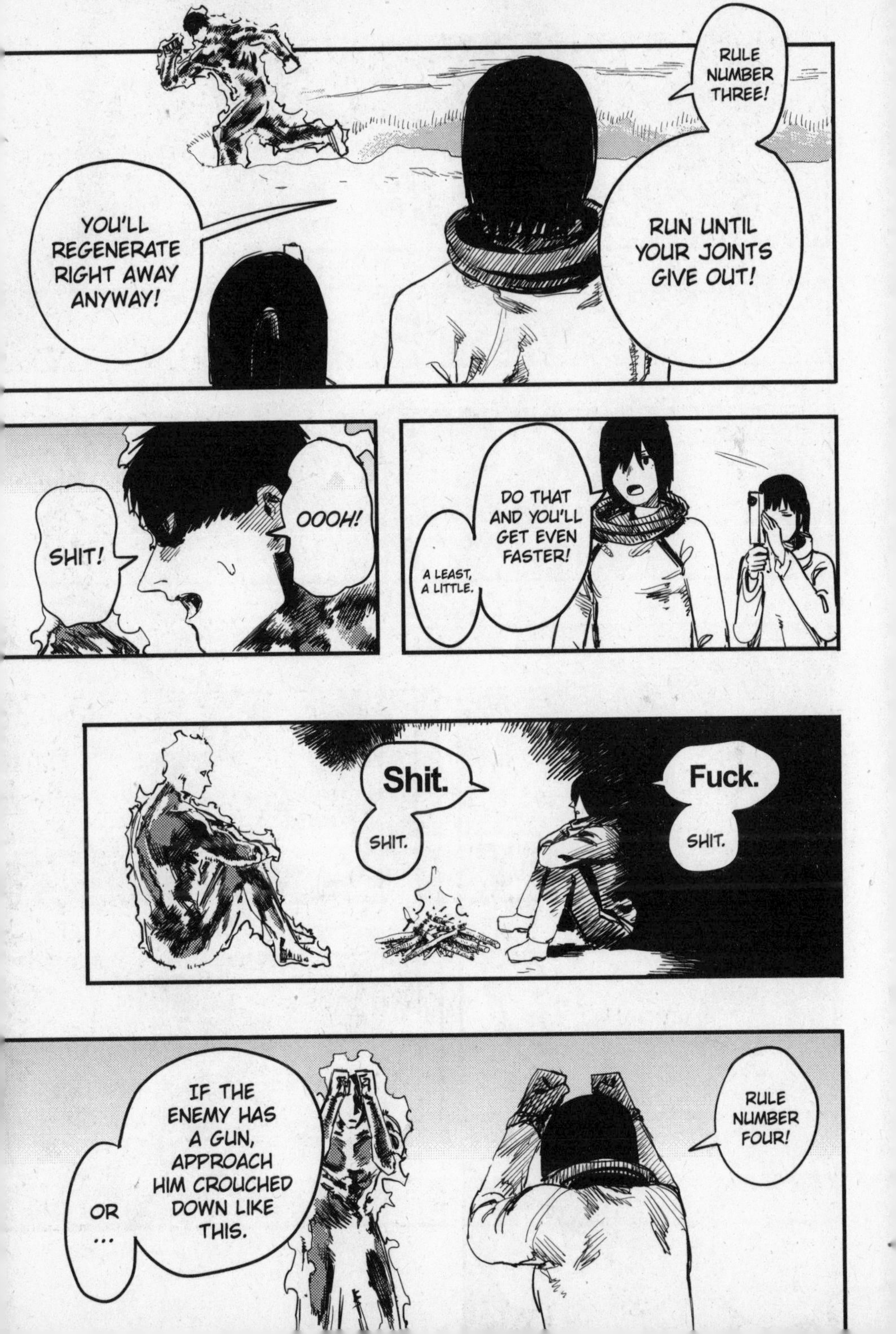
RULE NUMBER THREE!
RUN UNTIL YOUR JOINTS GIVE OUT!
YOU'LL REGENERATE RIGHT AWAY ANYWAY!
DO THAT AND YOU'LL GET EVEN FASTER!
A LEAST, A LITTLE.
OOOH!
SHIT!
Fuck.
SHIT.
Shit.
SHIT.
RULE NUMBER FOUR!
IF THE ENEMY HAS A GUN, APPROACH HIM CROUCHED DOWN LIKE THIS.
OR ...

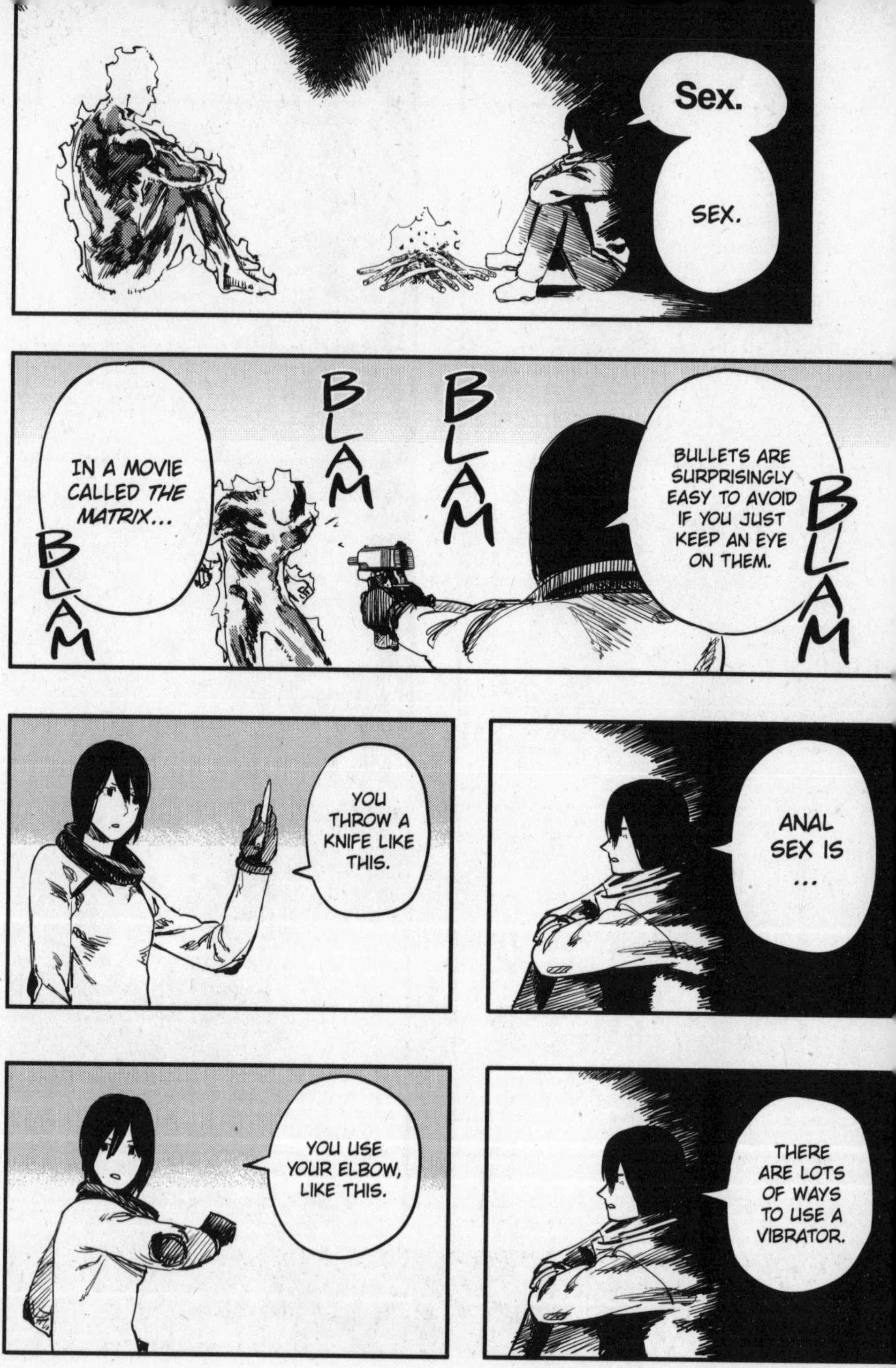
Sex.
SEX.
BLAM
BULLETS ARE SURPRISINGLY EASY TO AVOID IF YOU JUST KEEP AN EYE ON THEM.
BLAM
BLAM
IN A MOVIE CALLED *THE MATRIX*...
BLAM
ANAL SEX IS ...
YOU THROW A KNIFE LIKE THIS.
THERE ARE LOTS OF WAYS TO USE A VIBRATOR.
YOU USE YOUR ELBOW, LIKE THIS.

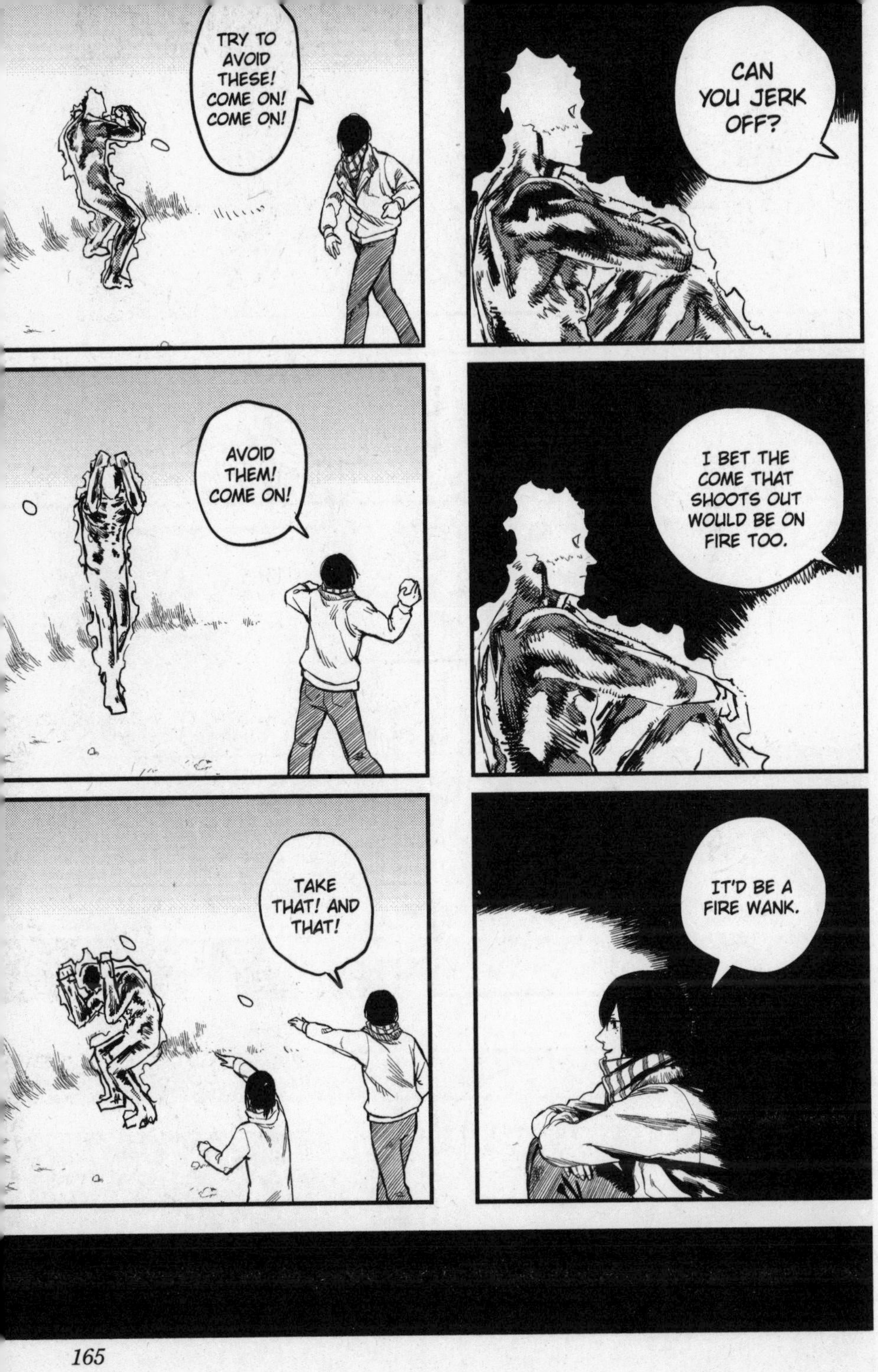
CAN YOU JERK OFF?
TRY TO AVOID THESE! COME ON! COME ON!
I BET THE COME THAT SHOOTS OUT WOULD BE ON FIRE TOO.
AVOID THEM! COME ON!
IT'D BE A FIRE WANK.
TAKE THAT! AND THAT!

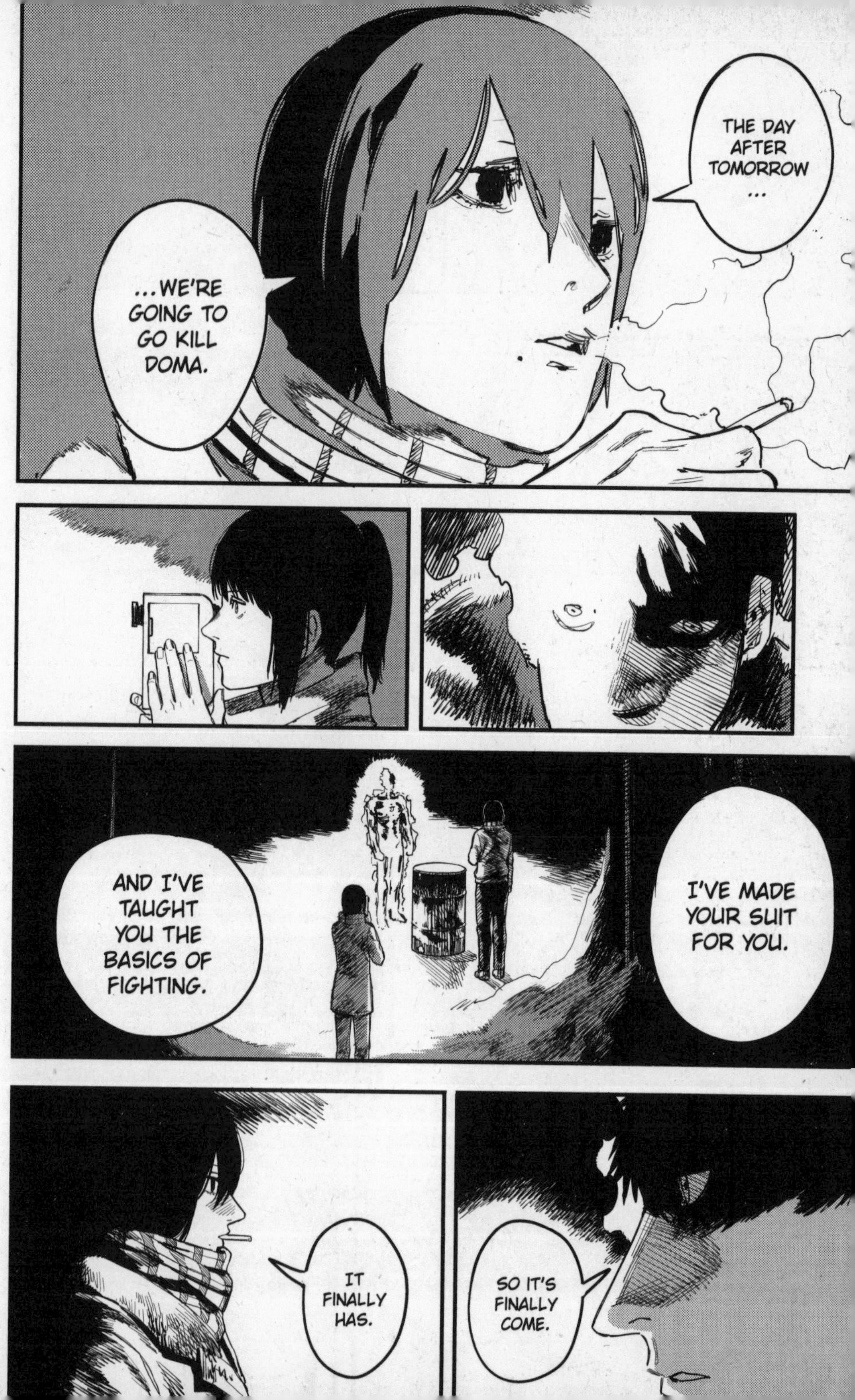
THE DAY AFTER TOMORROW...
...WE'RE GOING TO GO KILL DOMA.
I'VE MADE YOUR SUIT FOR YOU.
AND I'VE TAUGHT YOU THE BASICS OF FIGHTING.
SO IT'S FINALLY COME.
IT FINALLY HAS.

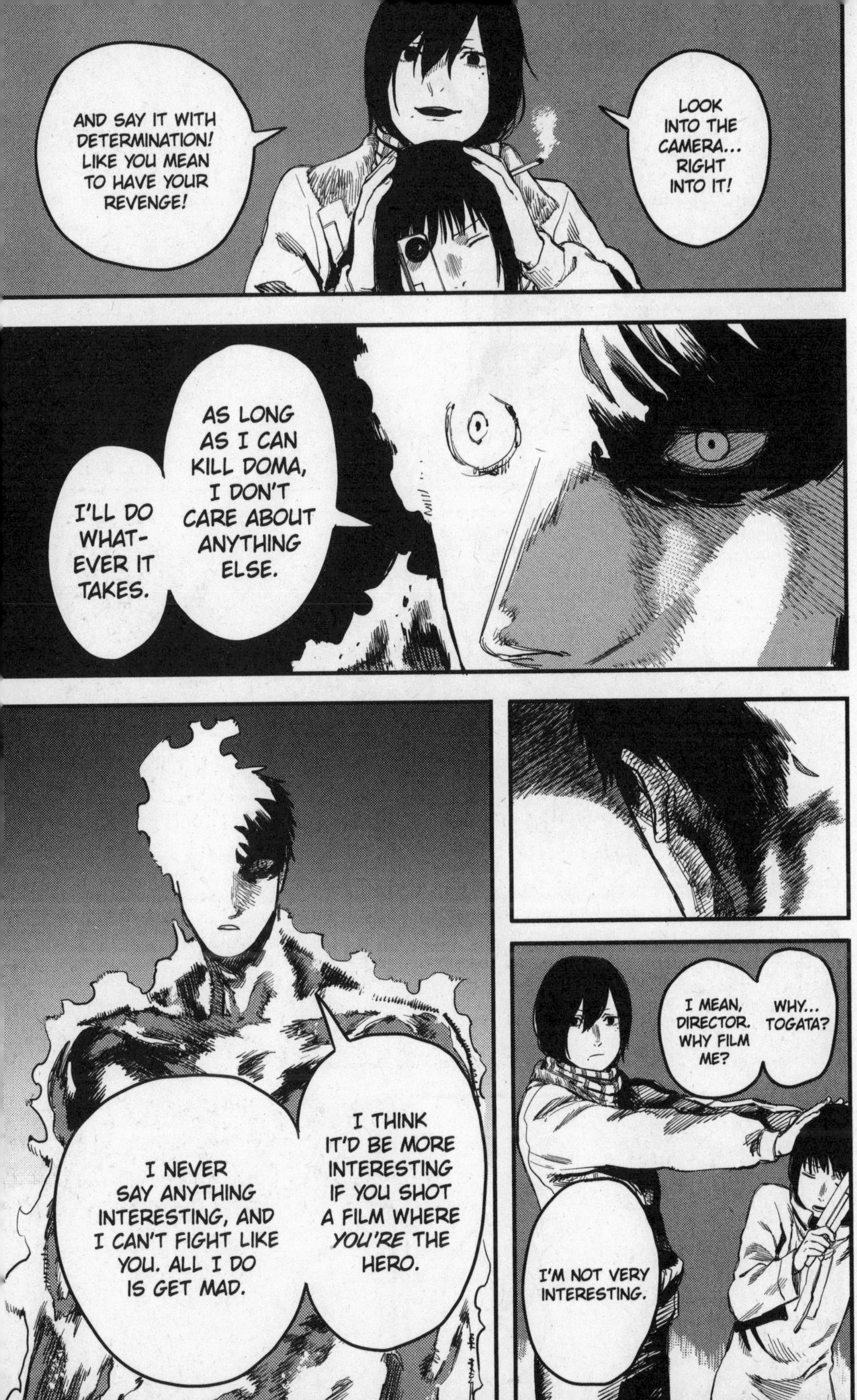
LOOK INTO THE CAMERA... RIGHT INTO IT!
AND SAY IT WITH DETERMINATION! LIKE YOU MEAN TO HAVE YOUR REVENGE!
AS LONG AS I CAN KILL DOMA, I DON'T CARE ABOUT ANYTHING ELSE.
I'LL DO WHATEVER IT TAKES.
WHY... TOGATA?
I MEAN, DIRECTOR. WHY FILM ME?
I'M NOT VERY INTERESTING.
I THINK IT'D BE MORE INTERESTING IF YOU SHOT A FILM WHERE *YOU'RE* THE HERO.
I NEVER SAY ANYTHING INTERESTING, AND I CAN'T FIGHT LIKE YOU. ALL I DO IS GET MAD.

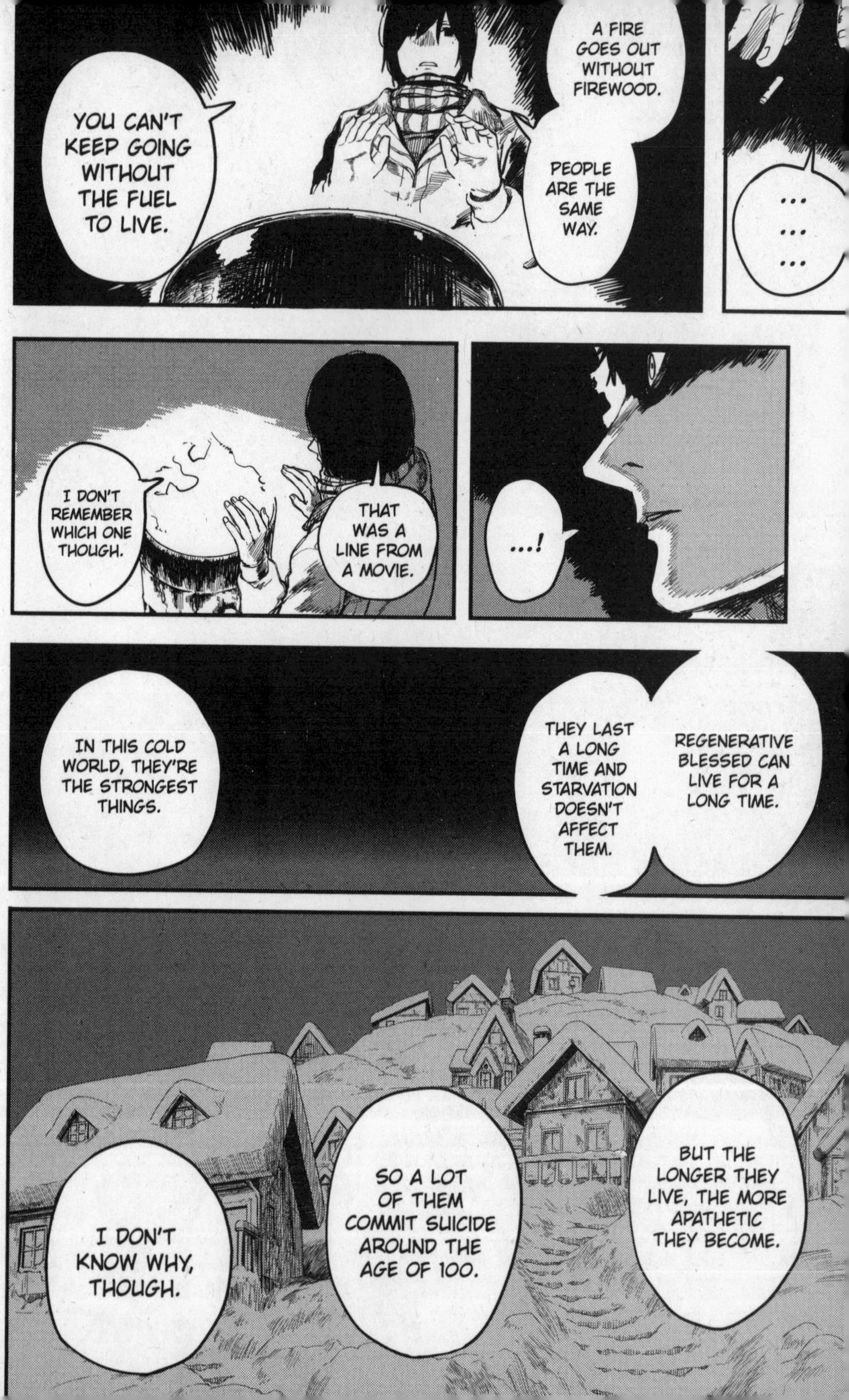
...
...
...
A FIRE GOES OUT WITHOUT FIREWOOD.
PEOPLE ARE THE SAME WAY.
YOU CAN'T KEEP GOING WITHOUT THE FUEL TO LIVE.
...!
THAT WAS A LINE FROM A MOVIE.
I DON'T REMEMBER WHICH ONE THOUGH.
REGENERATIVE BLESSED CAN LIVE FOR A LONG TIME.
THEY LAST A LONG TIME AND STARVATION DOESN'T AFFECT THEM.
IN THIS COLD WORLD, THEY'RE THE STRONGEST THINGS.
BUT THE LONGER THEY LIVE, THE MORE APATHETIC THEY BECOME.
SO A LOT OF THEM COMMIT SUICIDE AROUND THE AGE OF 100.
I DON'T KNOW WHY, THOUGH.

THE REASON I'VE BEEN ABLE TO LIVE FOR 300 YEARS IS THANKS TO MOVIES.
MOVIES ARE INCREDIBLE.
THEY TELL ALL SORTS OF STORIES.
YOU MEET ALL KINDS OF CHARACTERS.
ANYTHING CAN HAPPEN IN THEM.
A BLACK MAN CAN BE KILLED DUE TO DISCRIMINATION.
A LIFE CAN GO DOWN THE DRAIN DUE TO DRUGS.
SOMEONE CAN SHOOT THEIR OWN CHILD TO DEATH!
AS LONG AS IT'S INTERESTING, ANYTHING GOES...
...IN MOVIES.

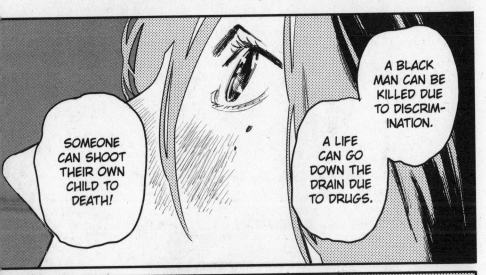

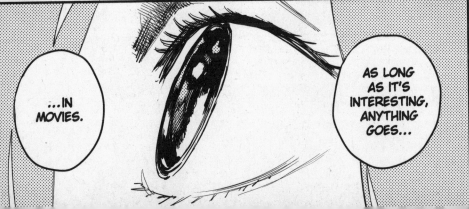

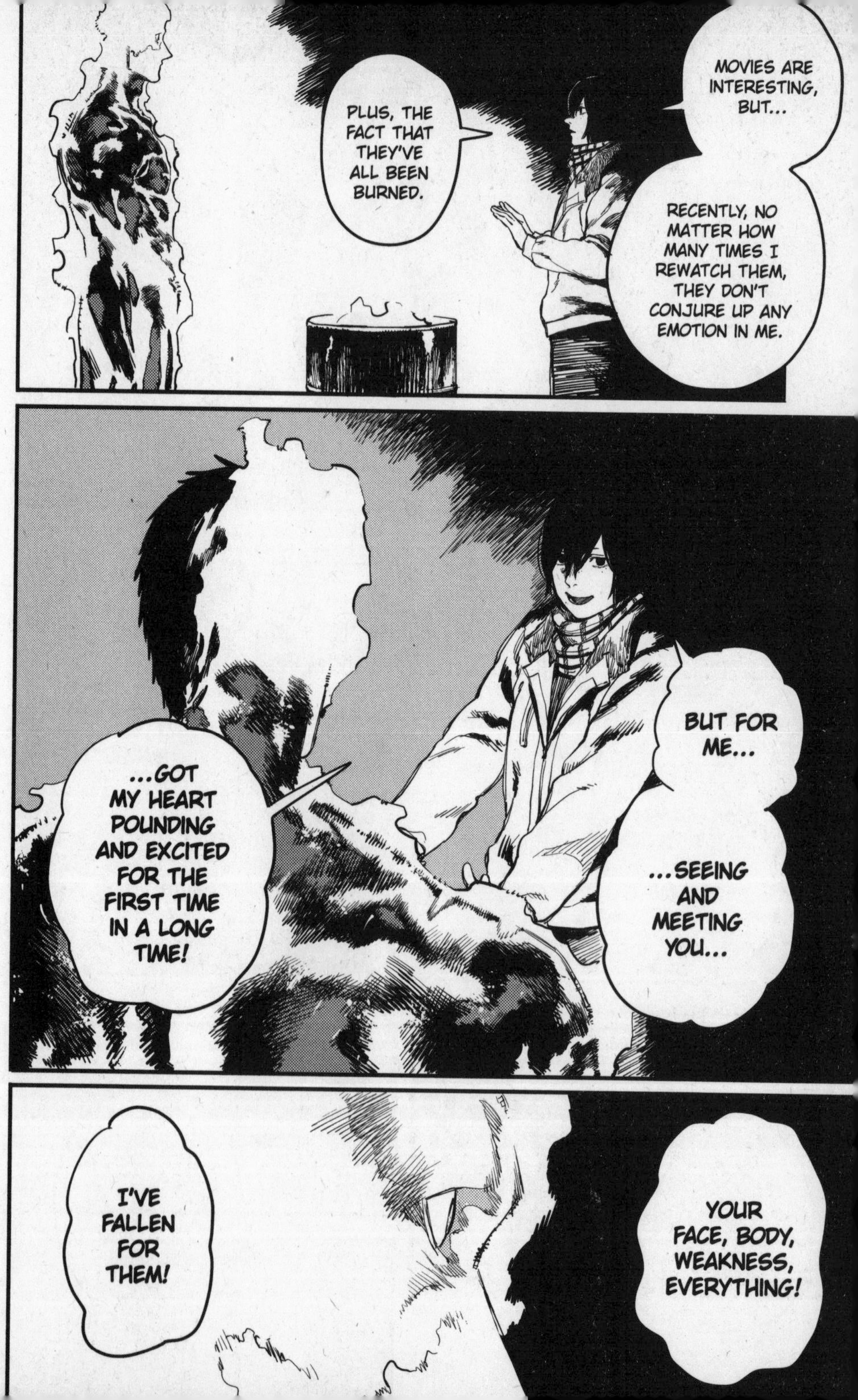
MOVIES ARE INTERESTING, BUT...
RECENTLY, NO MATTER HOW MANY TIMES I REWATCH THEM, THEY DON'T CONJURE UP ANY EMOTION IN ME.
PLUS, THE FACT THAT THEY'VE ALL BEEN BURNED.
BUT FOR ME...
...SEEING AND MEETING YOU...
...GOT MY HEART POUNDING AND EXCITED FOR THE FIRST TIME IN A LONG TIME!
YOUR FACE, BODY, WEAKNESS, EVERYTHING!
I'VE FALLEN FOR THEM!

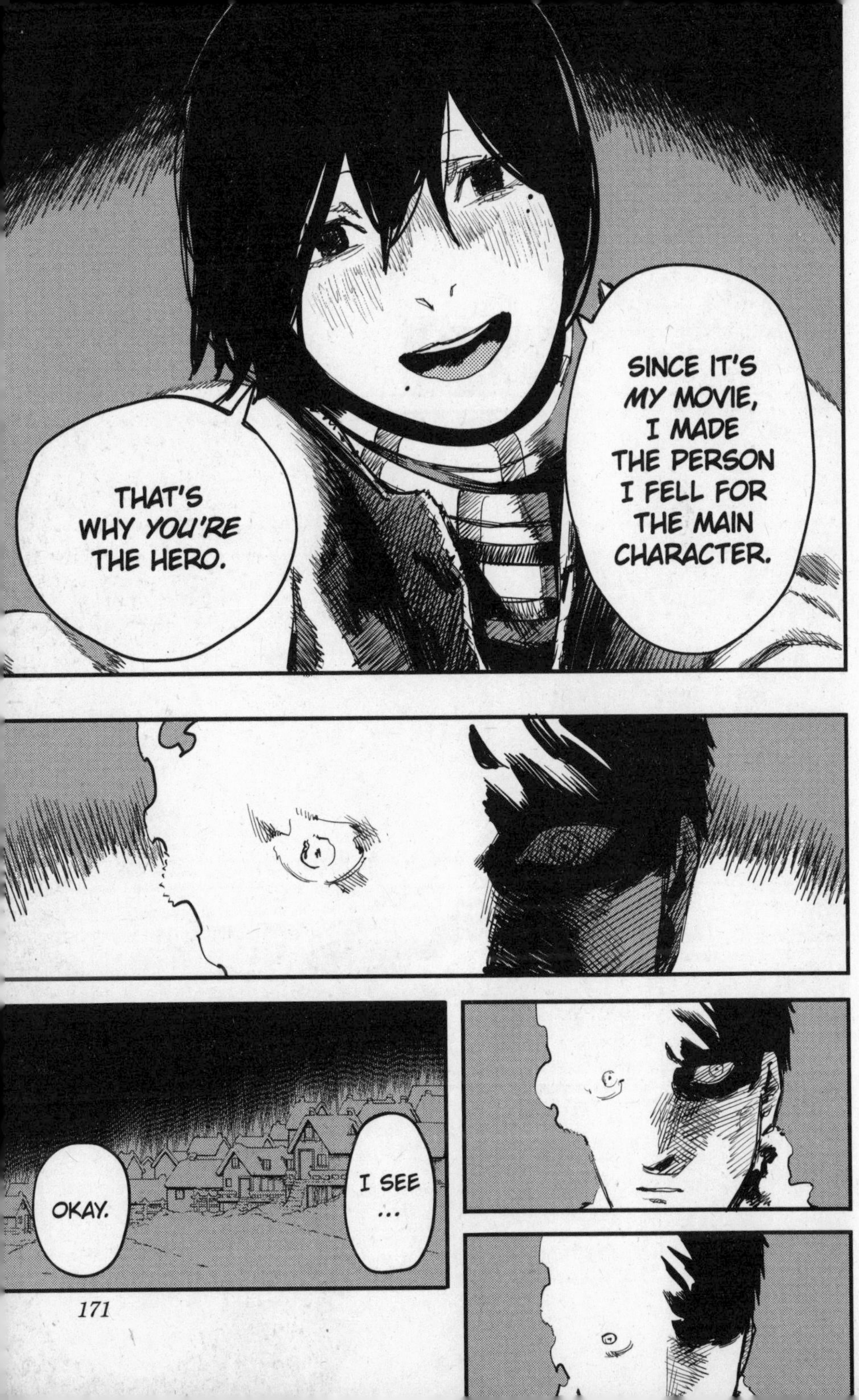
SINCE IT'S *MY* MOVIE, I MADE THE PERSON I FELL FOR THE MAIN CHARACTER.
THAT'S WHY *YOU'RE* THE HERO.
I SEE ...
OKAY.

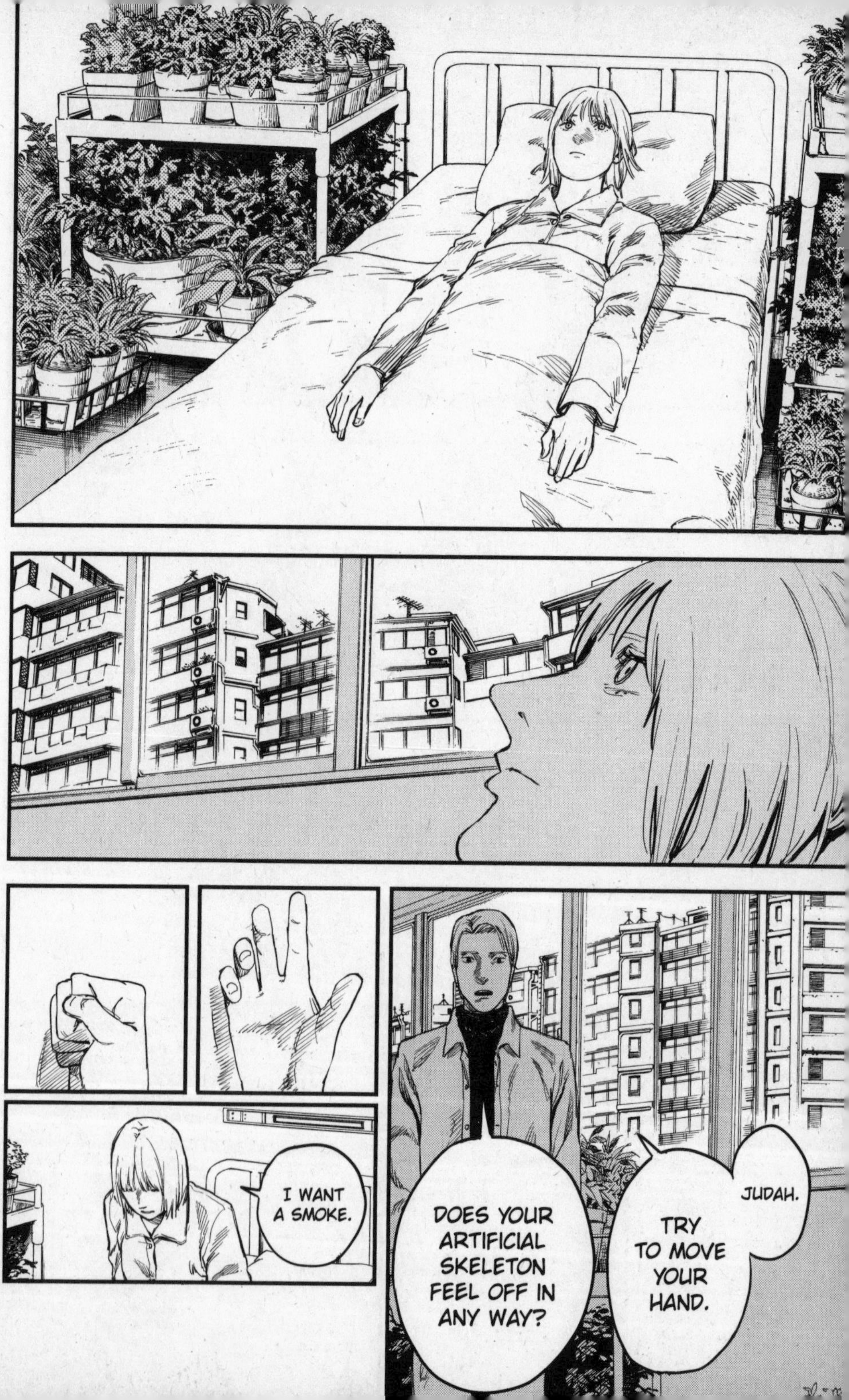
JUDAH.
TRY TO MOVE YOUR HAND.
DOES YOUR ARTIFICIAL SKELETON FEEL OFF IN ANY WAY?
I WANT A SMOKE.

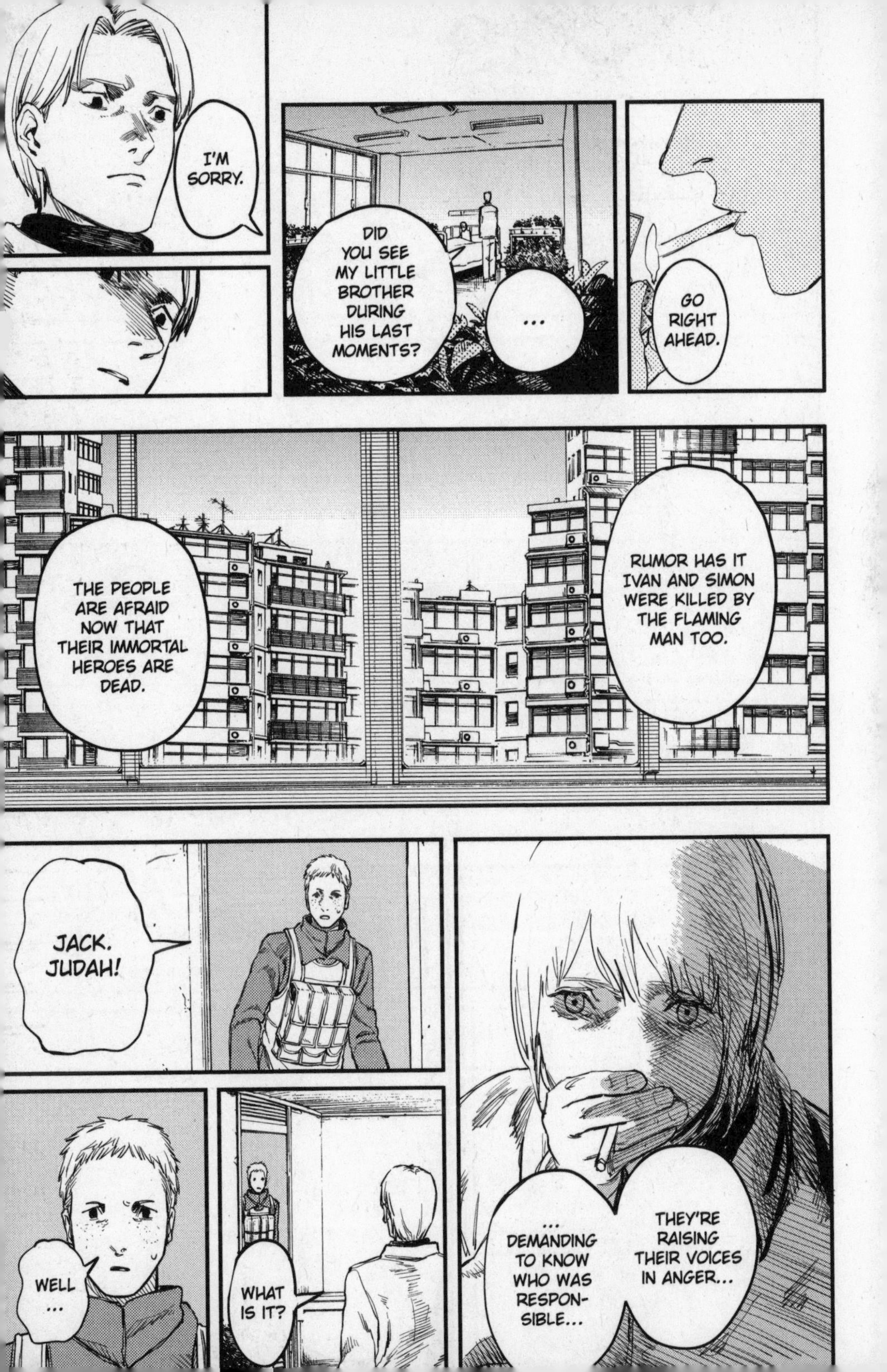
GO RIGHT AHEAD.
DID YOU SEE MY LITTLE BROTHER DURING HIS LAST MOMENTS?
...
I'M SORRY.
RUMOR HAS IT IVAN AND SIMON WERE KILLED BY THE FLAMING MAN TOO.
THE PEOPLE ARE AFRAID NOW THAT THEIR IMMORTAL HEROES ARE DEAD.
THEY'RE RAISING THEIR VOICES IN ANGER...
... DEMANDING TO KNOW WHO WAS RESPONSIBLE...
JACK. JUDAH!
WHAT IS IT?
WELL ...

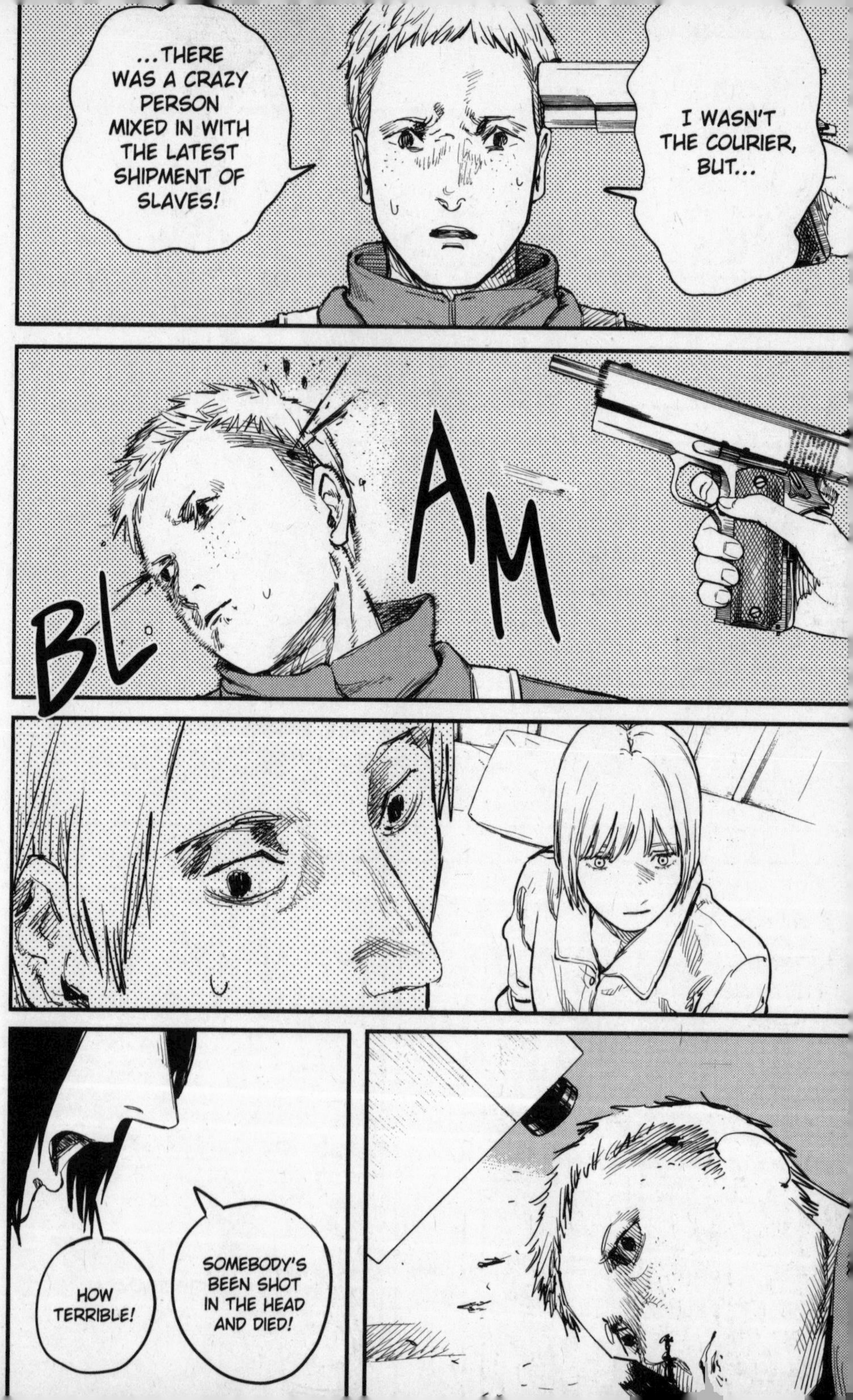
I WASN'T THE COURIER, BUT...
...THERE WAS A CRAZY PERSON MIXED IN WITH THE LATEST SHIPMENT OF SLAVES!
BLAM
SOMEBODY'S BEEN SHOT IN THE HEAD AND DIED!
HOW TERRIBLE!

THAT'S THE PERSON WHO KILLED IVAN AND SIMON.

WHAT ?!

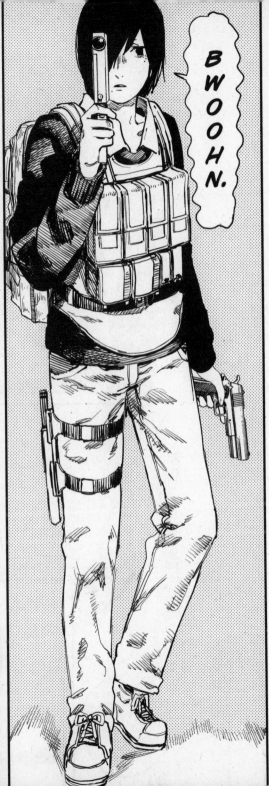

BWOOHN.

YEP!

I'M THE PERSON WHO KILLED IVAN AND SIMON!

AND NOW I HAVE A PROPOSAL!

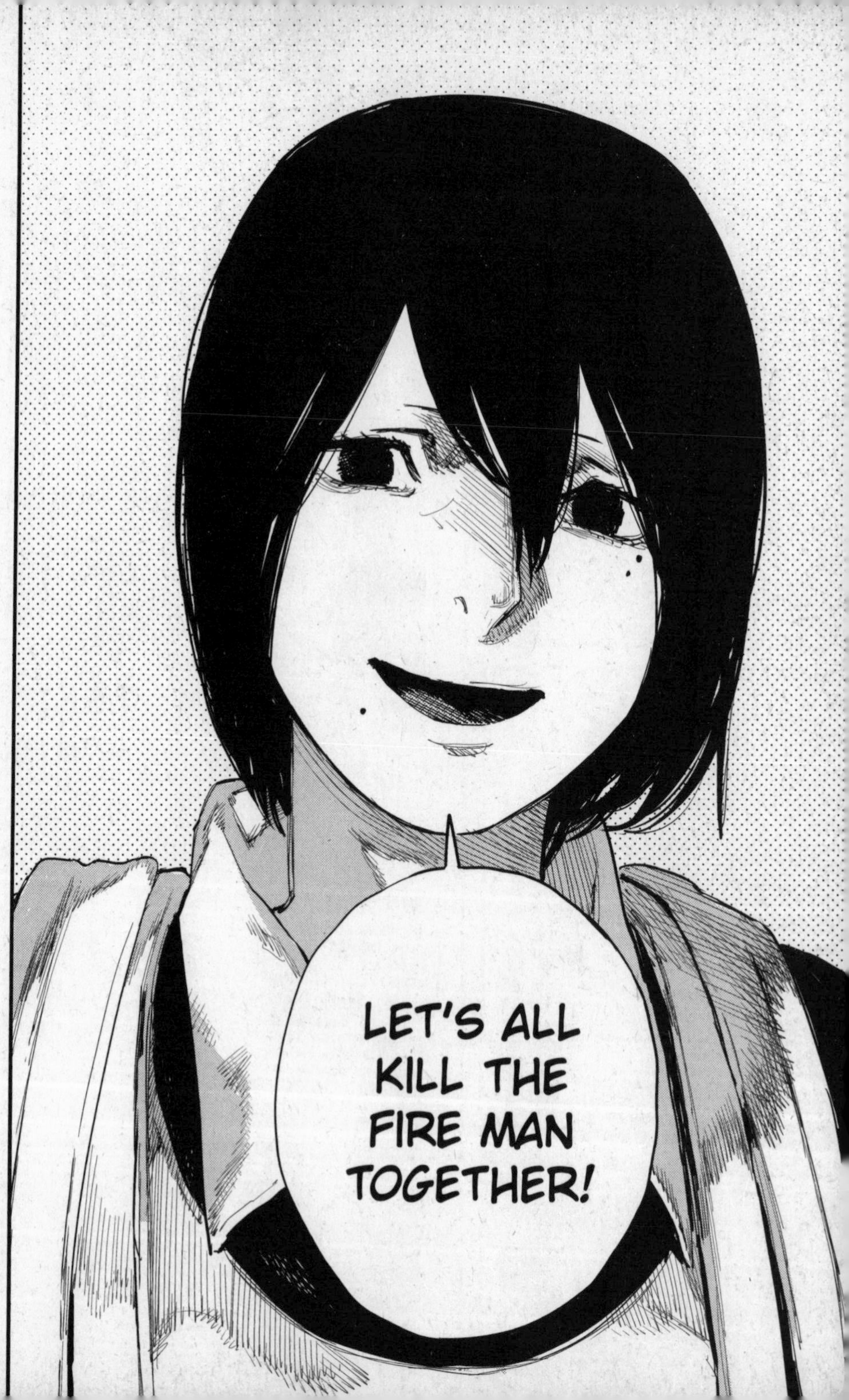
LET'S ALL KILL THE FIRE MAN TOGETHER!

FIRE PUNCH

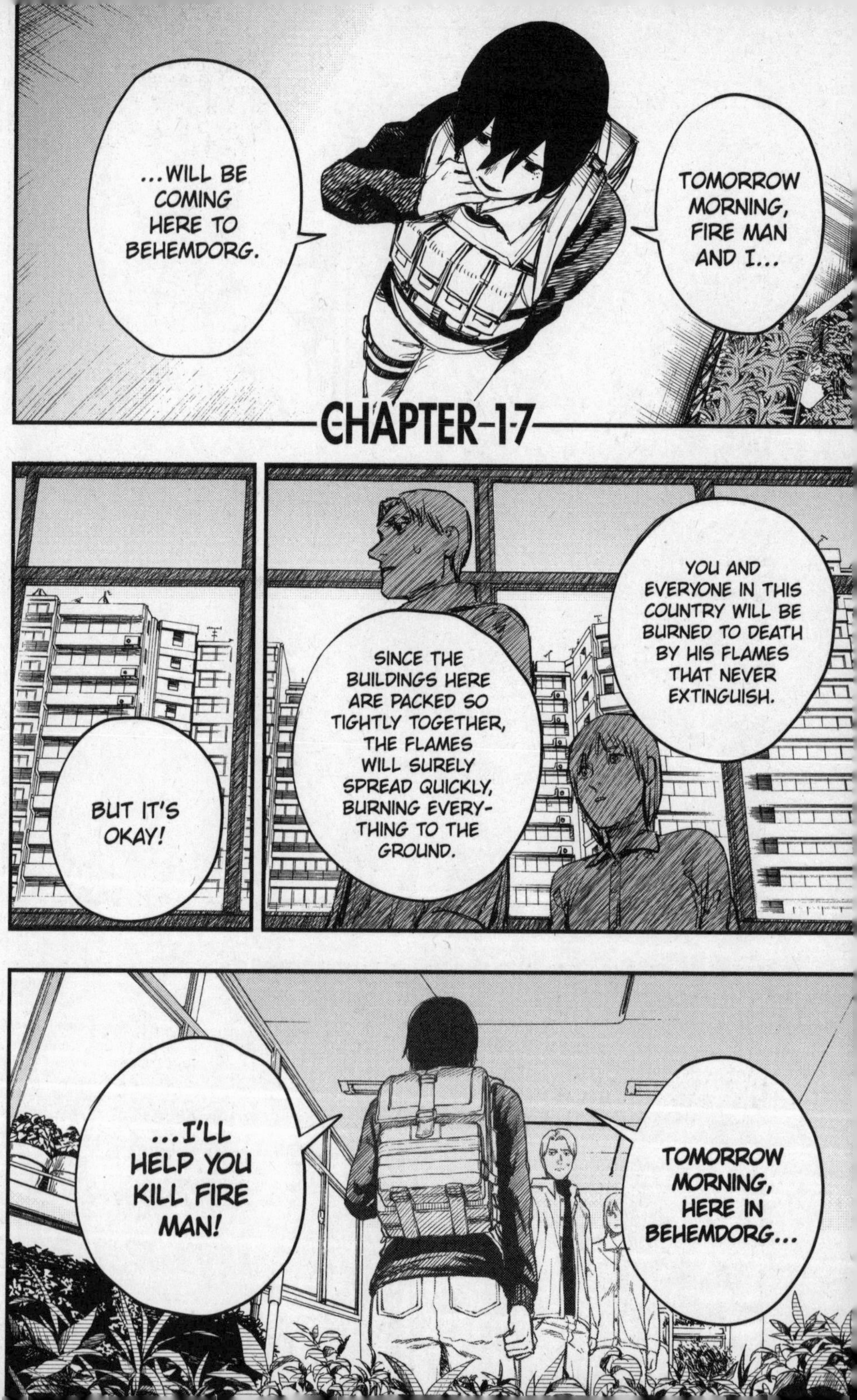
TOMORROW MORNING, FIRE MAN AND I...
...WILL BE COMING HERE TO BEHEMDORG.
CHAPTER 17
YOU AND EVERYONE IN THIS COUNTRY WILL BE BURNED TO DEATH BY HIS FLAMES THAT NEVER EXTINGUISH.
SINCE THE BUILDINGS HERE ARE PACKED SO TIGHTLY TOGETHER, THE FLAMES WILL SURELY SPREAD QUICKLY, BURNING EVERY-THING TO THE GROUND.
BUT IT'S OKAY!
TOMORROW MORNING, HERE IN BEHEMDORG...
...I'LL HELP YOU KILL FIRE MAN!

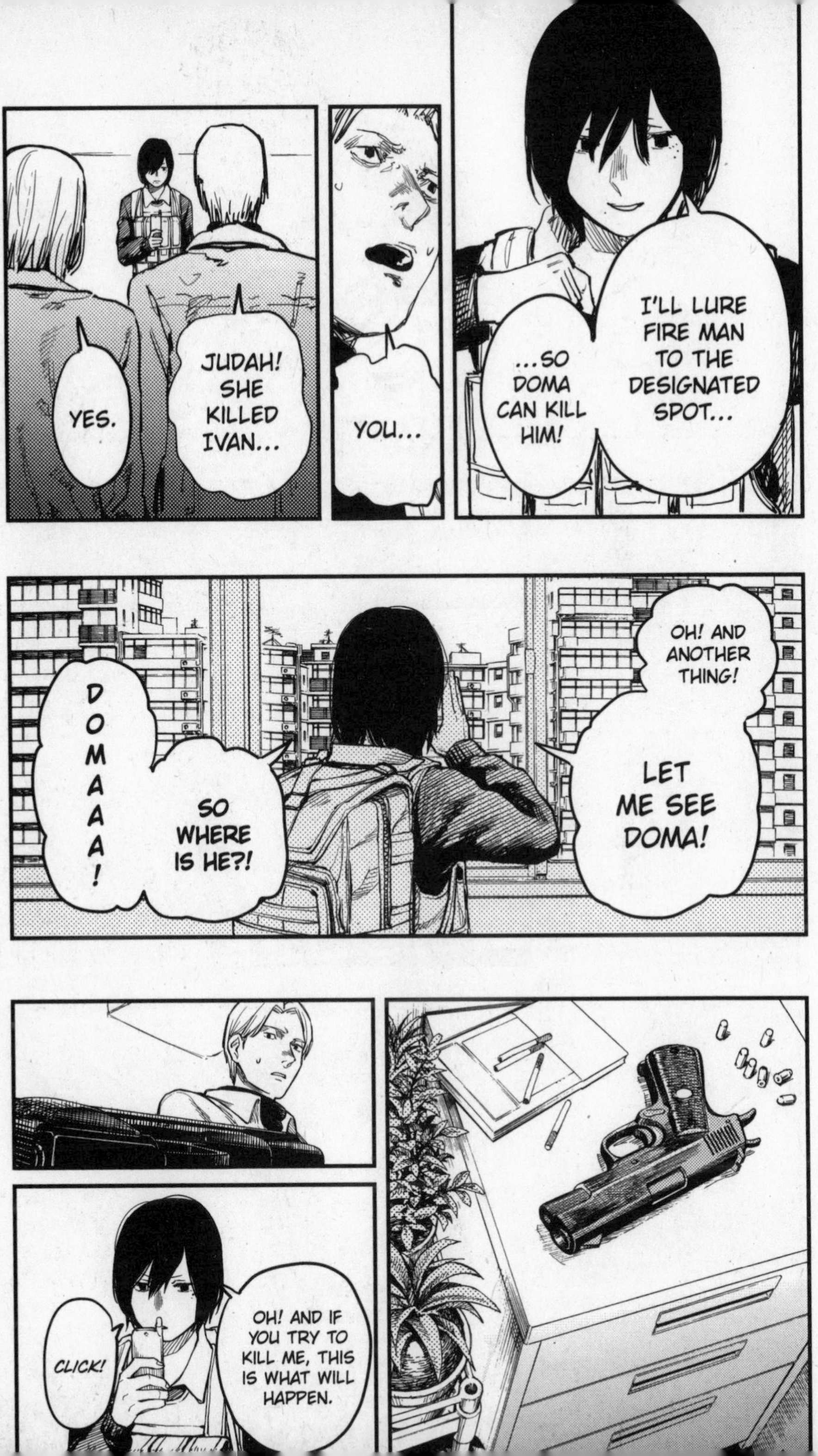
I'LL LURE FIRE MAN TO THE DESIGNATED SPOT...
...SO DOMA CAN KILL HIM!
YOU...
JUDAH! SHE KILLED IVAN...
YES.
OH! AND ANOTHER THING!
LET ME SEE DOMA!
SO WHERE IS HE?!
DOMAAA!
OH! AND IF YOU TRY TO KILL ME, THIS IS WHAT WILL HAPPEN.
CLICK!

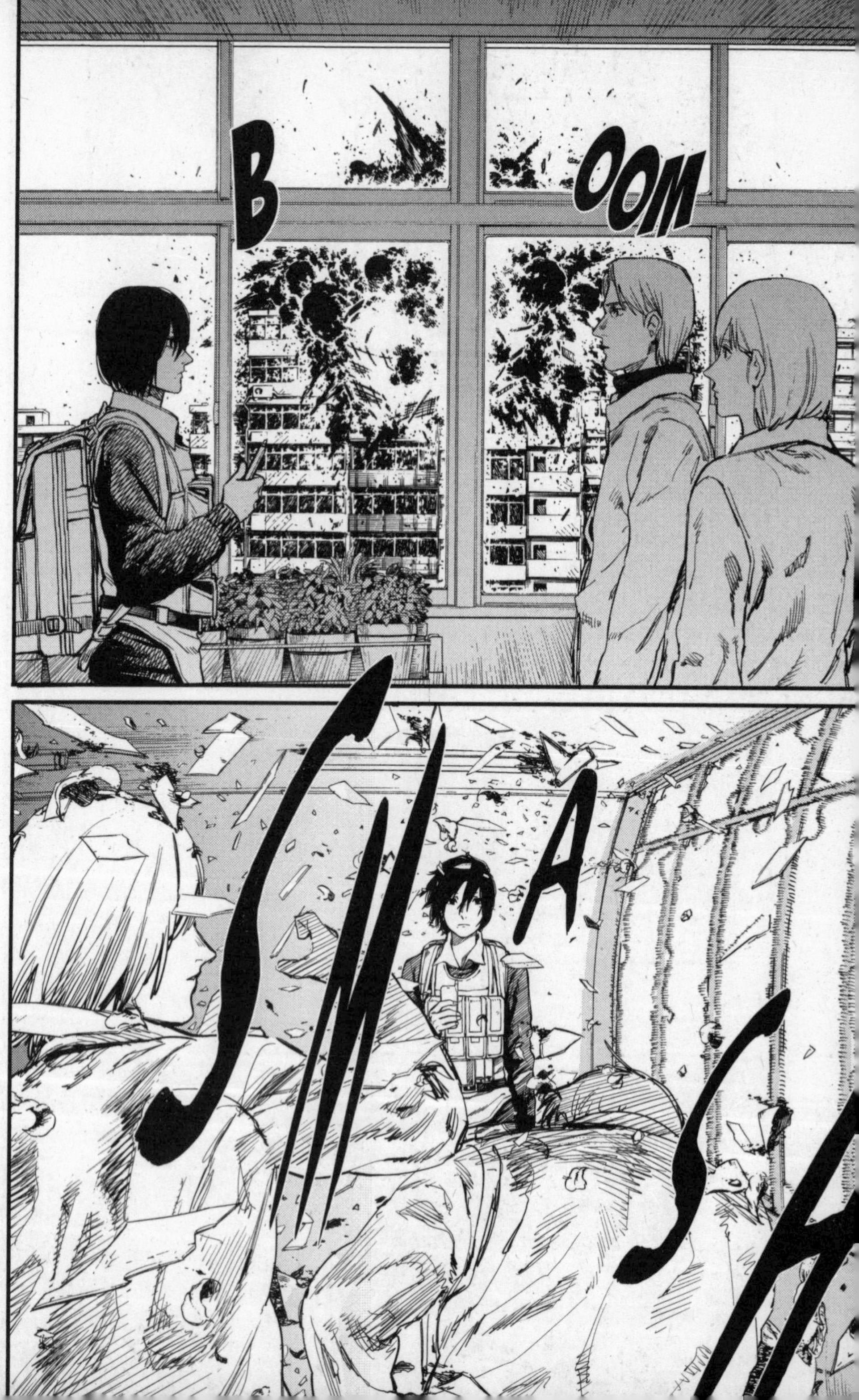
BOOM
SMASH

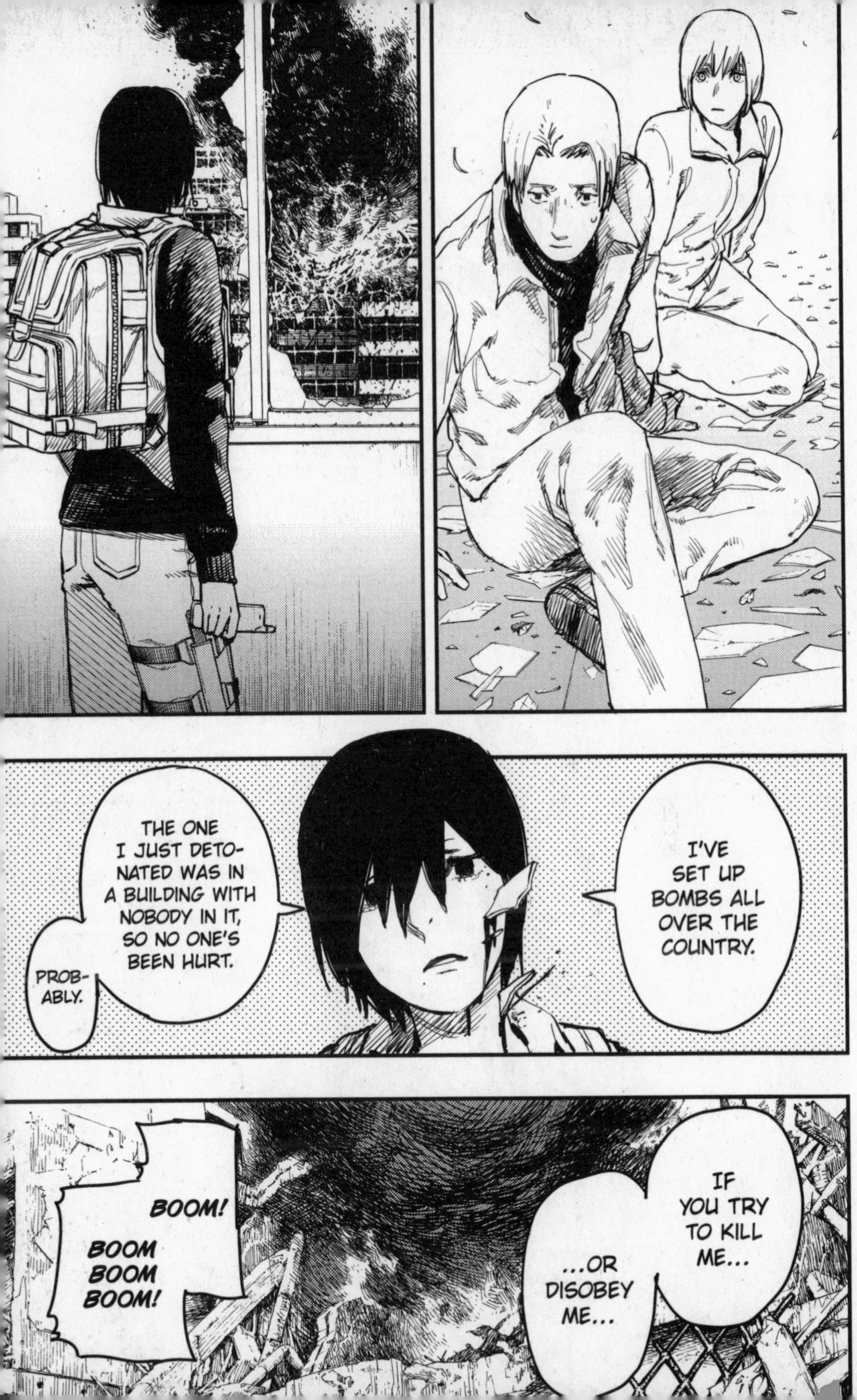
I'VE SET UP BOMBS ALL OVER THE COUNTRY.
THE ONE I JUST DETONATED WAS IN A BUILDING WITH NOBODY IN IT, SO NO ONE'S BEEN HURT.
PROBABLY.
IF YOU TRY TO KILL ME...
...OR DISOBEY ME...
BOOM!
BOOM BOOM BOOM!

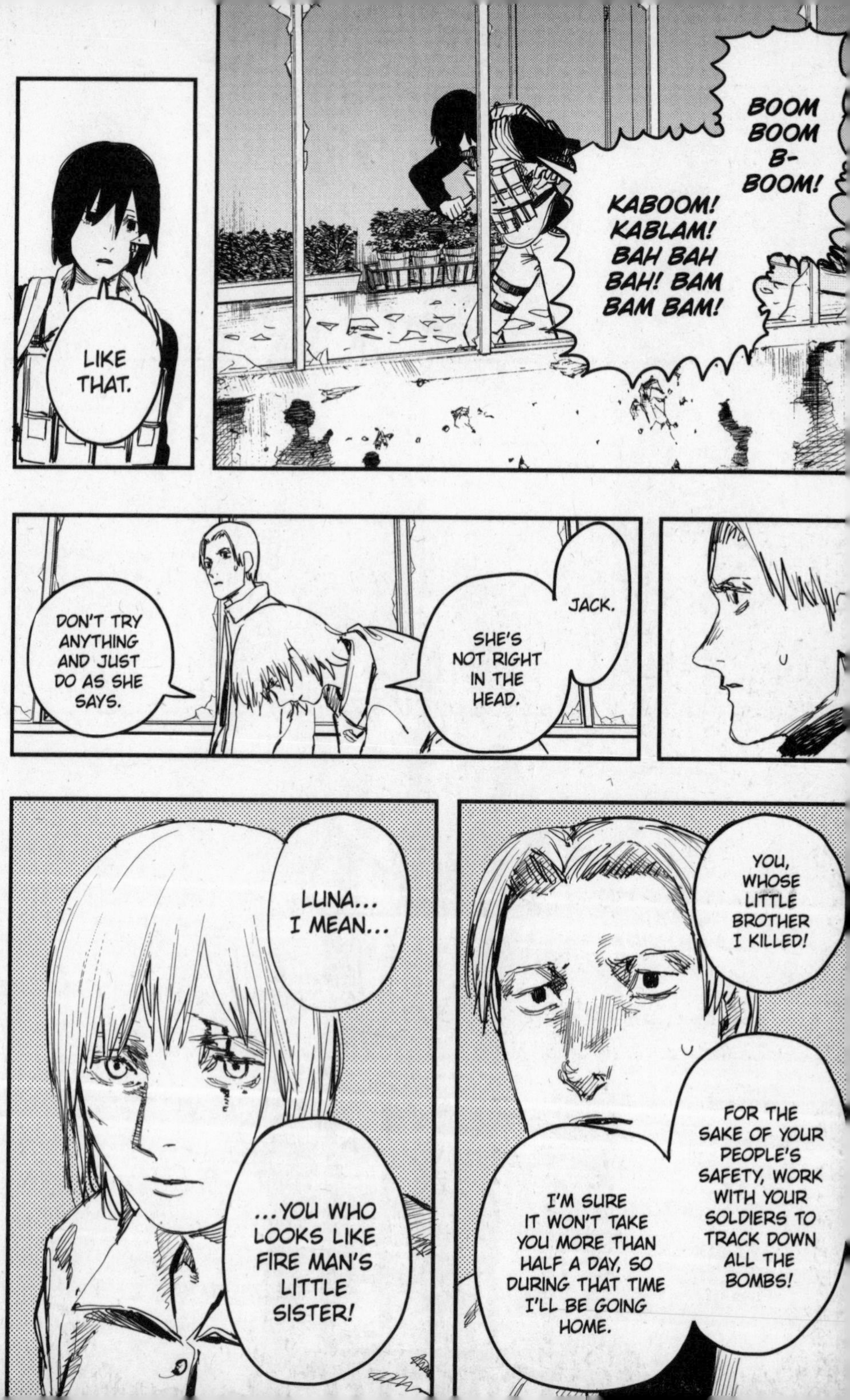
BOOM BOOM B-BOOM!
KABOOM! KABLAM! BAH BAH BAH! BAM BAM BAM!
LIKE THAT.
JACK.
SHE'S NOT RIGHT IN THE HEAD.
DON'T TRY ANYTHING AND JUST DO AS SHE SAYS.
YOU, WHOSE LITTLE BROTHER I KILLED!
FOR THE SAKE OF YOUR PEOPLE'S SAFETY, WORK WITH YOUR SOLDIERS TO TRACK DOWN ALL THE BOMBS!
I'M SURE IT WON'T TAKE YOU MORE THAN HALF A DAY, SO DURING THAT TIME I'LL BE GOING HOME.
LUNA... I MEAN...
...YOU WHO LOOKS LIKE FIRE MAN'S LITTLE SISTER!

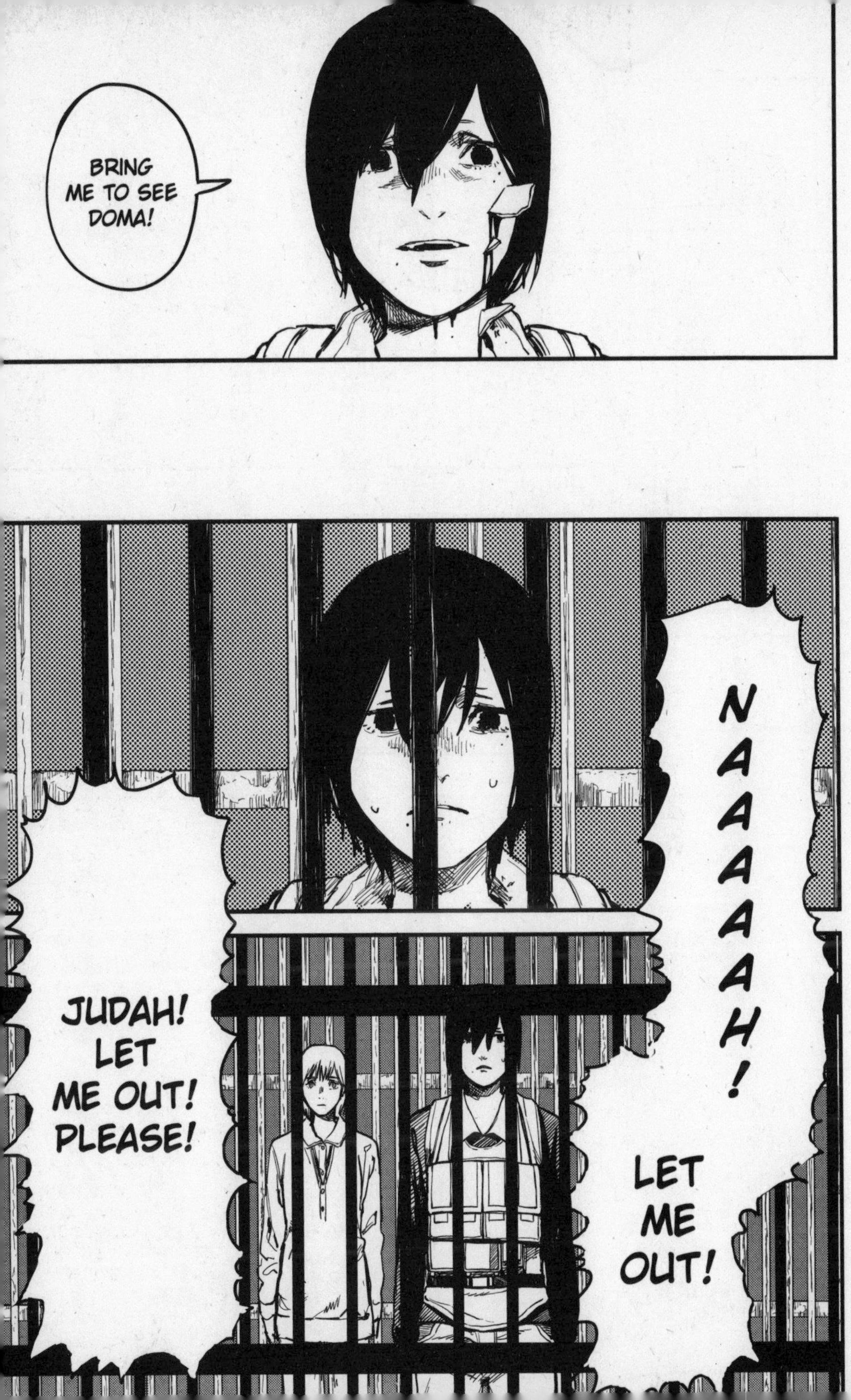

BRING ME TO SEE DOMA!
NAAAAAH!
LET ME OUT!
JUDAH! LET ME OUT! PLEASE!

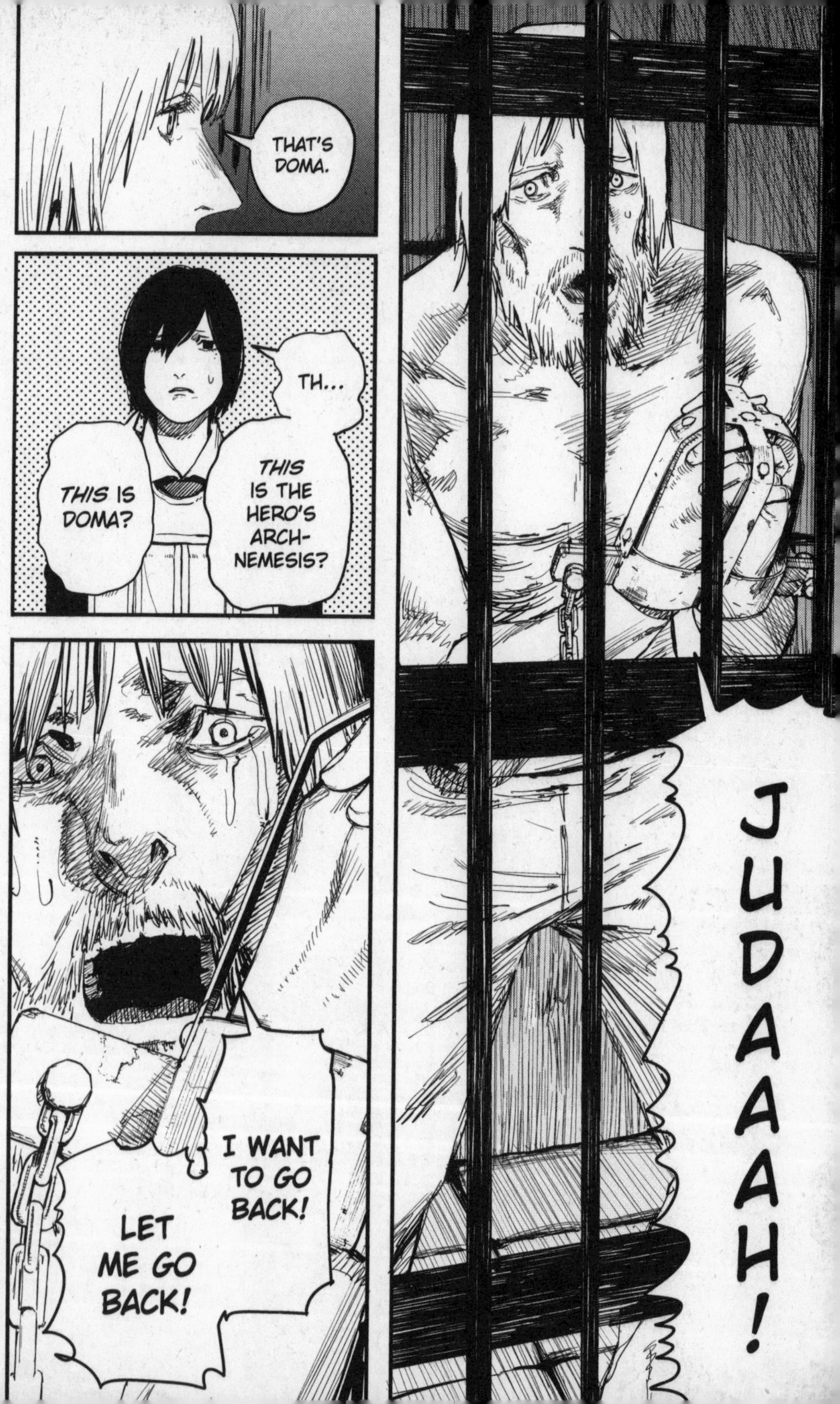
JUDAAAH!
THAT'S DOMA.
TH...
THIS IS THE HERO'S ARCH-NEMESIS?
THIS IS DOMA?
I WANT TO GO BACK!
LET ME GO BACK!

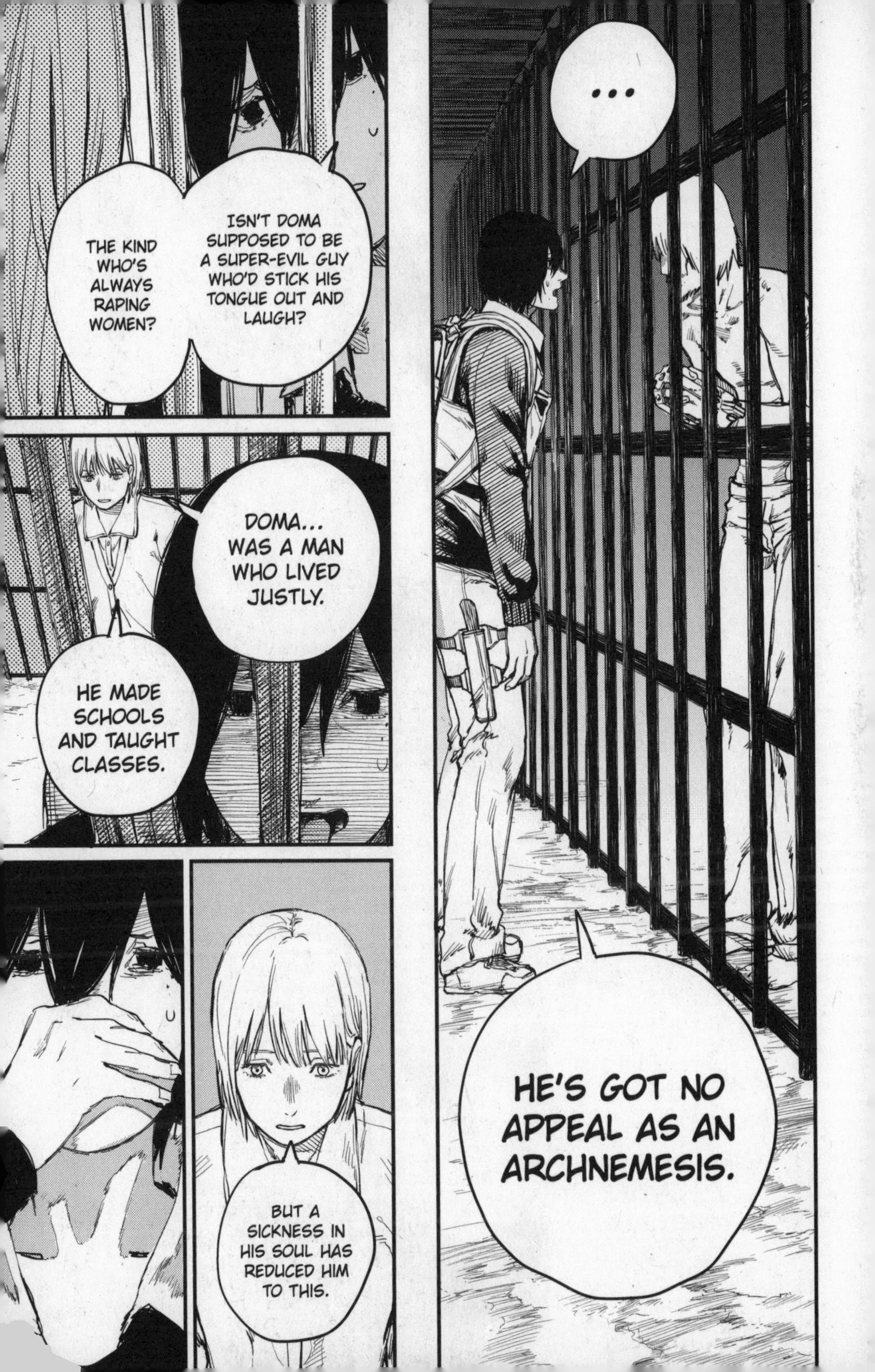
...
HE'S GOT NO APPEAL AS AN ARCHNEMESIS.
ISN'T DOMA SUPPOSED TO BE A SUPER-EVIL GUY WHO'D STICK HIS TONGUE OUT AND LAUGH?
THE KIND WHO'S ALWAYS RAPING WOMEN?
DOMA... WAS A MAN WHO LIVED JUSTLY.
HE MADE SCHOOLS AND TAUGHT CLASSES.
BUT A SICKNESS IN HIS SOUL HAS REDUCED HIM TO THIS.

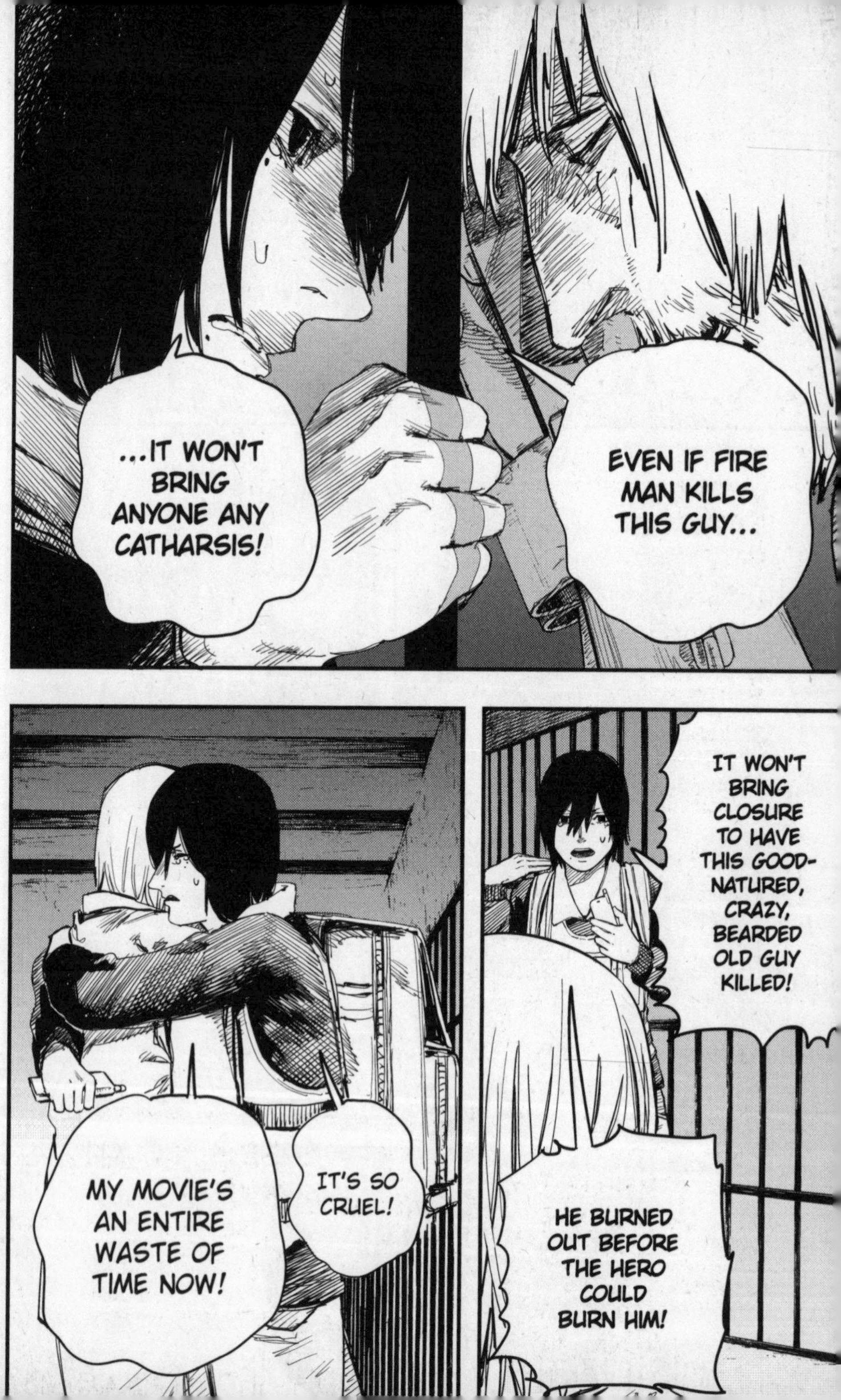
EVEN IF FIRE MAN KILLS THIS GUY...
...IT WON'T BRING ANYONE ANY CATHARSIS!
IT WON'T BRING CLOSURE TO HAVE THIS GOOD-NATURED, CRAZY, BEARDED OLD GUY KILLED!
HE BURNED OUT BEFORE THE HERO COULD BURN HIM!
IT'S SO CRUEL!
MY MOVIE'S AN ENTIRE WASTE OF TIME NOW!

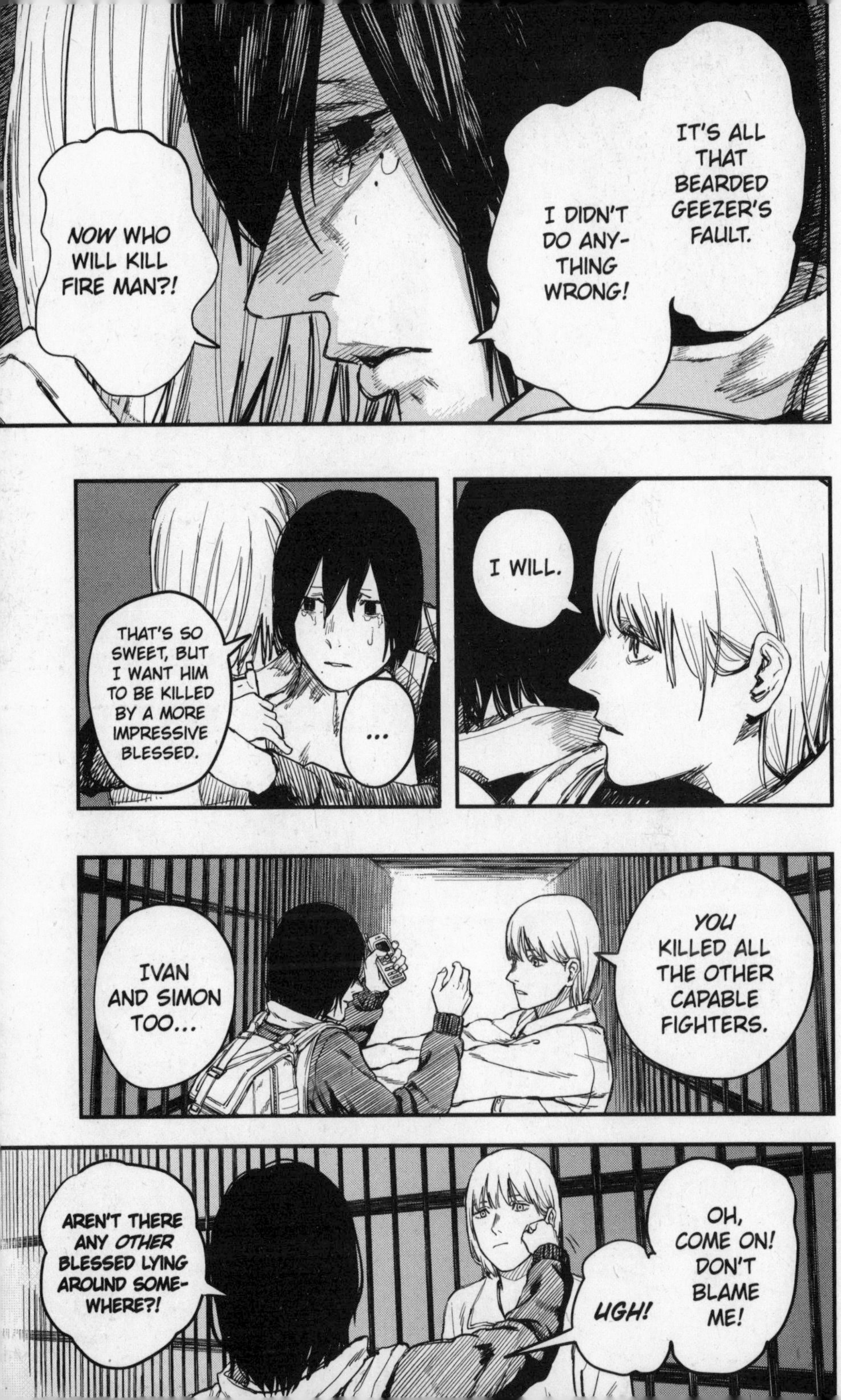
IT'S ALL THAT BEARDED GEEZER'S FAULT.
I DIDN'T DO ANYTHING WRONG!
NOW WHO WILL KILL FIRE MAN?!
I WILL.
...
THAT'S SO SWEET, BUT I WANT HIM TO BE KILLED BY A MORE IMPRESSIVE BLESSED.
YOU KILLED ALL THE OTHER CAPABLE FIGHTERS.
IVAN AND SIMON TOO...
OH, COME ON! DON'T BLAME ME!
UGH!
AREN'T THERE ANY *OTHER* BLESSED LYING AROUND SOMEWHERE?!

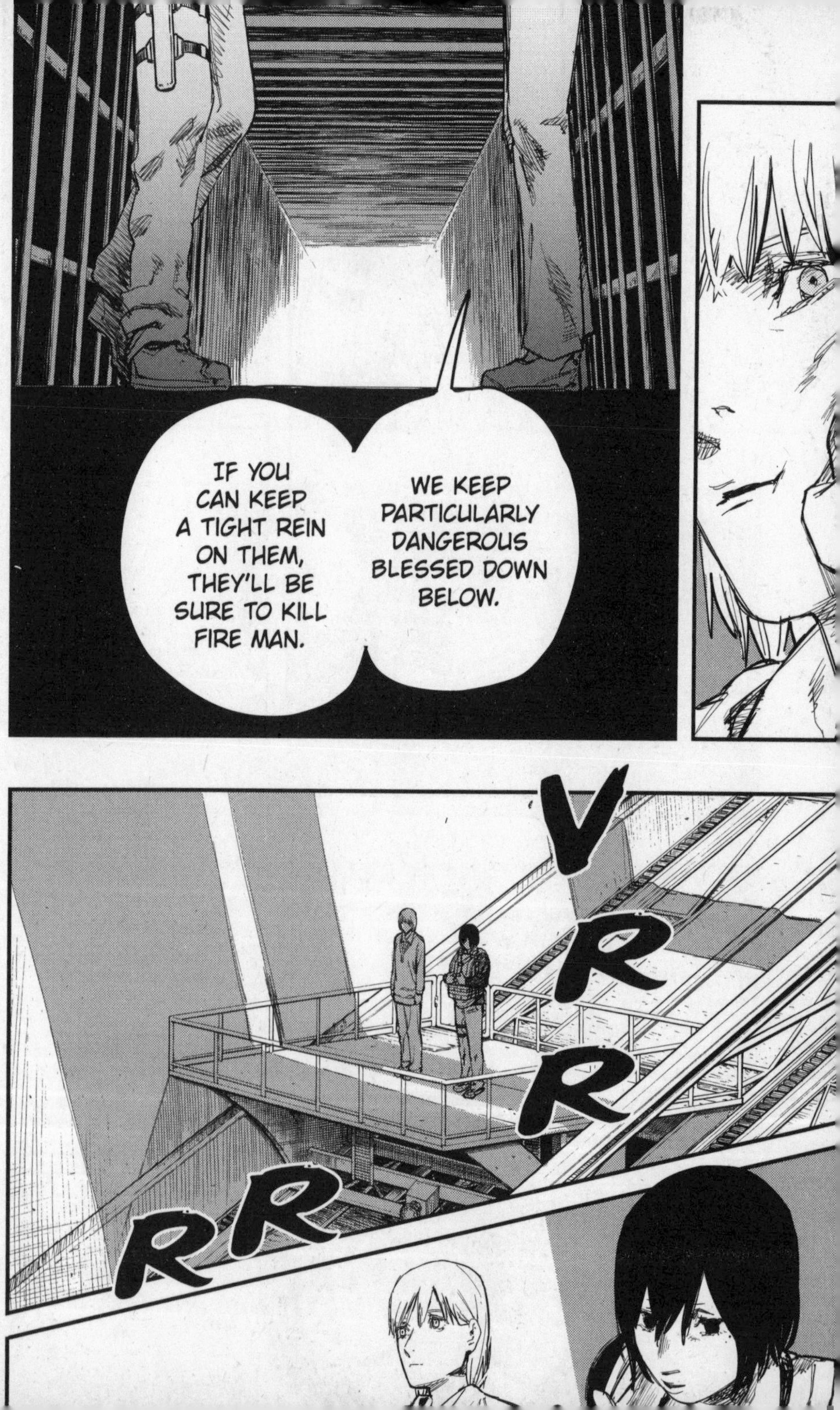
WE KEEP PARTICULARLY DANGEROUS BLESSED DOWN BELOW.
IF YOU CAN KEEP A TIGHT REIN ON THEM, THEY'LL BE SURE TO KILL FIRE MAN.
VRRRRR

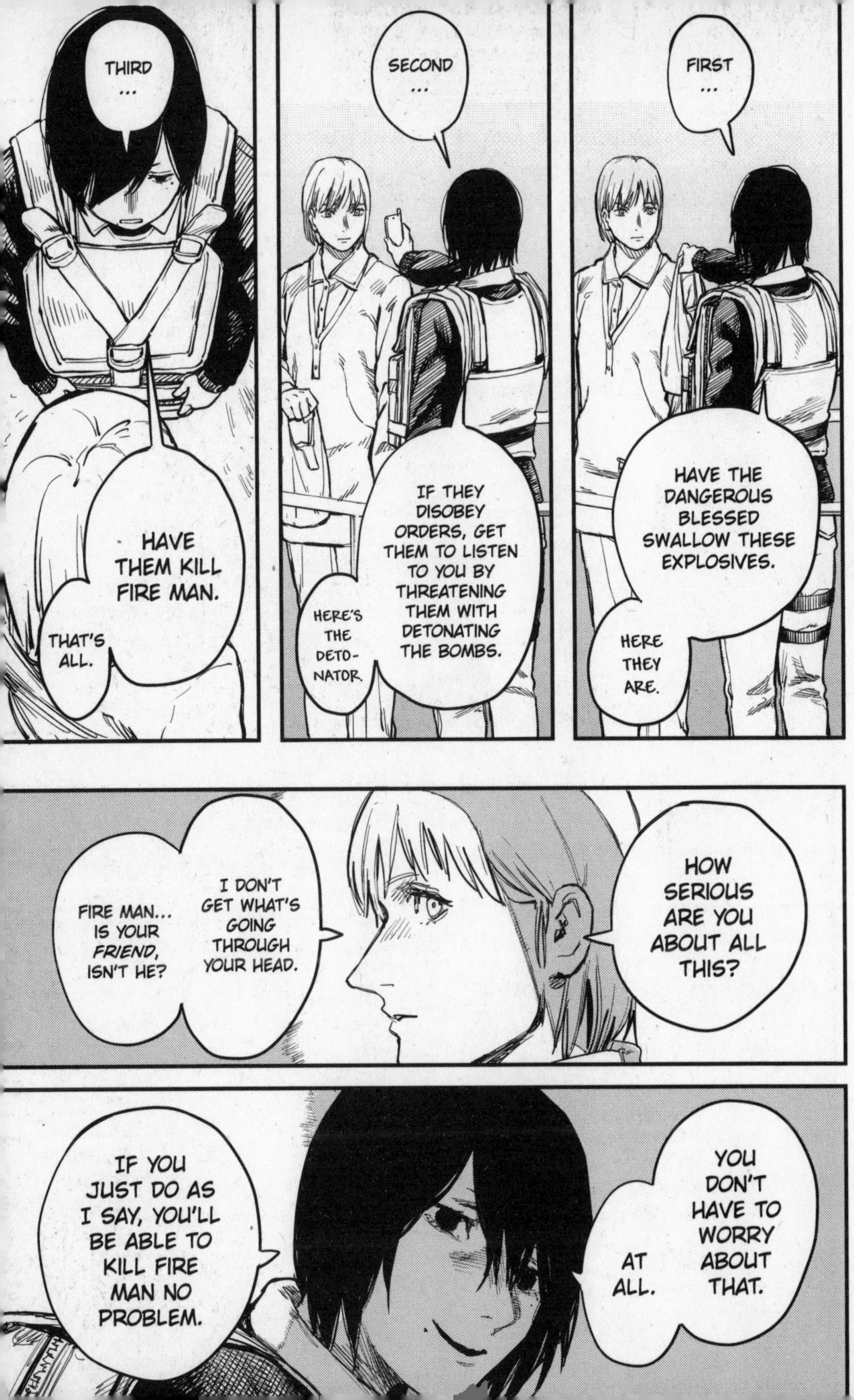
FIRST ...
HAVE THE DANGEROUS BLESSED SWALLOW THESE EXPLOSIVES.
HERE THEY ARE.
SECOND ...
IF THEY DISOBEY ORDERS, GET THEM TO LISTEN TO YOU BY THREATENING THEM WITH DETONATING THE BOMBS.
HERE'S THE DETONATOR.
THIRD ...
HAVE THEM KILL FIRE MAN.
THAT'S ALL.
HOW SERIOUS ARE YOU ABOUT ALL THIS?
I DON'T GET WHAT'S GOING THROUGH YOUR HEAD.
FIRE MAN... IS YOUR *FRIEND*, ISN'T HE?
YOU DON'T HAVE TO WORRY ABOUT THAT.
AT ALL.
IF YOU JUST DO AS I SAY, YOU'LL BE ABLE TO KILL FIRE MAN NO PROBLEM.

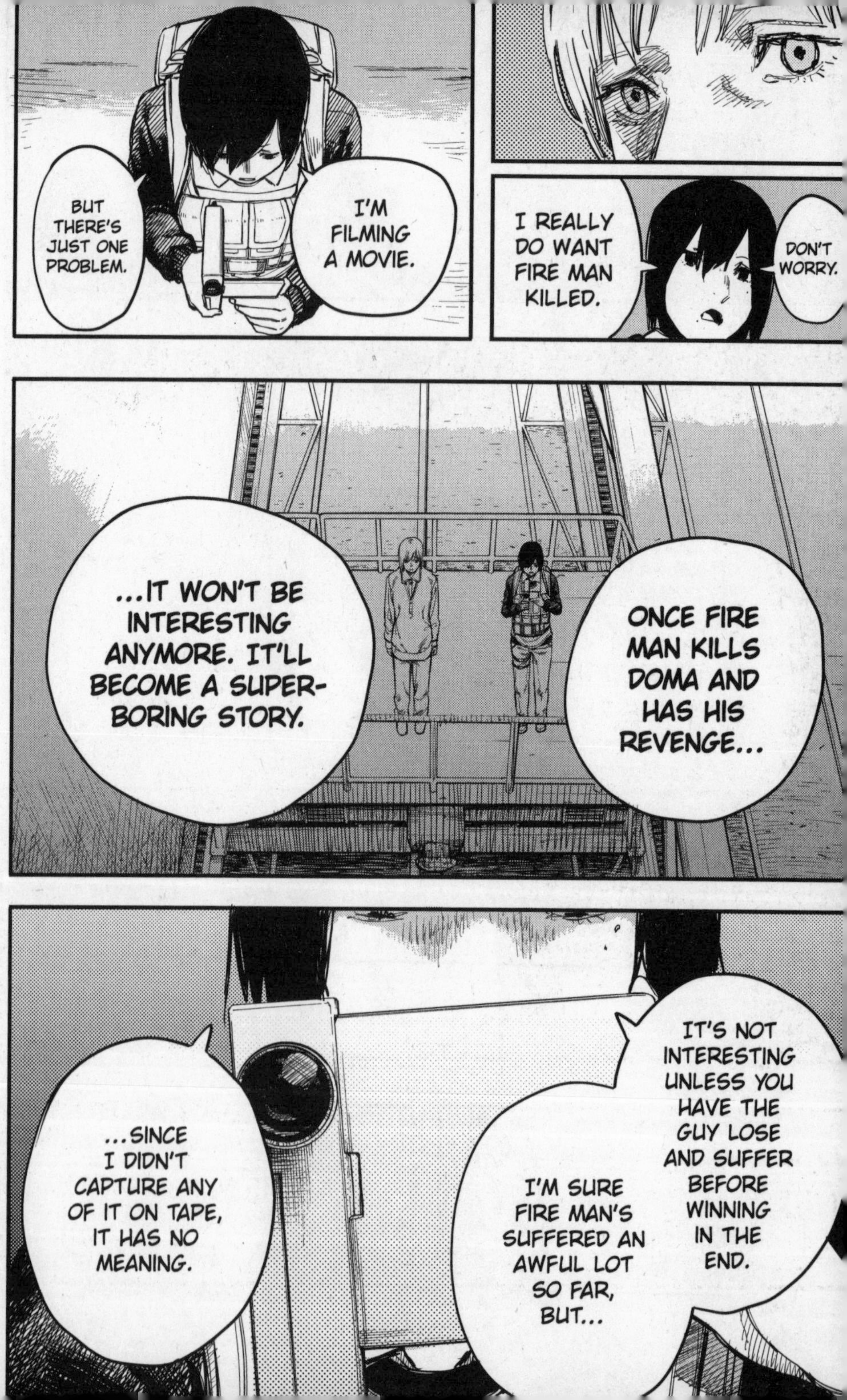
DON'T WORRY.
I REALLY DO WANT FIRE MAN KILLED.
I'M FILMING A MOVIE.
BUT THERE'S JUST ONE PROBLEM.
ONCE FIRE MAN KILLS DOMA AND HAS HIS REVENGE...
...IT WON'T BE INTERESTING ANYMORE. IT'LL BECOME A SUPER-BORING STORY.
IT'S NOT INTERESTING UNLESS YOU HAVE THE GUY LOSE AND SUFFER BEFORE WINNING IN THE END.
I'M SURE FIRE MAN'S SUFFERED AN AWFUL LOT SO FAR, BUT...
...SINCE I DIDN'T CAPTURE ANY OF IT ON TAPE, IT HAS NO MEANING.

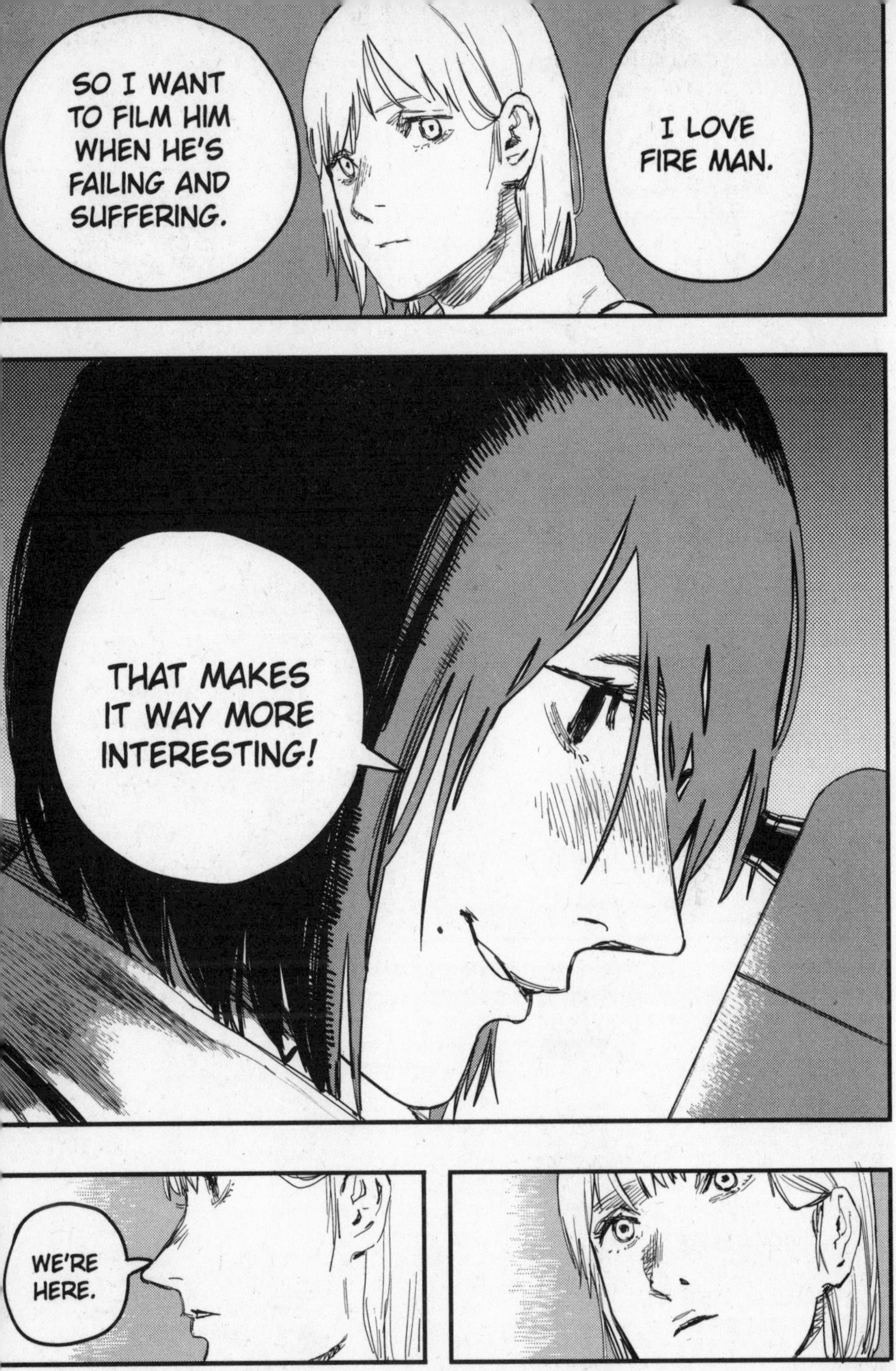
I LOVE FIRE MAN.
SO I WANT TO FILM HIM WHEN HE'S FAILING AND SUFFERING.
THAT MAKES IT WAY MORE INTERESTING!
WE'RE HERE.

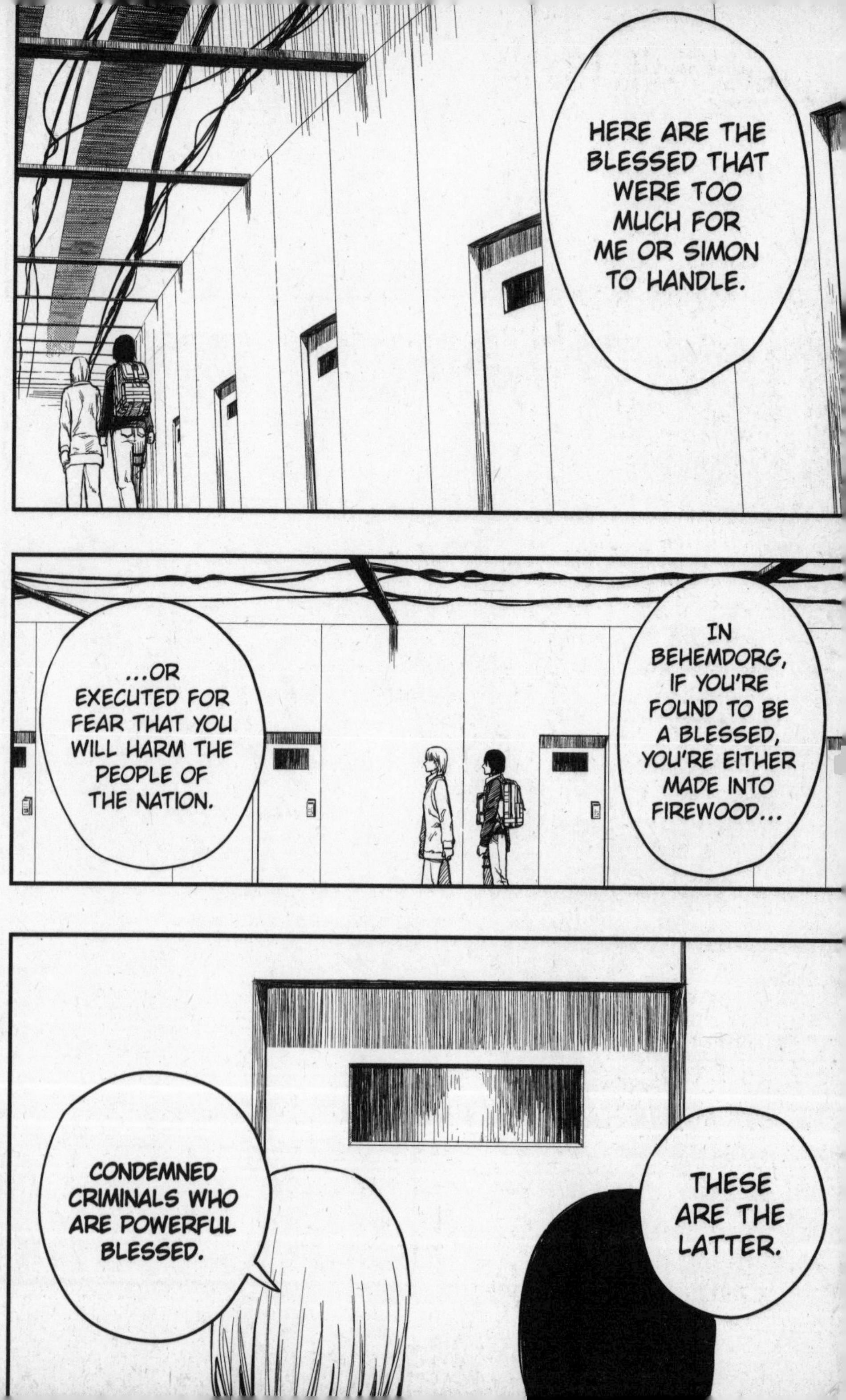
HERE ARE THE BLESSED THAT WERE TOO MUCH FOR ME OR SIMON TO HANDLE.
IN BEHEMDORG, IF YOU'RE FOUND TO BE A BLESSED, YOU'RE EITHER MADE INTO FIREWOOD...
...OR EXECUTED FOR FEAR THAT YOU WILL HARM THE PEOPLE OF THE NATION.
THESE ARE THE LATTER.
CONDEMNED CRIMINALS WHO ARE POWERFUL BLESSED.

CHAPTER 18

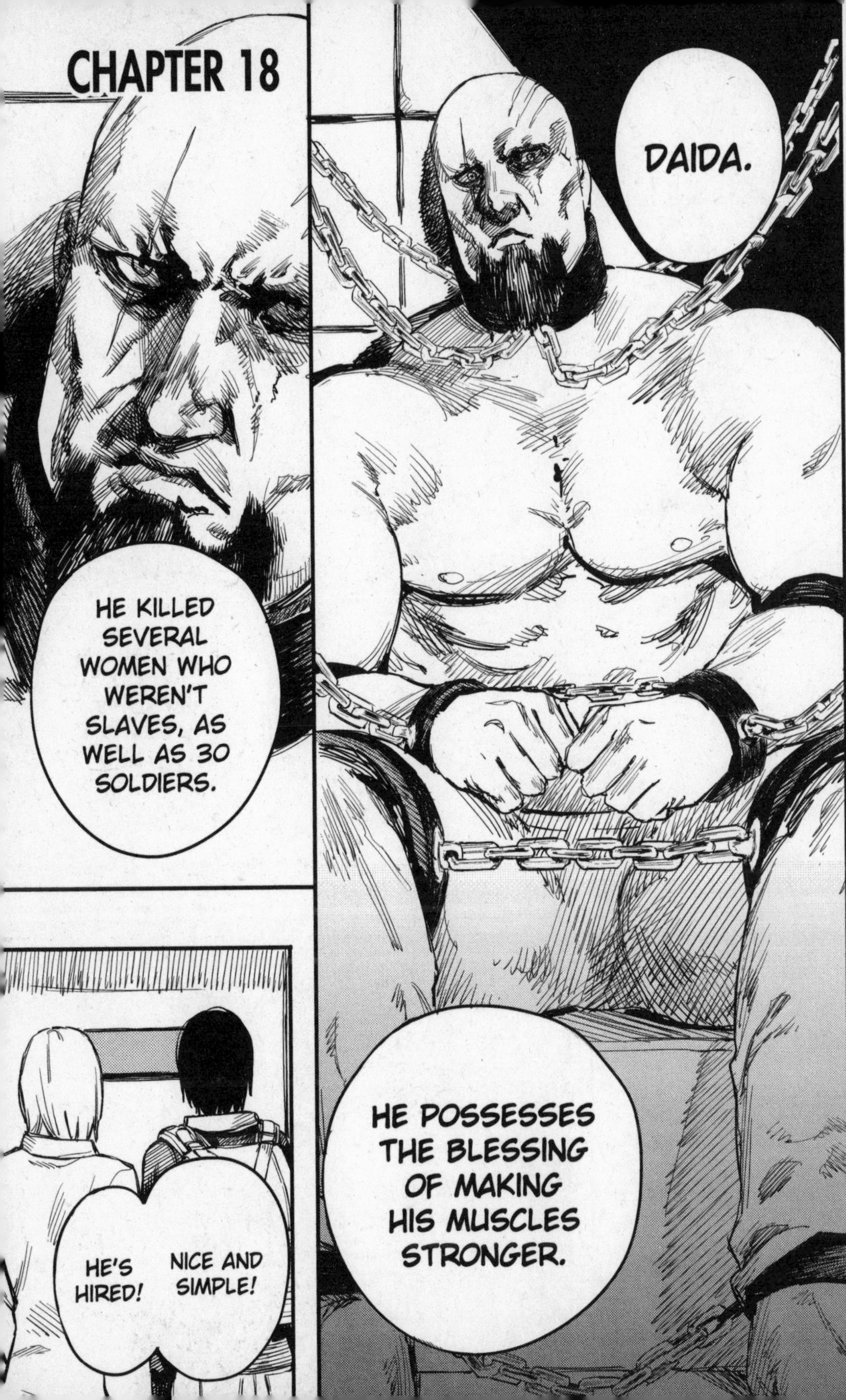
DAIDA.
HE POSSESSES THE BLESSING OF MAKING HIS MUSCLES STRONGER.
HE KILLED SEVERAL WOMEN WHO WEREN'T SLAVES, AS WELL AS 30 SOLDIERS.
NICE AND SIMPLE!
HE'S HIRED!

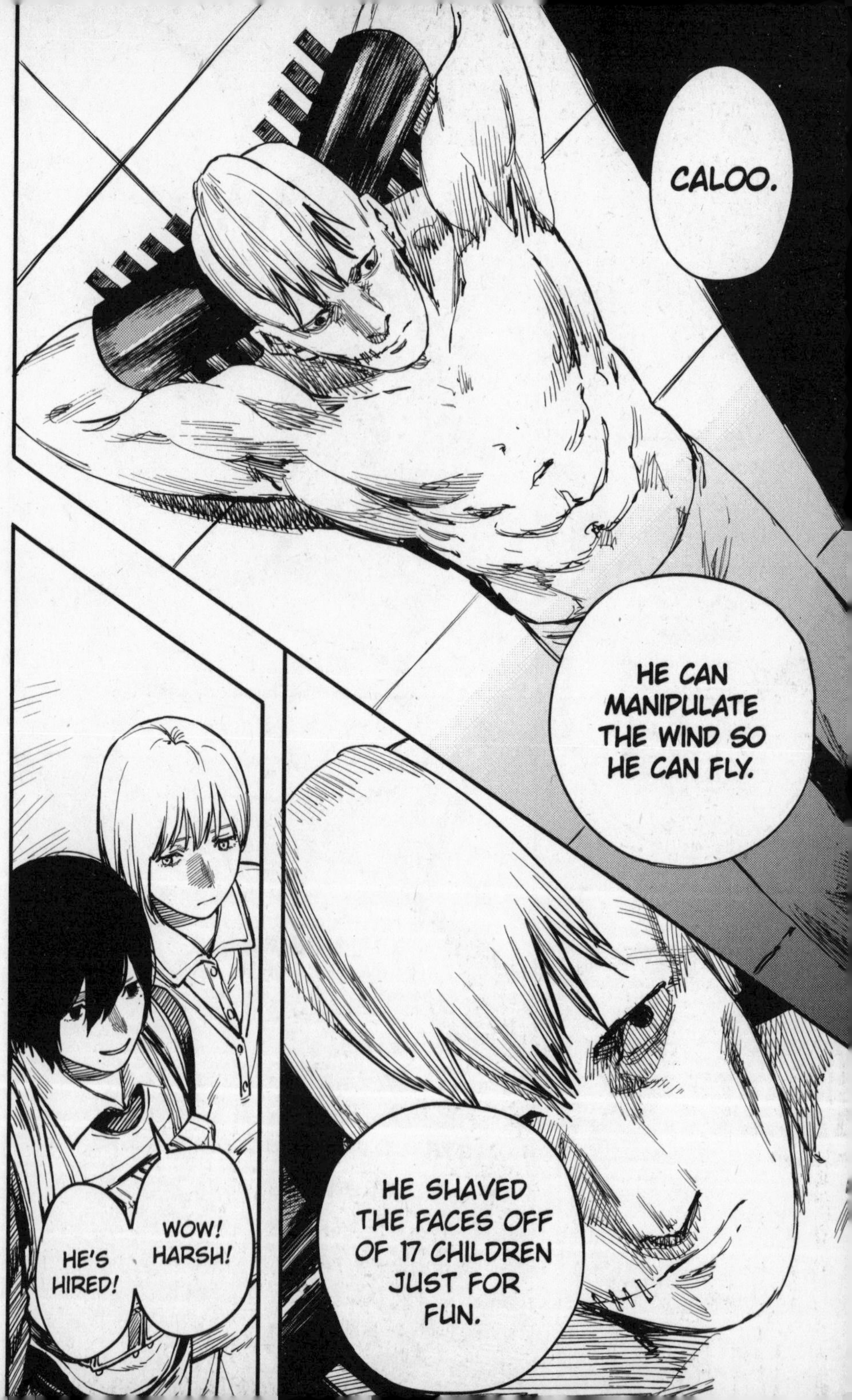
CALOO.
HE CAN MANIPULATE THE WIND SO HE CAN FLY.
HE SHAVED THE FACES OFF OF 17 CHILDREN JUST FOR FUN.
WOW! HARSH!
HE'S HIRED!

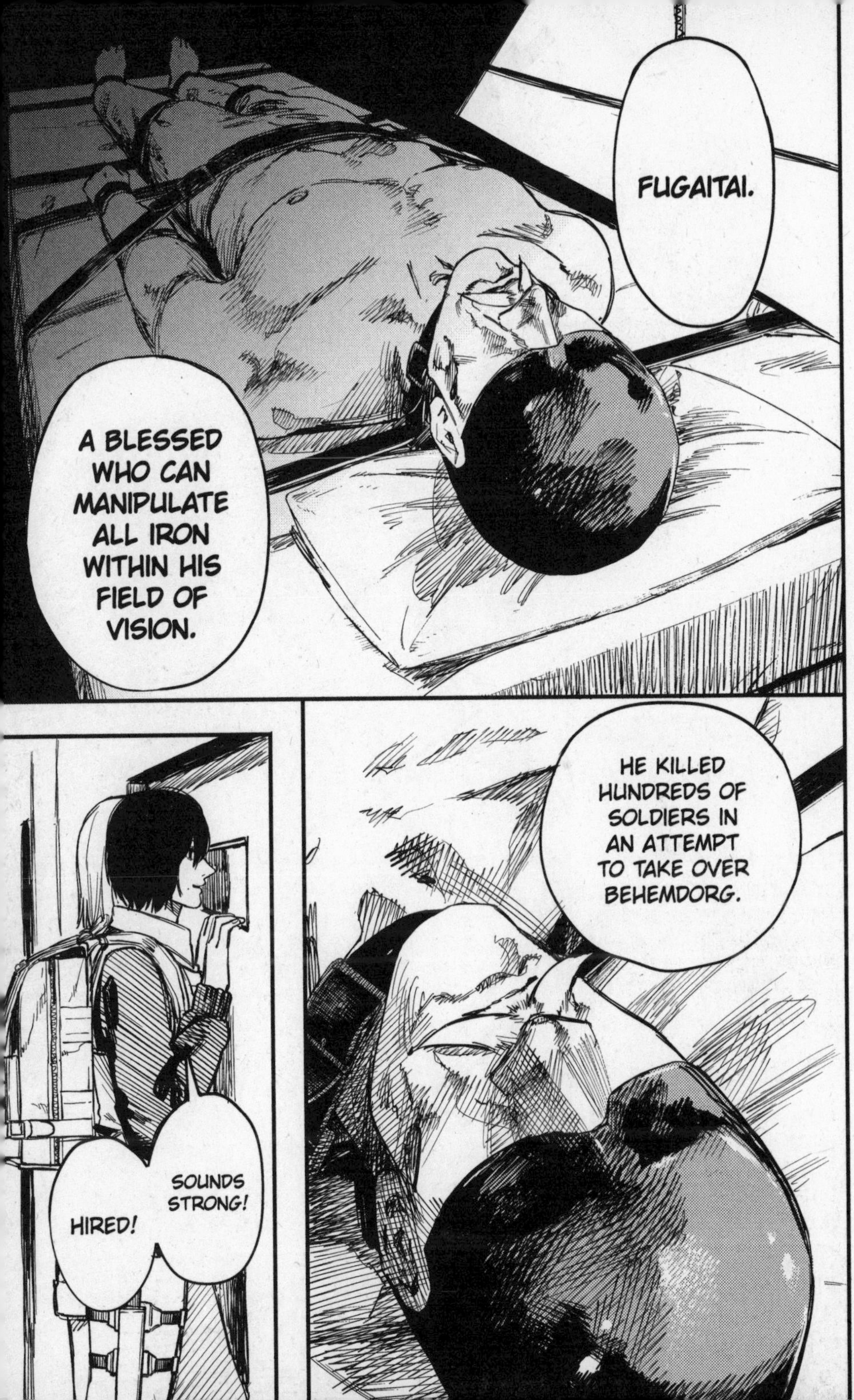
FUGAITAI.
A BLESSED WHO CAN MANIPULATE ALL IRON WITHIN HIS FIELD OF VISION.
HE KILLED HUNDREDS OF SOLDIERS IN AN ATTEMPT TO TAKE OVER BEHEMDORG.
SOUNDS STRONG!
HIRED!

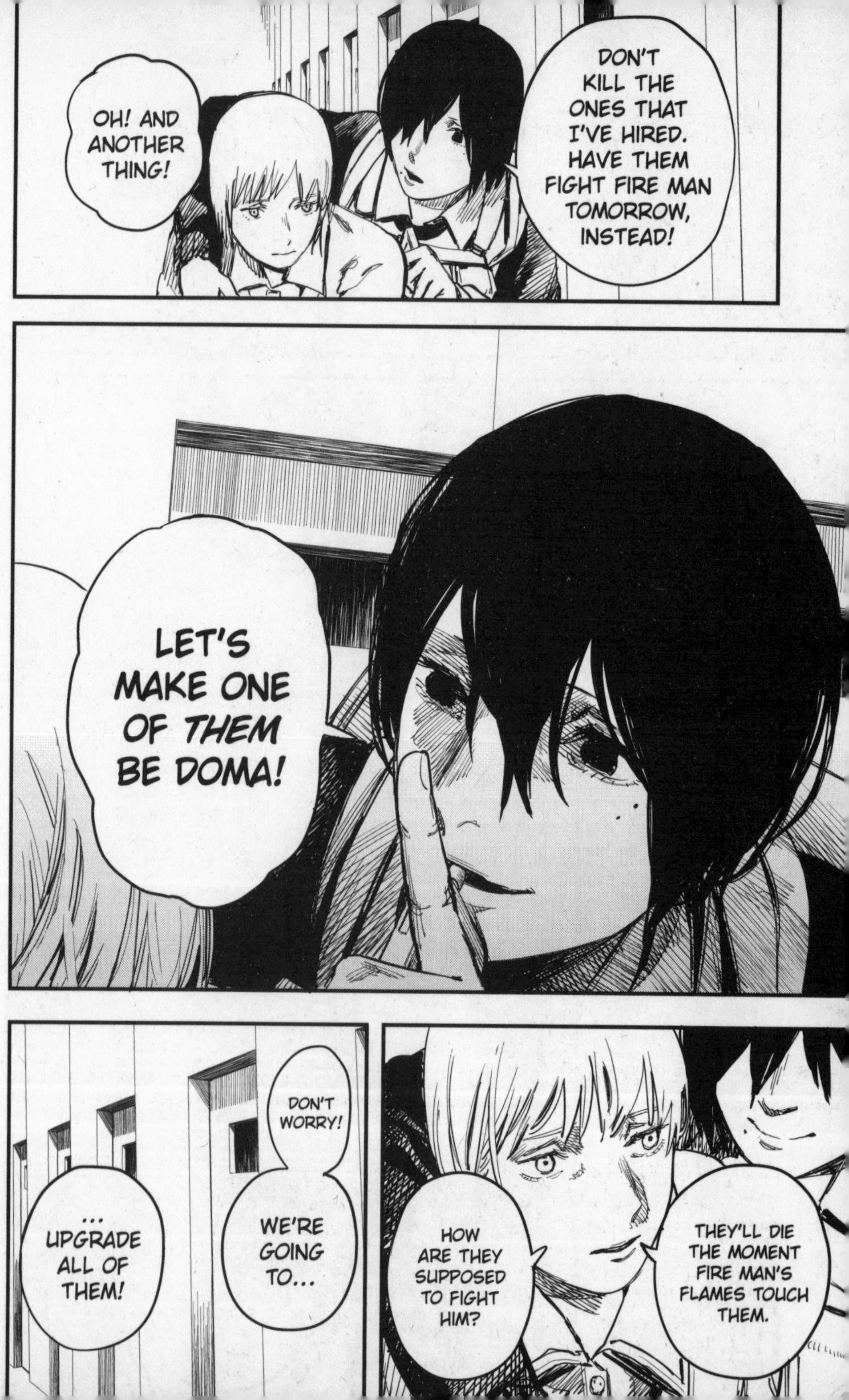
DON'T KILL THE ONES THAT I'VE HIRED. HAVE THEM FIGHT FIRE MAN TOMORROW, INSTEAD!
OH! AND ANOTHER THING!
LET'S MAKE ONE OF *THEM* BE DOMA!
THEY'LL DIE THE MOMENT FIRE MAN'S FLAMES TOUCH THEM.
HOW ARE THEY SUPPOSED TO FIGHT HIM?
DON'T WORRY!
WE'RE GOING TO...
...UPGRADE ALL OF THEM!

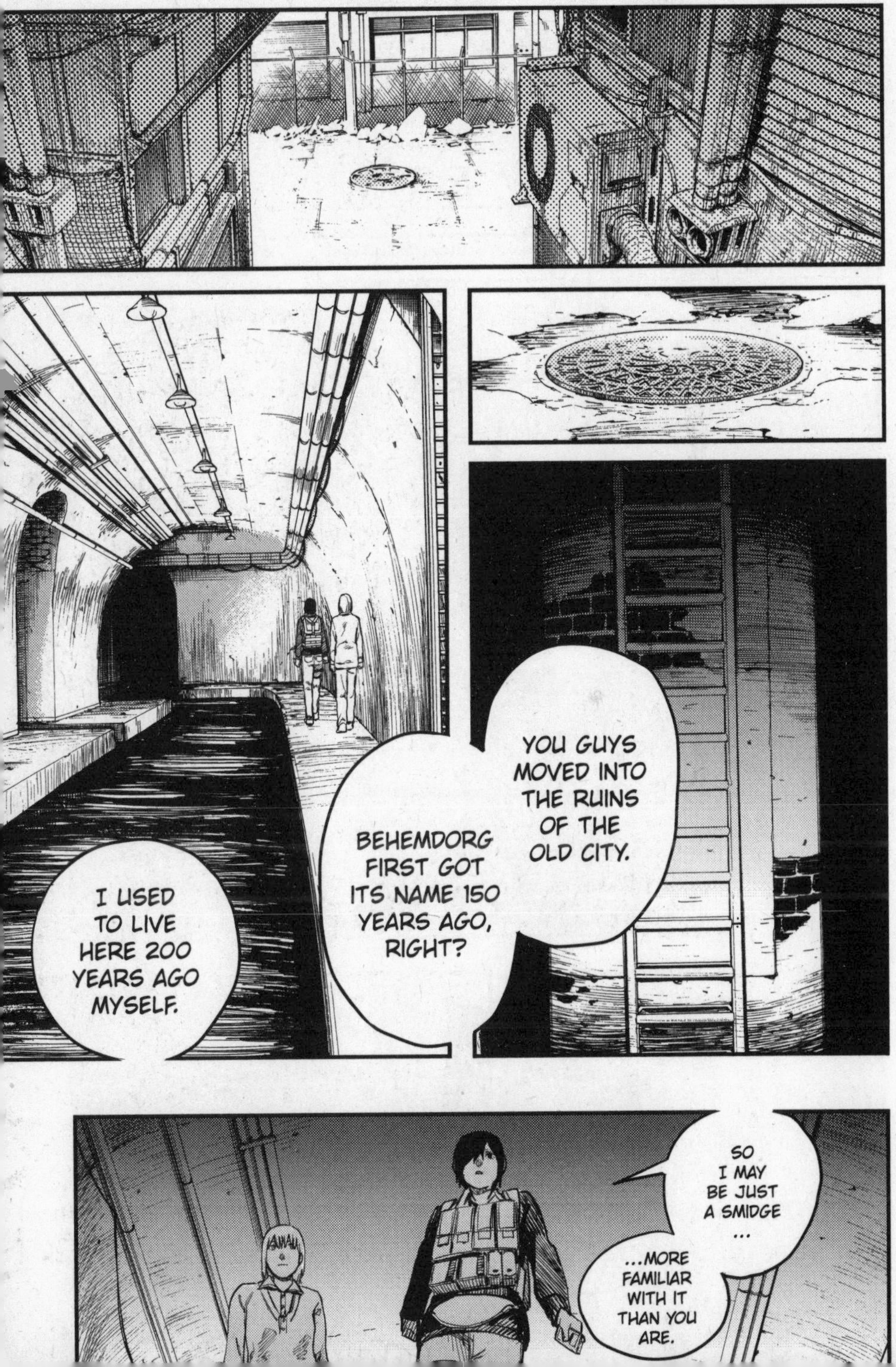
YOU GUYS MOVED INTO THE RUINS OF THE OLD CITY.
BEHEMDORG FIRST GOT ITS NAME 150 YEARS AGO, RIGHT?
I USED TO LIVE HERE 200 YEARS AGO MYSELF.
SO I MAY BE JUST A SMIDGE ...
...MORE FAMILIAR WITH IT THAN YOU ARE.

HERE.
IT'S JUST A WALL.
WAIT AND WATCH.
AHEM!
A.
LO.
HO.
MO.
RA.

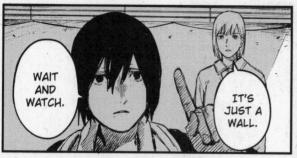

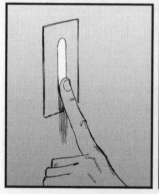

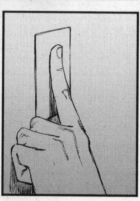

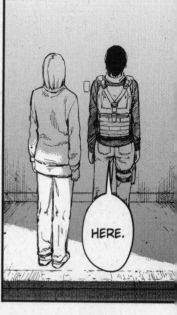

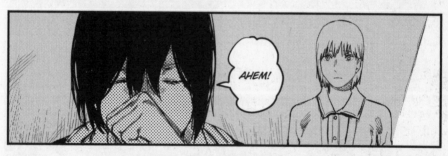

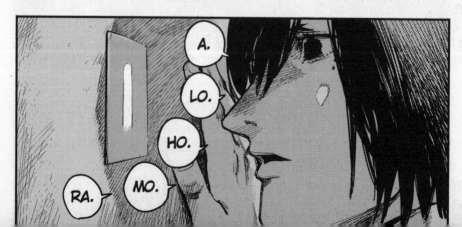

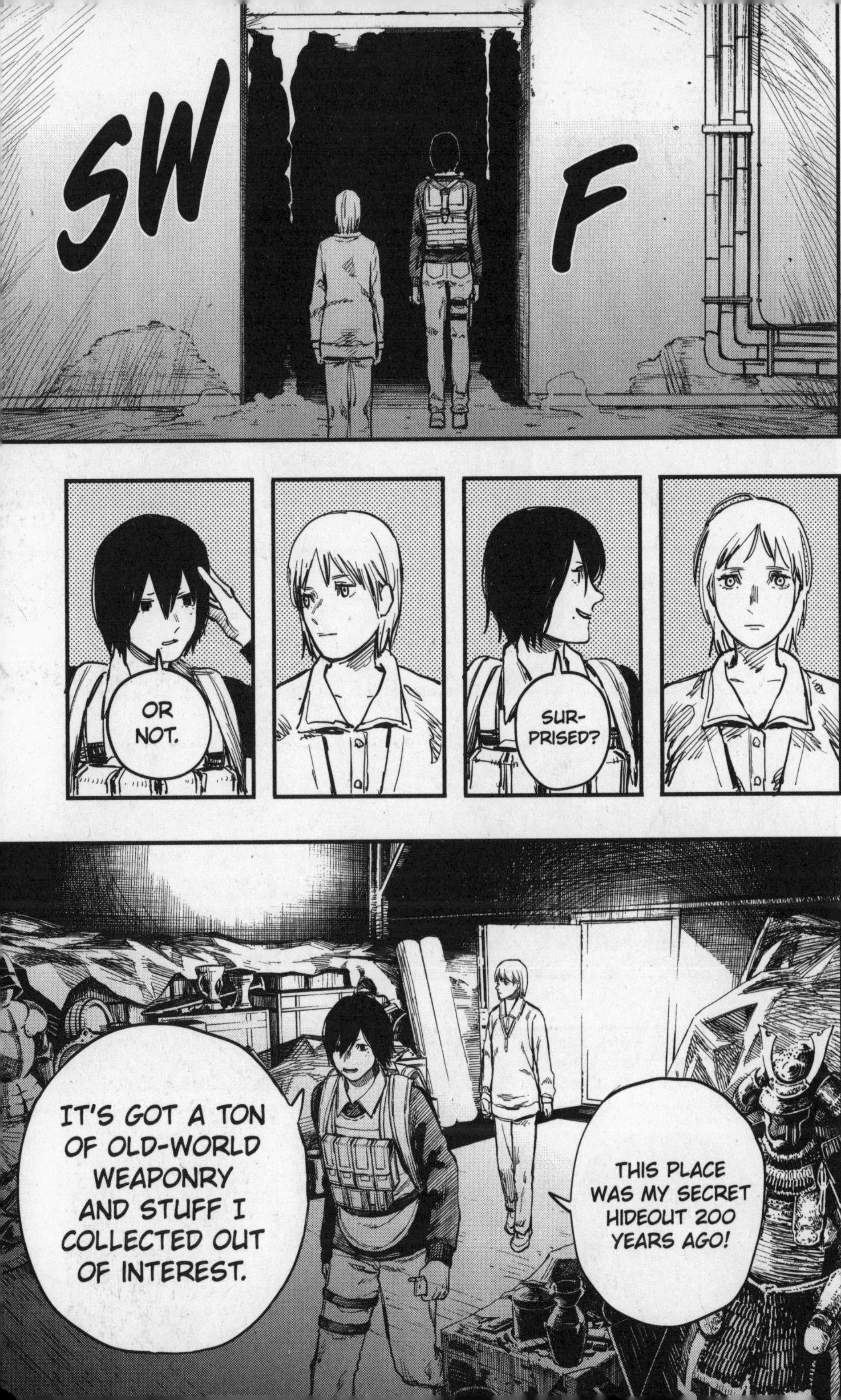
SW
F
SURPRISED?
OR NOT.
THIS PLACE WAS MY SECRET HIDEOUT 200 YEARS AGO!
IT'S GOT A TON OF OLD-WORLD WEAPONRY AND STUFF I COLLECTED OUT OF INTEREST.

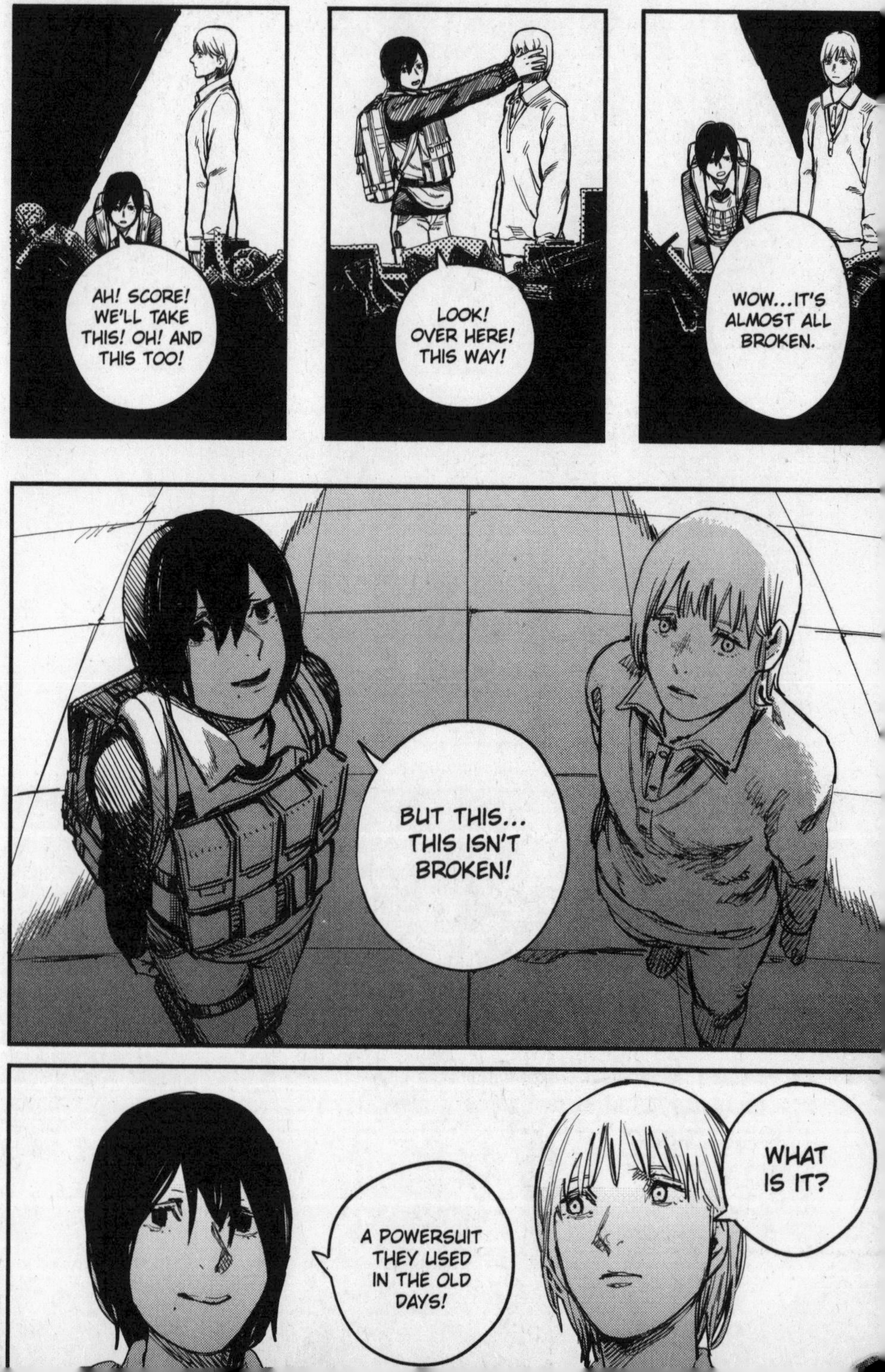
WOW...IT'S ALMOST ALL BROKEN.
LOOK! OVER HERE! THIS WAY!
AH! SCORE! WE'LL TAKE THIS! OH! AND THIS TOO!
BUT THIS... THIS ISN'T BROKEN!
WHAT IS IT?
A POWERSUIT THEY USED IN THE OLD DAYS!

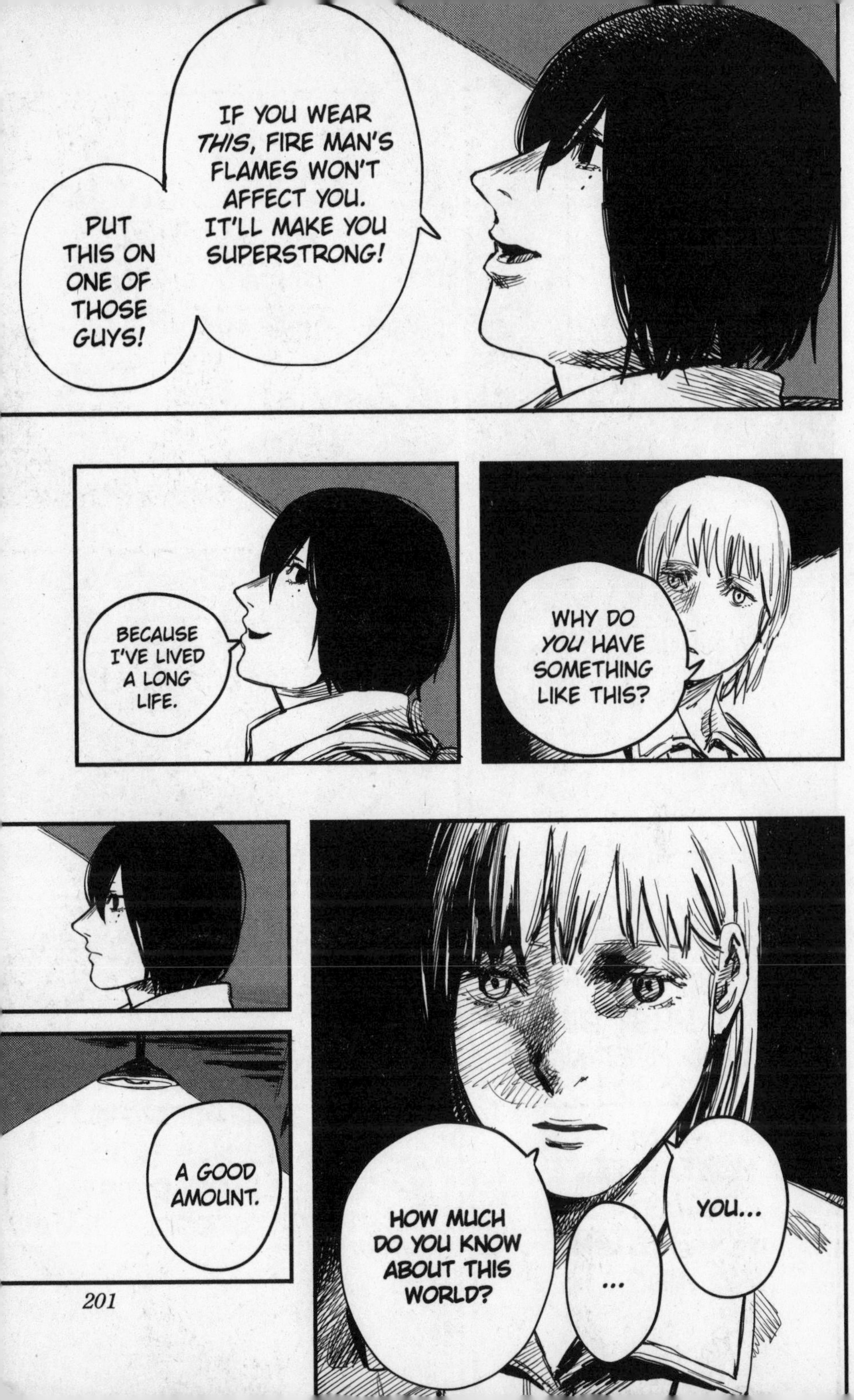
IF YOU WEAR *THIS*, FIRE MAN'S FLAMES WON'T AFFECT YOU. IT'LL MAKE YOU SUPERSTRONG!
PUT THIS ON ONE OF THOSE GUYS!
WHY DO *YOU* HAVE SOMETHING LIKE THIS?
BECAUSE I'VE LIVED A LONG LIFE.
YOU...
...
HOW MUCH DO YOU KNOW ABOUT THIS WORLD?
A GOOD AMOUNT.

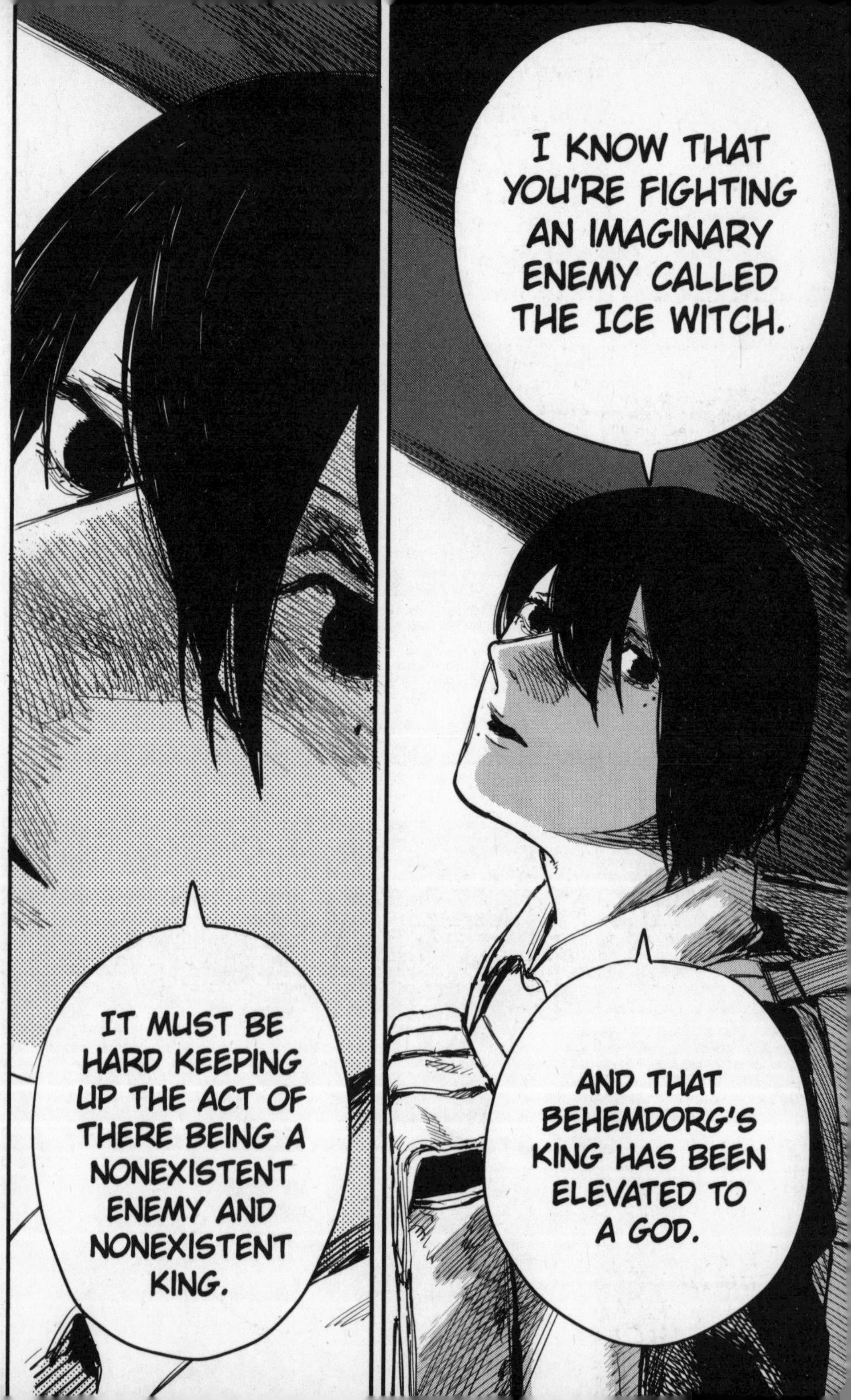
I KNOW THAT YOU'RE FIGHTING AN IMAGINARY ENEMY CALLED THE ICE WITCH.
AND THAT BEHEMDORG'S KING HAS BEEN ELEVATED TO A GOD.
IT MUST BE HARD KEEPING UP THE ACT OF THERE BEING A NONEXISTENT ENEMY AND NONEXISTENT KING.

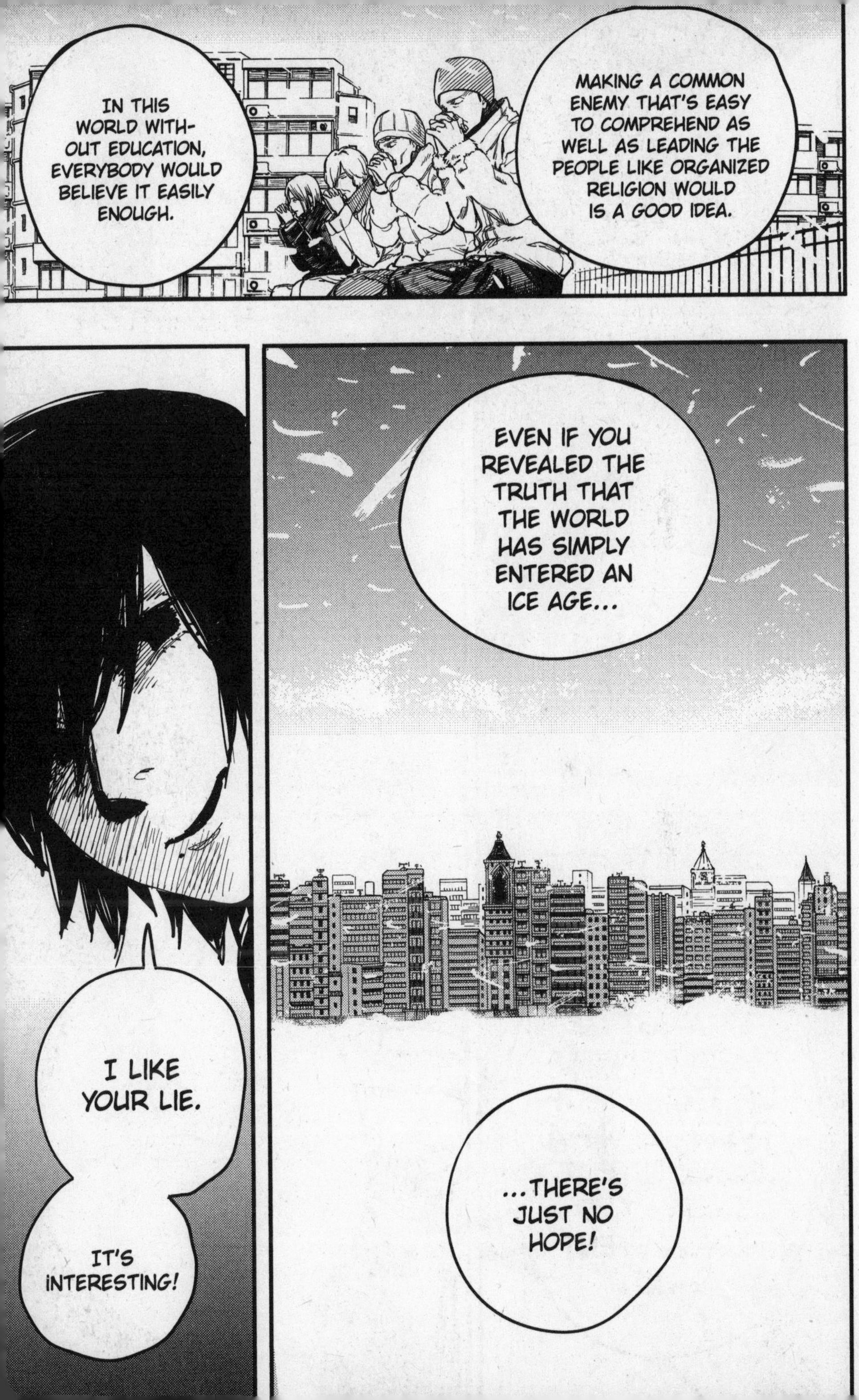
MAKING A COMMON ENEMY THAT'S EASY TO COMPREHEND AS WELL AS LEADING THE PEOPLE LIKE ORGANIZED RELIGION WOULD IS A GOOD IDEA.
IN THIS WORLD WITH-OUT EDUCATION, EVERYBODY WOULD BELIEVE IT EASILY ENOUGH.
EVEN IF YOU REVEALED THE TRUTH THAT THE WORLD HAS SIMPLY ENTERED AN ICE AGE...
...THERE'S JUST NO HOPE!
I LIKE YOUR LIE.
IT'S INTERESTING!

...CAN MANKIND SURVIVE IN THIS WORLD?

HOW MUCH LONGER...

SO TELL ME.

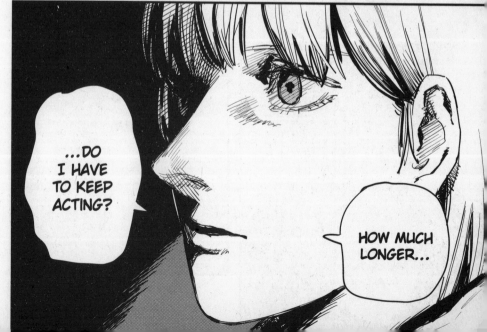

...DO I HAVE TO KEEP ACTING?

HOW MUCH LONGER...

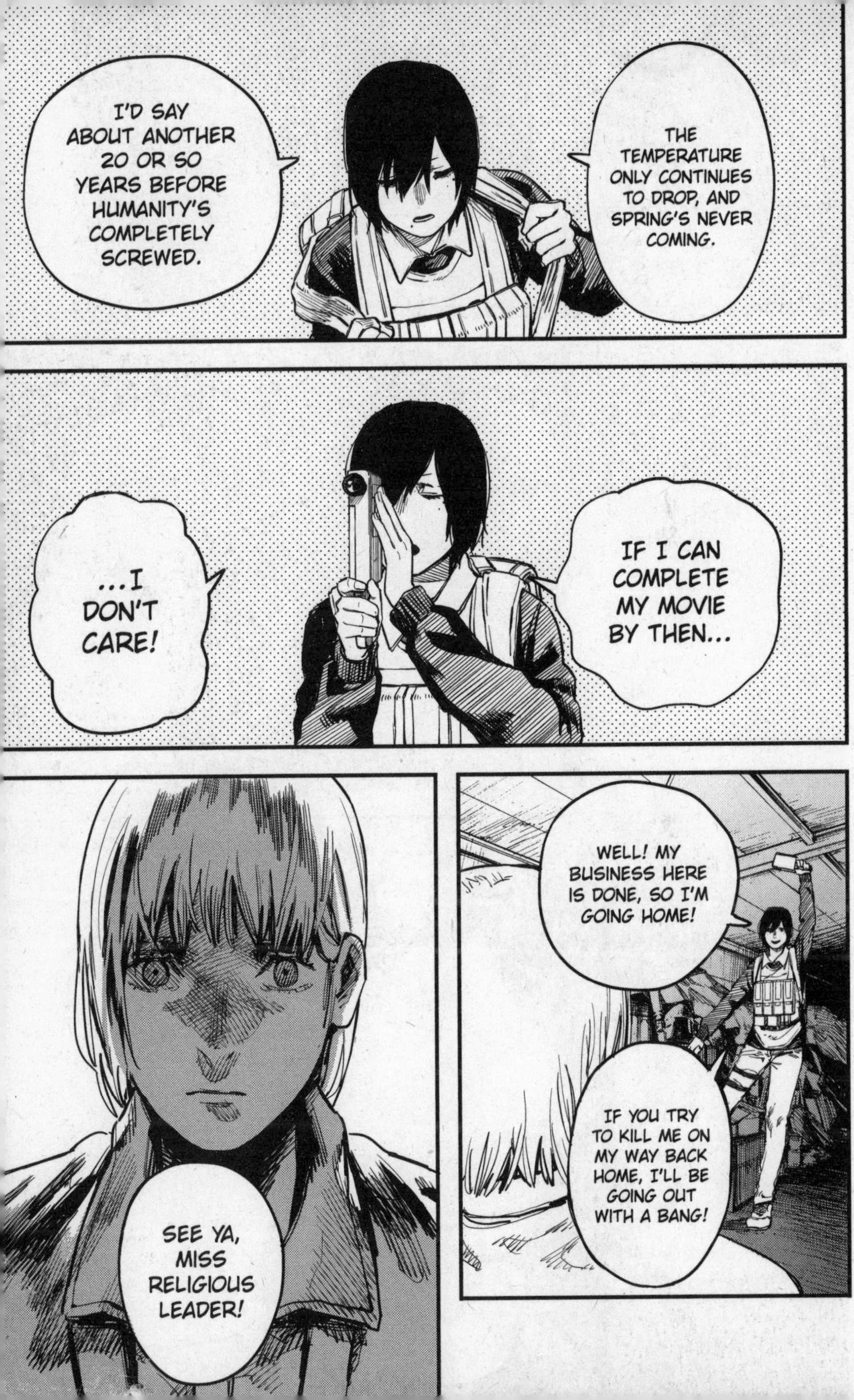
THE TEMPERATURE ONLY CONTINUES TO DROP, AND SPRING'S NEVER COMING.
I'D SAY ABOUT ANOTHER 20 OR SO YEARS BEFORE HUMANITY'S COMPLETELY SCREWED.
IF I CAN COMPLETE MY MOVIE BY THEN...
...I DON'T CARE!
WELL! MY BUSINESS HERE IS DONE, SO I'M GOING HOME!
IF YOU TRY TO KILL ME ON MY WAY BACK HOME, I'LL BE GOING OUT WITH A BANG!
SEE YA, MISS RELIGIOUS LEADER!

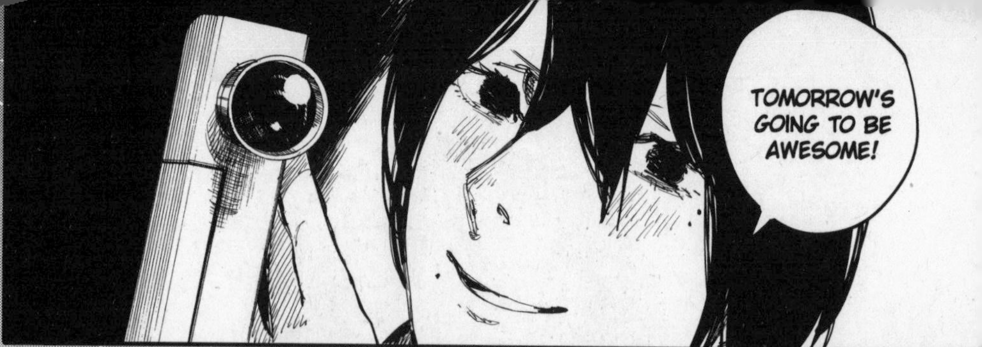
TOMORROW'S GOING TO BE AWESOME!

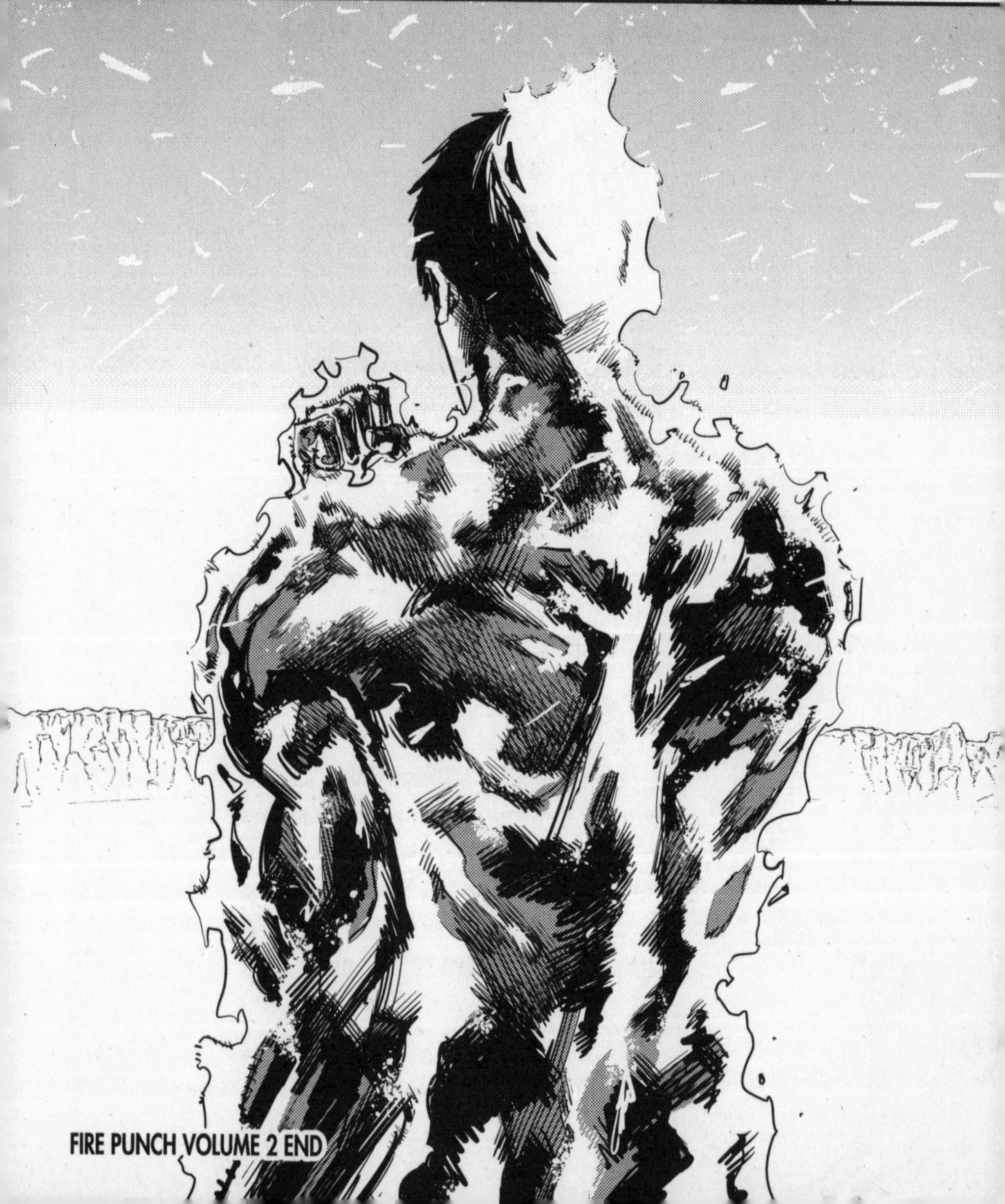
FIRE PUNCH VOLUME 2 END

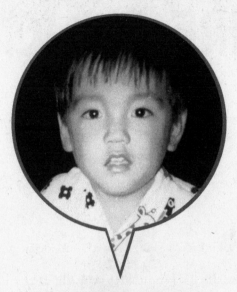

TATSUKI FUJIMOTO

I once walked the perimeter of Japan.

Tatsuki Fujimoto won Honorable Mention in the November 2013 Shueisha Crown Newcomers' Awards for his debut one-shot story "Love Is Blind," which was published in volume 13 of *Jump SQ.19*. Fujimoto's follow-up series, *Fire Punch*, is the creator's first English-language release.

FIRE PUNCH

Volume 2
VIZ Signature Edition

Story and Art by Tatsuki Fujimoto

Translation: Christine Dashiell
Touch-Up Art & Lettering: Snir Aharon
Design: Julian [JR] Robinson
Editor: Jennifer LeBlanc

FIRE PUNCH © 2016 by Tatsuki Fujimoto
All rights reserved.
First published in Japan in 2016 by SHUEISHA Inc., Tokyo.
English translation rights arranged by SHUEISHA Inc.

The stories, characters and incidents mentioned in
this publication are entirely fictional.

Printed in the U.S.A.

Published by VIZ Media, LLC
P.O. Box 77010
San Francisco, CA 94107

10 9 8 7 6 5 4 3 2 1
First printing, April 2018

viz.com

PARENTAL ADVISORY
FIRE PUNCH is rated M for Mature. Contains graphic
violence and sexual situations, and is recommended
for mature readers.
ratings.viz.com

vizsignature.com